The Guinness Book of

Golf

FACTS AND FEATS

The Guinness Book of

Golf

FACTS AND FEATS

Andrew Swales

GUINNESS PUBLISHING

Text design and layout: Mitchell Associates

Cover design: Ad Vantage Studios

Printed and bound in Great Britain by
The Bath Press, Bath

A catalogue record of this book is available from the
British Library.

ISBN 085112-604-9

Contents

Acknowledgements

Ed Abelson

David Begg

European PGA Tour (Ian Barker, Vanessa Brannetti, Bill Hodge, Helen Hudson, Valerie Steele)

Tom Eveling

Sheila Fairclough (Women's European Tour)

Tony Greer (Sony Ranking/IMG)

Sal Johnson

Peter Lewis (Royal & Ancient Library)

Kathryn Murphy (Augusta National GC)

PGA Tour (Communications Dept. United States)

Charles Richards (Guinness Publishing)

Sandra Spear

USGA (Suzanne Colson, media relations)

USPGA (Kathy Jordan's office)

Laurence Viney

Bibliography

An Illustrated History of the Masters 1934-80, Dawson Taylor

British Open Champions, Michael Hobbs

Golf Magazine's *Encyclopedia of Golf* (1993)

The Guinness Golf Facts & Feats, Donald Steel (1982)

History of the Open Golf Championship 1920-92, The Guardian

History of the PGA Tour, Al Barkow (to 1988)

LPGA Player Guide 1995

Magazines: *Golf Digest* (US), *Golf Monthly*, *Golf Weekly*, *Golf World*, *Today's Golfer*

Media Guides: European Tour, European Senior Tour, PGA Tour (US), PGA Senior Tour (US), Women's European Tour

Official History of the Ryder Cup 1927-89, Michael Williams

Official US Open Almanac, Sal Johnson

Player Guides (British Open, US Open, USPGA)

Royal & Ancient Book of Golf Records, (Laurence Viney)

Story of the Open Golf Championship 1860-1950, Charles Mortimer & Fred Pignon

USGA Record Books 1895-1959, 1960-1980, 1981-89

USPGA Media Guide 1995

World of Professional Golf, Mark McCormack (annuals 1984-91)

Introduction

Golf is all about tradition. It's a game where the prestige and honour gained in victory can at times be more important than the accumulation of wealth certain tournaments bring with it.

A British Open champion at St Andrews will gain more satisfaction from looking at his name inscribed on the famous claret jug trophy than by counting the number of noughts on the winner's cheque.

That is why much of this book concentrates on the 'big five' – British Open, US Open, USPGA, US Masters and of course the Ryder Cup; events in which the champions are guaranteed a place in history.

Ireland's Philip Walton, who holed the putt that clinched the 1995 Ryder Cup for Europe, may never win a British or US Open, yet his name has already been etched into golfing folklore. Walton wasn't paid a penny for playing in that match at Oak Hill, but his position of importance in the game's rich history is assured.

Sandy Lyle summed up perfectly what tradition is all about after winning the 1987 Players' Championship at Sawgrass in Florida. When asked if there was any difference between winning this tournament, an extremely prestigious title in its own right, and the 1985 British Open, he replied: 'Oh yes, about a hundred years.'

Lyle is one of over 30 players highlighted here in the chapter reserved for golf's champions, a chapter which celebrates the achievements of the game's all-time greats as well as the leading players of the last 20 to 30 years.

The latter sections of this book pay tribute to the leading women and top amateur players who have left their mark on the game. The American and European professional Tours are also included, together with the most important championships in other parts of the world. All information has been updated to 1 January 1996.

ANDREW SWALES, March 1996

THE FOUR MAJOR CHAMPIONSHIPS

British Open
United States Open
United States Masters
USPGA Championship

In order to avoid confusion, I have referred to Britain's Open Championship as the British Open. Traditionalists will argue that it should simply be titled The Open, but equally there are many on the other side of the Atlantic who like to call their own National Open 'The Open', rather than the US Open . . .

BRITISH OPEN

Note: Between 1860 and 1881 tournaments staged at Prestwick were played over three rounds of 12 holes. The first 18-hole course to be used for The Open was St Andrews in 1873. Amateurs are referred to as 'Mr'.

From 1860 through to 1969, players are associated by their club. British clubs are named in full while those attached to overseas clubs are listed by country. Most players were connected to clubs in their own country, although there were one or two anomalies. For example, Percy Alliss (the father of BBC commentator Peter Alliss) is listed as being attached to a German club in 1928, 1930 and 1931 despite obviously being British. By 1932 he was back in this country and representing Beaconsfield. From 1970 onwards golfers are listed by nationality.

Tom Morris senior, oldest winner of the British Open title

1860 - Willie Park (at Prestwick)

Willie Park (Musselburgh)	55-59-60	174
Tom Morris sr (Prestwick)	58-59-59	176
Andrew Strath (St Andrews)	*	180
Robert Andrew (Perth)	*	191
George Brown (Blackheath)	*	192

* - Individual round scores not known.

1861 - Tom Morris sr (at Prestwick)

Tom Morris sr (Prestwick)	54-56-53	163
Willie Park (Musselburgh)	54-54-59	167
William Dow (Musselburgh)	59-58-54	171
David Park (Musselburgh)	58-57-57	172
Robert Andrew (Perth)	58-61-56	175

1862 - Tom Morris sr (at Prestwick)

Tom Morris sr (Prestwick)	52-55-56	163
Willie Park (Musselburgh)	59-59-58	176
Charles Hunter (Prestwick)	60-60-58	178
William Dow (Musselburgh)	60-58-63	181
Mr James Knight (Prestwick)	62-61-63	186

1863 - Willie Park (at Prestwick)

Willie Park (Musselburgh)	56-54-58	168
Tom Morris sr (Prestwick)	56-58-56	170
David Park (Musselburgh)	55-63-54	172
Andrew Strath (St Andrews)	61-55-58	174
George Brown (St Andrews)	58-61-57	176

1864 - Tom Morris sr (at Prestwick)

Tom Morris sr (Prestwick)	54-58-55	167
Andrew Strath (St Andrews)	56-57-56	169
Robert Andrew (Perth)	57-58-60	175

Willie Park (Musselburgh)	55-67-55	177
William Dow (Musselburgh)	56-58-67	181

1865 - Andrew Strath (at Prestwick)

Andrew Strath (St Andrews)	55-54-53	162
Willie Park (Musselburgh)	56-52-56	164
William Dow (Musselburgh)	*	171
Robert Kirk (St Andrews)	64-54-55	173
Tom Morris sr (St Andrews)	57-61-56	174

* - Individual round scores not known.

1866 - Willie Park (at Prestwick)

Willie Park (Musselburgh)	54-56-59	169
David Park (Musselburgh)	58-57-56	171
Robert Andrew (Perth)	58-59-59	176
Tom Morris sr (St Andrews)	61-58-59	178
Robert Kirk (St Andrews)	60-62-58	180

1867 - Tom Morris sr (at Prestwick)

Tom Morris sr (St Andrews)	58-54-58	170
Willie Park (Musselburgh)	58-56-58	172
Andrew Strath (St Andrews)	61-57-56	174
Tom Morris jr (St Andrews)	58-59-58	175
Robert Kirk (St Andrews)	57-60-60	177

Tom Morris junior, winner of four British Opens

1868- Tom Morris jr (at Prestwick)

Tom Morris jr (St Andrews)	50-55-52	157
Robert Andrew (Perth)	53-54-52	159
Wille Park (Musselburgh)	58-50-54	162
Robert Kirk (St Andrews)	56-59-56	171
John Allan (Westwood Ho)	54-55-63	172

1869 -Tom Morris jr (at Prestwick)

Tom Morris jr (St Andrews)	51-54-49	154
Tom Morris sr (St Andrews)	54-50-53	157
Mr S Mure Fergusson (R&A*)	57-54-54	165
Robert Kirk (St Andrews)	53-58-57	168
David Strath (St Andrews)	53-56-60	169
* - Royal & Ancient		

1870 -Tom Morris jr (at Prestwick)

Tom Morris jr (St Andrews)	47-51-51	149
Bob Kirk (Royal Blackheath)	52-52-57	161
David Strath (St Andrews)	54-49-58	161
Tom Morris sr (St Andrews)	56-52-54	162
Mr William Doleman (Musselburgh)	57-56-58	171

1871- NO TOURNAMENT

1872- Tom Morris jr (at Prestwick)

Tom Morris jr (St Andrews)	57-56-53	166
David Strath (St Andrews)	56-52-61	169
Mr William Doleman (Musselburgh)	63-60-54	177
Tom Morris sr (St Andrews)	62-60-57	179
David Park (Musselburgh)	61-57-61	179

1873- Tom Kidd (at St Andrews)

Tom Kidd (St Andrews)	91-88	179
Jamie Anderson (St Andrews)	91-89	180
Tom Morris jr (St Andrews)	94-89	183
Bob Kirk (Royal Blackheath)	91-92	183
David Strath (St Andrews)	97-90	187

1874- Mungo Park (at Musselburgh)

Mungo Park (Musselburgh)	75-84	159
Tom Morris jr (St Andrews)	83-78	161
George Paxton (Musselburgh)	80-82	162
Bob Martin (St Andrews)	85-79	164
Jamie Anderson (St Andrews)	82-83	165

1875- Willie Park   (at Prestwick)

Willie Park (Musselburgh)	56-59-51	166
Bob Martin (St Andrews)	56-58-54	168
Mungo Park (Musselburgh)	59-57-55	171
Robert Ferguson (Musselburgh)	58-56-58	172
James Rennie (St Andrews)	61-59-57	177

1876- Bob Martin (at St Andrews)

Bob Martin (St Andrews)	86-90	176
David Strath (North Berwick)	86-90	176
Play-Off: Strath refused to play-off		
Willie Park (Musselburgh)	94-89	183
Tom Morris sr (St Andrews)	90-95	185
W Thompson (Elie)	90-95	185
Mungo Park (Musselburgh)	95-90	185

1877- Jamie Anderson (at Musselburgh)

Jamie Anderson (St Andrews)	82-78	160
Bob Pringle (Musselburgh)	82-80	162
Bob Ferguson (Musselburgh)	80-84	164
William Cosgrove (Musselburgh)	80-84	164
David Strath (North Berwick)	85-81	166
William Brown (Musselburgh)	80-86	166

1878- Jamie Anderson (at Prestwick)

Jamie Anderson (St Andrews)	53-53-51	157
Bob Kirk (St Andrews)	53-55-51	159
JOF Morris (St Andrews)	50-56-55	161
Bob Martin (St Andrews)	57-53-55	165
Mr John Ball (Hoylake)	53-57-55	165

1879- Jamie Anderson (at St Andrews)

Jamie Anderson (St Andrews)	84-85	169
James Allan (Westward Ho!)	88-84	172
Andrew Kirkaldy (St Andrews)	86-86	172
George Paxton (Musselburgh)	*	174
Tom Kidd (St Andrews)	*	175

* - *Individual round scores not known.*

1880- Bob Ferguson (at Musselburgh)

Bob Ferguson (Musselburgh)	81-81	162
Peter Paxton (Musselburgh)	81-86	167
Ned Cosgrove (Musselburgh)	82-86	168
George Paxton (Musselburgh)	85-84	169
Bob Pringle (Musselburgh)	90-79	169
David Brown (Musselburgh)	86-83	169

1881- Bob Ferguson (at Prestwick)

Bob Ferguson (Musselburgh)	53-60-57	170
Jamie Anderson (St Andrews)	57-60-56	173
Ned Cosgrove (Musselburgh)	61-59-57	177
Bob Martin (St Andrews)	57-62-59	178
Tom Morris sr (St Andrews)	58-65-58	181
W Campbell (Musselburgh)	60-56-65	181
Willie Park jr (Musselburgh)	66-57-58	181

1882- Bob Ferguson (at St Andrews)

Bob Ferguson (Musselburgh)	83-88	171
Willie Fernie (Dumfries)	88-86	174
Jamie Anderson (St Andrews)	87-88	175
John Kirkaldy (St Andrews)	86-89	175
Bob Martin (St Andrews)	89-86	175
Mr Fitz Boothby (St Andrews)	86-89	175

1883- Willie Fernie (at Musselburgh)

Willie Fernie (Dumfries)	75-84	159
Bob Ferguson (Musselburgh)	78-81	159

Play-Off: Fernie 158 (81-77);
Ferguson 159 (82-77)

William Brown (Musselburgh)	83-77	160
Bob Pringle (Musselburgh)	79-82	161
Willie Campbell (Musselburgh)	80-83	163
George Paxton (Musselburgh)	80-83	163

1884- Jack Simpson (at Prestwick)

Jack Simpson (Carnoustie)	78-82	160
D Rolland (Elie)	81-83	164
Willie Fernie (Felixstowe)	80-84	164
Willie Campbell (Musselburgh)	84-85	169
Willie Park jr (Musselburgh)	86-83	169

1885- Bob Martin (at St Andrews)

Bob Martin (St Andrews)	84-87	171
Archie Simpson (Carnoustie)	83-89	172

David Ayton (St Andrews)	89-84	173
Willie Fernie (Felixstowe)	89-85	174
Willie Park jr (Musselburgh)	86-88	174
Bob Simpson (Carnoustie)	85-89	174

1886 David Brown (at Musselburgh)

David Brown (Musselburgh)	79-78	157
Willie Campbell (Musselburgh)	78-81	159
Ben Campbell (Musselburgh)	79-81	160
Archie Simpson (Carnoustie)	82-79	161
Willie Park jr (Musselburgh)	84-77	161
Thomas Gossett (Musselburgh)	80-81	161
Bob Ferguson (Musselburgh)	82-79	161

1887- Willie Park jr (at Prestwick)

Willie Park jr (Musselburgh)	82-79	161
Bob Martin (St Andrews)	81-81	162
Willie Campbell (Prestwick)	77-87	164
Mr J E Laidlay (Hon. Company)	86-80	166
Ben Sayers (North Berwick)	83-85	168
Archie Simpson (Carnoustie)	81-87	168

1888- Jack Burns (at St Andrews)

Jack Burns (Warwick)	86-85	171
D Anderson jr (St Andrews)	86-86	172
Ben Sayers (North Berwick)	85-87	172
Willie Campbell (Prestwick)	84-90	174
Mr Leslie Balfour (Edinburgh)	86-89	175

1889- Willie Park jr (at Musselburgh)

Willie Park jr (Musselburgh)	78-77	155
Andrew Kirkaldy (St Andrews)	77-78	155

Play-Off: Park jr 158 (82-76);
Kirkaldy 163 (85-78)

Ben Sayers (North Berwick)	79-80	159
Mr J E Laidlay (Hon. Company)	81-81	162
David Brown (Musselburgh)	82-80	162

1890- Mr John Ball jr (at Prestwick)

Mr John Ball jr (Royal Liverpool)	82-82	164
Willie Fernie (Troon)	85-82	167
Archie Simpson (Carnoustie)	85-82	167
Willie Park jr (Musselburgh)	90-80	170
Andrew Kirkaldy (St Andrews)	81-89	170

1891- Hugh Kirkaldy (at St Andrews)

Hugh Kirkaldy (St Andrews)	83-83	166
Andrew Kirkaldy (St Andrews)	84-84	168
Willie Fernie (Troon)	84-84	168
Mr R Mure Fergusson (R&A*)	86-84	170
WD More (Chester)	84-87	171

* - *Royal & Ancient*

1892- Mr Harold Hilton (at Muirfield)

Mr Harold Hilton (R. Liverpool)	78-81-72-74	305
Mr John Ball jr (R. Liverpool)	75-80-74-79	308
Hugh Kirkaldy (St Andrews)	77-83-73-75	308
Alex Herd (Huddersfield)	77-78-77-76	308
J Kay (Seaton Carew)	82-78-74-78	312
Ben Sayers (North Berwick)	80-76-81-75	312

1893- Willie Auchterlonie (at Prestwick)

Willie Auchterlonie (St Andrews)	78-81-81-82	322
Mr J E Laidlay (Hon. Company)	80-83-80-81	324
Alex Herd (Huddersfield)	82-81-78-84	325
Andrew Kirkaldy (St Andrews)	85-82-82-77	326
Hugh Kirkaldy (St Andrews)	83-79-82-82	326

1894- JH Taylor (at Sandwich, St George's)

JH Taylor (Winchester)	84-80-81-81	326
D Rolland (Limpsfield)	86-79-84-82	331
Andrew Kirkaldy (St Andrews)	86-79-83-84	332
A Toogood (Eltham)	84-85-82-82	333
Willie Fernie (Troon)	84-84-86-80	334
Ben Sayers (North Berwick)	85-81-84-84	334
Harry Vardon (Bury)	86-86-82-80	334

1895- JH Taylor (at St Andrews)

JH Taylor (Winchester)	86-78-80-78	322
Alex Herd (Huddersfield)	82-77-82-85	326
Andrew Kirkaldy (St Andrews)	81-83-84-84	332
G Pulford (Hoylake)	84-81-83-86	334
Archie Simpson (Aberdeen)	88-85-78-85	336

1896- Harry Vardon (at Muirfield)

Harry Vardon (Ganton)	83-78-78-77	316
JH Taylor (Winchester)	77-78-81-80	316
Play-Off: Vardon 157; Taylor 161		
Mr FG Tait (Black Watch)	83-75-84-77	319
Willie Fernie (Troon)	78-79-82-80	319
Alex Herd (Huddersfield)	72-84-79-85	320

1897- Mr Harold Hilton (at Hoylake, Royal Liverpool)

Mr Harold Hilton (Royal Liverpool)	80-75-84-75	314
James Braid (Romford)	80-74-82-79	315
Mr FG Tait (Black Watch)	79-79-80-79	317
G Pulford (Hoylake)	80-79-79-79	317
Alex Herd (Huddersfield)	78-81-79-80	318

1898- Harry Vardon (at Prestwick)

Harry Vardon (Ganton)	79-75-77-76	307
Willie Park jr (Musselburgh)	76-75-78-79	308
Mr Harold Hilton (R. Liverpool)	76-81-77-75	309
JH Taylor (Winchester)	78-78-77-79	312
Mr FG Tait (Black Watch)	81-77-75-82	315

1899- Harry Vardon (at Sandwich, St George's)

Harry Vardon (Ganton)	76-76-81-77	310
Jack White (Seaford)	79-79-82-75	315
Andrew Kirkaldy (St Andrews)	81-79-82-77	319
JH Taylor (Richmond)	77-76-83-84	320
James Braid (Romford)	78-78-85-81	322
Willie Fernie (Troon)	79-83-82-78	322

1900- JH Taylor (at St Andrews)

JH Taylor (Richmond)	79-77-78-75	309
Harry Vardon (Ganton)	79-81-80-77	317
James Braid (Romford)	82-81-80-79	322
Jack White (Seaford)	80-81-82-80	323
Willie Auchterlonie (St Andrews)	81-85-80-80	326

1901- James Braid (at Muirfield)

James Braid (Romford)	79-76-74-80	309
Harry Vardon (Ganton)	77-78-79-78	312
JH Taylor (Richmond)	79-83-74-77	313
Mr Harold Hilton (Royal Liverpool)	89-80-75-76	320
Alex Herd (Huddersfield)	87-81-81-76	325

1902- Alex Herd (at Hoylake, Royal Liverpool)

Alex Herd (Huddersfield)	77-76-73-81	307
Harry Vardon (Ganton)	72-77-80-79	308
James Braid (Romford)	78-76-80-74	308
Mr Robert Maxwell (Tantallon)	79-77-79-74	309
Tom Vardon (St George's)	80-76-78-79	313

1903- Harry Vardon (at Prestwick)

Harry Vardon (Totteridge)	73-77-72-78	300
Tom Vardon (St George's)	76-81-75-74	306
Jack White (Sunningdale)	77-78-74-79	308
Alex Herd (Huddersfield)	73-83-76-77	309
James Braid (Romford)	77-79-79-75	310

1904- Jack White (at Sandwich, Royal St George's)

Jack White (Sunningdale)	80-75-72-69	296
JH Taylor (Mid-Surrey)	77-78-74-68	297
James Braid (Walton Heath)	77-80-69-71	297
Tom Vardon (R. St George's)	77-77-75-72	301
Harry Vardon (South Herts)	76-73-79-74	302

1905- James Braid (at St Andrews)

James Braid (Walton Heath)	81-78-78-81	318
Rowland Jones (Wimbledon Pk)	81-77-87-78	323
JH Taylor (Mid-Surrey)	80-85-78-80	323
James Kinnell (Purley Downs)	82-79-82-81	324
Ernest Gray (Littlehampton)	82-81-84-78	325
Arnaud Massy (N. Berwick)	81-80-82-82	325

1906- James Braid (at Muirfield)

James Braid (Walton Heath)	77-76-74-73	300
JH Taylor (Mid-Surrey)	77-72-75-80	304
Harry Vardon (South Herts)	77-73-77-78	305
Mr John Graham jr (Royal Liverpool)	71-79-78-78	306
Rowland Jones (Wimbledon Pk)	74-78-73-83	308

1907- Arnaud Massy (at Hoylake, Royal Liverpool)

Arnaud Massy (France)	76-81-78-77	312
JH Taylor (Mid-Surrey)	79-79-76-80	314
Tom Vardon (R. St George's)	81-81-80-75	317
G Pulford (Hoylake)	81-78-80-78	317
James Braid (Walton Heath)	82-85-75-76	318
Ted Ray (Ganton)	83-80-79-76	318

1908- James Braid (at Prestwick)

James Braid (Walton Heath)	70-72-77-72	291
T Ball (West Lancashire)	76-73-76-74	299
Ted Ray (Ganton)	79-71-75-76	301
Alex Herd (Huddersfield)	74-74-79-75	302
Harry Vardon (South Herts)	79-78-74-75	306
D Kinnell (Prestwick)	75-73-80-78	306

1909- JH Taylor (at Deal, Royal Cinque Ports)

JH Taylor (Mid-Surrey)	74-73-74-74	295
James Braid (Walton Heath)	79-75-73-74	301
T Ball (West Lancashire)	74-75-76-76	301
C Johns (Southdown)	72-76-79-75	302
TG Renouf (Manchester)	76-78-76-73	303

1910- James Braid (at St Andrews)

James Braid (Walton Heath)	76-73-74-76	299
Alex Herd (Huddersfield)	78-74-75-76	303
George Duncan (Hanger Hill)	73-77-71-83	304
L Ayton (Bishop's Stortford)	78-76-75-77	306
J Robson (West Surrey)	75-80-77-76	308
Willie Smith (Mexico)	77-71-80-80	308
Ted Ray (Ganton)	76-77-74-81	308

1911- Harry Vardon (at Sandwich, Royal St George's)

Harry Vardon (South Herts)	74-74-75-80	303
Arnaud Massy (France)	75-78-74-76	303

Play-Off: Vardon won when Massy conceded on 35th hole

Mr Harold Hilton (R. Liverpool)	76-74-78-76	304
Alex Herd (Coombe Hill)	77-73-76-78	304
James Braid (Walton Heath)	78-75-74-78	305

Ted Ray (Ganton)	76-72-79-78	305
JH Taylor (Mid-Surrey)	72-76-78-79	305

1912- Ted Ray (at Muirfield)

Ted Ray (Oxhey)	71-73-76-75	295
Harry Vardon (South Herts)	75-72-81-71	299
James Braid (Walton Heath)	77-71-77-78	303
George Duncan (Hanger Hill)	72-77-78-78	305
Alex Herd (Coombe Hill)	76-81-76-76	309
L Ayton (Bishop's Stortford)	74-80-75-80	309

1913- JH Taylor (Hoylake, Royal Liverpool)

JH Taylor (Mid-Surrey)	73-75-77-79	304
Ted Ray (Ganton)	73-74-81-84	312
Michael Moran (Royal Dublin)	76-74-89-74	313
Harry Vardon (South Herts)	79-75-79-80	313
TG Renouf (Manchester)	75-78-84-78	315
John J McDermott (USA)	75-80-77-83	315

1914- Harry Vardon (at Prestwick)

Harry Vardon (South Herts)	73-77-78-78	306
JH Taylor (Mid-Surrey)	74-78-74-83	309
H Simpson (St Anne's Old Links)	77-80-78-75	310
Abe Mitchell (Sonning)	76-78-79-79	312
Tom Williamson (Notts)	75-79-79-79	312

No Championship 1915-19 (World War I)

1920- George Duncan (at Deal, Royal Cinque Ports)

George Duncan (Hanger Hill)	80-80-71-72	303
Alex Herd (Coombe Hill)	72-81-77-75	305
Ted Ray (Oxhey)	72-83-78-73	306
Abe Mitchell (North Foreland)	74-73-84-76	307
Len Holland (Northamptonshire)	80-78-71-79	308

1921- Jock Hutchison (at St Andrews)

Jock Hutchison (USA)	72-75-79-70	296
Mr RH Wethered (R&A)	78-75-72-71	296

Play-Off: Hutchison 150 (74-76); Wethered 159 (77-82)

Tom Kerrigan (USA)	74-80-72-72	298
Arthur Havers (West Lancashire)	76-74-77-72	299
George Duncan (Hanger Hill)	74-75-78-74	301

1922- Walter Hagen (at Sandwich, Royal St George's)

Walter Hagen (USA)	76-73-79-72	300
George Duncan (Hanger Hill)	76-75-81-69	301
Jim Barnes (USA)	75-76-77-73	301
Jock Hutchison (USA)	79-74-73-76	302
Charles Whitcombe (Dorchester)	77-79-72-75	303

1923- Arthur Havers (at Troon)

Arthur Havers (Coombe Hill)	73-73-73-76	295
Walter Hagen (USA)	76-71-74-75	296
Macdonald Smith (USA)	80-73-69-75	297
J Kirkwood (Australia)	72-79-69-78	298
T Fernie (Turnberry)	73-78-74-75	300

1924- Walter Hagen (at Hoylake, Royal Liverpool)

Walter Hagen (USA)	77-73-74-77	301
Ernest Whitcombe (Came Down)	77-70-77-78	302
Frank Ball (Langley Park)	78-75-74-77	304
Macdonald Smith (USA)	76-74-77-77	304
JH Taylor (Mid-Surrey)	75-74-79-79	307

1925- Jim Barnes (at Prestwick)

Jim Barnes (USA)	70-77-79-74	300
Ted Ray (Oxhey)	77-76-75-73	301
Archie Compston (North Manchester)	76-75-75-75	301
Macdonald Smith (USA)	76-69-76-82	303
Abe Mitchell (unattached)	77-76-75-77	305

1926- Mr Bobby Jones jr (at Royal Lytham & St Anne's)

Mr Bobby Jones jr (USA)	72-72-73-74	291
Al Watrous (USA)	71-75-69-78	293
Mr George Von Elm (USA)	75-72-76-72	295
Walter Hagen (USA)	68-77-74-76	295
Abe Mitchell (unattached)	78-78-72-71	299
T Barber (Cavendish)	77-73-78-71	299

1927- Mr Bobby Jones jr (at St Andrews)

Mr Bobby Jones jr (USA)	68-72-73-72	285
Aubrey Boomer (France)	76-70-73-72	291
Fred Robson (Cooden Beach)	76-72-69-74	291
Ernest Whitcombe (Bournemouth)	74-73-73-73	293
Joe Kirkwood (USA)	72-72-75-74	293

The great Bobby Jones, who won three British Open titles as an amateur, after his win at St Andrews in 1927

Walter Hagen: always a smile on his face

1928- Walter Hagen (at Sandwich, Royal St George's)

Walter Hagen (USA)	75-73-72-72	292
Gene Sarazen (USA)	72-76-73-73	294
Archie Compston (unattached)	75-74-73-73	295
Percy Alliss (Germany)	75-76-75-72	298
Fred Robson(Cooden Beach)	79-73-73-73	298

1929- Walter Hagen (at Muirfield)

Walter Hagen (USA)	75-67-75-75	292
Johnny Farrell (USA)	72-75-76-75	298
Leo Diegel (USA)	71-69-82-77	299
Abe Mitchell (unattached)	72-72-78-78	300
Percy Alliss (Germany)	69-76-76-79	300

1930- Mr Bobby Jones jr (at Hoylake, Royal Liverpool)

Mr Bobby Jones jr (USA)	70-72-74-75	291
Macdonald Smith (USA)	70-77-75-71	293
Leo Diegel (Mexico)	74-73-71-75	293
Horton Smith (USA)	72-73-78-73	296
Fred Robson (Cooden Beach)	71-72-78-75	296

1931- Tommy Armour (at Carnoustie)

Tommy Armour (USA)	73-75-77-71	296
Jose Jurado (Argentina)	76-71-73-77	297
Percy Alliss (Germany)	74-78-73-73	298
Gene Sarazen (USA)	74-76-75-73	298
Johnny Farrell (USA)	72-77-75-75	299
Macdonald Smith (USA)	75-77-71-76	299

1932- Gene Sarazen (at Sandwich, Prince's)

Gene Sarazen (USA)	70-69-70-74	283
Macdonald Smith (USA)	71-76-71-70	288
Arthur Havers (Sandy Lodge)	74-71-68-76	289
Alf Padgham (R.Ashdown Forest)	76-72-74-70	292
Percy Alliss (Beaconsfield)	71-71-78-72	292
Charles Whitcombe (Crews Hill)	71-73-73-75	292

1933- Densmore Shute (at St Andrews)

Densmore Shute (USA)	73-73-73-73	292
Craig Wood (USA)	77-72-68-75	292

Play-Off: Shute 149 (75-74); Wood 154 (78-76)

Gene Sarazen (USA)	72-73-73-75	293
Leo Diegel (USA)	75-70-71-77	293
Syd Easterbrook (Knowle)	73-72-71-77	293

1934- Henry Cotton (at Sandwich, Royal St George's)

Henry Cotton (Belgium)	67-65-72-79	283
SF Brews (South Africa)	76-71-70-71	288
Alf Padgham (Sundridge Park)	71-70-75-74	290
Macdonald Smith (USA)	77-71-72-72	292
Marcel Dallemagne (France)	71-73-71-77	292
Joe Kirkwood (USA)	74-69-71-78	292

1935- Alf Perry (at Muirfield)

Alf Perry (Leatherhead)	69-75-67-72	283
Alf Padgham (Sundridge Park)	70-72-74-71	287
Charles Whitcombe (Crews Hill)	71-68-73-76	288

Three-times Open winner Henry Cotton, seen here playing in the 1933 1,500 Guineas Southport Dunlop tournament

The 1935 Open winner Alf Perry (right) is congratulated by Wimbledon champion Fred Perry at Harrod's, in London

Mr Lawson Little (USA)	75-71-74-69	289
B Gadd (Brand Hall)	72-75-71-71	289

1936- Alf Padgham (at Hoylake, Royal Liverpool)

Alf Padgham (Sundridge Park)	73-72-71-71	287
James Adams (Romford)	71-73-71-73	288
Marcel Dallemagne (France)	73-72-75-69	289
Henry Cotton (Belgium)	73-72-70-74	289
Percy Alliss (Templenewsam)	74-72-74-71	291
Gene Sarazen (USA)	73-75-70-73	291
Tom Green (Burnham Beeches)	74-72-70-75	291

1937- Henry Cotton (at Carnoustie)

Henry Cotton (Ashridge)	74-73-72-71	290
Reg Whitcombe (Parkstone)	72-70-74-76	292
C. Lacey (USA)	76-75-70-72	293
Charles Whitcombe (Crews Hill)	73-71-74-76	294
Byron Nelson (USA)	75-76-71-74	296

1938- Reg Whitcombe (at Sandwich, Royal St George's)

Reg Whitcombe (Parkstone)	71-71-75-78	295
James Adams (R. Liverpool)	70-71-78-78	297

Henry Cotton (Ashridge)	74-73-77-74	298
Allan Dailey (Wanstead)	73-72-80-78	303
Jack Busson (Pannal)	71-69-83-80	303
Alf Padgham (Sundridge Park)	74-72-75-82	303
Dick Burton (Sale)	71-69-78-85	303

1939- Dick Burton (at St Andrews)

Dick Burton (Sale)	70-72-77-71	290
Johnny Bulla (USA)	77-71-71-73	292
Sam King (Knole Park)	74-72-75-73	294
Reg Whitcombe (Parkstone)	71-75-74-74	294
Alf Perry (Leatherhead)	71-74-73-76	294
Bill Shankland (Templenewsam)	72-73-72-77	294
John Fallon (Huddersfield)	71-73-71-79	294

No Championship 1940-45 (World War Two)

1946- Sam Snead (at Andrews)

Sam Snead (USA)	71-70-74-75	290
Bobby Locke (South Africa)	69-74-75-76	294
Johnny Bulla (USA)	71-72-72-79	294
Norman von Nida (Australia)	70-76-74-75	295
Charlie Ward (Little Aston)	73-73-73-76	295
Henry Cotton (Royal Mid-Surrey)	70-70-76-79	295
Dai Rees (Hindhead)	75-67-73-80	295

1947- Fred Daly (at Hoylake, Royal Liverpool)

Fred Daly (Balmoral)	73-70-78-72	293
Reg Horne (Hendon)	77-74-72-71	294
Mr Frank Stranahan (USA)	71-79-72-72	294
Bill Shankland (Templenewsam)	76-74-75-70	295
Dick Burton (Coombe Hill)	77-71-77-71	296

1948- Henry Cotton (at Muirfield)

Henry Cotton (Royal Mid-Surrey)	71-66-75-72	284
Fred Daly (Balmoral)	72-71-73-73	289
Norman von Nida (Australia)	71-72-76-71	290
Jack Hargreaves (S. Coldfield)	76-68-73-73	290
Charlie Ward (Little Aston)	69-72-75-74	290
Roberto de Vicenzo (Argentina)	70-73-72-75	290

1949- Bobby Locke (at Sandwich, Royal St George's)

Bobby Locke (South Africa)	69-76-68-70	283
Harry Bradshaw (Kilcroney)	68-77-68-70	283

Ben Hogan played in the British Open only once – and won it

**1952- Bobby Locke (at Royal Lytham &
St Anne's)**

Bobby Locke (South Africa)	69-71-74-73	287
Peter Thomson (Australia)	68-73-77-70	288
Fred Daly (Balmoral)	67-69-77-76	289
Henry Cotton (Royal Mid-Surrey)	75-74-74-71	294
A Cerda (Argentina)	73-73-76-73	295
Sam King (Knole Park)	71-74-74-76	295

1953- Ben Hogan (at Carnoustie)

Ben Hogan (USA)	73-71-70-68	282
Mr Frank Stranahan (USA)	70-74-73-69	286
A Cerda (Argentina)	75-71-69-71	286
Peter Thomson (Australia)	72-72-71-71	286
Dai Rees (South Herts)	72-70-73-71	286

1954- Peter Thomson (at Birkdale)

Peter Thomson (Australia)	72-71-69-71	283
Bobby Locke (South Africa)	74-71-69-70	284
Syd Scott (Carlisle City)	76-67-69-72	284
Dai Rees (South Herts)	72-71-69-72	284
James Adams (Royal Mid-Surrey)	73-75-69-69	286
Jim Turnesa (USA)	72-72-71-71	286
A Cerda (Argentina)	71-71-73-71	286

Play-Off: Locke 135 (67-68);
Bradshaw 147 (74-73)

Roberto de Vicenzo (Argentina)	68-75-73-69	285
Charlie Ward (Little Aston)	73-71-70-72	286
Sam King (Knole Park)	71-69-74-72	286

1950- Bobby Locke (at Troon)

Bobby Locke (South Africa)	69-72-70-68	279
Roberto de Vicenzo (Argentina)	72-71-68-70	281
Fred Daly (Balmoral)	75-72-69-66	282
Dai Rees (South Herts)	71-68-72-71	282
E Moore (South Africa)	74-68-73-68	283
Max Faulkner (Royal Mid-Surrey)	72-70-70-71	283

1951- Max Faulkner (at Royal Portrush)

Max Faulkner (unattached)	71-70-70-74	285
A Cerda (Argentina)	74-72-71-70	287
Charlie Ward (Little Aston)	75-73-74-68	290
James Adams (Wentworth)	68-77-75-72	292
Fred Daly (Balmoral)	74-70-75-73	292

*A happy Peter Thomson after winning his first British Open
at Birkdale in 1954, pictured with his wife Lois*

1955- Peter Thomson (at St Andrews)

Peter Thomson (Australia)	71-68-70-72	281
John Fallon (Huddersfield)	73-67-73-70	283
F Jowle (Edgbaston)	70-71-69-74	284
Bobby Locke (South Africa)	74-69-70-72	285
Ken Bousfield (Coombe Hill)	71-75-70-70	286
A Cerda (Argentina)	73-71-71-71	286
Bernard Hunt (Hartsbourne)	70-71-74-71	286
F van Donck (Belgium)	71-72-71-72	286
Harry Weetman (Croham Hurst)	71-71-70-74	286

1956- Peter Thomson (at Hoylake, Royal Liverpool)

Peter Thomson (Australia)	70-70-72-74	286
F van Donck (Belgium)	71-74-70-74	289
Roberto de Vicenzo (Mexico)	71-70-79-70	290
Gary Player (South Africa)	71-76-73-71	291
John Panton (Glenbervie)	74-76-72-70	292

1957- Bobby Locke (at St Andrews)

Bobby Locke (South Africa)	69-72-68-70	279
Peter Thomson (Australia)	73-69-70-70	282
Eric Brown (Buchanan Castle)	67-72-73-71	283
A Miguel (Spain)	72-72-69-72	285
Dave Thomas (Sudbury)	72-74-70-70	286
Mr WD Smith (Prestwick)	71-72-72-71	286
F van Donck (Belgium)	72-68-74-72	286
Tom Haliburton (Wentworth)	72-73-68-73	286

1958- Peter Thomson (at Royal Lytham & St Anne's)

Peter Thomson (Australia)	66-72-67-73	278
Dave Thomas (Sudbury)	70-68-69-71	278
Play-Off: Thomson 139 (68-71); Thomas 143 (69-74)		
Eric Brown (Buchanan Castle)	73-70-65-71	279
Christy O'Connor (Killarney)	67-68-73-71	279
Leopoldo Ruiz (Argentina)	71-65-72-73	281
F van Donck (Belgium)	70-70-67-74	281

1959- Gary Player (at Muirfield)

Gary Player (South Africa)	75-71-70-68	284
F van Donck (Belgium)	70-70-73-73	286
F Bullock (Prestwick St Nicholas)	68-70-74-74	286
Syd Scott (Roehampton)	73-70-73-71	287
Christy O'Connor (Royal Dublin)	73-74-72-69	288
John Panton (Glenbervie)	72-72-71-73	288

Mr RR Jack (Dullatur)	71-75-68-74	288
Sam King (Knole Park)	70-74-68-76	288

1960- Kel Nagle (at St Andrews)

Kel Nagle (Australia)	69-67-71-71	278
Arnold Palmer (USA)	70-71-70-68	279
Bernard Hunt (Hartsbourne)	72-73-71-66	282
Harold Henning (S Africa)	72-72-69-69	282
Roberto de Vicenzo (Mexico)	67-67-75-73	282

1961- Arnold Palmer (at Birkdale)

Arnold Palmer (USA)	70-73-69-72	284
Dai Rees (South Herts)	68-74-71-72	285
Neil Coles (Coombe Hill)	70-77-69-72	288
Christy O'Connor (Royal Dublin)	71-77-67-73	288
Eric Brown (unattached)	73-76-70-70	289
Kel Nagle (Australia)	68-75-75-71	289

1962- Arnold Palmer (at Troon)

Arnold Palmer (USA)	71-69-67-69	276
Kel Nagle (Australia)	71-71-70-70	282
Brian Huggett (Romford)	75-71-74-69	289
Phil Rodgers (USA)	75-70-72-72	289
Bob Charles (New Zealand)	75-70-70-75	290

1963- Bob Charles (at Royal Lytham & St Anne's)

Bob Charles (New Zealand)	68-72-66-71	277
Phil Rodgers (USA)	67-68-73-69	277
Play-Off: Charles 140 (69-71); Rodgers 148 (72-76)		
Jack Nicklaus (USA)	71-67-70-70	278
Kel Nagle (Australia)	69-70-73-71	283
Peter Thomson (Australia)	67-69-71-78	285

1964- Tony Lema (at St Andrews)

Tony Lema (USA)	73-68-68-70	279
Jack Nicklaus (USA)	76-74-66-68	284
Roberto de Vicenzo (Argentina)	76-72-70-67	285
Bernard Hunt (Hartsbourne)	73-74-70-70	287
Bruce Devlin (Australia)	72-72-73-73	290

1965- Peter Thomson (at Royal Birkdale)

Peter Thomson (Australia)	74-68-72-71	285
Brian Huggett (Romford)	73-68-76-70	287
Christy O'Connor (Royal Dublin)	69-73-74-71	287
Roberto de Vicenzo (Argentina)	74-69-73-72	288
Bernard Hunt (Hartsbourne)	74-74-70-71	289
Kel Nagle (Australia)	74-70-73-72	289
Tony Lema (USA)	68-72-75-74	289

1966- Jack Nicklaus (at Muirfield)

Jack Nicklaus (USA)	70-67-75-70	282
Dave Thomas (Dunham Forest)	72-73-69-69	283
Doug Sanders (USA)	71-70-72-70	283
Gary Player (South Africa)	72-74-71-69	286
Bruce Devlin (Australia)	73-69-74-70	286
Kel Nagle (Australia)	72-68-76-70	286
Phil Rodgers (USA)	74-66-70-76	286

1967- Roberto de Vicenzo (at Hoylake, Royal Liverpool)

Roberto de Vicenzo (Argentina)	70-71-67-70	278
Jack Nicklaus (USA)	71-69-71-69	280
Clive Clark (Sunningdale)	70-73-69-72	284
Gary Player (South Africa)	72-71-67-74	284
Tony Jacklin (Potters Bar)	73-69-73-70	285

A second British Open victory for a delighted South African Gary Player in 1968

1968- Gary Player (at Carnoustie)

Gary Player (South Africa)	74-71-71-73	289
Jack Nicklaus (USA)	76-69-73-73	291
Bob Charles (New Zealand)	72-72-71-76	291
Billy Casper (USA)	72-68-74-78	292
Maurice Bembridge (Little Aston)	71-75-73-74	293

1969- Tony Jacklin (at Royal Lytham & St Anne's)

Tony Jacklin (Potters Bar)	68-70-70-72	280
Bob Charles (New Zealand)	66-69-75-72	282
Roberto de Vicenzo (Argentina)	72-73-66-72	283

Peter Thomson (Australia)	71-70-70-72	283
Christy O'Connor (Royal Dublin)	71-65-74-74	284

Jack Nicklaus (right) contested a play-off against Doug Sanders (left) in 1970 at St Andrews to clinch victory

1970- Jack Nicklaus (at St Andrews)

Jack Nicklaus (USA)	68-69-73-73	283
Doug Sanders (USA)	68-71-71-73	283
Play-Off: Nicklaus 72; Sanders 73		
Harold Henning (S Africa)	67-72-73-73	285
Lee Trevino (USA)	68-68-72-77	285
Tony Jacklin (GB&I)	67-70-73-76	286
Peter Oosterhuis (GB&I)	73-69-69-76	287
Neil Coles (GB&I)	65-74-72-76	287
Hugh Jackson (GB&I)	69-72-73-74	288
John Panton (GB&I)	72-73-73-71	289
Peter Thomson (Australia)	68-74-73-74	289
Tommy Horton (GB&I)	66-73-75-75	289

1971- Lee Trevino (at Royal Birkdale)

Lee Trevino (USA)	69-70-69-70	278
Liang Huan Lu (Taiwan)	70-70-69-70	279
Tony Jacklin (GB&I)	69-70-70-71	280
Craig DeFoy (GB&I)	72-72-68-69	281
Charles Coody (USA)	74-71-70-68	283
Jack Nicklaus (USA)	71-71-72-69	283
Billy Casper (USA)	70-72-75-67	284
Gary Player (South Africa)	71-70-71-72	284
Doug Sanders (USA)	73-71-74-67	285
Peter Thomson (Australia)	70-73-73-69	285

1972- Lee Trevino (at Muirfield)

Lee Trevino (USA)	71-70-66-71	278
Jack Nicklaus (USA)	70-72-71-66	279
Tony Jacklin (GB&I)	69-72-67-72	280
Doug Sanders (USA)	71-71-69-70	281
Brian Barnes (GB&I)	71-72-69-71	283
Gary Player (South Africa)	71-71-76-67	285
David Vaughan (GB&I)	74-73-70-69	286
Tom Weiskopf (USA)	73-74-70-69	286
Arnold Palmer (USA)	73-73-69-71	286
Guy Hunt (GB&I)	75-72-67-72	286

1973- Tom Weiskopf (at Troon)

Tom Weiskopf (USA)	68-67-71-70	276
Neil Coles (GB&I)	71-72-70-66	279
Johnny Miller (USA)	70-68-69-72	279
Jack Nicklaus (USA)	69-70-76-65	280
Bert Yancey (USA)	69-69-73-70	281
Peter Butler (GB&I)	71-72-74-69	286
Bob Charles (New Zealand)	73-71-73-71	288
Christy O'Connor (GB&I)	73-68-74-73	288
Lanny Wadkins (USA)	71-73-70-74	288
Lee Trevino (USA)	75-73-73-68	289
Gay Brewer (USA)	76-71-72-70	289
Harold Henning (South Africa)	73-73-73-70	289
Brian Barnes (GB&I)	76-67-70-76	289

1974- Gary Player (at Royal Lytham & St Anne's)

Gary Player (South Africa)	69-68-75-70	282
Peter Oosterhuis (GB&I)	71-71-73-71	286
Jack Nicklaus (USA)	74-72-70-71	287
Hubert Green (USA)	71-74-72-71	288
David Edwards (USA)	70-73-76-73	292
Liang Huan Lu (Taiwan)	72-72-75-73	292
Donald Swaelens (Belgium)	77-73-74-69	293
Tom Weiskopf (USA)	72-72-74-75	293
Bobby Cole (South Africa)	70-72-76-75	293
Johnny Miller (USA)	72-75-73-74	294

1975- Tom Watson (at Carnoustie)

Tom Watson (USA)	71-67-69-72	279
Jack Newton (Australia)	69-71-65-74	279
Play-Off: Watson 71; Newton 72		
Jack Nicklaus (USA)	69-71-68-72	280
Johnny Miller (USA)	71-69-66-74	280
Bobby Cole (South Africa)	72-66-66-76	280
Graham Marsh (Australia)	72-67-71-71	281
Peter Oosterhuis (GB&I)	68-70-71-73	282
Neil Coles (GB&I)	72-69-67-74	282
Hale Irwin (USA)	69-70-69-75	283
George Burns (USA)	71-73-69-71	284
John Mahaffey (USA)	71-68-69-76	284

'Supermex' Lee Trevino holds up the claret jug after a dramatic finale to the 1972 Championship at Muirfield

1976- Johnny Miller (at Royal Birkdale)

Johnny Miller (USA)	72-68-73-66	279
Jack Nicklaus (USA)	74-70-72-69	285
Seve Ballesteros (Sp)	69-69-73-74	285
Ray Floyd (USA)	76-67-73-70	286
Mark James (GB&I)	76-72-74-66	288
Hubert Green (USA)	72-70-78-68	288
Tom Kite (USA)	70-74-73-71	288
Christy O'Connor jr (GB&I)	69-73-75-71	288
Tommy Horton (GB&I)	74-69-72-73	288
Vicente Fernandez (Argentina)	79-71-69-70	289
Peter Butler (GB&I)	74-72-73-70	289
Norio Suzuki (Japan)	69-75-75-70	289
George Burns (USA)	75-69-75-70	289

1977- Tom Watson (at Turnberry)

Tom Watson (USA)	68-70-65-65	268
Jack Nicklaus (USA)	68-70-65-66	269
Hubert Green (USA)	72-66-74-67	279
Lee Trevino (USA)	68-70-72-70	280
George Burns (USA)	70-70-72-69	281
Ben Crenshaw (USA)	71-69-66-75	281
Arnold Palmer (USA)	73-73-67-69	282
Ray Floyd (USA)	70-73-68-72	283
John Schroeder (USA)	66-74-73-71	284
Mark Hayes (USA)	76-63-72-73	284
Tommy Horton (GB&I)	70-74-65-75	284
Johnny Miller (USA)	69-74-67-74	284

1978- Jack Nicklaus (at St Andrews)

Jack Nicklaus (USA)	71-72-69-69	281
Simon Owen (New Zealand)	70-75-67-71	283

Ray Floyd (USA)	69-75-71-68	283
Ben Crenshaw (USA)	70-69-73-71	283
Tom Kite (USA)	72-69-72-70	283
Peter Oosterhuis (GB&I)	72-70-69-73	284
Isao Aoki (Japan)	68-71-73-73	285
Bob Shearer (Australia)	71-69-74-71	285
John Schroeder (USA)	74-69-70-72	285
Nick Faldo (GB&I)	71-72-70-72	285

1979- Seve Ballesteros (at Royal ͟͟͟͟ St Anne's)

	͟͟͟	287
	͟͟-70-70-73	288
Hale Irwin (USA)	68-68-75-78	289
Graham Marsh (Australia)	74-68-75-74	291
Isao Aoki (Japan)	70-74-72-75	291
Bob Byman (USA)	73-70-72-76	291
Bob Charles (New Zealand)	78-72-70-72	292
Jumbo Ozaki (Japan)	75-69-75-73	292
Greg Norman (Australia)	73-71-72-76	292

1980- Tom Watson (at Muirfield)

Tom Watson (USA)	68-70-64-69	271
Lee Trevino (USA)	68-67-71-69	275
Ben Crenshaw (USA)	70-70-68-69	277
Jack Nicklaus (USA)	73-67-71-69	280
Carl Mason (GB&I)	72-69-70-69	280
Craig Stadler (USA)	72-70-69-71	282
Andy Bean (USA)	71-69-70-72	282
Hubert Green (USA)	77-69-64-72	282
Ken Brown (GB&I)	70-68-68-76	282
Jack Newton (Australia)	69-71-73-70	283
Gil Morgan (USA)	70-70-71-72	283

1981- Bill Rogers (at Sandwich, Royal St George's)

Bill Rogers (USA)	72-66-67-71	276
Bernhard Langer (West Germany)	73-67-70-70	280
Ray Floyd (USA)	74-70-69-70	283
Mark James (GB&I)	72-70-68-73	283
Sam Torrance (GB&I)	72-69-73-70	284
Bruce Lietzke (USA)	76-69-71-69	285
Manuel Pinero (Spain)	73-74-68-70	285
Howard Clark (GB&I)	72-76-70-68	286
Ben Crenshaw (USA)	72-67-76-71	286
Brian Jones (Australia)	73-76-66-71	286

1982- Tom Watson (at Royal Troon)

Tom Watson (USA)	69-71-74-70	284
Peter Oosterhuis (GB&I)	74-67-74-70	285

Nick Price (South Africa)	69-69-74-73	285
Tom Purtzer (USA)	76-66-75-69	286
Nick Faldo (GB&I)	73-73-71-69	286
Masahiro Kuramoto (Japan)	71-73-71-71	286
Des Smyth (GB&I)	70-69-74-73	286
Fuzzy Zoeller (USA)	73-71-73-70	287
Sandy Lyle (GB&I)	74-66-73-74	287
Jack Nicklaus (USA)	77-70-72-69	288
͟͟pett (USA)	67-66-78-77	288

1983- Tom Watson (at Royal Birkdale)

Tom Watson (USA)	67-68-70-70	275
Hale Irwin (USA)	69-68-72-67	276
Andy Bean (USA)	70-69-70-67	276
Graham Marsh (Australia)	69-70-74-64	277
Lee Trevino (USA)	69-66-73-70	278
Seve Ballesteros (Spain)	71-71-69-68	279
Harold Henning (South Africa)	71-69-70-69	279
Denis Durnian (GB&I)	73-66-74-67	280
Christy O'Connor jr (GB&I)	72-69-71-68	280
Bill Rogers (USA)	67-71-73-69	280
Nick Faldo (GB&I)	68-68-71-73	280

1984- Seve Ballesteros (at St Andrews)

Seve Ballesteros (Spain)	69-68-70-69	276
Bernhard Langer (West Germany)	71-68-68-71	278
Tom Watson (USA)	71-68-66-73	278
Fred Couples (USA)	70-69-74-68	281
Lanny Wadkins (USA)	70-69-73-69	281
Greg Norman (Australia)	67-74-74-67	282
Nick Faldo (GB&I)	69-68-76-69	282
Mark McCumber (USA)	74-67-72-70	283
Graham Marsh (Australia)	70-74-73-67	284
Sam Torrance (GB&I)	74-74-66-70	284
Ronan Rafferty (GB&I)	74-72-67-71	284
Hugh Baiocchi (South Africa)	72-70-70-72	284
Ian Baker-Finch (Australia)	68-66-71-79	284

1985- Sandy Lyle (at Sandwich, Royal St George's)

Sandy Lyle (GB&I)	68-71-73-70	282
Payne Stewart (USA)	70-75-70-68	283
Jose Rivero (Spain)	74-72-70-68	284
Christy O'Connor jr (GB&I)	64-76-72-72	284
Mark O'Meara (USA)	70-72-70-72	284
David Graham (Australia)	68-71-70-75	284
Bernhard Langer (West Germany)	72-69-68-75	284
Anders Forsbrand (Sweden)	70-76-69-70	285
DA Weibring (USA)	69-71-74-71	285
Tom Kite (USA)	73-73-67-72	285

1986- Greg Norman (at Turnberry)

Greg Norman (Australia)	74-63-74-69	280
Gordon J Brand (GB&I)	71-68-75-71	285
Bernhard Langer (West Germany)	72-70-76-68	286
Ian Woosnam (GB&I)	70-74-70-72	286
Nick Faldo (GB&I)	71-70-76-70	287
Seve Ballesteros (Spain)	76-75-73-64	288
Gary Koch (USA)	73-72-72-71	288
Fuzzy Zoeller (USA)	75-73-72-69	289
Brain Marchbank (GB&I)	78-70-72-69	289
Tommy Nakajima (Japan)	74-67-71-77	289

1987- Nick Faldo (at Muirfield)

Nick Faldo (GB&I)	68-69-71-71	279
Rodger Davis (Australia)	64-73-74-69	280
Paul Azinger (USA)	68-68-71-73	280
Ben Crenshaw (USA)	73-68-72-68	281
Payne Stewart (USA)	71-66-72-72	281
David Frost (South Africa)	70-68-70-74	282
Tom Watson (USA)	69-69-71-74	283
Ian Woosnam (GB&I)	71-69-72-72	284
Nick Price (Zimbabwe)	68-71-72-73	284
Craig Stadler (USA)	69-69-71-75	284

1988- Seve Ballesteros (at Royal Lytham & St Anne's)

Seve Ballesteros (Spain)	67-71-70-65	273
Nick Price (Zimbabwe)	70-67-69-69	275
Nick Faldo (GB&I)	71-69-68-71	279
Fred Couples (USA)	73-69-71-68	281
Gary Koch (USA)	71-72-70-68	281
Peter Senior (Australia)	70-73-70-69	282
David Frost (South Africa)	71-75-69-68	283
Payne Stewart (USA)	73-75-68-67	283
Isao Aoki (Japan)	72-71-73-67	283
Sandy Lyle (GB&I)	73-69-67-74	283

1989- Mark Calcavecchia (at Royal Troon)

Mark Calcavecchia (USA)	71-68-68-68	275
Greg Norman (Australia)	69-70-72-64	275
Wayne Grady (Australia)	68-67-69-71	275

Calcavecchia won four-hole play-off

Tom Watson (USA)	69-68-68-72	277
Jodie Mudd (USA)	73-67-68-70	278
David Feherty (GB&I)	71-67-69-72	279
Fred Couples (USA)	68-71-68-72	279
Eduardo Romero (Argentina)	68-70-75-67	280
Paul Azinger (USA)	68-73-67-72	280
Payne Stewart (USA)	72-65-69-74	280

1990- Nick Faldo (at St Andrews)

Nick Faldo (GB&I)	67-65-67-71	270
Mark McNulty (Zimbabwe)	74-68-68-65	275

Ian Baker-Finch of Australia, champion in 1991

Payne Stewart (USA)	68-68-68-71	275
Ian Woosnam (GB&I)	68-69-70-69	276
Jodie Mudd (USA)	72-66-72-66	276
Ian Baker-Finch (Australia)	68-72-64-73	277
Greg Norman (Australia)	66-66-76-69	277
Steve Pate (USA)	70-68-72-69	279
Corey Pavin (USA)	71-69-68-71	279
Donnie Hammond (USA)	70-71-68-70	279
David Graham (Australia)	72-71-70-66	279

1991- Ian Baker-Finch (at Royal Birkdale)

Ian Baker-Finch (Australia)	71-71-64-66	272
Mike Harwood (Australia)	68-70-69-67	274
Mark O'Meara (USA)	71-68-67-69	275
Fred Couples (USA)	72-69-70-64	275
Jodie Mudd (USA)	72-70-72-63	277
Eamonn Darcy (GB&I)	73-68-66-70	277
Bob Tway (USA)	75-66-70-66	277
Craig Parry (Australia)	71-70-69-68	278
Greg Norman (Australia)	74-68-71-66	279
Bernhard Langer (Germany)	71-71-70-67	279
Seve Ballesteros (Spain)	66-73-69-71	279

1992- Nick Faldo   (at Muirfield)

Nick Faldo(GB&I)	66-64-69-73	272
John Cook (USA)	66-67-70-70	273
Jose-Maria Olazabal (Spain)	70-67-69-68	274

Nick Price celebrates his eagle putt at the 17th on the way to winning at Turnberry in 1994

Steve Pate (USA)	64-70-69-73	276
Donnie Hammond (USA)	70-65-70-74	279
Andrew Magee (USA)	67-72-70-70	279
Ernie Els (South Africa)	66-69-70-74	279
Ian Woosnam (GB&I)	65-73-70-71	279
Gordon Brand jr (GB&I)	65-68-72-74	279
Malcolm Mackenzie (GB&I)	71-67-70-71	279
Robert Karlsson (Sweden)	70-68-70-71	279

1993- Greg Norman (at Sandwich, Royal St George's)

Greg Norman (Australia)	66-68-69-64	267
Nick Faldo (GB&I)	69-63-70-67	269
Bernhard Langer (Germany)	67-66-70-67	270
Corey Pavin (USA)	68-66-68-70	272
Peter Senior (Australia)	66-69-70-67	272
Nick Price (Zimbabwe)	68-70-67-69	274
Ernie Els (South Africa)	68-69-69-68	274
Paul Lawrie (GB&I)	72-68-69-65	274
Wayne Grady (Australia)	74-68-64-69	275
Fred Couples (USA)	68-66-72-69	275
Scott Simpson (USA)	68-70-71-66	275

1994- Nick Price (at Turnberry)

Nick Price (Zimbabwe)	69-66-67-66	268
Jesper Parnevik (Sweden)	68-66-68-67	269
Fuzzy Zoeller (USA)	71-66-64-70	271
Anders Forsbrand (Sweden)	72-71-66-64	273
Mark James (GB&I)	72-67-66-68	273
David Feherty (GB&I)	68-69-66-70	273
Brad Faxon (USA)	69-65-67-73	274
Colin Montgomerie (GB&I)	72-69-65-69	275
Tom Kite (USA)	71-69-66-69	275
Nick Faldo (GB&I)	75-66-70-64	275

1995- John Daly (at St Andrews)

John Daly (USA)	67-71-73-71	282
Costantino Rocca (Italy)	69-70-70-73	282
Daly won four-hole play-off		
Michael Campbell (New Zealand)	71-71-65-76	283
Mark Brooks (USA)	70-69-73-71	283
Steven Bottomley (GB&I)	70-72-72-69	283
Vijay Singh (Fiji)	68-72-73-71	284
Steve Elkington (Australia)	72-69-69-74	284
Corey Pavin (USA)	69-70-72-74	285
Mark James (GB&I)	72-75-68-70	285
Bob Estes (USA)	72-70-71-72	285

Mark Hayes: first player to shoot 63 in the British Open

BRITISH OPEN SUMMARY

Most Victories:	6 -	Harry Vardon (1896-98-99-1903-11-14)
	5 -	James Braid (1901-05-06-08-10)
		JH Taylor (1894-95-1900-09-13)
		Peter Thomson (1954-55-56-58-65)
		Tom Watson (1975-77-80-82-83)
Oldest Champions:		Tom Morris sr (46 yrs, 99 dys, 1867)
		Roberto de Vicenzo (44 yrs, 93 dys, 1967)
Youngest Champions:		Tom Morris jr (17 yrs, 5 mths, 8 dys, 1868) - won 4 times in a row
		Willie Auchterlonie (21 yrs, 24 days, 1893)
		Seve Ballesteros (22 yrs, 3 mths, 12 days, 1979)
Widest Winning Margin:	13 -	Tom Morris sr (1862)
	12 -	Tom Morris jr (1870)
(Since 2nd World War):	6 -	Arnold Palmer (1962)
		Johnny Miller (1976)
Lowest 72-Hole Totals:	267 -	Greg Norman (1993 at Royal St George's)
	268 -	Tom Watson (1977 at Turnberry)
		Nick Price (1994 at Turnberry)
Best 18-Hole Round:	63 -	7 times (first by Mark Hayes, Turnberry, 1977)

SHORT PUTTS

Bradshaw's bottle

One of the most unfortunate incidents in Open history came at Sandwich in 1949. At the 5th hole in round two, the drive of Ireland's Harry Bradshaw finished inside a broken bottle. Unable to decide whether his ball was in an unplayable position or not, Bradshaw went ahead and played the ball as it lay. The result was a double-bogey six, en route to a 77. Yet the significance of this incident did not become apparent until the end of the regulation 72 holes when Bradshaw was tied for first place with Bobby Locke. The pair contested a 36-hole play-off the following day when Locke won by 12 strokes.

Small blunders

Possibly the best remembered missed putt of all time was that of Doug Sanders on the final hole at St Andrews in 1970. Then, he stood over a putt of about one yard to win the title by a single shot, only to miss it comfortably. A day later he lost an 18-hole play-off to Jack Nicklaus 72-73. Yet 37 years earlier on the very same green, another American, Leo Diegel, missed a similar length putt which, had he holed it, would have got him into a play-off. But probably the smallest blunder of all time was Hale Irwin's missed putt of about one inch in the 1983 Open at Royal Birkdale. At the par-three 14th in round three, Irwin carelessly took his eye off the ball as he went to complete the formality of tapping-in. But his putter head never came in contact with the ball and Irwin called a one shot penalty on himself. He registered a bogey. Twenty-four hours later he'd tied for second, one stroke behind winner Tom Watson.

Jones genius

One of the greatest Open shots of all time was played by amateur Bobby Jones, who after 70 holes of the 1926 contest at Royal Lytham & St Anne's was tied for the lead with fellow American Al Watrous. The penultimate hole is one of the more testing par fours in links golf. It was here that Jones hooked his drive into a shallow bunker some 170 yards from the green. The only route to the pin was over sandhills, yet from a difficult lie over treacherous landscape and into the wind, Jones managed to fly his ball to within 15 feet of the flag. He made par, while an obviously shaken Watrous three-putted for a five. Jones made a more conventional par four at the last where his playing partner made another bogey after finding sand himself. Jones had won by two strokes. And on Lytham's 17th hole, a bronze plaque now marks the spot from where Jones played his remarkable 'championship-winning' shot.

Whew! That was close

Irishman Fred Daly looked a comfortable winner as he sat in the clubhouse at Hoylake, Royal Liverpool, in 1947. The only player left who could beat him was American amateur Frank Stranahan who needed to eagle the final hole - a par four to tie. From the centre of the fairway, Stranahan had to sink his second shot from around 160 yards. Straight on line, his ball landed about ten feet from the flag and rolled to within inches of the cup, perfect on length, just a little to the left. Daly had won, but only in a dramatic finish.

Hsieh hell

In the final round of the 1983 Open (Royal Birkdale) Taiwan's Yu-Shu Hsieh covered the first 16 holes in a respectable level par. In normal circumstances, the 17th shouldn't have created a problem, in fact being a par five it was one of the easier birdie opportunities on the course. But not for Hsieh who needed five shots to rid himself of a sandbank just short of the green. He finally got down in 11 (six over par) and completed his round with a 78 (+7) for a 72-hole total of 295.

Palmer's missed opportunity

When Arnold Palmer arrived at St Andrews in 1960 he was seeking the grand slam having won the first two legs, the US Masters and US Open, earlier in the year. If he could win the British as well he would equal the achievement of Ben Hogan in 1953. Hogan remains the only player in history to win three majors in the same year. After 36 holes Palmer trailed leader Roberto de Vicenzo by seven and the eventual champion, Kel Nagle, by five. After three rounds he'd reduced the gap on new-leader Nagle to four, after Vicenzo had blown up with a 75. Yet with two holes to play in the final round it was down to just two strokes. Palmer, playing just ahead of Nagle, made a par four at the dangerous Road Hole (17th) before pitching to within four feet of

the flag at 18, where he closed with a birdie. Nagle, meanwhile, was back on the 17th green needing a six-footer for par. The cool Australian firmly holed out to take a one-stroke lead up the last. A par four at the reasonably easy 18th gave him a one-stroke edge over Palmer who had come so close to emulating Hogan.

Hot stuff

Australian Ian Baker-Finch needed only 61 strokes to play 18 consecutive holes in his Championship winning year of 1991. First, he covered the back-nine of Saturday's third round in 32, before going out in 29 on the final day. His last two rounds were 64-66 and he eventually won by two strokes from fellow Aussie Mike Harwood.

Age doesn't matter

At the famous Postage Stamp hole (the 126-yard 8th) at Royal Troon in 1973, 71-year-old American Gene Sarazen and 19-year-old English amateur David J Russell both scored holes in one. They came within an hour of each other in round one. The following day both players made birdie 2s at the same hole - Sarazen holing out from a greenside bunker.

Over par

Sandy Lyle's victory in 1985 was the most recent occasion in any of the four major championships that the winner completed 72-holes over par. The 27-year-old Scotsman had rounds of 68-71-73-70 for a two-over-par total of 282 at Royal St George's GC, Sandwich.

American blues at Lytham

As yet, no American professional has won the title at Royal Lytham & St Anne's. In eight stagings of the event on the Fylde coast, the only American winner was an amateur, Bobby Jones in 1926. Since then, the seven titles have been shared by South Africa (Locke & Player), Spain (Ballesteros - twice), Australia (Thomson), New Zealand (Charles) and Britain (Jacklin).

British blushes at Birkdale

While the Americans have struggled at Lytham, the Brits have drawn a blank at Royal Birkdale, which staged the first of its seven Opens in 1954. The winners have either been American (Arnold Palmer, Lee Trevino, Johnny Miller & Tom Watson) or Australian (Peter Thomson (twice) & Ian Baker-Finch).

What a difference a day makes

Up until 1965, the championship traditionally finished on a Friday - when the last two rounds were played on the final day (not including play-offs). From 1966 through to 1979, the last scheduled day was Saturday (one round a day Wednesday through Saturday). Since 1980, the British Open has ended on a Sunday and for one year only - 1988 - bad weather meant the tournament had to be extended into the Monday.

Early fright

Bill Rogers, champion at Royal St George's in 1981, nearly missed out. On the first morning, the American came within 30 seconds of being disqualified for being late on the first tee. While travelling to the course, his car had been held up for almost half-an-hour at a level crossing.

Opening shots

The first Open Championship was held at Prestwick on October 17th 1860, although the word Open was slightly misleading because entries were limited to Scotland. However, by 1861, it was decided that the Championship belt should be open to any player in the world.

In 1870, the Championship belt became the property of Tom Morris jr who had won the tournament three years in a row. After a gap of one year, the Open returned in 1872, when the golfers played for a cup, jointly donated by the three most influential clubs of that time - St Andrews, Prestwick and Musselburgh. That famous claret jug is still the prize today.

Changing rewards

It is highly unlikely that any of today's leading players would ever fall upon hard times. But this is what happened to Jamie Anderson, the winner of three successive Open titles from 1877 to 1879. The life of a professional in those days was difficult and did not offer great rewards. At the time of his death in 1905, Anderson was living in a poor house in Perth.

Smashing time

Alf Padgham endured an unnerving experience during his title winning year of 1936. Having left his clubs in the professional's shop overnight, he arrived at Hoylake early on the final morning to find that they were still locked away and there was no one there with a key to open up. Fearing that a late start would amount to disqualification, there was little alternative but to smash the shop window with a brick in order to retrieve the clubs. Padgham played the final 36 holes that day in 142 strokes - two rounds of 71.

Duncan back from obscurity

After 36 holes of the 1920 Championship at Deal in Kent, George Duncan was some 13 strokes behind leader Abe Mitchell after carding two rounds of 80. Duncan was one of the early starters in round three, and while his 71 was certainly a vast improvement on his first two rounds, it didn't seem likely that he would move into contention. But this is exactly what happened. Few players scored well in round three, particularly Mitchell who slumped to an 84. Duncan had made-up 13 strokes on Mitchell in just 18 holes, and now lay just two strokes off the pace. Duncan closed with a 72 to win by two strokes, overtaking a number of players, including third round leader Len Holland who shot 79.

Lee's present

After winning in 1971 at Royal Birkdale, Lee Trevino donated £2,000 of his £5,500 first prize to a Formby orphanage.

Some finish

One of the great finishes of all time came in 1878 when the eventual champion Jamie Anderson arrived at the 15th tee at Prestwick knowing he needed to play the last four holes in just 16 strokes to beat JOF Morris who was the leader in the clubhouse with a 36-hole total of 161.

At the 15th he holed out with a long iron for a three, made four at 16, and then produced one of the most remarkable shots of all time at 17. Although not a particularly great stroke, his ball struck a bank beside the green and rolled into the cup for a hole-in-one. He then scored five on the final hole to post a final total of 157, four better than Morris. However, the drama had not ended because Bob Kirk later came to the final hole with a chance to tie Anderson only to miss out by one stroke.

What a way to start

At the opening hole of the 1976 Championship at Royal Birkdale, South African Bobby Cole took five putts from around 40 feet. Cole, who the previous year at Carnoustie had missed out on a play-off by just one shot, left his first putt four feet short. His second went 30 inches past, his third was also 30 inches too strong and his fourth over shot the hole by two feet. The long, hot summer had made the greens faster than normal. Cole finished 17 shots behind champion Johnny Miller.

CLASSIC MOMENTS

SIX OF THE BEST

1) 1926, Bobby Jones, par-4, 17th at Royal Lytham & St Anne's: *From a shallow bunker to the left of the 17th fairway and 170 yards from the green, Jones hit a high shot to within 12 feet of the cup. From a likely bogey five, Jones managed to make a match-winning four. (see Jones Genius)*

2) 1954, Peter Thomson, par-5 16th at Royal Birkdale: *After a splendid drive, Thomson slightly miscued his fairway wood second shot, leaving his ball in a bunker about 25 yards from the pin. Yet from a potentially difficult situation, the 24-year-old Australian exploded to within two feet of the flag and holed the putt. Thomson went on to win the first of his five Open titles by one stroke.*

3) 1968, Gary Player, par-5 14th at Carnoustie: *With five holes remaining, Player was tied for the lead with Bob Charles and Billy Casper, and two strokes ahead of Jack Nicklaus. His drive at the hole named Spectacles, left him a three-wood shot to the green. From there he hammered his ball over the two Spectacle-looking bunkers, to rest no more than two feet from the pin. Player duly got his eagle three which gave him some day light over the rest of the field. He eventually won by two strokes from Nicklaus and Charles.*

4) 1977, Tom Watson, par-4 18th at Turnberry: *The classic head-to-head duel between Tom Watson and Jack Nicklaus reached its climax on the 72nd fairway. A short missed putt by Nicklaus on the 17th green had given Watson the lead for the first time on that final afternoon. At 18, Watson took a 1-iron off the tee for safety and was sitting pretty in the fairway. Nicklaus, however, had used his driver in the hope of gaining extra-length but had blocked his tee shot out right, leaving his ball inches from oblivion yet just about playable. Watson hit his second shot first. His 7-iron was right on line. It landed a mere three feet from the cup. It was the stroke that clinched Watson the title, although there was still more drama to come. Nicklaus, somehow, managed to find the green from his tough lie with an 8-iron and then incredibly holed a 20-foot putt for a birdie three. However, Watson was close enough to the hole to shut the door on Nicklaus by a single stroke.*

5) 1984, Seve Ballesteros, par-4 17th at St Andrews: *Seve Ballesteros denied Tom Watson a third successive title by making one of the greatest finishes ever seen in an Open championship. Although not paired together for the final round both players stood at 11 under par on the 71st tee. The 17th (Road Hole) at St Andrews is one of the great holes in golf. Despite being a par-4, it is a difficult green to find in two. Length isn't the problem. A deep bunker threatens the front left of the green, while to overshoot on the right will take the ball onto the road from which the hole gets its name. And even if a player tries to get up and down in two from short of the green for par, the contours of the putting surface are likely to cause grief. You simply can't get a conservative par four here. And so it was. Having driven into rough on the left side of the fairway, the Spaniard then played one of the bravest strokes of his career. A towering 6-iron found the putting surface. On most holes an inch perfect shot means landing the ball three feet from the cup, but at the Road Hole, it means 'just' finding the green. Seve got his par - the first time he'd achieved that all week. That put the pressure on Watson, who minutes later overdid his approach. His ball landed on the green but then kicked forward onto the road and bounced against the wall that lay beyond the tarmac. It came to rest two feet away from it. Watson was unable to make par. While all this was going on Seve had made birdie at 18 to win his second Open title. But for most on-lookers, it was his second to 17 that did the damage.*

6) 1994, Nick Price, par-5 17th at Turnberry: *While Nick Price was walking onto the 71st green to survey a putt of around 50 feet, tournament leader Jesper Parnevik was bogeying the final hole. It meant that Price was now only one stroke behind the Swede and having reached the 17th green in two, he had an outside chance of making an eagle. A birdie four, however, looked the more likely scenario. But his slightly downhill putt had the perfect line and pace. It rolled in for a three, giving the Zimbabwean the outright lead. A par four at 18 earned Price the greatest prize of his life.*

UNITED STATES OPEN

Note: From 1895 through to 1969, players are associated by their club. United States clubs are named in full while those attached to overseas clubs are listed by country. Most players were connected to clubs in their own country, although there were one or two exceptions.

1895- Horace Rawlins (at Newport GC, Rhode Island)

Horace Rawlins (Newport)	45-46-41-41	173
Willie Dunn (Shinnecock Hills)	43-46-44-42	175
James Foulis (Chicago)	46-43-44-43	176
Mr AW Smith (Toronto)	47-43-44-42	176
WF Davis (Newport)	45-49-42-42	178

Note: The first US Open was played on a nine-hole course.

1896- James Foulis (at Shinnecock Hills GC, New York)

James Foulis (Chicago)	78-74	152
Horace Rawlins (Sadaquada)	79-76	155
Joe Lloyd (Essex County)	76-81	157
George Douglas (Brookline)	79-79	158
Mr AW Smith (Toronto)	78-80	158

1897- Joe Lloyd (at Chicago GC, Wheaton, Illinois)

Joe Lloyd (Essex County)	83-79	162
Willie Anderson (Watch Hill)	79-84	163
James Foulis (Chicago)	80-88	168
Willie Dunn (New York)	87-81	168
WT Hoare (Pittsburgh)	82-87	169

1898- Fred Herd (at Myopia Hunt Club, Hamilton, Mass.)

Fred Herd (Washington Park)	84-85-75-84	328
Alex Smith (Washington Park)	78-86-86-85	335
Willie Anderson (Baltusrol)	81-82-87-86	336
Joe Lloyd (Essex County)	87-80-86-86	339
Willie Smith (Shinnecock Hills)	82-91-85-82	340

1899- Willie Smith (at Baltimore CC, Maryland)

Willie Smith (Midlothian)	77-82-79-77	315
George Low (Dyker Meadow)	82-79-89-76	326
Val Fitzjohn (Otsego)	85-80-79-82	326
WH Way (Detroit)	80-85-80-81	326
Willie Anderson (New York)	77-81-85-84	327

1900- Harry Vardon (at Chicago GC, Wheaton, Illinois)

Harry Vardon (England)	79-78-76-80	313
JH Taylor (England)	76-82-79-78	315
David Bell (Midlothian)	78-83-83-78	322
Laurie Auchterlonie (Glen View)	84-82-80-81	327
Willie Smith (Midlothian)	82-83-79-83	327

1901- Willie Anderson (at Myopia Hunt Club, Hamilton, Mass.)

Willie Anderson (Pittsfield)	84-83-83-81	331
Alex Smith (Washington Park)	82-82-87-80	331

Play-Off: Anderson 85; Smith 86

Willie Smith (Midlothian)	84-86-82-81	333
Stewart Gardner (Garden City)	86-82-81-85	334
Laurie Auchterlonie (Garden City)	81-85-86-83	335
Bernard Nicholls (Boston)	84-85-83-83	335

1902- Laurie Auchterlonie (at The Garden City GC, New York)

Laurie Auchterlonie (Chicago)	78-78-74-77	307
Stewart Gardner (Garden City)	82-76-77-78	313
Mr Walter J Travis (Garden City)	82-82-75-74	313
Willie Smith (Chicago)	82-79-80-75	316
John Shippen (New York)	83-81-75-79	318
Willie Anderson (Montclair)	79-82-76-81	318

1903- Willie Anderson (at Baltusrol GC, Springfield, New Jersey)

Willie Anderson (Apawamis)	73-76-76-82	307
David Brown (Wollaston)	79-77-75-76	307

Play-Off: Anderson 82; Brown 84

Stewart Gardner (Garden City)	77-77-82-79	315
Alex Smith (Nassau)	77-77-81-81	316
Donald J Ross (Oakley)	79-79-78-82	318

1904- Willie Anderson (at Glen View Club, Illinois)

Willie Anderson (Apawamis)	75-78-78-72	303
Gilbert Nicholls (St Louis)	80-76-79-73	308
Fred Mackenzie (Onwentsia)	76-79-74-80	309
Laurie Auchterlonie (Glen View)	80-81-75-78	314
Bernard Nicholls (Elyria)	80-77-79-78	314

1905- Willie Anderson (at Myopia Hunt Club, Hamilton, Mass.)

Willie Anderson (Apawamis)	81-80-76-77	314
Alex Smith (Nassau)	76-80-80-80	316
Peter Robertson (Oakmont)	79-80-81-77	317
Percy Barrett (Canada)	81-80-77-79	317
Stewart Gardner (Garden City)	78-78-85-77	318

1906- Alex Smith (at Onwentsia Club, Lake Forest, Illinois)

Alex Smith (Nassau)	73-74-73-75	295
Willie Smith (Mexico)	73-81-74-74	302
Laurie Auchterlonie (Glen View)	76-78-75-76	305
James Maiden (Toledo)	80-73-77-75	305
Willie Anderson (Onwentsia)	73-76-74-84	307

1907- Aleck Ross (at Philadelphia Cricket Club, Pennsylvania)

Aleck Ross (Brae-Burn)	76-74-76-76	302
Gilbert Nicholls (Woodland)	80-73-72-79	304
Aleck Campbell (T.Country Club)	78-74-78-75	305
Jack Hobens (Englewood)	76-75-73-85	309
Peter Robertson (Oakmont)	81-77-78-74	310
George Low (Baltusrol)	78-76-79-77	310
Fred McLeod (Midlothian)	79-77-79-75	310

1908- Fred McLeod (at Myopia Hunt Club, Hamilton, Mass.)

Fred McLeod (Midlothian)	82-82-81-77	322
Willie Smith (Mexico)	77-82-85-78	322
Play-Off: McLeod 77; Smith 83		
Alex Smith (Nassau)	80-83-83-81	327
Willie Anderson (Onwentsia)	85-86-80-79	330
John Jones (Myopia)	81-81-87-82	331

1909- George Sargent (at Englewood GC, New Jersey)

George Sargent (Hyde Manor)	75-72-72-71	290
Tom McNamara (Wollaston)	73-69-75-77	294
Alex Smith (Wykagyl)	76-73-74-72	295
Isaac Mackie (Fox Hills)	77-75-74-73	299

Willie Anderson (St Louis)	79-74-76-70	299
Jack Hobens (Englewood)	75-78-72-74	299

1910- Alex Smith (at Philadelphia Cricket Club, Pennsylvania)

Alex Smith (Wykagyl)	73-73-79-73	298
John J McDermott (Merchantville)	74-74-75-75	298
Macdonald Smith (Claremont)	74-78-75-71	298
Play-Off: Alex Smith 71; McDermott 75; Macdonald Smith 77)		
Fred McLeod (St Louis)	78-70-78-73	299
Tom McNamara (Boston)	73-78-73-76	300
Gilbert Nicholls (Wilmington)	73-75-77-75	300

1911- John J McDermott (at Chicago GC, Wheaton, Illinois)

John J McDermott (Atlantic City)	81-72-75-79	307
Mike J Brady (Wollaston)	76-77-79-75	307
George O Simpson (Wheaton)	76-77-79-75	307
Play-Off: McDermott 80; Brady 82; Simpson 85		
Fred McLeod (St Louis)	77-72-76-83	308
Gilbert Nicholls (Wilmington)	76-78-74-81	309
Jock Hutchison (Allegheny)	80-77-73-79	309

1912- John J McDermott (at the Country Club of Buffalo, New York)

John J McDermott (Atlantic City)	74-75-74-71	294
Tom McNamara (Boston)	74-80-73-69	296
Alex Smith (Wykagyl)	77-70-77-75	299
Mike J Brady (Wollaston)	72-75-73-79	299
Aleck Campbell (Brookline)	74-77-80-71	302

1913- Mr Francis Ouimet (at The Country Club, Brookline, Mass.)

Mr Francis Ouimet (Woodland)	77-74-74-79	304
Harry Vardon (England)	75-72-78-79	304
Ted Ray (England)	79-70-76-79	304
Play-Off: Ouimet 72; Vardon 77; Ray 78		
Walter Hagen (Rochester)	73-78-76-80	307
Jim Barnes (Tacoma)	74-76-78-79	307
Macdonald Smith (Wykagyl)	71-79-80-77	307
Louis Tellier (France)	76-76-79-76	307

1914- Walter Hagen (at Midlothian CC, Blue Island, Illinois)

Walter Hagen (Rochester)	68-74-75-73	290
Mr Charles Evans jr (Edgewater)	76-74-71-70	291

Two US Open champions from Great Britain –
Harry Vardon (left) and Ted Ray

George Sargent (Chevy Chase)	74-77-74-72	297
Fred McLeod (Columbia)	78-73-75-71	297
Mr Francis Ouimet (Woodland)	69-76-75-78	298
Mike J Brady (Wollaston)	78-72-74-74	298
James A Donaldson (Glen View)	72-79-74-73	298

1915- Mr Jerome D Travers (at Baltusrol GC, Springfield, New Jersey)

Mr JD Travers (Upper Montclair)	76-72-73-76	297
Tom McNamara (Boston)	78-71-74-75	298
Bob MacDonald (Buffalo)	72-77-73-78	300
Jim Barnes (Whitemarsh Valley)	71-75-76-79	301
Louis Tellier (Canoe Brook)	75-71-76-79	301

1916- Mr Charles Evans jr (at Minikahda Club, Minneapolis, Minnesota

Mr Charles Evans jr (Edgewater)	70-69-74-73	286
Jock Hutchison (Allegheny)	73-75-72-68	288
Jim Barnes (Whitemarsh Valley)	71-74-71-74	290
Wilfrid Reid (Wilmington)	70-72-79-72	293
Gilbert Nicholls (Great Neck)	73-76-71-73	293
George Sargent (Interlachen)	75-71-72-75	293

NO TOURNAMENT 1917-18 (World War I)

1919- Walter Hagen (at Brae Burn CC, West Newton, Mass.)

Walter Hagen (Oakland Hills)	78-73-75-75	301
Mike J Brady (Oakley)	74-74-73-80	301
Play-Off: Hagen 77; Brady 78		
Jock Hutchison (Glen View)	78-76-76-76	306
Tom McNamara (New York)	80-73-79-74	306
George McLean (Great Neck)	81-75-76-76	308
Louis Tellier (Brae Burn)	73-78-82-75	308

1920- Ted Ray (at Inverness Club, Toledo, Ohio)

Ted Ray (England)	74-73-73-75	295
Harry Vardon (England)	74-73-71-78	296
Jack Burke (Town & Country)	75-77-72-72	296
Leo Diegel (Lake Shore)	72-74-73-77	296
Jock Hutchison (Glen View)	69-76-74-77	296

1921- Jim Barnes (at Columbia CC, Chevy Chase, Maryland)

Jim Barnes (Pelham)	69-75-73-72	289
Walter Hagen (New York)	79-73-72-74	298
Fred McLeod (Columbia)	74-74-76-74	298
Mr Charles Evans jr (Edgewater)	73-78-76-75	302
Mr Bobby Jones jr (Atlanta)	78-71-77-77	303
Emmett French (Youngstown)	75-77-74-77	303
Alex Smith (Shennecossett)	75-75-79-74	303

1922- Gene Sarazen (at Skokie CC, Glencoe, Illinois)

Gene Sarazen (Highland)	72-73-75-68	288
John Black (Oakland)	71-71-75-72	289
Mr Bobby Jones jr (Atlanta)	74-72-70-73	289
William Mehlhorn (Shreveport)	73-71-72-74	290
Walter Hagen (New York)	68-77-74-72	291

1923- Mr Bobby Jones jr (at Inwood CC, New York)

Mr Bobby Jones jr (Atlanta)	71-73-76-76	296
Robert Cruickshank (Sha'maxon)	73-72-78-73	296
Play-Off: Jones 76; Cruickshank 78		
Jock Hutchison (Glen View)	70-72-82-78	302
Jack Forrester (Hollywood)	75-73-77-78	303
John Farrell (Quaker Ridge)	76-77-75-76	304
Francis Gallett (Port Washington)	76-72-77-79	304

Mr WM Reekie (Upper Montclair)   80-74-75-75   304

1924- Cyril Walker (at Oakland Hills CC, Birmingham, Michigan)

Cyril Walker (Englewood)	74-74-74-75	297
Mr Bobby Jones jr (Atlanta)	74-73-75-78	300
William Mehlhorn (Normandy)	72-75-76-78	301
Robert Cruickshank (Sha'maxon)	77-72-76-78	303
Walter Hagen (New York)	75-75-76-77	303
Macdonald Smith (San Francisco)	78-72-77-76	303

1925- Willie MacFarlane (at Worcester CC, Mass.)

Willie MacFarlane (Oak Ridge)	74-67-72-78	291
Mr Bobby Jones jr (Atlanta)	77-70-70-74	291

Play-Off: Macfarlane 147 (75-72); Jones 148 (75-73)

Johnny Farrell (Quaker Ridge)	71-74-69-78	292
Mr Francis Ouimet (Woodland)	70-73-73-76	292
Gene Sarazen (Fresh Meadow)	72-72-75-74	293
Walter Hagen (Pasadena)	72-76-71-74	293

1926- Mr Bobby Jones jr (at Scioto CC, Columbus, Ohio)

Mr Bobby Jones jr (Atlanta)	70-79-71-73	293
Joe Turnesa (Fairview)	71-74-72-77	294
William Mehlhorn (Chicago)	68-75-76-78	297
Gene Sarazen (Fresh Meadow)	78-77-72-70	297
Leo Diegel (Mountain View Farm)	72-76-75-74	297
Johnny Farrell (Quaker Ridge)	76-79-69-73	297

1927- Tommy Armour (at Oakmont CC, Pennsylvania)

Tommy Armour (Congressional)	78-71-76-76	301
Harry Cooper (El Serreno)	74-76-74-77	301

Play-Off: Armour 76; Cooper 79

Gene Sarazen (Fresh Meadow)	74-74-80-74	302
Emmett French (Southern Pines)	75-79-77-73	304
Bill Mehlhorn (New York)	75-77-80-73	305

1928- Johnny Farrell (at Olympia Fields CC, Matteson, Illinois)

Johnny Farrell (Quaker Ridge)	77-74-71-72	294
Mr Bobby Jones jr (Atlanta)	73-71-73-77	294

Play-Off: Farrell 143 (70-73); Jones 144 (73-71)

Roland Hancock (Wilmington)	74-77-72-72	295
Walter Hagen (New York City)	75-72-73-76	296
Mr G. Von Elm (Tam O'Shanter)	74-72-76-74	296

1929- Mr Bobby Jones jr (at Winged Foot GC, Mamaroneck, New York)

Mr Bobby Jones jr (Atlanta)	69-75-71-79	294
Al Espinosa (Glencoe)	70-72-77-75	294

Play-Off: Jones 141 (72-69); Espinosa 164 (80-84)

Gene Sarazen (Fresh Meadow)	71-71-76-78	296
Densmore Shute (Worthington)	73-71-76-76	296
Tommy Armour (Tam O'Shanter)	74-71-76-76	297
Mr G. Von Elm (Tam O'Shanter)	79-70-74-74	297

1930- Mr Bobby Jones jr (at Interlachen CC, Minneapolis, Minnesota)

Mr Bobby Jones jr (Atlanta)	71-73-68-75	287
Macdonald Smith (Lakeville)	70-75-74-70	289
Horton Smith (Cragston)	72-70-76-74	292
Harry Cooper (Glen Elyn)	72-72-73-76	293
Johnny Golden (Wee Burn)	74-73-71-76	294

1931- Billy Burke (at Inverness Club, Toledo, Ohio)

Billy Burke (Round Hill)	73-72-74-73	292
George Von Elm (unattached)	75-69-73-75	292

Play-Off: Burke 149 (73-76)/148 (77-71); Von Elm 149 (75-74)/149 (76-73)

Leo Diegel (Mexico)	75-73-74-72	294
Wiffy Cox (Brooklyn)	75-74-75-72	296
Bill Mehlhorn (Pinewald)	77-73-75-71	296
Gene Sarazen (Lakeville)	74-78-74-70	296

1932- Gene Sarazen (at Fresh Meadow CC, Flushing, New York)

Gene Sarazen (Lakeville)	74-76-70-66	286
Robert Cruickshank (Willowbrook)	78-74-69-68	289

Philip Perkins (unattached)	76-69-74-70	289
Leo Diegel (Mexico)	73-74-73-74	294
Wiffy Cox (Brooklyn)	80-73-70-72	295

1933- Mr Johnny Goodman (at North Shore GC, Glen View, Illinois)

Mr Johnny Goodman (Omaha)	75-66-70-76	287
Ralph Guldahl (St Louis)	76-71-70-71	288
Craig Wood (Hollywood)	73-74-71-72	290
Walter Hagen (unattached)	73-76-77-66	292
Tommy Armour (Medinah)	68-75-76-73	292

1934- Olin Dutra (at Merion Cricket Club, Ardmore, Pennsylvania)

Olin Dutra (Brentwood)	76-74-71-72	293
Gene Sarazen (New York City)	73-72-73-76	294
Wiffy Cox (Dyker Beach)	71-75-74-75	295
Robert Cruickshank (CC.Virginia)	71-71-77-76	295
Harry Cooper (Glen Oak)	76-74-74-71	295

1935- Sam Parks jr (at Oakmont CC, Pennsylvania)

Sam Parks jr (South Hills)	77-73-73-76	299
Jimmy Thomson (Lakewood)	73-73-77-78	301
Walter Hagen (Detroit)	77-76-73-76	302
Denny Shute (Chicago)	78-73-76-76	303
Ray Mangrum (Los Angeles)	76-76-72-79	303

1936- Tony Manero (at Baltusrol GC, Springfield, New Jersey)

Tony Manero (Sedgefield)	73-69-73-67	282
Harry Cooper (Glen Oak)	71-70-70-73	284
Clarence Clark (Forest Hill Field)	69-75-71-72	287
Macdonald Smith (Glendale)	73-73-72-70	288
Henry Picard (Hershey)	70-71-74-74	289
Wiffy Cox (Kenwood)	74-74-69-72	289
Ky Laffoon (Northmoor)	71-74-70-74	289

1937- Ralph Guldahl (at Oakland Hills CC, Birmingham, Michigan)

Ralph Guldahl (Chicago)	71-69-72-69	281
Sam Snead (Greenbrier)	69-73-70-71	283
Robert Cruickshank (CC.Virginia)	73-73-67-72	285
Harry Cooper (Chicago)	72-70-73-71	286
Ed Dudley (Philadelphia)	70-70-71-76	287

1938- Ralph Guldahl (at Cherry Hills Club, Denver, Colorado)

Ralph Guldahl (Braidburn)	74-70-71-69	284

Dick Metz (Mill Road Farm)	73-68-70-79	290
Harry Copper (Chicopee)	76-69-76-71	292
Toney Penna (Dayton)	78-72-74-68	292
Byron Nelson (Reading)	77-71-74-72	294
Emery Zimmerman (Columbia)	72-71-73-78	294

1939- Byron Nelson (at Philadelphia CC, Pennsylvania)

Byron Nelson (Reading)	72-73-71-68	284
Craig Wood (Winged Foot)	70-71-71-72	284
Densmore Shute (Huntington)	70-72-70-72	284

Play-Off *: Nelson 68-70; Wood 68-73; Shute 76

Mr Marvin Ward (Spokane)	69-73-71-72	285
Sam Snead (Greenbrier)	68-71-73-74	286

* - 18-hole play-off extended to 36 holes after a tie

1940- Lawson Little (at Canterbury GC, Cleveland, Ohio)

Lawson Little (Bretton Woods)	72-69-73-73	287
Gene Sarazen (Brookfield Center)	71-74-70-72	287

Play-Off: Little 70; Sarazen 73

Horton Smith (Oak Park)	69-72-78-69	288
Craig Wood (Winged Foot)	72-73-72-72	289
Ben Hogan (Century)	70-73-74-73	290
Ralph Guldahl (Chicago)	73-71-76-70	290
Lloyd Mangrum (Oak Park)	75-70-71-74	290
Byron Nelson (Inverness)	72-74-70-74	290

1942-45 No Tournament

1941- Craig Wood (at Colonial Club, Fort Worth, Texas)

Craig Wood (Winged Foot)	73-71-70-70	284
Densmore Shute (Chicago)	69-75-72-71	287
Johnny Bulla (Chicago)	75-71-72-71	289
Ben Hogan (Hershey)	74-77-68-70	289
Herman Barron (Fenway)	75-71-74-71	291
Paul Runyan (Metropolis)	73-72-71-75	291

1946- Lloyd Mangrum (at Canterbury GC, Cleveland, Ohio)

Lloyd Mangrum (L.Angeles)	74-70-68-72	284
Byron Nelson (Toledo)	71-71-69-73	284
Victor Ghezzi (Knoxville)	71-69-72-72	284

Play-Off *: Mangrum 72-72; Nelson 72-73; Ghezzi 72-73

Herman Barron (Fenway)	72-72-72-69	285
Ben Hogan (Hershey)	72-68-73-72	285

* - 18-hole play-off extended to 36 holes after tie

1947- Lew Worsham (St. Louis CC, Clayton, Missouri)

Lew Worsham (Oakmont)	70-70-71-71	282
Sam Snead (Cascades)	72-70-70-70	282

Play-Off: Worsham 69; Snead 70

Bobby Locke (South Africa)	68-74-70-73	285
Ed Oliver jr (Wilmington)	73-70-71-71	285
Mr Marvin Ward (Spokane)	69-72-73-73	287

1948- Ben Hogan (at Riviera CC, Los Angeles, California)

Ben Hogan (Hershey)	67-72-68-69	276
Jimmy Demaret (Houston)	71-70-68-69	278
Jim Turnesa (Elmsford)	71-69-70-70	280
Bobby Locke (South Africa)	70-69-73-70	282
Sam Snead (Greenbrier)	69-69-73-72	283

1949- Cary Middlecoff (at Medinah CC, Illinois)

Cary Middlecoff (Colonial)	75-67-69-75	286
Clayton Heafner (Eastwood)	72-71-71-73	287
Sam Snead (Greenbrier)	73-73-71-70	287
Jim Turnesa (Briar Hall)	78-69-70-72	289
Bobby Locke (South Africa)	74-71-73-71	289

1950- Ben Hogan (at Merion GC, Ardmore, Pennsylvania)

Ben Hogan (Hershey)	72-69-72-74	287
(Tam O'Shanter)		
Lloyd Mangrum	72-70-69-76	287
George Fazio (Woodmont)	73-72-72-70	287

Play-Off: Hogan 69; Mangrum 73; Fazio 75

E.J Harrison (St Andrews)	72-67-73-76	288
Joe Kirkwood jr	71-74-74-70	289
(Kirkwood G.R)		
Jim Ferrier (Chicago)	71-69-74-75	289
Henry Ransom (St Andrews)	72-71-73-73	289

1951- Ben Hogan (at Oakland Hills CC, Birmingham, Michigan)

Ben Hogan (Hershey)	76-73-71-67	287
Clayton Heafner (Eastwood)	72-75-73-69	289
Bobby Locke (South Africa)	73-71-74-73	291
Lloyd Mangrum	75-74-74-70	293
(Tam O'Shanter)		
Julius Boros (Mid Pines)	74-74-71-74	293

1952- Julius Boros (at Northwood Club, Dallas, Texas)

Julius Boros (Mid Pines)	71-71-68-71	281
Ed Oliver jr (Cog Hill)	71-72-70-72	285
Ben Hogan (Tamarisk)	69-69-74-74	286
Johnny Bulla (Westmoreland)	73-68-73-73	287
George Fazio (Pine Valley)	71-69-75-75	290

1953- Ben Hogan (at Oakmont CC, Pennsylvania)

Ben Hogan (Tamarisk)	67-72-73-71	283
Sam Snead (Greenbrier)	72-69-72-76	289
Lloyd Mangrum	73-70-74-75	292
(Tam O'Shanter)		
Pete Cooper (Century)	78-75-71-70	294
George Fazio (Pine Valley)	70-71-77-76	294
Jimmy Demaret (Concord)	71-76-71-76	294

1954- Ed Furgol (Baltusrol GC, Springfield, New Jersey)

Ed Furgol (Westwood)	71-70-71-72	284
Gene Littler (Thunderbird)	70-69-76-70	285
Dick Mayer (St Petersburg)	72-71-70-73	286
Lloyd Mangrum	72-71-72-71	286
(Tam O'Shanter)		
Bobby Locke (South Africa)	74-70-74-70	288

1955- Jack Fleck (at Olympic CC, San Francisco, California)

Jack Fleck	76-69-75-67	287
(Davenport Municipal)		
Ben Hogan (Fort Worth)	72-73-72-70	287

Play-Off: Fleck 69; Hogan 72

Sam Snead (Greenbrier)	79-69-70-74	292
Tommy Bolt (Chattanooga)	67-77-75-73	292
Julius Boros (Mid Pines)	76-69-73-77	295
Bob Rosburg (Palo Alto)	78-74-67-76	295

1956- Cary Middlecoff (at Oak Hill CC, Rochester, New York)

Cary Middlecoff (Riverlake)	71-70-70-70	281
Julius Boros (Mid Pines)	71-71-71-69	282
Ben Hogan (Fort Worth)	72-68-72-70	282
Ed Furgol (Westwood)	71-70-73-71	285
Peter Thomson (Australia)	70-69-75-71	285
Ted Kroll (Fort Lauderdale)	72-70-70-73	285

1957- Dick Mayer (at Inverness Club, Toledo, Ohio)

Dick Mayer (St Petersburg)	70-68-74-70	282
Cary Middlecoff (Riverlake)	71-75-68-68	282

Play-Off: Mayer 72; Middlecoff 79

Jimmy Demaret (Concord)	68-73-70-72	283
Julius Boros (Mid Pines)	69-75-70-70	284
Walter Burkemo	74-73-72-65	284
(Franklin Hills)		

1958- Tommy Bolt (at Southern Hills CC, Tulsa, Oklahoma)

Tommy Bolt (Paradise)	71-71-69-72	283
Gary Player (South Africa)	75-68-73-71	287
Julius Boros (Mid Pines)	71-75-72-71	289

Gene Littler (Singing Hills) 74-73-67-76 290
Walter Burkemo 75-74-70-72 291
(Franklin Hills)
Bob Rosburg (Silverado) 75-74-72-70 291

1959- Billy Casper (at Winged Foot GC, Mamaroneck, New York)

Billy Casper (Apple Valley) 71-68-69-74 282
Bob Rosburg (Palo Alto) 75-70-67-71 283
Claude Harmon 72-71-70-71 284
(Winged Foot)
Mike Souchak (Grossinger) 71-70-72-71 284
Doug Ford (Paradise) 72-69-72-73 286
Ernie Vossler (Midland) 72-70-72-72 286
Arnold Palmer 71-69-72-74 286
(Laurel Valley)

1960- Arnold Palmer (at Cherry Hills CC, Englewood, Colorado)

Arnold Palmer 72-71-72-65 280
(Laurel Valley)
Mr Jack Nicklaus (Scioto) 71-71-69-71 282
E.J Harrison (Old Warson) 74-70-70-69 283
Julius Boros (Mid Pines) 73-69-68-73 283
Mike Souchak (Grossinger) 68-67-73-75 283
Ted Kroll (DeSoto Lakes) 72-69-75-67 283
Jack Fleck (El Caballero) 70-70-72-71 283
Dow Finsterwald (Tequesta) 71-69-70-73 283

1961- Gene Littler (at Oakland Hills CC, Birmingham, Michigan)

Gene Littler (Singing Hills) 73-68-72-68 281
Bob Goalby (Paradise) 70-72-69-71 282
Doug Sanders (Ojai) 72-67-71-72 282
Mike Souchak (Grossinger) 73-70-68-73 284
Mr Jack Nicklaus (Scioto) 75-69-70-70 284

1962- Jack Nicklaus (at Oakmont CC, Pennsylvania)

Jack Nicklaus 72-70-72-69 283
(Tucson National)
Arnold Palmer 71-68-73-71 283
(CC of Miami)
Play-Off: Nicklaus 71; Palmer 74
Phil Rodgers (La Jolla) 74-70-69-72 285
Bobby Nichols (Midland) 70-72-70-73 285
Gay Brewer (Paradise) 73-72-73-69 287

1963- Julius Boros (at The Country Club, Brookline, Mass.)

Julius Boros (Mid Pines) 71-74-76-72 293
Jacky Cupit (Mountain View) 70-72-76-75 293
Arnold Palmer 73-69-77-74 293
(Laurel Valley)

Play-Off: Boros 70; Cupit 73; Palmer 76
Paul Harney (Sunset Oaks) 78-70-73-73 294
Billy Maxwell (Tropicana) 73-73-75-74 295
Bruce Crampton (Australia) 74-72-75-74 295
Tony Lema (San Leandro) 71-74-74-76 295

1964- Ken Venturi (at Congressional CC, Washington, DC)

Ken Venturi (Paradise) 72-70-66-70 278
Tommy Jacobs 72-64-70-76 282
(Bermuda Dunes)
Bob Charles (De Soto Lakes) 72-72-71-68 283
Billy Casper 71-74-69-71 285
(Bermuda Dunes)
Gay Brewer (Dallas) 76-69-73-68 286
Arnold Palmer 68-69-75-74 286
(Laurel Valley)

1965- Gary Player (at Bellerive CC, St Louis, Missouri)

Gary Player (South Africa) 70-70-71-71 282
Kel Nagle (Australia) 68-73-72-69 282
Play-Off: Player 71; Nagle 74

Billy Casper pictured after his second US Open win in 1966

Tony Jacklin (far left) at work during the early stages of his US Open victory at Hazeltine in 1970

Frank Beard (Seneca)	74-69-70-71	284
Julius Boros (Mid Pines)	72-75-70-70	287
Al Geiberger (Carlton Oaks)	70-76-70-71	287

1966- Billy Casper (at Olympic CC, San Francisco, California)

Billy Casper (Peacock Gap)	69-68-73-68	278
Arnold Palmer (Laurel Valley)	71-66-70-71	278
Play-Off: Casper 69; Palmer 73		
Jack Nicklaus (Scioto)	71-71-69-74	285
Tony Lema (Marco Island)	71-74-70-71	286
Dave Marr (Goodyear)	71-74-68-73	286

1967- Jack Nicklaus (at Baltusrol GC, Springfield, New Jersey)

Jack Nicklaus (Scioto)	71-67-72-65	275
Arnold Palmer (Laurel Valley)	69-68-73-69	279
Don January (Dallas)	69-72-70-70	281
Billy Casper (Bonita)	69-70-71-72	282
Lee Trevino (Horizon Hills)	72-70-71-70	283

1968- Lee Trevino (at Oak Hill CC, Rochester, New York)

Lee Trevino (Horizon Hills)	69-68-69-69	275
Jack Nicklaus (Scioto)	72-70-70-67	279
Bert Yancey (Killearn)	67-68-70-76	281
Bobby Nichols (Louisville)	74-71-68-69	282
Don Bies (Seattle)	70-70-75-69	284
John Spray (Cedar Rapids)	73-75-71-65	284

1969- Orville Moody (at Champions GC, Houston, Texas)

Orville Moody (Yukon)	71-70-68-72	281
Deane Beman (Bethesda)	68-69-73-72	282
Al Geiberger (Santa Barbara)	68-72-72-70	282
Bob Rosburg (Westwood)	70-69-72-71	282
Bob Murphy (Bartow)	66-72-74-71	283

1970- Tony Jacklin (at Hazeltine National GC, Chaska, Minnesota)

Tony Jacklin (GB&I)	71-70-70-70	281
Dave Hill (USA)	75-69-71-73	288
Bob Lunn (USA)	77-72-70-70	289
Bob Charles (New Zealand)	76-71-75-67	289
Ken Still (USA)	78-71-71-71	291
Miller Barber (USA)	75-75-72-70	292
Gay Brewer (USA)	75-71-71-76	293
Billy Casper (USA)	75-75-71-73	294
Larry Ziegler (USA)	75-73-73-73	294
Bruce Devlin (Australia)	75-75-71-73	294
Lee Trevino (USA)	77-73-74-70	294

1971- Lee Trevino (at Merion GC, Ardmore, Pennsylvania)

Lee Trevino (USA)	70-72-69-69	280
Jack Nicklaus (USA)	69-72-68-71	280

Play-Off: Trevino 68; Nicklaus 71

Bob Rosburg (USA)	71-72-70-69	282
Jim Colbert (USA)	69-69-73-71	282
Mr Jim Simons (USA)	71-71-65-76	283
Johnny Miller (USA)	70-73-70-70	283
George Archer (USA)	71-70-70-72	283
Ray Floyd (USA)	71-75-67-71	284
Gay Brewer (USA)	70-70-73-72	285
Bert Yancey (USA)	75-69-69-72	285
Larry Hinson (USA)	71-71-70-73	285
Bobby Nichols (USA)	69-72-69-75	285

1972 -Jack Nicklaus (at Pebble Beach GL, California)

Jack Nicklaus (USA)	71-73-72-74	290
Bruce Crampton (Australia)	74-70-73-76	293
Arnold Palmer (USA)	77-68-73-76	294
Lee Trevino (USA)	74-72-71-78	295
Homero Blancas (USA)	74-70-76-75	295
Kermit Zarley (USA)	71-73-73-79	296
Johnny Miller (USA)	74-73-71-79	297
Tom Weiskopf (USA)	73-74-73-78	298
Cesar Sanudo (USA)	72-72-78-77	299
Chi Chi Rodriguez (USA)	71-75-78-75	299

1973- Johnny Miller (at Oakmont CC, Pennsylvania)

Johnny Miller (USA)	71-69-76-63	279
John Schlee (USA)	73-70-67-70	280
Tom Weiskopf (USA)	73-69-69-70	281
Arnold Palmer (USA)	71-71-68-72	282
Lee Trevino (USA)	70-72-70-70	282
Jack Nicklaus (USA)	71-69-74-68	282
Lanny Wadkins (USA)	74-69-75-65	283
Julius Boros (USA)	73-69-68-73	283
Jerry Heard (USA)	74-70-66-73	283
Jim Colbert (USA)	70-68-74-72	284

1974- Hale Irwin (at Winged Foot GC, Mamaroneck, New York)

Hale Irwin (USA)	73-70-71-73	287
Forrest Fezler (USA)	75-70-74-70	289
Bert Yancey (USA)	76-69-73-72	290
Lou Graham (USA)	71-75-74-70	290
Tom Watson (USA)	73-71-69-79	292
Arnold Palmer (USA)	73-70-73-76	292
Jim Colbert (USA)	72-77-69-74	292
Gary Player (South Africa)	70-73-77-73	293
Tom Kite (USA)	74-70-77-72	293

Brian Allin (USA)	76-71-74-73	294
Jack Nicklaus (USA)	75-74-76-69	294

1975- Lou Graham (at Medinah CC, Illinois)

Lou Graham (USA)	74-72-68-73	287
John Mahaffey (USA)	73-71-72-71	287

Play-Off: Graham 71; Mahaffey 73

Bob Murphy (USA)	74-73-72-69	288
Hale Irwin (USA)	74-71-73-70	288
Ben Crenshaw (USA)	70-68-76-74	288
Frank Beard (USA)	74-69-67-78	288
Jack Nicklaus (USA)	72-70-75-72	289
Peter Oosterhuis (GB&I)	69-73-72-75	289
Tom Watson (USA)	67-68-78-77	290
Arnold Palmer (USA)	69-75-73-73	290
Pat Fitzsimons (USA)	67-73-73-77	290

1976- Jerry Pate (at Atlanta Athletic Club, Georgia)

Jerry Pate (USA)	71-69-69-68	277
Al Geiberger (USA)	70-69-71-69	279
Tom Weiskopf (USA)	73-70-68-68	279
Butch Baird (USA)	71-71-71-67	280
John Mahaffey (USA)	70-68-69-73	280
Hubert Green (USA)	72-70-71-69	282
Tom Watson (USA)	74-72-68-70	284
Ben Crenshaw (USA)	72-68-72-73	285
Lyn Lott (USA)	71-71-70-73	285
Johnny Miller (USA)	74-72-69-71	286

1977- Hubert Green (at Southern Hills CC, Tulsa, Oklahoma)

Hubert Green (USA)	69-67-72-70	278
Lou Graham (USA)	72-71-68-68	279
Tom Weiskopf (USA)	71-71-68-71	281
Tom Purtzer (USA)	69-69-72-72	282
Jay Haas (USA)	72-68-71-72	283
Gary Jacobson (USA)	73-70-67-73	283
Tom Watson (USA)	74-72-71-67	284
Lynn Lott (USA)	73-73-68-70	284
Terry Diehl (USA)	69-68-73-74	284
Al Geiberger (USA)	70-71-75-69	285
Peter Oosterhuis (GB&I)	71-70-74-70	285
Mike McCullough (USA)	73-73-69-70	285
Jack Nicklaus (USA)	74-68-71-72	285
Rod Funseth (USA)	69-70-72-74	285
Gary Player (South Africa)	72-67-71-75	285

1978- Andy North (at Cherry Hills CC, Englewood, Colorado)

Andy North (USA)	70-70-71-74	285
JC Snead (USA)	70-72-72-72	286
Dave Stockton (USA)	71-73-70-72	286
Tom Weiskopf (USA)	77-73-70-68	288

Hale Irwin (USA)	69-74-75-70	288
Tom Watson (USA)	74-75-70-70	289
Andy Bean (USA)	72-72-71-74	289
Bill Kratzert (USA)	72-74-70-73	289
Jack Nicklaus (USA)	73-69-74-73	289
Johnny Miller (USA)	78-69-68-74	289
Gary Player (South Africa)	71-71-70-77	289

1979- Hale Irwin (at the Inverness Club, Toledo, Ohio)

Hale Irwin (USA)	74-68-67-75	284
Gary Player (South Africa)	73-73-72-68	286
Jerry Pate (USA)	71-74-69-72	286
Bill Rogers (USA)	71-72-73-72	288
Larry Nelson (USA)	71-68-76-73	288
Tom Weiskopf (USA)	71-74-67-76	288
David Graham (Australia)	73-73-70-73	289
Tom Purtzer (USA)	70-69-75-76	290
Jack Nicklaus (USA)	74-77-72-68	291
Keith Fergus (USA)	70-77-72-72	291

1980- Jack Nicklaus (at Baltusrol GC, Springfield, New Jersey)

Jack Nicklaus (USA)	63-71-70-68	272
Isao Aoki (Japan)	68-68-68-70	274
Keith Fergus (USA)	66-70-70-70	276
Tom Watson (USA)	71-68-67-70	276
Lon Hinkle (USA)	66-70-69-71	276
Mike Reid (USA)	69-67-75-69	280
Mark Hayes (USA)	66-71-69-74	280
Andy North (USA)	68-75-72-67	282
Hale Irwin (USA)	70-70-73-69	282
Ed Sneed (USA)	72-70-70-70	282
Mike Morley (USA)	73-68-69-72	282

1981- David Graham (at Merion GC, Ardmore, Pennsylvania)

David Graham (Australia)	68-68-70-67	273
Bill Rogers (USA)	70-68-69-69	276
George Burns (USA)	69-66-68-73	276
John Cook (USA)	68-70-71-70	279
John Schroeder (USA)	71-68-69-71	279
Frank Conner (USA)	71-72-69-68	280
Lon Hinkle (USA)	69-71-70-70	280
Sam Rachels (USA)	70-71-69-70	280
Jack Nicklaus (USA)	69-68-71-72	280
Chi Chi Rodriguez (USA)	68-73-67-72	280

1982- Tom Watson (at Pebble Beach GL, California)

Tom Watson (USA)	72-72-68-70	282
Jack Nicklaus (USA)	74-70-71-69	284
Bobby Clampett (USA)	71-73-72-70	286

Dan Pohl (USA)	72-74-70-70	286
Bill Rogers (USA)	70-73-69-74	286
Gary Koch (USA)	78-73-69-67	287
Jay Haas (USA)	75-74-70-68	287
Lanny Wadkins (USA)	73-76-67-71	287
David Graham (Australia)	73-72-69-73	287
Calvin Peete (USA)	71-72-72-73	288
Bruce Devlin (Australia)	70-69-75-74	288

1983- Larry Nelson (at Oakmont CC, Pennsylvania)

Larry Nelson (USA)	75-73-65-67	280
Tom Watson (USA)	72-70-70-69	281
Gil Morgan (USA)	73-72-70-68	283
Calvin Peete (USA)	75-68-70-73	286
Seve Ballesteros (Spain)	69-74-69-74	286
Hal Sutton (USA)	73-70-73-71	287
Lanny Wadkins (USA)	72-73-74-69	288
David Graham (Australia)	74-75-73-69	291
Ralph Landrum (USA)	75-73-69-74	291
Chip Beck (USA)	73-74-74-71	292
Craig Stadler (USA)	76-74-73-69	292
Andy North (USA)	73-71-72-76	292

1984- Fuzzy Zoeller (at Winged Foot GC, Mamaroneck, New York)

Fuzzy Zoeller (USA)	71-66-69-70	276
Greg Norman (Australia)	70-68-69-69	276

Play-Off: Zoeller 67; Norman 75

Curtis Strange (USA)	69-70-74-68	281
Johnny Miller (USA)	74-68-70-70	282
Jim Thorpe (USA)	68-71-70-73	282
Hale Irwin (USA)	68-68-69-79	284
Peter Jacobsen (USA)	72-73-73-67	285
Mark O'Meara (USA)	71-74-71-69	285
Fred Couples (USA)	69-71-74-72	286
Lee Trevino (USA)	71-72-69-74	286

1985- Andy North (at Oakland Hills CC, Birmingham, Michigan)

Andy North (USA)	70-65-70-74	279
Denis Watson (South Africa)	72-65-73-70	280
Dave Barr (Canada)	70-68-70-72	280
TC Chen (Taiwan)	65-69-69-77	280
Lanny Wadkins (USA)	70-72-69-70	281
Payne Stewart (USA)	70-70-71-70	281
Seve Ballesteros (Spain)	71-70-69-71	281
Johnny Miller (USA)	74-71-68-69	282
Fuzzy Zoeller (USA)	71-69-72-71	283
Corey Pavin (USA)	72-68-73-70	283
Jack Renner (USA)	72-69-72-70	283
Rick Fehr (USA)	69-67-73-74	283

Payne Stewart (right) congratulates the 1986 champion Ray Floyd after his victory at Shinnecock Hills

1986- Ray Floyd (at Shinnecock Hills GC, Southampton, New York)

Ray Floyd (USA)	75-68-70-66	279
Lanny Wadkins (USA)	74-70-72-65	281
Chip Beck (USA)	75-73-68-65	281
Lee Trevino (USA)	74-68-69-71	282
Hal Sutton (USA)	75-70-66-71	282
Ben Crenshaw (USA)	76-69-69-69	283
Payne Stewart (USA)	76-68-69-70	283
Jack Nicklaus (USA)	77-72-67-68	284
Bernhard Langer (West Germany)	74-70-70-70	284
Mark McCumber (USA)	74-71-68-71	284
Bob Tway (USA)	70-73-69-72	284

1987- Scott Simpson (at The Olympic Club, San Francisco, California)

Scott Simpson (USA)	71-68-70-68	277
Tom Watson (USA)	72-65-71-70	278
Seve Ballesteros (Spain)	68-75-68-71	282
Bobby Wadkins (USA)	71-71-70-71	283
Curtis Strange (USA)	71-72-69-71	283
Bernhard Langer (West Germany)	69-69-73-72	283
Ben Crenshaw (USA)	67-72-72-72	283
Larry Mize (USA)	71-68-72-72	283
Dan Pohl (USA)	75-71-69-69	284
Tommy Nakajima (Japan)	68-70-74-72	284

Mac O'Grady (USA)	71-69-72-72	284
Jim Thorpe (USA)	70-68-73-73	284
Lennie Clements (USA)	70-70-70-74	284

1988- Curtis Strange (at The Country Club, Brookline, Mass.)

Curtis Strange (USA)	70-67-69-72	278
Nick Faldo (GB&I)	72-67-68-71	278

Play-Off: Strange 71; Faldo 75

Steve Pate (USA)	72-69-72-67	280
Mark O'Meara (USA)	71-72-66-71	280
D.A Weibring (USA)	71-69-68-72	280
Paul Azinger (USA)	69-70-76-66	281
Scott Simpson (USA)	69-66-72-74	281
Fuzzy Zoeller (USA)	73-72-71-66	282
Bob Gilder (USA)	68-69-70-75	282
Payne Stewart (USA)	73-73-70-67	283
Fred Couples (USA)	72-67-71-73	283

Curtis Strange holds the trophy after beating Nick Faldo in a play-off at The Country Club, Brookline in 1988

1989- Curtis Strange (at Oak Hill CC, Rochester, New York)

Curtis Strange (USA)	71-64-73-70	278
Ian Woosnam (GB&I)	70-68-73-68	279
Chip Beck (USA)	71-69-71-68	279

Scotland's Colin Montgomerie came close at Oakmont in 1994, losing out in a three-way play-off

Mark McCumber (USA)	70-68-72-69	279
Brian Claar (USA)	71-72-68-69	280
Jumbo Ozaki (Japan)	70-71-68-72	281
Scott Simpson (USA)	67-70-69-75	281
Peter Jacobsen (USA)	71-70-71-70	282
Hubert Green (USA)	69-72-74-68	283
Paul Azinger (USA)	71-72-70-70	283
Jose-Maria Olazabal (Spain)	69-72-70-72	283
Tom Kite (USA)	67-69-69-78	283

1990- Hale Irwin (at Medinah CC, Illinois)

Hale Irwin (USA)	69-70-74-67	280
Mike Donald (USA)	67-70-72-71	280

Play-Off: Irwin 74-3; Donald 74-4

Billy Ray Brown (USA)	69-71-69-72	281
Nick Faldo (GB&I)	72-72-68-69	281
Tim Simpson (USA)	66-69-75-73	283
Mark Brooks (USA)	68-70-72-73	283
Greg Norman (Australia)	72-73-69-69	283
Scott Hoch (USA)	70-73-69-72	284
Tom Sieckmann (USA)	70-74-68-72	284
Craig Stadler (USA)	71-70-72-71	284
Fuzzy Zoeller (USA)	73-70-68-73	284
Steve Jones (USA)	67-76-74-67	284
Jose-Maria Olazabal (Spain)	73-69-69-73	284

1991- Payne Stewart (at Hazeltine National GC, Minneapolis, Minnesota)

Payne Stewart (USA)	67-70-73-72	282
Scott Simpson (USA)	70-68-72-72	282

Play-Off: Stewart 75; Simpson 77

Fred Couples (USA)	70-70-75-70	285
Larry Nelson (USA)	73-72-72-68	285
Fuzzy Zoeller (USA)	72-73-74-67	286
Scott Hoch (USA)	69-71-74-73	287
Nolan Henke (USA)	67-71-77-73	288
Ray Floyd (USA)	73-72-76-68	289
Jose-Maria Olazabal (Spain)	73-71-75-70	289
Corey Pavin (USA)	71-67-79-72	289

1992- Tom Kite (at Pebble Beach GL, California)

Tom Kite (USA)	71-72-70-72	285
Jeff Sluman (USA)	73-74-69-71	287
Colin Montgomerie (GB&I)	70-71-77-70	288
Nick Price (South Africa)	71-72-77-71	291
Nick Faldo (GB&I)	70-76-68-77	291
Jay Don Blake (USA)	70-74-75-73	292
Bob Gilder (USA)	73-70-75-74	292
Billy Andrade (USA)	72-74-72-74	292
Mike Hulbert (USA)	74-73-70-75	292
Tom Lehman (USA)	69-74-72-77	292
Joey Sindelar (USA)	74-72-68-78	292
Ian Woosnam (GB&I)	72-72-69-79	292

1993- Lee Janzen (at Baltusrol GC, Springfield, New Jersey)

Lee Janzen (USA)	67-67-69-69	272
Payne Stewart (USA)	70-66-68-70	274
Paul Azinger (USA)	71-68-69-69	277
Craig Parry (Australia)	66-74-69-68	277
Scott Hoch (USA)	66-72-72-68	278

Tom Watson (USA)	70-66-73-69	278
Ernie Els (South Africa)	71-73-68-67	279
Ray Floyd (USA)	68-73-70-68	279
Fred Funk (USA)	70-72-67-70	279
Nolan Henke (USA)	72-71-67-69	279

1994- Ernie Els (at Oakmont CC, Pennsylvania)

Ernie Els (South Africa)	69-71-66-73	279
Loren Roberts (USA)	76-69-64-70	279
Colin Montgomerie (GB&I)	71-65-73-70	279

Play-Off: Els 74-4-4; Roberts 74-4-5;
Montgomerie 78

Curtis Strange (USA)	70-70-70-70	280
John Cook (USA)	73-65-73-71	282
Clark Dennis (USA)	71-71-70-71	283
Greg Norman (Australia)	71-71-69-72	283
Tom Watson (USA)	68-73-68-74	283
Jeff Maggert (USA)	71-68-75-70	284

Frank Nobilo (New Zealand)	69-71-68-76	284
Jeff Sluman (USA)	72-69-72-71	284
Duffy Waldorf (USA)	74-68-73-69	284

1995- Corey Pavin (at Shinnecock Hills GC, Southampton, New York)

Corey Pavin (USA)	72-69-71-68	280
Greg Norman (Australia)	68-67-74-73	282
Tom Lehman (USA)	70-72-67-74	283
Bill Glasson (USA)	69-70-76-69	284
Neal Lancaster (USA)	70-72-77-65	284
Jeff Maggert (USA)	69-72-77-66	284
Phil Mickelson (USA)	68-70-72-74	284
Jay Haas (USA)	70-73-72-69	284
Davis Love III (USA)	72-68-73-71	284
Bob Tway (USA)	69-69-72-75	285
Frank Nobilo (New Zealand)	72-72-70-71	285
Vijay Singh (Fiji)	70-71-72-72	285

US OPEN SUMMARY

Most Victories:	4 -	Willie Anderson (1901-03-04-05)
		Mr Bobby Jones (1923-26-29-30)
		Ben Hogan (1948-50-51-53)
		Jack Nicklaus (1962-67-72-80)
	3 -	Hale Irwin (1974-79-90)
Oldest Champions:		Hale Irwin (45 yrs, 0 mths, 15 dys, 1990)
		Ray Floyd (43 yrs, 9 mths, 11 dys, 1986)
		Ted Ray (43 yrs, 4 mths, 16 dys, 1920)
Youngest Champion:		John J McDermott (19 yrs, 10 mths, 14 dys, 1911)
Widest Winning Margins:	11 -	Willie Smith (1899)
	9 -	Jim Barnes (1921)
(Since 2nd World War):	7 -	Tony Jacklin (1970)
Lowest 72-Hole Totals:	272 -	Jack Nicklaus (1980 at Baltusrol)
		Lee Janzen (1993 at Baltusrol)
	273 -	David Graham (1981 at Merion)
Best 18-Hole Round:	63 -	3 times (first by Johnny Miller at Oakmont, 1973)

SHORT PUTTS

The US Open is run by the United States Golf Association (USGA). Formed at a meeting in New York City, on December 22nd 1894, the USGA governs the amateur side of the game in the United States. It is America's equivalent of the Royal and Ancient Golf Club (R&A) of St Andrews in Scotland, which is the ruling body for Great Britain & Ireland. And in consultation with the R&A the USGA write and interpret the rules of golf, as well as administer America's national handicapping system.

When the USGA was formed there were only five member clubs - Newport CC, Rhode Island, New York; Shinnecock Hills GC, Long Island, New York; The Country Club, Brookline, Massachusetts; St Andrews, New York and Chicago GC. Nowadays there are over five and a half thousand affiliated member clubs.

Hubert Green survived the trauma of a death threat to win the US Open in 1977

Other important tournaments conducted by the USGA include the US Amateur Championship, US Women's Open and the Walker Cup (joint venture with the R&A). Today, the USGA has its offices at Far Hills, New Jersey.

Defying doctor's orders

When Ken Venturi won in 1964 he defied doctor's orders to do so. Towards the end of round three, the severe heat and humidity at Congressional Country Club was beginning to take its toll on 33-year-old Venturi. Back in the locker room, Venturi was given liquid and salt tablets in an effort to get him ready for the afternoon's final round. He was even advised by Dr John Everett to withdraw from the tournament. But Venturi was not giving up now - he was just two strokes off the lead. For the final 18 holes Dr Everett walked around the course with Venturi, carrying ice packs in case the golfer collapsed through heat exhaustion. Yet despite feeling physically unwell, Venturi held his game together superbly, fired a par round of 70 and won by four strokes. For the 1965 tournament, the USGA decided that only one round should be scheduled each day.

Man for the big occasion

Andy North only won three Tour events in his career - yet two of them were US Opens (1978 & 1985). And strangely, both were achieved with bogeys on the 72nd hole. His other victory was the 1977 Westchester Classic.

Death threat

1977 champion Hubert Green played the last four holes of the tournament under the threat of death. A woman had called the FBI to say that three men were making their way to Southern Hills Country Club in Tulsa, to assassinate Green, who was leading the tournament. Green was told of this threat as he left the 14th green. He was offered three alternatives - withdraw from the tournament, suspend play or carry on. He chose the latter joking that the threat probably came from an old girlfriend. Green hung-on grimly over the closing four holes, making a birdie, two pars and a bogey at 18, where he needed to hole out from four feet for a one shot victory.

Last of a kind

The last amateur to win a professional Major

Championship was Johnny Goodman who won the 1933 US Open at North Shore Country Club, Illinois.

Three-in-a-row
Willie Anderson (1903-05) is the only player to have won three successive US Open titles. Yet with one round to go in 1990 Curtis Strange had a great opportunity to equal Anderson's feat. After 54 holes at Medinah Country Club, Strange was just two strokes behind joint-leaders Billy Ray Brown and Mike Donald. But after bogeying the second hole in round four, Strange slumped to a three-over-par 75 to finish in a tie for 25th.

Shaky finale
Probably the poorest finish any champion has made in recent years came from Hale Irwin in 1979. Irwin covered the last five holes in four-over-par, including a double-bogey at 17 and a bogey at 18 - yet he still won by two strokes. He played the last nine in 40.

Major collapse
After 43 holes of the 1992 Open at Pebble Beach, Gil Morgan was 12-under-par and held a seven-stroke lead. But then his game fell apart. He played the next seven holes in nine-over-par, finished the round with a 77, and despite still holding a one-stroke lead going into the final day, proceeded to post an 81 in round four. He ended up in a tie for 13th, eight strokes behind champion Tom Kite. In the same tournament, American Mark Brooks was just one stroke behind leader Gil Morgan with 18 holes to play. But on a day of strong gusting winds, the 31-year-old Texan carded a disastrous 12-over-par 84 in the final round, 12 strokes worse than playing partner Kite. Brooks finished 44th.

Day of the Jacklin
When England's Tony Jacklin won at Hazeltine in 1970, he led at the end of each round - the last champion to do so. He was two strokes ahead after round one, led by three shots on day two, was four strokes in front after the third round, before winning by seven. He broke par every day carding 71-70-70-70 for a 72-hole total of 281 (seven under par).

Palmer blows-up
With just nine holes to play in 1966 at the Olympic Club in San Francisco, Arnold Palmer enjoyed a massive seven-stroke lead over nearest challenger Billy Casper. He had reached the turn in 32 and was looking to set a new scoring record for the tournament. But bogey followed bogey on the way home. He hooked his drive at 10, dropped another at 13, bunkered his tee shot at the par-three 15th, hooked another from the tee at 16 and made a fifth bogey at 17. In the middle of all this calamity he managed to birdie the 12th and then saved par brilliantly at 18 after yet another poor drive. But a back-nine of 39, coupled with Casper's home journey of 32, meant a tie and an 18-hole play-off the following day. Yet despite his trauma in round four, Palmer somehow managed to force his way into a two-stroke lead in the play-off through 10 holes. But, then, once again, it all went sour. He came home in 40 (five over par), which included a double-bogey seven at the par five 16th, his 73 four strokes worse than Casper.

Perfect Pate
Few Championships are won in such dramatic style as the 1976 Open at Atlanta Athletic Club. Arriving at the 72nd hole, 22-year-old Tour rookie Jerry Pate held a slender one-stroke lead over playing partner John Mahaffey. Both players drove into rough at the final hole, leaving themselves difficult carries over water to the green. Mahaffey went first with a wood, but his ball fell short and he found the lake. It was now upto Pate, who still needed a par to beat Al Geiberger and Tom Weiskopf. Both these players were safely in the clubhouse. Without any thought of laying-up short of the water, in the hope of getting down in two from there for a scrambling par, Pate went straight for the green. From 194 yards away, he took a 5-iron and played one of the greatest shots of all time. He put his ball within three feet of the pin, holed the birdie putt and won by two strokes. And like Jack Nicklaus 14 years earlier, his first Tour victory came in the US Open.

Controversial Hill
Hazeltine National in Chaska, Minnesota, was such an unpopular choice of venue in 1970, it was severely criticised by the players. But one golfer who took his comments too far was Dave Hill, who eventually finished runner-up. The outspoken Hill said the land needed: "Eighty acres of corn plus a few cows. They ruined a good farm when they built this course. Plow it up and start over again. If I had to play this course every day for fun I'd find another game." He was fined $150. When the Open returned to Hazeltine in 1991, its layout had changed considerably.

Gil Morgan made a spectacular start to the 1992 US Open before suffering an equally dramatic collapse

No Ray of hope

The highest score ever recorded at a single hole in the US Open was 19. The unfortunate holder of this unwanted record is Ray Ainsley who was 15-over-par at the 16th hole in 1938 at Cherry Hills, Denver, Colorado. Ainsley's ball had landed in a fast-moving creek near the green. He made numerous attempts to get the submerged ball out of the water, which was moving his ball downstream and further away from the hole. The ball eventually came to rest on a dry patch. From there Ainsley knocked it onto the fairway, then played it onto the green and single-putted. When asked afterwards why he hadn't taken a drop under penalty, Ainsley said that he thought he had to play the ball as it lay. He missed the cut by 17 shots with rounds of 76 and 96.

Smoking his way to success

American Billy Burke smoked 32 cigars en route to his victory in 1931 which required four play-off rounds - 144 holes in all.

Ball trouble

In the third round of the 1946 Open at Canterbury GC in Ohio, Byron Nelson's caddie, Eddie Martin, accidentally kicked his player's ball while getting underneath a spectator rope on the edge of the 15th fairway. It cost Nelson a one-stroke penalty and ultimately the Championship. Nelson lost in a play-off.

First ace

Jack Hobens made the first hole-in-one in US Open history when he holed his tee-shot at the 147-yard par-3 10th in the second round in 1907 at Philadelphia Cricket Club. Hobens led the tournament through 54 holes before collapsing to a 12-over-par 85 in the final round. He finished fourth.

Four at Oak Hill

Within the space of two hours in 1989, four players had aced the 167-yard 6th hole in the second round at Oak Hill. Doug Weaver was the first to hole out at 8:15 am. He was followed by Mark Wiebe, Jerry Pate and Nick Price. Pate made his while Price waited on the tee just one group behind.

Chen's costly double hit

No Asian golfer has ever won a major championship. Yet TC Chen of Taiwan came mighty close at Oakland Hills in 1985. Leading by two with 18 holes remaining, Chen had increased that lead to four strokes after four holes of the final round. But at the 5th it all went wrong. Attempting to play from heavy rough close to the green, his club got caught up in the thick grass and as he followed through on the shot his clubface jumped up and hit the ball for a second time. The result was a one shot penalty. Clearly affected by this unlikely mistake, Chen went on to make a quadruple-bogey eight on this par four hole. At the same hole, Chen's playing partner, Andy North, made par, and from being four behind just 10 minutes earlier, the American was now suddenly joint-leader. But Chen's misery didn't stop there. He three-putted the 6th and made bogeys at both 7 and 8. Chen finally carded a seven-over-par 77 to finish one-stroke behind champion North. At the same Championship, Denis Watson was penalised two strokes when he waited too long for a putt to drop into the hole in round one. At the eighth, his putt from around 12 feet came to rest on the lip of the cup. But instead of tapping it in, Watson waited 25-30 seconds

CLASSIC MOMENTS

SIX OF THE BEST

1) 1955, Jack Fleck, par-4 18th at the Olympic Club: *Little-known Jack Fleck caused one of the big surprises of all time by beating the great Ben Hogan in a play-off for the 1955 US Open. Yet to get into that play-off, Fleck had to make birdie at the tricky 18th; the key shot being his 7-iron approach that came to rest about eight feet from the flag. Fleck rolled in the putt and, as they say, the rest is history.*

2) 1960, Arnold Palmer, par-4 1st at Cherry Hills: *It might seem a strange choice to select a player's opening tee shot as being of great significance but when Arnold Palmer stood on the first tee in the final round in 1960 he was seven strokes off the pace and in 15th place. It was vital he made a good start if he was to stand any hope of making a final day charge. The first hole is not quite 350 yards in length. Palmer had tried to drive the green in his three previous rounds and had failed each time. Once more he attempted it and to the delight of his army of followers, he finally succeeded in reaching the putting surface. He didn't quite make an eagle, but two putts were good enough for an opening birdie. That thunderous first drive inspired Palmer to birdie six of the first seven holes en route to a front nine of 30. At the end of the day, Palmer was champion by two strokes after a final round of 65.*

3) 1972, Jack Nicklaus, par-3, 17th at Pebble Beach: *The Golden Bear came to the 71st tee with a three-stroke lead over Bruce Crampton. Playing the tough 17th into a strong wind, Nicklaus drilled a 1-iron that struck the pin*

and came to rest six inches away for a Championship clinching birdie two.

4) 1976, Jerry Pate, par-4 18th at Atlanta Athletic Club: *Needing at least a par to beat Tom Weiskopf and Al Geiberger, who were already in the clubhouse, Pate's drive at the 72nd hole had landed in the rough over 190 yards from the flag. His shot to the green was fraught with danger - a lake guarded the front of the putting surface. Yet with the confidence of youth, 22-year-old Pate calmly took out a 5-iron and drilled his ball to within three feet of the cup. The resulting birdie three earned him a two-stroke victory.*

5) 1982, Tom Watson, par-3 17th at Pebble Beach: *With Jack Nicklaus already finished at four-under-par, Watson arrived at the 71st hole tied with the great man and in search of his first US Open title. But Watson's tee-shot was pulled left of the green, his ball landing in heavy rough. A bogey looked inevitable. Yet Watson pulled-out a sand-wedge lobbed his ball on to the green and watched it roll into the hole for a birdie two and a one-stroke lead. Another birdie at the par-five 18th earned him a two-stroke victory.*

6) 1983, Larry Nelson, par-3 16th at Oakmont: *All square with co-leader Tom Watson with three holes to play, Nelson rolled in a tie-breaking 60-foot birdie-putt on the roller-coaster 16th green. He went on to beat runner-up Watson by one stroke. After 36-holes Nelson had been seven strokes off the pace but closed with rounds of 65 and 67 to claim the title.*

before the ball eventually toppled into the hole. As he left the green Watson was told by a USGA official that he'd been penalised two shots for delaying play while waiting for the ball to drop. Like Chen, Watson was a joint runner-up one stroke behind North.

Special exemption

The USGA award a handful of special exemptions each year to players who haven't already qualified for the Championship through the 'normal' channels. Most of these exemptions are given to players who are former winners of the event but whose 10-year exemption period has run out. By 1990, the 10-year exemption of 1979 winner Hale Irwin had just expired, so the USGA offered him a place in the tournament. He grabbed the opportunity with both hands winning the event after a play-off to become the only champion who ever needed a special invite.

First Open
Eleven golfers contested the first US Open, played over a nine-hole course at Newport Golf Club on Rhode Island in 1895. The tournament was contested over four rounds and completed in one day (October 4th).

Brits on Tour
Britain's top two golfers at the turn of the century, Harry Vardon and JH Taylor, made one of their rare US Open appearances in 1900. Vardon was in the States at the time promoting his new golf ball, the 'Vardon Flyer' by Spalding, as well as playing a number of exhibitions across the country. Taylor just happened to be there on business and the pair finished first and second in the Open. Vardon edged out Taylor by two strokes with third place going to David Bell a distant seven shots behind JH, illustrating the strength of British golf at that time.

All in the clubs
When Jack Fleck beat Ben Hogan in a play-off to win the 1955 Championship, he did so using a set of Ben Hogan Signature golf clubs.

Not one to boast about
In 1993 at Baltusrol, Joey Sindelar became the first player in the history of the US Open, to lead the tournament after 18 holes, yet still miss the 36-hole cut. His four-under-par 66 in round one gave

him a share of the lead with Craig Parry and Scott Hoch. But a 79 on day two meant he was on his way home - one stroke below the hatchet line.

Cheeky chappy
In 1980, a gate-crasher named Barry Bremen managed to convince officials he was Chuck Moran, a bona-fide competitor at Baltusrol. He took a courtesy car to the course, hit balls on the practice range, chatted to 'fellow' competitors and even had his photograph taken with Jack Nicklaus. Bremen, a 7-handicapper, joined the action at the 4th hole, teaming-up with Jim Thorpe and Bobby Nichols. He managed to play through to the end of his round before being caught by a USGA official.

Charitable Player
After winning the 1965 US Open in a play-off, Gary Player donated $5,000 of his prize-money to cancer research and $20,000 to the USGA to help junior golf. His cheque for winning the title was $26,000.

Cooper's wasted opportunity
Harry Cooper, one of the best players never to win a major championship, missed an excellent chance to take the 1927 US Open at Oakmont. The Englishman three-putted the 71st green. This allowed Tommy Armour the opportunity to force a play-off by birdieing the final hole from 10 feet. The following day's play-off was won by Armour (76 to 79).

Jim Barnes, winner of the first two USPGA titles in 1916 and 1919

USPGA CHAMPIONSHIP

Matchplay
Note: All semi-final & final matches contested over 36 holes. No tournament 1917-18-43.

1916 -   **Jim Barnes (at Siwanoy CC, Bronxville, New York)**

Semi-Finals:	Jim Barnes	bt	Willie McFarlane	6&5
	Jock Hutchison	bt	Walter Hagen	2 up
Final:	Jim Barnes	bt	Jock Hutchison	1 up

1919 -   **Jim Barnes (at Engineers CC, Roslyn, Long Island, New York)**

Semi-Finals:	Jim Barnes	bt	Bob McDonald	5&4
	Fred McLeod	bt	George McLean	3&2
Final:	Jim Barnes	bt	Fred McLeod	6&5

1920 -   **Jock Hutchison (at Flossmoor CC, Chicago, Illinois)**

Semi-Finals:	Jock Hutchison	bt	Harry Hampton	4&3
	Douglas Edgar	bt	George McLean	8&6
Final:	Jock Hutchison	bt	Douglas Edgar	1 up

1921 -   **Walter Hagen (at Inwood CC, Far Rockaway, New York)**

Semi-Finals:	Walter Hagen	bt	Cyril Walker	5&4
	Jim Barnes	bt	Emmett French	5&4
Final:	Walter Hagen	bt	Jim Barnes	3&2

1922 -   **Gene Sarazen (at Oakmont CC, Oakmont, Pennsylvania)**

Semi-Finals:	Gene Sarazen	bt	Bobby Cruickshank	3&2
	Emmett French	bt	John Golden	8&7
Final:	Gene Sarazen	bt	Emmett French	4&3

1923 -   **Gene Sarazen (at Pelham GC, Pelham Manor, New York)**

Semi-Finals:	Gene Sarazen	bt	Bobby Cruickshank	6&5
	Walter Hagen	bt	George McLean	12&11
Final:	Gene Sarazen	bt	Walter Hagen	at 38th

1924 -   **Walter Hagen (at French Springs GC, French Lick, Indiana)**

Semi-Finals:	Walter Hagen	bt	Ray Derr	8&7
	Jim Barnes	bt	Larry Nabholtz	1 up
Final:	Walter Hagen	bt	Jim Barnes	2 up

1925 -   **Walter Hagen (at Olympia Fields CC, Olympia Fields, Illinois)**

Semi-Finals:	Walter Hagen	bt	Harry Cooper	3&1
	Bill Mehlhorn	bt	Mortie Dutra	8&6
Final:	Walter Hagen	bt	Bill Mehlhorn	6&5

1926 -   **Walter Hagen (at Salisbury Golf Links, Westbury, Long Island, NY)**

Semi-Finals:	Walter Hagen	bt	Johnny Farrell	6&5
	Leo Diegel	bt	John Golden	1 up
Final:	Walter Hagen	bt	Leo Diegel	5&3

1927 -   **Walter Hagen (at Cedar Crest CC, Dallas, Texas)**

Semi-Finals:	Walter Hagen	bt	Al Espinosa	at 37th
	Joe Turnesa	bt	John Golden	7&6
Final:	Walter Hagen	bt	Joe Turnesa	1 up

1928 -   Leo Diegel   (at Five Farms CC, Baltimore, Maryland)

Semi-Finals:	Leo Diegel	bt	Gene Sarazen	9&8
	Al Espinosa	bt	Horton Smith	6&5
Final:	Leo Diegel	bt	Al Espinosa	6&5

1929 -   Leo Diegel   (at Hillcrest CC, Los Angeles, California)

Semi-Finals:	Leo Diegel	bt	Walter Hagen	3&2
	Johnny Farrell	bt	Al Watrous	6&5
Final:	Leo Diegel	bt	Johnny Farrell	6&4

1930 -   Tommy Armour   (at Fresh Meadows CC, Flushing, New York)

Semi-Finals:	Tommy Armour	bt	Charles Lacey	1 up
	Gene Sarazen	bt	Joe Kirkwood	5&4
Final:	Tommy Armour	bt	Gene Sarazen	1 up

1931 -   Tom Creavy   (at Wannamoisett CC, Rumford, Rhode Island)

Semi-Finals:	Tom Creavy	bt	Gene Sarazen	5&3
	Densmore Shute	bt	Billy Burke	1 up
Final:	Tom Creavy	bt	Densmore Shute	2&1

1932 -   Olin Dutra   (at Keller GC, St Paul, Minnesota)

Semi-Finals:	Olin Dutra	bt	Ed Dudley	3&2
	Frank Walsh	bt	Tom Creavy	at 38th
Final:	Olin Dutra	bt	Frank Walsh	4&3

1933 -   Gene Sarazen   (at Blue Mound CC, Milwaukee, Wisconsin)

Semi-Finals:	Gene Sarazen	bt	Johnny Farrell	5&4
	Willie Goggin	bt	Jimmy Hines	1 up
Final:	Gene Sarazen	bt	Willie Goggin	5&4

1934 -   Paul Runyan   (at Park Club of Buffalo, Williamsville, New York)

Semi-Finals:	Paul Runyan	bt	Gene Kunes	4&2
	Craig Wood	bt	Densmore Shute	2&1
Final:	Paul Runyan	bt	Craig Wood	at 38th

1935 -   Johnny Revolta   (at Twin Hills CC, Oklahoma City, Oklahoma)

Semi-Finals:	Johnny Revolta	bt	Al Zimmerman	4&3
	Tommy Armour	bt	Al Watrous	2&1
Final:	Johnny Revolta	bt	Tommy Armour	5&4

1936 -   Densmore Shute   (at Pinehurst CC, Pinehurst, North Carolina)

Semi-Finals:	Densmore Shute	bt	Bill Mehlhorn	1 up
	Jimmy Thomson	bt	Craig Wood	4&3
Final:	Densmore Shute	bt	Jimmy Thomson	3&2

1937 -   Densmore Shute   (at Pittsburgh Field, Aspinwall, Pennsylvania)

Semi-Finals:	Densmore Shute	bt	Tony Manero	3&2
	Harold McSpaden	bt	Ky Laffoon	2&1
Final:	Densmore Shute	bt	Harold McSpaden	at 37th

1938 -   Paul Runyan   (at Shawnee CC, Shawnee-on-Delaware, Pennsyvania)

Semi-Finals:	Paul Runyan	bt	Henry Picard	4&3
	Sam Snead	bt	Jimmy Hines	1 up
Final:	Paul Runyan	bt	Sam Snead	8&7

1939 -	Henry Picard (at Pomonok CC, Flushing, New York)			
Semi-Finals:	Henry Picard	bt	Dick Metz	1 up
	Byron Nelson	bt	Dutch Harrison	9&8
Final:	Henry Picard	bt	Byron Nelson	at 37th

1940 -	Byron Nelson (at Hershey CC, Hershey, Pennsylvania)			
Semi-Finals:	Byron Nelson	bt	Ralph Guldahl	1 up
	Sam Snead	bt	Harold McSpaden	5&4
Final:	Byron Nelson	bt	Sam Snead	1 up

1941 -	Vic Ghezzi (at Cherry Hills Club, Denver, Colorado)			
Semi-Finals:	Vic Ghezzi	bt	Lloyd Mangrum	1 up
	Byron Nelson	bt	Gene Sarazen	2&1
Final:	Vic Ghezzi	bt	Byron Nelson	at 38th

1942 -	Sam Snead (at Seaview CC, Atlantic City, New Jersey)			
Semi-Finals:	Sam Snead	bt	Jimmy Demaret	3&2
	Jim Turnesa	bt	Byron Nelson	at 37th
Final:	Sam Snead	bt	Jim Turnesa	2&1

1944 -	Bob Hamilton (at Manito G&CC, Spokane, Washington)			
Semi-Finals:	Bob Hamilton	bt	George Schneiter	1 up
	Byron Nelson	bt	Charles Congdon	8&7
Final:	Bob Hamilton	bt	Byron Nelson	1 up

1945 -	Byron Nelson (at Moraine CC, Dayton, Ohio)			
Semi-Finals:	Byron Nelson	bt	Claude Harmon	5&4
	Sam Byrd	bt	Clarence Doser	7&6
Final:	Byron Nelson	bt	Sam Byrd	4&3

1946 -	Ben Hogan (at Portland GC, Portland, Oregan)			
Semi-Finals:	Ben Hogan	bt	Jimmy Demaret	10&9
	Ed Oliver	bt	Harold McSpaden	6&5
Final:	Ben Hogan	bt	Ed Oliver	6&4

1947 -	Jim Ferrier (at Plum Hollow CC, Detroit, Michigan)			
Semi-Finals:	Jim Ferrier	bt	Art Bell	10&9
	Chick Harbert	bt	Vic Ghezzi	6&5
Final:	Jim Ferrier	bt	Chick Harbert	2&1

1948 -	Ben Hogan (at Norwood Hills CC, St Louis, Mo.)			
Semi-Finals:	Ben Hogan	bt	Jimmy Demaret	2&1
	Mike Turnesa	bt	Claude Harmon	at 37th
Final:	Ben Hogan	bt	Mike Turnesa	7&6

1949 -	Sam Snead (at Hermitage CC, Richmond, Virginia)			
Semi-Finals:	Sam Snead	bt	Jim Ferrier	3&2
	Johnny Palmer	bt	Lloyd Mangrum	6&5
Final:	Sam Snead	bt	Johnny Palmer	3&2

1950 -	Chandler Harper (at Scioto CC, Columbus, Ohio)			
Semi-Finals:	Chandler Harper	bt	Jimmy Demaret	2&1
	Henry Williams	bt	Henry Picard	at 38th
Final:	Chandler Harper	bt	Henry Williams	4&3

1951 - Sam Snead (at Oakmont CC, Oakmont, Pennsylvania)

Semi-Finals:	Sam Snead	bt	Charles Bassler	9&8
	Walter Burkemo	bt	Ellsworth Vines	at 37th
Final:	Sam Snead	bt	Walter Burkemo	7&6

1952 - Jim Turnesa (at Big Spring CC, Louisville, Kentucky)

Semi-Finals:	Jim Turnesa	bt	Ted Kroll	4&2
	Chick Harbert	bt	Bob Hamilton	2&1
Final:	Jim Turnesa	bt	Chick Harbert	1 up

1953 - Walter Burkemo (at Birmingham CC, Birmingham, Michigan)

Semi-Finals:	Walter Burkemo	bt	Claude Harmon	1 up
	Felice Torza	bt	Jack Isaacs	at 39th
Final:	Walter Burkemo	bt	Felice Torza	2&1

1954 - Chick Harbert (at Keller GC, St Paul, Minnesota)

Semi-Finals:	Chick Harbert	bt	Tommy Bolt	1 up
	Walter Burkemo	bt	Cary Middlecoff	at 37th
Final:	Chick Harbert	bt	Walter Burkemo	4&3

1955 - Doug Ford (at Meadowbrook CC, Northville, Michigan)

Semi-Finals:	Doug Ford	bt	Shelly Mayfield	4&3
	Cary Middlecoff	bt	Tommy Bolt	4&3
Final:	Doug Ford	bt	Cary Middlecoff	4&3

1956 - Jack Burke jr (at Blue Hill G&CC, Canton, Mass.)

Semi-Finals:	Jack Burke jr	bt	Ed Furgol	at 37th
	Ted Kroll	bt	William Johnston	10&8
Final:	Jack Burke jr	bt	Ted Kroll	3&2

1957 - Lionel Hebert (at Miami Valley GC, Dayton Ohio)

Semi-Finals:	Lionel Hebert	bt	Walter Burkemo	3&1
	Dow Finsterwald	bt	Don Whitt	2 up
Final:	Lionel Hebert	bt	Dow Finsterwald	2&1

Strokeplay

1958- Dow Finsterwald (at Llanerch CC, Havertown, Pennsylvania)

Dow Finsterwald	67-72-70-67	276
Billy Casper	73-67-68-70	278
Sam Snead	73-67-67-73	280
Jack Burke Jr	70-72-69-70	281
Tommy Bolt	72-70-73-70	285
Julius Boros	72-68-73-72	285
Jay Hebert	68-71-73-73	285

1959- Bob Rosburg (at Minneapolis GC, St Louis Park, Minnesota)

Bob Rosburg	71-72-68-66	277
Jerry Barber	69-65-71-73	278
Doug Sanders	72-66-68-72	278
Dow Finsterwald	71-68-71-70	280
Bob Goalby	72-69-72-68	281
Mike Souchak	69-67-71-74	281
Ken Venturi	70-72-70-69	281

1960- Jay Hebert (at Firestone CC, Akron, Ohio)

Jay Hebert	72-67-72-70	281
Jim Ferrier	71-74-66-71	282
Doug Sanders	70-71-69-73	283
Sam Snead	68-73-70-72	283
Don January	70-70-72-72	284

1961- Jerry Barber (at Olympia Fields CC, Olympia Fields, Illinois)

Jerry Barber	69-67-71-70	277
Don January	72-66-67-72	277

Play-Off: Barber 67, January 68

Doug Sanders	70-68-74-68	280
Ted Kroll	72-68-70-71	281
Wes Ellis Jr	71-71-68-72	282
Doug Ford	69-73-74-66	282
Gene Littler	71-70-72-69	282
Arnold Palmer	73-72-69-68	282
Johnny Pott	71-73-67-71	282
Art Wall	67-72-73-70	282

1962- Gary Player (at Aronimink GC, Newtown Square, Pennsylvania)

Gary Player	72-67-69-70	278
Bob Goalby	69-72-71-67	279
George Bayer	69-70-71-71	281
Jack Nicklaus	71-74-69-67	281
Doug Ford	69-69-73-71	282

The Rodman Wanamaker Trophy, which is awarded to the USPGA champion

1963- Jack Nicklaus (at Dallas Athletic Club, Dallas, Texas)

Jack Nicklaus	69-73-69-68	279
Dave Ragan	75-70-67-69	281
Bruce Crampton	70-73-65-74	282
Dow Finsterwald	72-72-66-72	282
Al Geiberger	72-73-69-70	284
Billy Maxwell	73-71-69-71	284

1964- Bobby Nichols (at Columbus CC, Columbus, Ohio)

Bobby Nichols	64-71-69-67	271
Jack Nicklaus	67-73-70-64	274
Arnold Palmer	68-68-69-69	274
Mason Rudolph	73-66-68-69	276
Tom Nieporte	68-71-68-72	279
Ken Venturi	72-65-73-69	279

1965- Dave Marr (at Laurel Valley GC, Ligonier, Pennsylvania)

Dave Marr	70-69-70-71	280
Billy Casper	70-70-71-71	282
Jack Nicklaus	69-70-72-71	282
Bo Wininger	73-72-72-66	283
Gardner Dickinson	67-74-69-74	284

1966- Al Geiberger (at Firestone CC, Akron, Ohio)

Al Geiberger	68-72-68-72	280
Dudley Wysong	74-72-66-72	284
Billy Casper	73-73-70-70	286
Gene Littler	75-71-71-69	286
Gary Player	73-70-70-73	286

1967- Don January (at Columbine CC, Denver, Colorado)

Don January	71-72-70-68	281
Don Massengale	70-75-70-66	281

(Play-Off: January 69, Massengale 71)

Jack Nicklaus	67-75-69-71	282
Dan Sikes	69-70-70-73	282
Julius Boros	69-76-70-68	283
Al Geiberger	73-71-69-70	283

1968- Julius Boros (at Pecan Valley CC, San Antonio, Texas)

Julius Boros	71-71-70-69	281
Bob Charles	72-70-70-70	282
Arnold Palmer	71-69-72-70	282
George Archer	71-69-74-69	283
Marty Fleckman	66-72-72-73	283

1969- Ray Floyd (at NCR CC, Dayton, Ohio)

Ray Floyd	69-66-67-74	276

Gary Player	71-65-71-70	277
Bert Greene	71-68-68-71	278
Jimmy Wright	71-68-69-71	279
Miller Barber	73-75-64-68	280
Larry Ziegler	69-71-70-70	280

1970- Dave Stockton (at Southern Hills CC, Tulsa, Oklahoma)

Dave Stockton	70-70-66-73	279
Bob Murphy	71-73-71-66	281
Arnold Palmer	70-72-69-70	281
Larry Hinson	69-71-74-68	282
Gene Littler	72-71-69-70	282
Bruce Crampton	73-75-68-67	283
Jack Nicklaus	68-76-73-66	283
Ray Floyd	71-73-65-75	284
Dick Lotz	72-70-75-67	284
Billy Maxwell	72-71-73-69	285
Mason Rudolph	71-70-73-71	285

1971- Jack Nicklaus (at PGA National, Palm Beach Gardens, Florida)

Jack Nicklaus	69-69-70-73	281
Billy Casper	71-73-71-68	283
Tommy Bolt	72-74-69-69	284
Miller Barber	72-68-75-70	285
Gary Player	71-73-68-73	285
Gibby Gilbert	74-67-72-73	286
Dave Hill	74-71-71-70	286
Jim Jamieson	72-72-72-70	286
Jerry Heard	73-71-72-71	287
Bob Lunn	72-70-73-72	287
Fred Marti	72-71-74-70	287
Bob Rosburg	74-72-70-71	287

1972- Gary Player (at Oakland Hills CC, Birmingham, Michigan)

Gary Player	71-71-67-72	281
Tommy Aaron	71-71-70-71	283
Jim Jamieson	69-72-72-70	283
Billy Casper	73-70-67-74	284
Ray Floyd	69-71-74-70	284
Sam Snead	70-74-71-69	284
Gay Brewer	71-70-70-74	285
Jerry Heard	69-70-72-74	285
Phil Rodgers	71-72-68-74	285
Doug Sanders	72-72-68-73	285

1973- Jack Nicklaus (at Canterbury GC, Cleveland, Ohio)

Jack Nicklaus	72-68-68-69	277
Bruce Crampton	71-73-67-70	281
Mason Rudolph	69-70-70-73	282
JC Snead	71-74-68-69	282

Lanny Wadkins	73-69-71-69	282
Don Iverson	67-72-70-74	283
Dan Sikes	72-68-72-71	283
Tom Weiskopf	70-71-71-71	283
Hale Irwin	76-72-68-68	284
Sam Snead	71-71-71-71	284
Kermit Zarley	76-71-68-69	284

1974- Lee Trevino (at Tanglewood GC, Clemmons, North Carolina)

Lee Trevino	73-66-68-69	276
Jack Nicklaus	69-69-70-69	277
Bobby Cole	69-68-71-71	279
Hubert Green	68-68-73-70	279
Dave Hill	74-69-67-69	279
Sam Snead	69-71-71-68	279
Gary Player	73-64-73-70	280
Al Geiberger	70-70-75-66	281
Don Bies	73-71-68-70	282
John Mahaffey	72-72-71-67	282

1975- Jack Nicklaus (at Firestone CC, Akron, Ohio)

Jack Nicklaus	70-68-67-71	276
Bruce Crampton	71-63-75-69	278
Tom Weiskopf	70-71-70-68	279
Andy North	72-74-70-65	281
Billy Casper	69-72-72-70	283
Hale Irwin	72-65-73-73	283
Dave Hill	71-71-74-68	284
Gene Littler	76-71-66-71	284
Tom Watson	70-71-71-73	285
Buddy Allin	73-72-70-71	286
Ben Crenshaw	73-72-71-70	286
Ray Floyd	70-73-72-71	286
David Graham	72-70-70-74	286
Don January	72-70-71-73	286
John Schlee	71-68-75-72	286
Leonard Thompson	74-69-72-71	286

1976- Dave Stockton (at Congressional CC, Bethesda, Maryland)

Dave Stockton	70-72-69-70	281
Ray Floyd	72-68-71-71	282
Don January	70-69-71-72	282
David Graham	70-71-70-72	283
Jack Nicklaus	71-69-69-74	283
Jerry Pate	69-73-72-69	283
John Schlee	72-71-70-70	283
Charles Coody	68-72-67-77	284
Ben Crenshaw	71-69-74-70	284
Jerry McGee	68-72-72-72	284
Gil Morgan	66-68-75-75	284
Tom Weiskopf	65-74-73-72	284

1977- Lanny Wadkins (at Pebble Beach Links, Pebble Beach, California)

Lanny Wadkins	69-71-72-70	282
Gene Littler	67-69-70-76	282

Play-Off: Wadkins 4,4,3; Littler 4,4,4

Jack Nicklaus	69-71-70-73	283
Charles Coody	70-71-70-73	284
Jerry Pate	73-70-69-73	285
Al Geiberger	71-70-73-72	286
Lou Graham	71-73-71-71	286
Don January	75-69-70-72	286
Jerry McGee	68-70-77-71	286
Tom Watson	68-73-71-74	286

1978- John Mahaffey (at Oakmont CC, Oakmont, Pennsylvania)

John Mahaffey	75-67-68-66	276
Jerry Pate	72-70-66-68	276
Tom Watson	67-69-67-73	276

Play-Off: Mahaffey 4,3; Pate 4,4; Watson 4,4

Gil Morgan	76-71-66-67	280
Tom Weiskopf	73-67-69-71	280
Craig Stadler	70-74-67-71	282
Andy Bean	72-72-70-70	284
Graham Marsh	72-74-68-70	284
Lee Trevino	69-73-70-72	284
Fuzzy Zoeller	75-69-73-68	285

1979- David Graham (at Oakland Hills CC, Birmingham, Michigan)

David Graham	69-68-70-65	272
Ben Crenshaw	69-67-69-67	272

Play-Off: Graham 4,4,2; Crenshaw 4,4,4

Rex Caldwell	67-70-66-71	274
Ron Streck	68-71-69-68	276
Gibby Gilbert	69-72-68-69	278
Jerry Pate	69-69-69-71	278
Jay Haas	68-69-73-69	279
Don January	69-70-71-69	279
Howard Twitty	70-73-69-67	279
Lou Graham	69-74-68-69	280
Gary Koch	71-71-71-67	280

1980- Jack Nicklaus (at Oak Hill CC, Rochester, New York)

Jack Nicklaus	70-69-66-69	274
Andy Bean	72-71-68-70	281
Lon Hinkle	70-69-69-75	283
Gil Morgan	68-70-73-72	283
Curtis Strange	68-72-72-72	284
Howard Twitty	68-74-71-71	284
Lee Trevino	74-71-71-69	285
Bill Rogers	71-71-72-72	286
Bobby Walzel	68-76-71-71	286

Terry Diehl	72-72-68-76	288
Peter Jacobsen	71-73-74-70	288
Jerry Pate	72-73-70-73	288
Tom Watson	75-74-72-67	288
Tom Weiskopf	71-73-72-72	288

1981- Larry Nelson (at Atlanta Athletic Club, Duluth, Geogia)

Larry Nelson	70-66-66-71	273
Fuzzy Zoeller	70-68-68-71	277
Dan Pohl	69-67-73-69	278
Isao Aoki	75-68-66-70	279
Keith Fergus	71-71-69-68	279
Bob Gilder	74-69-70-66	279
Tom Kite	71-67-69-72	279
Bruce Lietzke	70-70-71-68	279
Jack Nicklaus	71-68-71-69	279
Greg Norman	73-67-68-71	279

1982- Ray Floyd (at Southern Hills CC, Tulsa, Oklahoma)

Ray Floyd	63-69-68-72	272
Lanny Wadkins	71-68-69-67	275
Fred Couples	67-71-72-66	276
Calvin Peete	69-70-68-69	276
Jay Haas	71-66-68-72	277
Greg Norman	66-69-70-72	277
Jim Simons	68-67-73-69	277
Bob Gilder	66-68-72-72	278
Lon Hinkle	70-68-71-71	280
Tom Kite	73-70-70-67	280
Jerry Pate	72-69-70-69	280
Tom Watson	72-69-71-68	280

1983- Hal Sutton (at Riviera CC, Los Angeles, California)

Hal Sutton	65-66-72-71	274
Jack Nicklaus	73-65-71-66	275
Peter Jacobsen	73-70-68-65	276
Pat McGowan	68-67-73-69	277
John Fought	67-69-71-71	278
Bruce Lietzke	67-71-70-71	279
Fuzzy Zoeller	72-71-67-69	279
Dan Pohl	72-70-69-69	280
Ben Crenshaw	68-66-71-77	282
Jay Haas	68-72-69-73	282
Mike Reid	69-71-72-70	282
Scott Simpson	66-73-70-73	282
Doug Tewell	74-72-69-67	282

1984- Lee Trevino (at Shoal Creek CC, Birmingham, Alabama)

Lee Trevino	69-68-67-69	273
Gary Player	74-63-69-71	277

Lee Trevino (second from right) wins the 1984 USPGA championship at the age of 44, the sixth Major title of his career

Lanny Wadkins	68-69-68-72	277
Calvin Peete	71-70-69-68	278
Seve Ballesteros	70-69-70-70	279
Gary Hallberg	69-71-68-72	280
Larry Mize	71-69-67-73	280
Scott Simpson	69-69-72-70	280
Hal Sutton	74-73-64-69	280
Russ Cochran	73-68-73-67	281
Tommy Nakajima	72-68-67-74	281
Victor Regalado	69-69-73-70	281

1985- Hubert Green (at Cherry Hills CC, Englewood, Colorado)

Hubert Green	67-69-70-72	278
Lee Trevino	66-68-75-71	280
Andy Bean	71-70-72-68	281
TM Chen	69-76-71-65	281
Nick Price	73-73-65-71	282
Fred Couples	70-65-76-72	283
Buddy Gardner	73-73-70-67	283
Corey Pavin	66-75-73-69	283
Tom Watson	67-70-74-72	283
Peter Jacobsen	66-71-75-72	284
Lanny Wadkins	70-69-73-72	284

1986- Bob Tway (at Inverness Club, Toledo, Ohio)

Bob Tway	72-70-64-70	276
Greg Norman	65-68-69-76	278
Peter Jacobsen	68-70-70-71	279
DA Weibring	71-72-68-69	280
Bruce Lietzke	69-71-70-71	281
Payne Stewart	70-67-72-72	281
David Graham	75-69-71-67	282
Mike Hulbert	69-68-74-71	282
Jim Thorpe	71-67-73-71	282
Doug Tewell	73-71-68-71	283

1987- Larry Nelson (at PGA National*, Palm Beach Gardens, Florida)

Larry Nelson	70-72-73-72	287
Lanny Wadkins	70-70-74-73	287

Play-Off: Nelson 4, Wadkins 5

Scott Hoch	74-74-71-69	288
DA Weibring	73-72-67-76	288
Mark McCumber	74-69-69-77	289
Don Pooley	73-71-73-72	289
Ben Crenshaw	72-70-74-74	290
Bobby Wadkins	68-74-71-77	290
Curtis Strange	70-76-71-74	291

Seve Ballesteros	72-70-72-78	292
David Frost	75-70-71-76	292
Tom Kite	72-77-71-72	292
Nick Price	76-71-70-75	292

* - Not the same course as the one which staged this championship in 1971 at PGA National. The venue which hosted the tournament 16 years earlier is now called Ballen Isles CC.

1988- Jeff Sluman (at Oak Tree GC, Edmond, Oklahoma)

Jeff Sluman	69-70-68-65	272
Paul Azinger	67-66-71-71	275
Tommy Nakajima	69-68-74-67	278
Nick Faldo	67-71-70-71	279
Tom Kite	72-69-71-67	279
Bob Gilder	66-75-71-68	280
Dave Rummells	73-64-68-75	280
Dan Pohl	69-71-70-71	281
Ray Floyd	68-68-74-72	282
Steve Jones	69-68-72-73	282
Kenny Knox	72-69-68-73	282
Greg Norman	68-71-72-71	282
Mark O'Meara	70-71-70-71	282
Payne Stewart	70-69-70-73	282

1989- Payne Stewart (at Kemper Lakes GC, Hawthorn Woods, Illinois)

Payne Stewart	74-66-69-67	276
Andy Bean	70-67-74-66	277
Mike Reid	66-67-70-74	277
Curtis Strange	70-68-70-69	277
Dave Rummells	68-69-69-72	278
Ian Woosnam	68-70-70-71	279
Scott Hoch	69-69-69-73	280
Craig Stadler	71-64-72-73	280
Nick Faldo	70-73-69-69	281
Ed Fiori	70-67-75-69	281
Tom Watson	67-69-74-71	281

1990- Wayne Grady (at Shoal Creek CC, Birmingham, Alabama)

Wayne Grady	72-67-72-71	282
Fred Couples	69-71-73-72	285
Gil Morgan	77-72-65-72	286
Bill Britton	72-74-72-71	289
Chip Beck	71-70-78-71	290
Billy Mayfair	70-71-75-74	290
Loren Roberts	73-71-70-76	290
Mark McNulty	74-72-75-71	292
Don Pooley	75-74-71-72	292
Tim Simpson	71-73-75-73	292
Payne Stewart	71-72-70-79	292

1991- John Daly (at Crooked Stick GC, Carmel, Indiana)

John Daly	69-67-69-71	276
Bruce Lietzke	68-69-72-70	279
Jim Gallagher jr	70-72-72-67	281
Kenny Knox	67-71-70-74	282
Bob Gilder	73-70-67-73	283
Steve Richardson	70-72-72-69	283
David Feherty	71-74-71-68	284
Ray Floyd	69-74-72-69	284
John Huston	70-72-70-72	284
Steve Pate	70-75-70-69	284
Craig Stadler	68-71-69-76	284
Hal Sutton	74-67-72-71	284

1992- Nick Price (at Bellerive CC, St Louis, Missouri)

Nick Price	70-70-68-70	278
John Cook	71-72-67-71	281
Nick Faldo	68-70-76-67	281
Jim Gallagher Jr	72-66-72-71	281
Gene Sauers	67-69-70-75	281
Jeff Maggert	71-72-65-74	282
Russ Cochran	69-69-76-69	283
Dan Forsman	70-73-70-70	283
Brian Claar	68-73-73-70	284
Anders Forsbrand	73-71-70-70	284
Duffy Waldorf	74-73-68-69	284

1993- Paul Azinger (at Inverness Club, Toledo, Ohio)

Paul Azinger	69-66-69-68	272
Greg Norman	68-68-67-69	272

Play-Off: Azinger 4,4; Norman 4,5

Nick Faldo	68-68-69-68	273
Vijay Singh	68-63-73-70	274
Tom Watson	69-65-70-72	276
John Cook	72-66-68-71	277
Bob Estes	69-66-69-73	277
Dudley Hart	66-68-71-72	277
Nolan Henke	72-70-67-68	277
Scott Hoch	74-68-68-67	277
Hale Irwin	68-69-67-73	277
Phil Mickelson	67-71-69-70	277
Scott Simpson	64-70-71-72	277

1994- Nick Price (at Southern Hills CC, Tulsa, Oklahoma)

Nick Price	67-65-70-67	269
Corey Pavin	70-67-69-69	275
Phil Mickelson	68-71-67-70	276
Nick Faldo	73-67-71-66	277
Greg Norman	71-69-67-70	277
John Cook	71-67-69-70	277

Steve Elkington	73-70-66-69	278
Jose Maria Olazabal	72-66-70-70	278
Ben Crenshaw	70-67-70-72	279
Tom Kite	72-68-69-70	279
Loren Roberts	69-72-67-71	279
Tom Watson	69-72-67-71	279
Ian Woosnam	68-72-73-66	279

1995- Steve Elkington (at Riviera CC, Los Angeles, California)

| Steve Elkington | 68-67-68-64 | 267 |
| Colin Montgomerie | 68-67-67-65 | 267 |

Play-Off: Elkington 3; Montgomerie 4

Ernie Els	66-65-66-72	269
Jeff Maggert	66-69-65-69	269
Brad Faxon	70-67-71-63	271
Bob Estes	69-68-68-68	273
Mark O'Meara	64-67-69-73	273
Jay Haas	69-71-64-70	274
Justin Leonard	68-66-70-70	274
Steve Lowery	69-68-68-69	274
Jeff Sluman	69-67-68-70	274
Craig Stadler	71-66-66-71	274

Steve Elkington (and daughter Annie) after his win in 1995

The moment the dream came true for Elkington as he defeats Colin Montgomerie in the play-off

USPGA CHAMPIONSHIP SUMMARY

Most Victories:	5 -	Walter Hagen (1921-24-25-26-27)
		Jack Nicklaus (1963-71-73-75-80)
	3 -	Gene Sarazen (1922-23-33)
		Sam Snead (1942-49-51)
Oldest Champions:		Julius Boros (48 yrs, 4 mths, 18 dys, 1968)
		Jerry Barber (45 yrs, 3 mths, 6 dys, 1961)
Youngest Champions:		Gene Sarazen (20 yrs, 5 mths, 22 dys, 1922)
		Tom Creavy (20 yrs, 7 mths 11 dys, 1931)
Widest Winning Margins	7 -	Jack Nicklaus (1980)
(strokeplay):	6 -	Nick Price (1994)
Lowest 72-Hole Totals:	267 -	Steve Elkington (Riviera, 1995)
		Colin Montgomerie (Riviera, 1995)
Best 18-Hole Round:	63 -	6 times (first by Bruce Crampton, Firestone, 1975)

SHORT PUTTS

The USPGA Championship is run by the Professional Golfers' Association of America, which was formed in 1916. Rodman Wanamaker, a department store magnate from Philadelphia, held a lunch at the Taplow Club in New York City on January 17th of that year, when he told a group of golf professionals that they should form their own organisation.

Three months later, having agreed on a constitution, the PGA of America was born. And in October 1916, Wanamaker donated a prize fund of $2,580 (and trophy) to be contested at the first USPGA Championship, which was won by Jim Barnes. The PGA, which started with just 35 charter members, all from the New York area, continues to look after the interests of America's club professionals. Today, its membership exceeds 23,000 nationwide. The PGA has its headquarters at Palm Beach Gardens, Florida.

Barber cuts down January

Possibly the most amazing finale to a USPGA Championship came in 1961 at Olympia Fields. On the last three greens of regulation play, 45-year-old Jerry Barber holed putts of 20 (birdie), 40 (par) and 60 (birdie) feet respectively to tie Don January, who had held a four-stroke lead with just three holes to play. Barber had nine single-putt greens in his final round 70. He then won the following day's play-off 67-68.

Tway's fight back

Bob Tway achieved one of the greatest fightbacks of recent times when he made-up a nine-stroke deficit on leader Greg Norman over the final two rounds at Inverness in 1986. Tway covered the last 36 holes in eight-under-par (64-70), to Norman's three-over (69-76), to win the tournament by two strokes.

Matchplay specialist

1953 champion Walter Burkemo had a surprisingly good record at matchplay, considering he only ever won one official strokeplay event on the US Tour (1957 Mayfair Inn Open). Apart from his victory, he was twice a runner-up (1951 & 1954) and a semi-finalist in 1957. In all he won 27 of his 33 matches (81.82%)

Stewart's late burst denies Reid

Payne Stewart birdied four of the final five holes to win in 1989 at Kemper Lakes. But even his great finish shouldn't have been enough to wrest the title from Mike Reid's grasp. Reid, who'd led from day one, bogied 16, double-bogied 17 and missed an eight-foot birdie attempt at 18, to end up in a tie for second place one stroke behind Stewart.

Successful brothers

Brothers Jay and Lionel Hebert won the title within three years of each other. First, in 1957, Lionel won the last matchplay version of the

Championship beating Dow Finsterwald in the final. Jay had lost at the quarter-final stage to Walter Burkemo, who was beaten in his next match by Lionel. Then in 1960, Jay took the title by one stroke, with Lionel finishing in a tie for 18th.

Daly's long drive to destiny

John Daly's victory at Crooked Stick in 1991 provided one of the greatest PGA stories of modern times. Daly, the ninth alternate for the Championship, was told he'd been moved up to first alternate at 5pm the day before the tournament was due to start. The 25-year-old American got into his car in Memphis and drove seven and a half hours to his hotel in Indianapolis where he discovered that Nick Price had withdrawn from the event. Price's wife was about to give birth. Daly was now playing in the tournament. Using Price's caddie, Squeaky Medlen, he won the Championship without having the opportunity to play a practice round.

Oldest champion

48-year-old Julius Boros, winner in 1968 at Pecan Valley Country Club, is the oldest winner of any of golf's four major championships.

The pain of it all

Twelve years before he won the 1964 USPGA Championship, Bobby Nichols, then 16, almost died in an horrific accident. Nichols was in a car full of teenagers when it crashed at 100 miles per hour. Nichols suffered a broken pelvis, twisted back, collapsed lung and an injured kidney. He was also unconscious for 13 days.

Preparing for battle

The day after winning the 1942 Championship, Sam Snead reported for duty with the United States Navy. He'd been called-up to serve his country in the Second World War.

The supreme scrambler

When Dave Stockton won his second USPGA title in 1976, he only hit three greens in regulation during the final nine holes. And on the 72nd green he holed a 10-footer for par to win by one stroke.

Time for a drink

One of the most bizarre moments in Championship history occurred in 1940, when Walter Hagen failed to arrive on the first tee, at his appointed time, for a second round match with Vic Ghezzi. Ghezzi went into the clubhouse where he found 47-year-old Hagen drinking scotch at the bar. Hagen, the king of gamesmanship, told Ghezzi: "I'll join you on the third." But an official informed Hagen he was not allowed to concede the opening two holes. So he downed his scotch and went to the first tee. An angry Ghezzi somehow managed to win the first two holes but lost the match 2&1. Hagen lost his third round contest to Harold McSpaden (1 up) and never again played in the Championship.

CLASSIC MOMENTS
SIX OF THE BEST

1) 1923, Gene Sarazen, par-4, 2nd extra-hole, Pelham: At the 38th hole of the 1923 final (matchplay) between Gene Sarazen and Walter Hagen, Sarazen left his tee shot perilously close to the out of bounds fence. Yet from heavy rough, he sailed his ball on to the green and to within two feet of the flag. This stroke unnerved Hagen who fluffed his approach shot into a greenside bunker. Sarazen duly holed his birdie putt to win the match and the title.

2) 1961, Jerry Barber, par-4, 18th at Olympia Fields: In near-darkness, Jerry Barber walked on to the 72nd green knowing he must hole his 60-foot birdie putt to force a play-off with leader Don January. In what was one of the most astonishing finishes in major championship history, Barber rolled in his putt for a three. The following day he beat January in the 18-hole play-off.

3) 1972, Gary Player, par-4, 16th at Oakland Hills: After pushing his tee shot down the right of the fairway, Player discovered that his line to the flag was blocked by a large tree. Having bogied the previous two holes, the South African was desperate to make par. Taking a 9-iron, he lofted his ball over the tree, to land it four feet from the hole. He then knocked in his birdie attempt and went on to win the title by two strokes.

Costly slip

Playing almost an hour in front of the third round leaders, Scott Hoch came to the final hole of the 1987 tournament convinced he needed a birdie-four to stand any chance of winning the title. And after three super shots at this par-five hole, he was left with an eight-footer for a four. But Hoch knocked his birdie attempt three feet past and missed the return. He took six. That three-putt green proved costly when at the end of the day, he had missed out on a play-off by one stroke.

4) 1978, John Mahaffey, par-4, 2nd extra-hole at Oakmont: It was an emotional moment for John Mahaffey when he knocked in his 12-foot putt for birdie at the second play-off hole to beat Tom Watson and Jerry Pate. Twice before Mahaffey had suffered the agony of losing a major championship over the closing few holes. This time he'd started the final round seven strokes off the pace, but had caught third round leader Tom Watson with a five-under-par 66. On the final hole of regulation play, Pate had a glorious opportunity to win the title but missed a par putt from four feet.

5) 1986, Bob Tway, par-4, 18th at the Inverness Club: Joint leaders and playing partners, Bob Tway and Greg Norman, had both played poor second shots to the 72nd green. Tway was in a greenside bunker, Norman on the fringe, some 25 feet from the flag. Tway's delicate stroke from sand landed on the edge of the putting surface and rolled all the way into the hole for a birdie three. And when Norman subsequently failed to sink his chip shot Tway captured his first major.

6) 1988, Jeff Sluman, par-5, 5th at Oak Tree: The diminutive Sluman had started the final round three strokes behind pacesetter Paul Azinger. But at the monster 590-yard, fifth, he holed out from 115 yards for an eagle three, it was the stroke that turned the Championship. Sluman went on to fire a six-under-par 65, for a three shot victory.

US MASTERS

1934- Horton Smith

Horton Smith	70-72-70-72	284
Craig Wood	71-74-69-71	285
Billy Burke	72-71-70-73	286
Paul Runyan	74-71-70-71	286
Ed Dudley	74-69-71-74	288

1935- Gene Sarazen

Gene Sarazen	68-71-73-70	282
Craig Wood	69-72-68-73	282
Play-Off: Sarazen 144 (71-73); Wood 149 (75-74)		
Olin Dutra	70-70-70-74	284
Henry Picard	67-68-76-75	286
Denny Shute	73-71-70-73	287

1936- Horton Smith

Horton Smith	74-71-68-72	285
Harry Cooper	70-69-71-76	286
Gene Sarazen	78-67-72-70	287
Bobby Cruickshank	75-69-74-72	290
Paul Runyan	76-69-70-75	290

1937- Byron Nelson

Byron Nelson	66-72-75-70	283
Ralph Guldahl	69-72-68-76	285
Ed Dudley	70-71-71-74	286
Harry Cooper	73-69-71-74	287
Ky Laffoon	73-70-74-73	290

1938- Henry Picard

Henry Picard	71-72-72-70	285
Ralph Guldahl	73-70-73-71	287
Harry Cooper	68-77-71-71	287
Paul Runyan	71-73-74-70	288
Byron Nelson	73-74-70-73	290

1939- Ralph Guldahl

Ralph Guldahl	72-68-70-69	279
Sam Snead	70-70-72-68	280
Billy Burke	69-72-71-70	282
Lawson Little	72-72-68-70	282
Gene Sarazen	73-66-72-72	283

1940- Jimmy Demaret

Jimmy Demaret	67-72-70-71	280
Lloyd Mangrum	64-75-71-74	284
Byron Nelson	69-72-74-70	285
Ed Dudley	73-72-71-71	287
Harry Cooper	69-75-73-70	287
Willie Goggin	71-72-73-71	287

Three times Masters champion Jimmy Demaret, pictured here in front of an admiring British gallery at Birkdale

1941- Craig Wood

Craig Wood	66-71-71-72	280
Byron Nelson	71-69-73-70	283
Sam Byrd	73-70-68-74	285
Ben Hogan	71-72-75-68	286
Ed Dudley	73-72-75-68	288

1942- Byron Nelson

Byron Nelson	68-67-72-73	280
Ben Hogan	73-70-67-70	280
Play-Off: Nelson 69, Hogan 70		
Paul Runyan	67-73-72-71	283
Sam Byrd	68-68-75-74	285
Horton Smith	67-73-74-73	287

1943-45 NO TOURNAMENT

1946- Herman Keiser

Herman Keiser	69-68-71-74	282
Ben Hogan	74-70-69-70	283
Bob Hamilton	75-69-71-72	287
Ky Laffoon	74-73-70-72	289
Jimmy Demaret	75-70-71-73	289
Jim Ferrier	74-72-68-75	289

1947- Jimmy Demaret

Jimmy Demaret	69-71-70-71	281
Byron Nelson	69-72-72-70	283
Frank Stranahan	73-72-70-68	283

Ben Hogan	75-68-71-70	284
Harold McSpaden	74-69-70-71	284

1948- Claude Harmon

Claude Harmon	70-70-69-70	279
Cary Middlecoff	74-71-69-70	284
Chick Harbert	71-70-70-76	287
Jim Ferrier	71-71-75-71	288
Lloyd Mangrum	69-73-75-71	288

1949- Sam Snead

Sam Snead	73-75-67-67	282
Johnny Bulla	74-73-69-69	285
Lloyd Mangrum	69-74-72-70	285
Johnny Palmer	73-71-70-72	286
Jim Turnesa	73-72-71-70	286

1950- Jimmy Demaret

Jimmy Demaret	70-72-72-69	283
Jim Ferrier	70-67-73-75	285
Sam Snead	71-74-70-72	287
Ben Hogan	73-68-71-76	288
Byron Nelson	75-70-69-74	288

1951- Ben Hogan

Ben Hogan	70-72-70-68	280
Skee Riegel	73-68-70-71	282
Lloyd Mangrum	69-74-70-73	286
Lew Worsham	71-71-72-72	286
Dave Douglas	74-69-72-73	288

1952- Sam Snead

Sam Snead	70-67-77-72	286
Jack Burke Jr	76-67-78-69	290
Al Besselink	70-76-71-74	291
Tommy Bolt	71-71-75-74	291
Jim Ferrier	72-70-77-72	291

1953- Ben Hogan

Ben Hogan	70-69-66-69	274
Ed Oliver	69-73-67-70	279
Lloyd Mangrum	74-68-71-69	282
Bob Hamilton	71-69-70-73	283
Tommy Bolt	71-75-68-71	285
Chick Harbert	68-73-70-74	285

1954- Sam Snead

Sam Snead	74-73-70-72	289
Ben Hogan	72-73-69-75	289
Play-Off: Snead 70, Hogan 71		
Billy Joe Patton	70-74-75-71	290
EJ Harrison	70-79-74-68	291
Lloyd Mangrum	71-75-76-69	291

1955- Cary Middlecoff

Cary Middlecoff	72-65-72-70	279
Ben Hogan	73-68-72-73	286
Sam Snead	72-71-74-70	287
Bob Rosburg	72-72-72-73	289
Mike Souchak	71-74-72-72	289
Julius Boros	71-75-72-71	289

1956- Jack Burke Jr

Jack Burke Jr	72-71-75-71	289
Ken Venturi	66-69-75-80	290
Cary Middlecoff	67-72-75-77	291
Lloyd Mangrum	72-74-72-74	292
Sam Snead	73-76-72-71	292

1957- Doug Ford

Doug Ford	72-73-72-66	283
Sam Snead	72-68-74-72	286
Jimmy Demaret	72-70-75-70	287
E Harvie Ward Jr	73-71-71-73	288
Peter Thomson	72-73-73-71	289

1958- Arnold Palmer

Arnold Palmer	70-73-68-73	284
Doug Ford	74-71-70-70	285
Fred Hawkins	71-75-68-71	285
Stan Leonard	72-70-73-71	286
Ken Venturi	68-72-74-72	286

1959- Art Wall

Art Wall	73-74-71-66	284
Cary Middlecoff	74-71-68-72	285
Arnold Palmer	71-70-71-74	286
Dick Mayer	73-75-71-68	287
Stan Leonard	69-74-69-75	287

1960- Arnold Palmer

Arnold Palmer	67-73-72-70	282
Ken Venturi	73-69-71-70	283
Dow Finsterwald	71-70-72-71	284
Billy Casper	71-71-71-74	287
Julius Boros	72-71-70-75	288

1961- Gary Player

Gary Player	69-68-69-74	280
Charles Coe	72-71-69-69	281
Arnold Palmer	68-69-73-71	281
Tommy Bolt	72-71-74-68	285
Don January	74-68-72-71	285

1962- Arnold Palmer

Arnold Palmer	70-66-69-75	280
Gary Player	67-71-71-71	280
Dow Finsterwald	74-68-65-73	280
Play-Off: Palmer 68, Player 71, Finsterwald 77		
Gene Littler	71-68-71-72	282
Mike Souchak	70-72-74-71	287
Jimmy Demaret	73-73-71-70	287
Jerry Barber	72-72-69-74	287
Billy Maxwell	71-73-72-71	287

1963- Jack Nicklaus

Jack Nicklaus	74-66-74-72	286
Tony Lema	74-69-74-70	287
Julius Boros	76-69-71-72	288
Sam Snead	70-73-74-71	288
Dow Finsterwald	74-73-73-69	289
Ed Furgol	70-71-74-74	289
Gary Player	71-74-74-70	289

1964- Arnold Palmer

Arnold Palmer	69-68-69-70	276
Dave Marr	70-73-69-70	282
Jack Nicklaus	71-73-71-67	282
Bruce Devlin	72-72-67-73	284
Billy Casper	76-72-69-69	286
Jim Ferrier	71-73-69-73	286
Paul Harney	73-72-71-70	286
Gary Player	69-72-72-73	286

1965- Jack Nicklaus

Jack Nicklaus	67-71-64-69	271
Arnold Palmer	70-68-72-70	280
Gary Player	65-73-69-73	280
Mason Rudolph	70-75-66-72	283
Dan Sikes	67-72-71-75	285

1966- Jack Nicklaus

Jack Nicklaus	68-76-72-72	288
Tommy Jacobs	75-71-70-72	288
Gay Brewer	74-72-72-70	288
Play-Off: Nicklaus 70, Jacobs 72, Brewer 78		
Arnold Palmer	74-70-74-72	290
Doug Sanders	74-70-75-71	290

1967- Gay Brewer

Gay Brewer	73-68-72-67	280
Bobby Nichols	72-69-70-70	281
Bert Yancey	67-73-71-73	284
Arnold Palmer	73-73-70-69	285
Julius Boros	71-70-70-75	286

1968- Bob Goalby

Bob Goalby	70-70-71-66	277
Roberto de Vicenzo	69-73-70-66	278
Bert Yancey	71-71-72-65	279
Bruce Devlin	69-73-69-69	280
Frank Beard	75-65-71-70	281
Jack Nicklaus	69-71-74-67	281

1969- George Archer

George Archer	67-73-69-72	281
Billy Casper	66-71-71-74	282
George Knudson	70-73-69-70	282
Tom Weiskopf	71-71-69-71	282
Charles Coody	74-68-69-72	283
Don January	74-73-70-66	283

1970- Billy Casper

Billy Casper	72-68-68-71	279
Gene Littler	69-70-70-70	279
Play-Off: Casper 69, Littler 74		
Gary Player	74-68-68-70	280
Bert Yancey	69-70-72-70	281
Tommy Aaron	68-74-69-72	283
Dave Hill	73-70-70-70	283
Dave Stockton	72-72-69-70	283
Jack Nicklaus	71-75-69-69	284
Frank Beard	71-76-68-70	285
Bob Lunn	70-70-75-72	287
Chi Chi Rodriguez	70-76-73-68	287

1971- Charles Coody

Charles Coody	66-73-70-70	279
Johnny Miller	72-73-68-68	281
Jack Nicklaus	70-71-68-72	281
Don January	69-69-73-72	283
Gene Littler	72-69-73-69	283
Gary Player	72-72-71-69	284
Ken Still	72-71-72-69	284
Tom Weiskopf	71-69-72-72	284

Frank Beard	74-73-69-70	286
Roberto de Vicenzo	76-69-72-69	286
Dave Stockton	72-73-69-72	286

1972- Jack Nicklaus

Jack Nicklaus	68-71-73-74	286
Bruce Crampton	72-75-69-73	289
Bobby Mitchell	73-72-71-73	289
Tom Weiskopf	74-71-70-74	289
Homero Blancas	76-71-69-74	290
Bruce Devlin	74-75-70-71	290
Jerry Heard	73-71-72-74	290
Jim Jamieson	72-70-71-77	290
Jerry McGee	73-74-71-72	290
Gary Player	73-75-72-71	291
Dave Stockton	76-70-74-71	291

1973- Tommy Aaron

Tommy Aaron	68-73-74-68	283
JC Snead	70-71-73-70	284
Jim Jamieson	73-71-70-71	285
Jack Nicklaus	69-77-73-66	285
Peter Oosterhuis	73-70-68-74	285
Bob Goalby	73-70-71-74	288
Johnny Miller	75-69-71-73	288
Bruce Devlin	73-72-72-72	289
Jumbo Ozaki	69-74-73-73	289
Gay Brewer	75-66-74-76	291
Gardner Dickinson	74-70-72-75	291
Don January	75-71-75-70	291
Chi Chi Rodriguez	72-70-73-76	291

1974- Gary Player

Gary Player	71-71-66-70	278
Dave Stockton	71-66-70-73	280
Tom Weiskopf	71-69-70-70	280
Jim Colbert	67-72-69-73	281
Hale Irwin	68-70-72-71	281
Jack Nicklaus	69-71-72-69	281
Bobby Nichols	73-68-68-73	282
Phil Rodgers	72-69-68-73	282
Maurice Bembridge	73-74-72-64	283
Hubert Green	68-70-74-71	283

1975- Jack Nicklaus

Jack Nicklaus	68-67-73-68	276
Johnny Miller	75-71-65-66	277
Tom Weiskopf	69-72-66-70	277
Hale Irwin	73-74-71-64	282
Bobby Nichols	67-74-72-69	282
Billy Casper	70-70-73-70	283
Dave Hill	75-71-70-68	284
Hubert Green	74-71-70-70	285
Tom Watson	70-70-72-73	285

The 1975 champion Jack Nicklaus is helped into his Green Jacket by defending champion Gary Player

Tom Kite	72-74-71-69	286	Ben Crenshaw	71-69-69-76	285
JC Snead	69-72-75-70	286	Ray Floyd	71-72-71-71	285
Lee Trevino	71-70-74-71	286	Hubert Green	67-74-72-72	285
			Don January	69-76-69-71	285
1976- Ray Floyd			Gene Littler	71-72-73-69	285
Ray Floyd	65-66-70-70	271	John Schlee	75-73-69-68	285
Ben Crenshaw	70-70-72-67	279			
Jack Nicklaus	67-69-73-73	282	**1978- Gary Player**		
Larry Ziegler	67-71-72-72	282	Gary Player	72-72-69-64	277
Charles Coody	72-69-70-74	285	Rod Funseth	73-66-70-69	278
Hale Irwin	71-77-67-70	285	Hubert Green	72-69-65-72	278
Tom Kite	73-67-72-73	285	Tom Watson	73-68-68-69	278
Billy Casper	71-76-71-69	287	Wally Armstrong	72-70-70-68	280
Roger Maltbie	72-75-70-71	288	Billy Kratzert	70-74-67-69	280
Graham Marsh	73-68-75-72	288	Jack Nicklaus	72-73-69-67	281
Tom Weiskopf	73-71-70-74	288	Hale Irwin	73-67-71-71	282
			David Graham	75-69-67-72	283
1977- Tom Watson			Joe Inman	69-73-72-69	283
Tom Watson	70-69-70-67	276			
Jack Nicklaus	72-70-70-66	278	**1979- Fuzzy Zoeller**		
Tom Kite	70-73-70-67	280	Fuzzy Zoeller	70-71-69-70	280
Rik Massengale	70-73-67-70	280	Ed Sneed	68-67-69-76	280
Hale Irwin	70-74-70-68	282	Tom Watson	68-71-70-71	280
David Graham	75-67-73-69	284	*Play-Off*: Zoeller 4-3, Sneed 4-4, Watson 4-4		
Lou Graham	75-71-69-69	284	Jack Nicklaus	69-71-72-69	281

Tom Kite	71-72-68-72	283
Bruce Lietzke	67-75-68-74	284
Craig Stadler	69-66-74-76	285
Leonard Thompson	68-70-73-74	285
Lanny Wadkins	73-69-70-73	285
Hubert Green	74-69-72-71	286
Gene Littler	74-71-69-72	286

1980- Seve Ballesteros

Seve Ballesteros	66-69-68-72	275
Gibby Gilbert	70-74-68-67	279
Jack Newton	68-74-69-68	279
Hubert Green	68-74-71-67	280
David Graham	66-73-72-70	281
Ben Crenshaw	76-70-68-69	283
Ed Fiori	71-70-69-73	283
Tom Kite	69-71-74-69	283
Larry Nelson	69-72-73-69	283
Jerry Pate	72-68-76-67	283
Gary Player	71-71-71-70	283

1981- Tom Watson

Tom Watson	71-68-70-71	280
Johnny Miller	69-72-73-68	282
Jack Nicklaus	70-65-75-72	282
Greg Norman	69-70-72-72	283
Tom Kite	74-72-70-68	284
Jerry Pate	71-72-71-70	284
David Graham	70-70-74-71	285
Ben Crenshaw	71-72-70-73	286
Ray Floyd	75-71-71-69	286
John Mahaffey	72-71-69-74	286

1982- Craig Stadler

Craig Stadler	75-69-67-73	284
Dan Pohl	75-75-67-67	284

Play-Off: Stadler 4, Pohl 5

Seve Ballesteros	73-73-68-71	285
Jerry Pate	74-73-67-71	285
Tom Kite	76-69-73-69	287
Tom Watson	77-69-70-71	287
Ray Floyd	74-72-69-74	289
Larry Nelson	79-71-70-69	289
Curtis Strange	74-70-73-72	289
Andy Bean	75-72-73-70	290
Mark Hayes	74-73-73-70	290
Tom Weiskopf	75-72-68-75	290
Fuzzy Zoeller	72-76-70-72	290

1983- Seve Ballesteros

Seve Ballesteros	68-70-73-69	280
Ben Crenshaw	76-70-70-68	284
Tom Kite	70-72-73-69	284
Ray Floyd	67-72-71-75	285

Tom Watson	70-71-71-73	285
Hale Irwin	72-73-72-69	286
Craig Stadler	69-72-69-76	286
Gil Morgan	67-70-76-74	287
Dan Pohl	74-72-70-71	287
Lanny Wadkins	73-70-73-71	287

1984- Ben Crenshaw

Ben Crenshaw	67-72-70-68	277
Tom Watson	74-67-69-69	279
David Edwards	71-70-72-67	280
Gil Morgan	73-71-69-67	280
Larry Nelson	76-69-66-70	281
Ronnie Black	71-74-69-68	282
David Graham	69-70-70-73	282
Tom Kite	70-68-69-75	282
Mark Lye	69-66-73-74	282
Fred Couples	71-73-67-72	283

1985- Bernhard Langer

Bernhard Langer	72-74-68-68	282
Seve Ballesteros	72-71-71-70	284
Ray Floyd	70-73-69-72	284

Ben Crenshaw celebrates victory at Augusta in 1984

Curtis Strange	80-65-68-71	284
Jay Haas	73-73-72-67	285
Gary Hallberg	68-73-75-70	286
Bruce Lietzke	72-71-73-70	286
Jack Nicklaus	71-74-72-69	286
Craig Stadler	73-67-76-70	286
Fred Couples	75-73-69-70	287
David Graham	74-71-71-71	287
Lee Trevino	70-73-72-72	287
Tom Watson	69-71-75-72	287

1986- Jack Nicklaus

Jack Nicklaus	74-71-69-65	279
Tom Kite	70-74-68-68	280
Greg Norman	70-72-68-70	280
Seve Ballesteros	71-68-72-70	281
Nick Price	79-69-63-71	282
Jay Haas	76-69-71-67	283
Tom Watson	70-74-68-71	283
Tommy Nakajima	70-71-71-72	284
Payne Stewart	75-71-69-69	284
Bob Tway	70-73-71-70	284

1987- Larry Mize

Larry Mize	70-72-72-71	285
Seve Ballesteros	73-71-70-71	285
Greg Norman	73-74-66-72	285

Play-Off: Mize 4-3, Norman 4-4, Ballesteros 5

Ben Crenshaw	75-70-67-74	286
Roger Maltbie	76-66-70-74	286
Jodie Mudd	74-72-71-69	286
Jay Haas	72-72-72-73	289
Bernhard Langer	71-72-70-76	289
Jack Nicklaus	74-72-73-70	289
Tom Watson	71-72-74-72	289
DA Weibring	72-75-71-71	289

1988- Sandy Lyle

Sandy Lyle	71-67-72-71	281
Mark Calcavecchia	71-69-72-70	282
Craig Stadler	76-69-70-68	283
Ben Crenshaw	72-73-67-72	284
Fred Couples	75-68-71-71	285
Greg Norman	77-73-71-64	285
Don Pooley	71-72-72-70	285
David Frost	73-74-71-68	286
Bernhard Langer	71-72-71-73	287
Tom Watson	72-71-73-71	287

1989- Nick Faldo

Nick Faldo	68-73-77-65	283
Scott Hoch	69-74-71-69	283

Play-Off: Faldo 5-3, Hoch 5-4

Ben Crenshaw	71-72-70-71	284

Greg Norman	74-75-68-67	284
Seve Ballesteros	71-72-73-69	285
Mike Reid	72-71-71-72	286
Jodie Mudd	73-76-72-66	287
Chip Beck	74-76-70-68	288
Jose-Maria Olazabal	77-73-70-68	288
Jeff Sluman	74-72-74-68	288

1990- Nick Faldo

Nick Faldo	71-72-66-69	278
Ray Floyd	70-68-68-72	278

Play-Off: Faldo 4-4, Floyd 4-5

John Huston	66-74-68-75	283
Lanny Wadkins	72-73-70-68	283
Fred Couples	74-69-72-69	284
Jack Nicklaus	72-70-69-74	285
Seve Ballesteros	74-73-68-71	286
Bill Britton	68-74-71-73	286
Bernhard Langer	70-73-69-74	286
Scott Simpson	74-71-68-73	286
Curtis Strange	70-73-71-72	286
Tom Watson	77-71-67-71	286

1991- Ian Woosnam

Ian Woosnam	72-66-67-72	277
Jose-Maria Olazabal	68-71-69-70	278
Ben Crenshaw	70-73-68-68	279
Steve Pate	72-73-69-65	279
Lanny Wadkins	67-71-70-71	279
Tom Watson	68-68-70-73	279
Ian Baker-Finch	71-70-69-70	280
Andrew Magee	70-72-68-70	280
Jodie Mudd	70-70-71-69	280
Hale Irwin	70-70-75-66	281
Tommy Nakajima	74-71-67-69	281

1992- Fred Couples

Fred Couples	69-67-69-70	275
Ray Floyd	69-68-69-71	277
Corey Pavin	72-71-68-67	278
Mark O'Meara	74-67-69-70	280
Jeff Sluman	65-74-70-71	280
Ian Baker-Finch	70-69-68-74	281
Nolan Henke	70-71-70-70	281
Larry Mize	73-69-71-68	281
Greg Norman	70-70-73-68	281
Steve Pate	73-71-70-67	281
Nick Price	70-71-67-73	281
Ted Schulz	68-69-72-72	281

1993- Bernhard Langer

Bernhard Langer	68-70-69-70	277
Chip Beck	72-67-72-70	281
John Daly	70-71-73-69	283

Steve Elkington	71-70-71-71	283	Corey Pavin	71-72-73-70	286
Tom Lehman	67-75-73-68	283	Ian Baker-Finch	71-71-71-74	287
Lanny Wadkins	69-72-71-71	283	Ray Floyd	70-74-71-72	287
Dan Forsman	69-69-73-73	284	John Huston	72-72-74-69	287
Jose-Maria Olazabal	70-72-74-68	284			
Brad Faxon	71-70-72-72	285			
Payne Stewart	74-70-72-69	285			

1995- Ben Crenshaw

Ben Crenshaw	70-67-69-68	274
Davis Love III	69-69-71-66	275

1994- Jose-Maria Olazabal

Jose-Maria Olazabal	74-67-69-69	279	Jay Haas	71-64-72-70	277
Tom Lehman	70-70-69-72	281	Greg Norman	73-68-68-68	277
Larry Mize	68-71-72-71	282	Steve Elkington	73-67-67-72	279
Tom Kite	69-72-71-71	283	David Frost	66-71-71-71	279
Jay Haas	72-72-72-69	285	Scott Hoch	69-67-71-73	280
Jim McGovern	72-70-71-72	285	Phil Mickelson	66-71-70-73	280
Loren Roberts	75-68-72-70	285	Curtis Strange	72-71-65-73	281
Ernie Els	74-67-74-71	286	Fred Couples	71-69-67-75	282
			Brian Henninger	70-68-68-76	282

UNITED STATES MASTERS SUMMARY

Most Victories:	6 -	Jack Nicklaus (1963-65-66-72-75-86)
	4 -	Arnold Palmer (1958-60-62-64)
Widest Winning Margins:	9 -	Jack Nicklaus (1965)
	8 -	Ray Floyd (1976)
	7 -	Cary Middlecoff (1955)
Lowest 72-Hole Totals:	271 -	Jack Nicklaus (1965)
		Ray Floyd (1976)
Best 18-Hole Round:	63 -	Nick Price (1986)
Oldest Champions:		Jack Nicklaus (46 yrs, 2 mths, 23 dys, 1986)
		Ben Crenshaw (43 yrs, 2 mths, 29 dys, 1995)
		Gary Player (42 yrs, 5 mths, 8 dys, 1978)
Youngest Champions:		Seve Ballesteros (23 yrs, 0 mths, 4 dys, 1980)
		Jack Nicklaus (23 yrs, 2 mths, 17 dys 1963)

SHORT PUTTS

Unlike golf's three other major championships, which are run by national organisations, the US Masters belongs to the members of one club - Augusta National in Georgia. The club was the brainchild of two men. Bobby Jones, who retired from competition in 1930 after winning the 'old grand slam' (US Open, US Amateur, British Open and British Amateur) and Clifford Roberts, a Wall Street banker and an acquaintance of Jones.

The pair hired Dr Alister MacKenzie, a famous Scottish golf course architect, to design the layout, a task he started in the Spring of 1931. A year later the club opened. But unlike most clubs, where the majority of members live and work in close proximity to the course, the purpose of building Augusta National, as the name implies, was to invite members from all over the country. A kind of golfing retreat for the wealthy. The only local members were those brought in to help with the normal day-to-day administrative activities associated with most clubs. Thus, the exclusive nature of Augusta National was born and by-and-large this atmosphere still exists today.

In the beginning
The inaugural event in 1934 was called the "First

Annual Invitation Tournament." And for that year only, what is now known as the front and back nines, were played in reverse. Bobby Jones came out of retirement to play in his own event - he finished a creditable 13th - and in all 72 golfers competed.

Reduced by war
1942 provided the smallest field in the event's history, just 42. Originally, 88 players had been invited but less than half were able to attend.

Scott Hoch in 1989, the year he lost out in a play-off against Nick Faldo

Hogan's blues
Herman Keiser was the surprise champion in 1946 thanks to Ben Hogan's misfortune on the final green which he three-putted from 12 feet to lose by one stroke.

Green Jacket
In 1949, Sam Snead became the first champion to be presented with the now-famous Green Jacket. And as a result of this new ceremony, all former winners were soon to be measured-up for their own green jackets and the Masters Champions Club came into being. The Champions gather for a celebratory dinner once a year during tournament week, when they all wear their jackets.

Amateur hour
In 1954, Billy Joe Patton, an amateur from North Carolina, missed out on a play-off with Sam Snead and Ben Hogan by one stroke. He had started the final round five shots off the pace but an outward half of 32 (4 under par) had helped him into a share of the lead. His golden run included a hole-in-one at the 190-yard par-3 6th. By the start of the homeward journey, most of the spectators were rooting for Patton but the fairytale was not going to happen. His undoing came at 13 where he took a double-bogey seven after putting his ball into Rae's Creek. He also bogied the par-5 15th after finding water again. He needed 39 strokes to complete the back nine, one swipe too many.

Two years later there was another amateur in the frame. And as chances go, Ken Venturi couldn't have been better placed. He was the clear overnight leader going into round four and despite reaching the turn in 38 (2 over par), 24-year-old Venturi still led by four. But once again, Augusta's back nine was to change all that. He made bogies at 10, 11, 12, 14, 15 and 17 to return in 42 strokes and a round of 80. When the dust had settled, Venturi had lost by one shot to Jack Burke jr who had started the final day eight behind. Four years later, as a professional, Venturi finished second once again after Arnold Palmer closed with two birdies to pip him by a single shot. Venturi never did wear the Green Jacket although he did win the US Open in 1964.

Wall's spectacular burst

One of the most astounding bursts of form came from 1959 champion Art Wall who birdied five of the last six holes to win by one. He holed from 15 feet at the 13th, from 20 feet at 14, two-putted for a birdie at 15, sank another 15 footer on the 17th and rolled one in from 12 feet at the last. Wall was round in 66 after starting the final day six shots off the pace.

Bogey-mania

Charles Coody bogied the final three holes in 1969 to finish two strokes behind winner George Archer. Ten years later Ed Sneed suffered a similar fate closing with three successive bogies before losing in a play-off to Fuzzy Zoeller.

Sad Sunday

One of the saddest days in Masters history came in 1968, with the now-famous wrong-score incident involving Roberto de Vicenzo. The Argentinian left the final green convinced that his final round '65' had earned him a play-off spot against Bob Goalby. But what Vicenzo didn't realise, was that he'd signed his card for a round of 66. Despite making a birdie three on the 17th hole, Vicenzo's playing partner Tommy Aaron had incorrectly written down a four, which when totalled up equalled 66. And having not checked his card closely enough when signing it Vicenzo had to accept a 66, under the rules of golf. Goalby was named champion, with Vicenzo finishing in second place one shot behind.

Oosty's brave challenge

Between 1980 and 1994, European golfers dominated the Masters winning the Green Jacket on no fewer than nine occasions. But back in 1973, England's Peter Oosterhuis came mighty close to becoming the first European winner at Augusta. With just 18 holes to play the tall Londoner led by three shots but his bogey six at the par-5 15th, ended his challenge on the final day. He eventually finished third, two strokes behind winner Tommy Aaron.

Floyd's feast on the fives

It has often been said that to win at Augusta, you must play well on the four par-5 holes (2nd, 8th, 13th & 15th). One man who achieved this with interest was 1976 champion Ray Floyd who covered the 16 holes in 14-under-par - that's one eagle and 12 birdies. His sequence reads as follows:

	2nd	8th	13th	15th
Rd 1	-1	-1	-1	-1
Rd 2	-1	-1	-1	-2
Rd 3	-1	-1	-1	-1
Rd 4	Ev	Ev	Ev	-1

Tom's troubles

Four times Tom Weiskopf finished runner-up at Augusta. Twice it was Jack Nicklaus who denied him (1972 and 1975), with Gary Player edging him out in 1974. Yet according to Weiskopf himself, his greatest opportunity to wear the Green Jacket came in 1969. On that occasion Weiskopf three-putted 13 times in 72 holes to finish one shot behind winner George Archer who had only one three-stab green.

Fuzzy joins select group

Only three champions have triumphed on their first visit to Augusta. The inaugural champion of 1934 Horton Smith was one, with Gene Sarazen the tournament's second winner in 1935 being another. Since then only Fuzzy Zoeller has enjoyed that distinction in 1979.

Seve survives stumble

With just nine holes left to play in 1980, Seve Ballesteros held an enormous 10 stroke lead. But just when it seemed that Seve would win by miles, the Spaniard faltered. He three-putted the 10th, made par at 11 and then found water at the short 12th where his tee shot just about cleared the stream only to roll back down into the drink. He eventually took a double-bogey five. His second shot to the par-5 13th also rolled into the stream in front of the green. After taking yet another drop under penalty, he two-putted for a bogey six. In the space of four holes he'd dropped four strokes. He also drove poorly at the 14th but a superb recovery managed to earn him a par. Coupled with Gibby Gilbert's late charge, Seve's lead was now suddenly down to two. However, the Spaniard birdied the par five 15th and closed with three straight pars. He was home in 39 and had won by four shots - Gilbert bogied 18. Not only was Seve the first European winner, he was also, at 23, the youngest-ever champion.

Strange possibilities

With just nine holes to play in 1985 Curtis Strange held a comfortable four-stroke lead. It looked as though the American was about to make history as 'the champion with the worst first round score'. Strange had opened his account that week with an 8-over-par 80, which left him 12 strokes behind first round leader Gary Hallberg. However, rounds of 65 and 68 quickly moved him up the leaderboard and with 18 holes to play he trailed pacesetter Ray Floyd by a single stroke. Strange needed only 31 strokes to cover the front nine on the final afternoon. But just when he seemed unstoppable, the Virginian finished the tournament as he had started it - by playing bogey golf. The killer holes were 13 and 15, both par 5s. In his search for tournament-clinching birdies, Strange bit off more than he could chew. His 4-wood approach to 13 landed in Rae's Creek and his four-iron attempt to reach the 15th green in two also found water. Both holes resulted in bogey 6s and another bogey at 18 left him two shots behind champion Bernhard Langer. Strange had played the back nine in 40 strokes. For the record, Craig Stadler remains the champion with the highest first round score - a 75 in 1982.

CLASSIC MOMENTS
SIX OF THE BEST

1) 1935, Gene Sarazen, par-5 15th: Probably the most famous single stroke of all time. Trailing by three strokes with four holes to play, Sarazen holed out from 220 yards with a 4-wood for an albatross two. Sarazen won the title in a play-off the following day.

2) 1957, Doug Ford, par-4 18th: Leading by one shot with just one hole to play, Ford looked to be in trouble when he hooked his approach shot into a greenside bunker at the final hole. The ball was almost buried, yet from an upslope in the front of the bunker he managed to blast the ball onto the green. The ball landed 10 feet from the flag before rolling all the way into the hole for a birdie three. He eventually won by three.

3) 1974, Gary Player, par-4 17th: Gary Player had a habit of playing match-winning strokes at the right time. Leading by one stroke through 70 holes, the South African fired a 9-iron approach to within nine inches of the cup at 17. The resulting tap-in birdie three confirmed Player as champion for the second time. A par on 18 gave him a two-shot victory.

4) 1975, Jack Nicklaus, par-3 16th: In the famous three-way dogfight of 1975, the key moment came at 16 where Nicklaus holed a monster 40-foot putt for a birdie two. That stroke moved him into a tie for the lead with Tom Weiskopf who was watching it all from the 16th tee. Weiskopf immediately followed that stroke by leaving his tee-shot short of the green, from where he took three more to get down. Nicklaus won the tournament by a stroke from Weiskopf and Johnny Miller.

5) 1987, Larry Mize, par 4 11th (2nd play-off hole): The shot that broke Greg Norman's heart. With both players having had two shots each on the second play-off hole, Norman was on the front right fringe of the putting surface, about 40 feet from the cup, while Mize's ball lay some 40 yards wide and right of the flag. With a sand wedge in his hands, Mize played a low pitch, the ball landed about a yard off the green, bounced onto the putting surface and rolled all the way into the hole. A birdie three from an almost impossible position. Norman, now needing to sink his putt to take the play-off to a third extra hole, never threatened the cup. Mize was an unlikely champion.

6) 1988, Sandy Lyle, par 4 18th: Possibly the greatest bunker shot of all time. Standing on the 72nd tee, Lyle knew he needed a birdie for victory or a par to take Mark Calcavecchia into a play-off. But after hitting his 1-iron tee shot into a fairway bunker, even a par four looked a remote possibility. The one thing in Lyle's favour, however, was that he'd found a decent lie. And from around 140 yards from the pin, Lyle fired a 7-iron over the flag, to land around 20 feet from the cup and from there the ball rolled back down the slope towards the hole before coming to rest 10 feet away. Lyle cooly sank the putt to become the first British player to wear the Green Jacket.

THE MAJOR CHAMPIONS

An alphabetical directory of all major winners

Player	Wins	Titles
Tommy Aaron	1	Masters 1973
Jamie Anderson	3	Br Open 1877, 1878, 1879
Willie Anderson	4	US Open 1901, 1903, 1904, 1905
George Archer	1	Masters 1969
Tommy Armour	3	US Open 1927; USPGA1930 Br Open 1931
Laurie Auchterlonie	1	US Open 1902
Willie Auchterlonie	1	Br Open 1893
Paul Azinger	1	USPGA 1993
Ian Baker-Finch	1	Br Open 1991
Seve Ballesteros	5	Br Open 1979,1984, 1988 Masters1980, 1983
Mr John Ball Jr	1	Br Open 1890
Jerry Barber	1	USPGA 1961
Jim Barnes	4	USPGA 1916, 1919 US Open 1921; Br Open 1925
Tommy Bolt	1	US Open 1958
Julius Boros	3	US Open 1952, 1963 USPGA 1968
James Braid	5	Br Open 1901, 1905, 1906, 1908, 1910
Gay Brewer	1	Masters 1967
David Brown	1	Br Open 1886
Billy Burke	1	US Open 1931
Jack Burke Jr	2	Masters 1956; USPGA 1956
Walter Burkemo	1	USPGA 1953
Jack Burns	1	Br Open 1888
Dick Burton	1	Br Open 1939
Mark Calcavecchia	1	Br Open 1989
Billy Casper	3	US Open 1959, 1966 Masters 1970
Bob Charles	1	Br Open 1963
Charles Coody	1	Masters 1971
Henry Cotton	3	Br Open 1934, 1937, 1948
Fred Couples	1	Masters 1992
Tom Creavy	1	USPGA 1931
Ben Crenshaw	2	Masters 1984, 1995
Fred Daly	1	Br Open 1947
John Daly	2	USPGA 1991; Br Open 1995
Jimmy Demaret	3	Masters 1940, 1947, 1950
Leo Diegel	2	USPGA 1928, 1929

Player	Wins	Titles
George Duncan	1	Br Open 1920
Olin Dutra	2	USPGA 1932; US Open 1934
Steve Elkington	1	USPGA 1995
Ernie Els	1	US Open 1994
Mr Charles Evans	1	US Open 1916
Nick Faldo	5	Br Open 1987, 1990, 1992 Masters 1989, 1990
Johnny Farrell	1	US Open 1928
Max Faulkner	1	Br Open 1951
Bob Ferguson	3	Br Open 1880, 1881, 1882
Willie Fernie	1	Br Open 1883
Jim Ferrier	1	USPGA 1947
Dow Finsterwald	1	USPGA 1958
Jack Fleck	1	US Open 1955
Ray Floyd	4	USPGA 1969, 1982 Masters 1976; US Open 1986
Doug Ford	2	USPGA 1955; Masters 1957
James Foulis	1	US Open 1896
Ed Furgol	1	US Open 1954
Al Geiberger	1	USPGA 1966
Vic Ghezzi	1	USPGA 1941
Bob Goalby	1	Masters 1968
Johnny Goodman	1	US Open 1933
Wayne Grady	1	USPGA 1990
David Graham	2	USPGA 1979; US Open 1981
Lou Graham	1	US Open 1975
Hubert Green	2	US Open 1977; USPGA 1985
Ralph Guldahl	3	US Open 1937, 1938 Masters 1939
Walter Hagen	11	US Open 1914, 1919 USPGA 1921, 1924, 1925, 1926, 1927 Br Open 1922, 1924, 1928, 1929
Bob Hamilton	1	USPGA 1944
Chick Harbert	1	USPGA 1954
Claude Harmon	1	Masters 1948
Chandler Harper	1	USPGA 1950
Arthur Havers	1	Br Open 1923
Jay Hebert	1	USPGA 1960
Lionel Hebert	1	USPGA 1957
Alex Herd	1	Br Open 1902
Fred Herd	1	US Open 1898

Player	Wins	Titles
Mr Harold Hilton	2	Br Open 1892, 1897
Ben Hogan	9	USPGA 1946, 1948
		US Open 1948, 1950,
		1951, 1953
		Masters 1951, 1953
		Br Open 1953
Jock Hutchison	2	USPGA 1920;
		Br Open 1921
Hale Irwin	3	US Open 1974, 1979,
		1990
Tony Jacklin	2	Br Open 1969;
		US Open 1970
Don January	1	USPGA 1967
Lee Janzen	1	US Open 1993
Mr Bobby Jones	7	US Open 1923, 1926,
		1929, 1930
		Br Open 1926, 1927, 1930
Herman Keiser	1	Masters 1946
Tom Kidd	1	Br Open 1873
Hugh Kirkaldy	1	Br Open 1891
Tom Kite	1	US Open 1992
Bernhard Langer	2	Masters 1985, 1993
Tony Lema	1	Br Open 1964
Lawson Little	1	US Open 1940
Gene Littler	1	US Open 1961
Bobby Locke	4	Br Open 1949, 1950,
		1952, 1957
Joe Lloyd	1	US Open 1897
Sandy Lyle	2	Br Open 1985;
		Masters 1988
Willie MacFarlane	1	US Open 1925
John Mahaffey	1	USPGA 1978
Tony Manero	1	US Open 1936
Lloyd Mangrum	1	US Open 1946
Dave Marr	1	USPGA 1965
Bob Martin	2	Br Open 1876, 1885
Arnaud Massy	1	Br Open 1907
Dick Mayer	1	US Open 1957
John J McDermott	2	US Open 1911, 1912
Fred McLeod	1	US Open 1908
Cary Middlecoff	3	US Open 1949, 1956
		Masters 1955
Johnny Miller	2	US Open 1973;
		Br Open 1976
Larry Mize	1	Masters 1987
Orville Moody	1	US Open 1969
Tom Morris Jr	4	Br Open 1868, 1869,
		1870, 1872
Tom Morris Sr	4	Br Open 1861, 1862,
		1864, 1867
Kel Nagle	1	Br Open 1960
Byron Nelson	5	Masters 1937, 1942
		US Open 1939
		USPGA 1940, 1945
Larry Nelson	3	USPGA 1981, 1987
		US Open 1983
Jack Nicklaus	18	US Open 1962, 1967,
		1972, 1980
		Masters 1963, 1965,
		1966, 1972, 1975, 1986
		USPGA 1963, 1971,
		1973, 1975, 1980
		Br Open 1966, 1970,
		1978
Bobby Nichols	1	USPGA 1964
Greg Norman	2	Br Open 1986, 1993
Andy North	2	US Open 1978, 1985
Jose-Maria Olazabal	1	Masters 1994
Mr Francis Ouimet	1	US Open 1913
Alf Padgham	1	Br Open 1936
Arnold Palmer	7	Masters 1958, 1960,
		1962, 1964
		US Open 1960
		Br Open 1961, 1962
Mungo Park	1	Br Open 1874
Willie Park Jr	2	Br Open 1887, 1889
Willie Park	4	Br Open 1860, 1863,
		1866, 1875
Sam Parks Jr	1	US Open 1935
Jerry Pate	1	US Open 1976
Corey Pavin	1	US Open 1995
Alf Perry	1	Br Open 1935
Henry Picard	2	Masters 1938;
		USPGA 1939
Gary Player	9	Br Open 1959, 1968, 1974
		Masters 1961, 1974, 1978
		USPGA 1962, 1972
		US Open 1965
Nick Price	3	USPGA 1992, 1994
		Br Open 1994
Horace Rawlins	1	US Open 1895
Ted Ray	2	Br Open 1912;
		US Open 1920
Johnny Revolta	1	USPGA 1935
Aleck Ross	1	US Open 1907
Bill Rogers	1	Br Open 1981
Bob Rosburg	1	USPGA 1959
Paul Runyan	2	USPGA 1934, 1938
Gene Sarazen	7	US Open 1922, 1932
		USPGA 1922, 1923, 1933
		Br Open 1932,
		Masters 1935
George Sargent	1	US Open 1909
Densmore Shute	3	Br Open 1933
		USPGA 1936, 1937
Jack Simpson	1	Br Open 1884

Player	Wins	Titles
Scott Simpson	1	US Open 1987
Jeff Sluman	1	USPGA 1988
Alex Smith	2	US Open 1906, 1910
Horton Smith	2	Masters 1934, 1936
Willie Smith	1	US Open 1899
Sam Snead	7	USPGA 1942, 1949, 1951
		Br Open 1946
		Masters 1949, 1952, 1954
Craig Stadler	1	Masters 1982
Payne Stewart	2	USPGA 1989;
		US Open 1991
Dave Stockton	2	USPGA 1970, 1976
Andrew Strath	1	Br Open 1865
Curtis Strange	2	US Open 1988, 1989
Hal Sutton	1	USPGA 1983
JH Taylor	5	Br Open 1894, 1895,
		1900, 1909, 1913
Peter Thomson	5	Br Open 1954, 1955,
		1956, 1958, 1965
Mr Jerome Travers	1	US Open 1915
Lee Trevino	6	US Open 1968, 1971
		Br Open 1971, 1972
		USPGA 1974, 1984
Jim Turnesa	1	USPGA 1952
Bob Tway	1	USPGA 1986
Harry Vardon	7	Br Open 1896, 1898,
		1899, 1903, 1911, 1914
		US Open 1900
Ken Venturi	1	US Open 1964
Roberto de Vicenzo	1	Br Open 1967
Lanny Wadkins	1	USPGA 1977
Cyril Walker	1	US Open 1924
Art Wall	1	Masters 1959
Tom Watson	8	Br Open 1975, 1977,
		1980, 1982, 1983
		Masters 1977, 1981
		US Open 1982
Tom Weiskopf	1	Br Open 1973
Reg Whitcombe	1	Br Open 1938
Jack White	1	Br Open 1904
Craig Wood	2	Masters 1941;
		US Open 1941
Ian Woosnam	1	Masters 1991
Lew Worsham	1	US Open 1947
Fuzzy Zoeller	2	Masters 1979;
		US Open 1984

MOST PROFESSIONAL MAJOR TITLES OF ALL TIME

	Masters	US Op	Br Op	USPGA	Total	
Jack Nicklaus	6	4	3	5	18	(1962-86)
Walter Hagen	-	2	4	5	11	(1914-29)
Ben Hogan	2	4	1	2	9	(1946-53)
Gary Player	3	1	3	2	9	(1959-78)
Tom Watson	2	1	5	-	8	(1975-83)
Mr Bobby Jones	-	4	3	-	7	(1923-30)
Arnold Palmer	4	1	2	-	7	(1958-64)
Gene Sarazen	1	2	1	3	7	(1922-35)
Sam Snead	3	-	1	3	7	(1942-54)
Harry Vardon	-	1	6	-	7	(1896-1914)
Lee Trevino	-	2	2	2	6	(1968-84)
Seve Ballesteros	2	-	3	-	5	(1979-88)
James Braid	-	-	5	-	5	(1901-10)
Nick Faldo	2	-	3	-	5	(1987-92)
Byron Nelson	2	1	-	2	5	(1937-45)
JH Taylor	-	-	5	-	5	(1894-1913)
Peter Thomson	-	-	5	-	5	(1954-65)
Willie Anderson	-	4	-	-	4	(1901-05)
Jim Barnes	-	1	1	2	4	(1916-25)
Ray Floyd	1	1	-	2	4	(1969-86)
Bobby Locke	-	-	4	-	4	(1949-57)
Tom Morris Jr	-	-	4	-	4	(1868-72)
Tom Morris Sr	-	-	4	-	4	(1861-67)
Willie Park	-	-	4	-	4	(1860-75)
Jamie Anderson	-	-	3	-	3	(1877-79)
Tommy Armour	-	1	1	1	3	(1927-31)
Julius Boros	-	2	-	1	3	(1952-68)
Billy Casper	1	2	-	-	3	(1959-70)
Henry Cotton	-	-	3	-	3	(1934-48)
Jimmy Demaret	3	-	-	-	3	(1940-50)
Bob Ferguson	-	-	3	-	3	(1880-82)
Ralph Guldahl	1	2	-	-	3	(1937-39)
Hale Irwin	-	3	-	-	3	(1974-90)
Cary Middlecoff	1	2	-	-	3	(1949-56)
Larry Nelson	-	1	-	2	3	(1981-87)
Nick Price	-	-	1	2	3	(1992-94)
Densmore Shute	-	-	1	2	3	(1933-37)

TWO MAJOR TITLES IN THE SAME YEAR

The following have all won two or more professional majors in the same calendar year:

Player	Year	Tournaments
Ben Hogan	1953	(Masters, US Open & British Open)
Gene Sarazen	1922	(US Open & USPGA)
Walter Hagen	1924	(British Open & USPGA)
Mr Bobby Jones	1926	(British Open & US Open)
Mr Bobby Jones	1930	(British Open & US Open)
Gene Sarazen	1932	(British Open & US Open)
Craig Wood	1941	(Masters & US Open)
Ben Hogan	1948	(USPGA & US Open)
Sam Snead	1949	(Masters & USPGA)
Ben Hogan	1951	(Masters & US Open)
Jack Burke Jr	1956	(Masters & USPGA)
Arnold Palmer	1960	(Masters & US Open)
Arnold Palmer	1962	(Masters & Br Open)
Jack Nicklaus	1963	(Masters & USPGA)
Jack Nicklaus	1966	(Masters & Br Open)
Lee Trevino	1971	(US Open & British Open)
Jack Nicklaus	1972	(Masters & US Open)
Gary Player	1974	(Masters & British Open)
Jack Nicklaus	1975	(Masters & USPGA)
Tom Watson	1977	(Masters & British Open)
Jack Nicklaus	1980	(US Open & USPGA)
Tom Watson	1982	(US Open & British Open)
Nick Faldo	1990	(Masters & British Open)
Nick Price	1994	(British Open & USPGA)

LONGEST GAP BETWEEN SUCCESSIVE MAJOR VICTORIES

Period	Player	Tournaments
11 yrs 9 dys	Julius Boros	1952 US Open - 1963 US Open
11 yrs 1 dy	Hale Irwin	1979 US Open - 1990 US Open
10 yrs 359 dys	Henry Cotton	1937 Br Open - 1948 Br Open
10 yrs 359 dys	Ben Crenshaw	1984 Masters - 1995 Masters

Period	Player	Tournaments
10 yrs 8 dys	Lee Trevino	1974 USPGA - 1984 USPGA
9 yrs 4 dys	JH Taylor	1900 Br Open - 1909 Br Open
9 yrs 3 dys	Bob Martin	1876 Br Open - 1885 Br Open
8 yrs 362 dys	Willie Park	1866 Br Open - 1875 Br Open
8 yrs 255 dys	Gene Sarazen	1923 USPGA - 1932 Br Open
8 yrs 53 dys	Hubert Green	1977 US Open - 1985 USPGA
8 yrs 49 dys	Ted Ray	1912 Br Open - 1920 US Open
8 yrs 20 dys	Harry Vardon	1903 Br Open - 1911 Br Open
7 yrs 362 dys	Bernhard Langer	1985 Masters - 1993 Masters
7 yrs 7 dys	Billy Casper	1959 US Open - 1966 US Open
7 yrs 4 dys	Peter Thomson	1958 Br Open - 1965 Br Open
6 yrs 364 dys	Jimmy Demaret	1940 Masters - 1947 Masters
6 yrs 363 dys	Andy North	1978 US Open - 1985 US Open
6 yrs 363 dys	Greg Norman	1986 Br Open - 1993 Br Open
6 yrs 238 dys	Ray Floyd	1969 USPGA - 1976 Masters
6 yrs 119 dys	Ray Floyd	1976 Masters - 1982 USPGA
6 yrs 0 dys	Dave Stockton	1970 USPGA -1976 USPGA
5 yrs 303 dys	Cary Middlecoff	1949 US Open - 1955 Masters
5 yrs 246 dys	Jack Nicklaus	1980 USPGA - 1986 Masters

LONGEST TIME-SPAN BETWEEN FIRST AND LAST MAJOR VICTORIES

Period	Player	Tournaments
23 yrs 300 dys	Jack Nicklaus	1962 US Open - 1986 Masters
19 yrs 12 dys	JH Taylor	1894 Br Open - 1913 Br Open
18 yrs 280 dys	Gary Player	1959 Br Open - 1978 Masters
18 yrs 6 dys	Harry Vardon	1896 Br Open - 1914 Br Open
16 yrs 302 dys	Ray Floyd	1969 USPGA - 1986 US Open
16 yrs 64 dys	Lee Trevino	1968 US Open - 1984 USPGA
16 yrs 37 dys	Julius Boros	1952 US Open - 1968 USPGA
16 yrs 2 dys	Hale Irwin	1974 US Open - 1990 US Open
14 yrs 328 dys	Willie Park	1860 Br Open - 1875 Br Open
14 yrs 262 dys	Walter Hagen	1914 US Open - 1929 Br Open
14 yrs 3 dys	Henry Cotton	1934 Br Open - 1948 Br Open
12 yrs 267 dys	Gene Sarazen	1922 US Open - 1935 Masters
11 yrs 316 dys	Sam Snead	1942 USPGA -1954 Masters

DEFENDING CHAMPIONS

KEY

Margin refers to the number of shots that the defender finished behind the new champion, or in the case of players successfully defending titles, their own winning margin. For example: -3 means three strokes behind the winner, +2 means a player has successfully defended his title with a winning margin of two strokes.

Year refers to the year in which they were defending their title. For example, the year 1967 means the player won the Championship in 1966.

Position. T5 stands for tied 5th.

Note: Unless otherwise stated, *Missed the Cut* refers to a '36-hole cut'

BRITISH OPEN

Year	Player	Position	Margin
1861	Willie Park	2	-4
1862	Tom Morris Sr	Won	+13
1863	Tom Morris Sr	2	-2
1864	Willie Park	4	-10
1865	Tom Morris Sr	5	-12
1866	Andrew Strath	T6	-13
1867	Willie Park	2	-2
1868	Tom Morris Sr	6	-19
1869	Tom Morris Jr	Won	+3
1870	Tom Morris Jr	Won	+12
1871	No Tournament		
1872	Tom Morris Jr	Won	+3
1873	Tom Morris Jr	T3	-4
1874	Tom Kidd	T8	-8
1875	Mungo Park	3	-5
1876	Willie Park	3	-7
1877	Bob Martin	*No record of Martin taking part in tournament*	
1878	Jamie Anderson	Won	+2
1879	Jamie Anderson	Won	+3
1880	Jamie Anderson	*Did not defend*	
1881	Bob Ferguson	Won	+3
1882	Bob Ferguson	Won	+3
1883	Bob Ferguson	2	(Play-off)
1884	Willie Fernie	T2	-4
1885	Jack Simpson	T13	-8
1886	Bob Martin	*Did not defend*	
1887	David Brown	9	-13
1888	Willie Park Jr	T11	-11
1889	Jack Burns	14	-15
1890	Willie Park Jr	T4	-6
1891	Mr John Ball Jr	T11	-11
1892	Hugh Kirkaldy	T2	-3
1893	Mr Harold Hilton	T8	-10
1894	Willie Auchterlonie	T23	-29
1895	JH Taylor	Won	+4
1896	JH Taylor	2	(Play-off)
1897	Harry Vardon	6	-6
1898	Mr Harold Hilton	3	-2
1899	Harry Vardon	Won	+5
1900	Harry Vardon	2	-8
1901	JH Taylor	3	-4
1902	James Braid	T2	-1
1903	Alex Herd	4	-9
1904	Harry Vardon	5	-6
1905	Jack White	T18	-17
1906	James Braid	Won	+4
1907	James Braid	T5	-6
1908	Arnaud Massy	T9	-17
1909	James Braid	T2	-6
1910	JH Taylor	T14	-13
1911	James Braid	T5	-2
1912	Harry Vardon	2	-4
1913	Ted Ray	2	-8
1914	JH Taylor	2	-3
1915-19	*No tournament due to First World War*		
1920	Harry Vardon	T14	-15
1921	George Duncan	5	-5
1922	Jock Hutchison	4	-2
1923	Walter Hagen	2	-1
1924	Arthur Havers	T29	-16
1925	Walter Hagen	*Did not defend*	
1926	Jim Barnes	T18	-16
1927	Mr Bobby Jones	Won	+6
1928	Mr Bobby Jones	*Did not defend*	
1929	Walter Hagen	Won	+6
1930	Walter Hagen	*Did not defend*	
1931	Mr Bobby Jones	*Did not defend*	
1932	Tommy Armour	T17	-17
1933	Gene Sarazen	T3	-1
1934	Densmore Shute	20	-18
1935	Henry Cotton	T7	-10
1936	Alf Perry	T50	-24
1937	Alf Padgham	T7	-8
1938	Henry Cotton	3	-3
1939	Reg Whitcombe	T3	-4
1940-4	*No tournament due to Second World War*		
1946	Richard Burton	12	-12
1947	Sam Snead	*Did not defend*	
1948	Fred Daly	2	-5
1949	Henry Cotton	*Did not defend*	
1950	Bobby Locke	Won	+2
1951	Bobby Locke	T6	-8
1952	Max Faulkner	T17	-13
1953	Bobby Locke	8	-9
1954	Ben Hogan	*Did not defend*	
1955	Peter Thomson	Won	+2

1956	Peter Thomson	Won	+3
1957	Peter Thomson	2	-3
1958	Bobby Locke	T16	-10
1959	Peter Thomson	T23	-10
1960	Gary Player	7	-6
1961	Kel Nagle	T5	5
1962	Arnold Palmer	Won	+6
1963	Arnold Palmer	T26	-17
1964	Bob Charles	T17	-18
1965	Tony Lema	T5	-4
1966	Peter Thomson	T8	-6
1967	Jack Nicklaus	2	-2
1968	Roberto de Vicenzo	T10	-8
1969	Gary Player	T23	-12
1970	Tony Jacklin	5	-3
1971	Jack Nicklaus	T5	-5
1972	Lee Trevino	Won	+1
1973	Lee Trevino	T10	-13
1974	Tom Weiskopf	T7	-11
1975	Gary Player	T32	-13
1976	Tom Watson	*Missed the 54-hole cut*	
1977	Johnny Miller	T9	-16
1978	Tom Watson	T14	-6
1979	Jack Nicklaus	T2	-3
1980	Seve Ballesteros	T19	-15
1981	Tom Watson	T23	-14
1982	Bill Rogers	T22	-10
1983	Tom Watson	Won	+1
1984	Tom Watson	T2	-2
1985	Seve Ballesteros	T39	-10
1986	Sandy Lyle	T30	-15
1987	Greg Norman	T35	-12
1988	Nick Faldo	3	-6
1989	Seve Ballesteros	T77	-24
1990	Mark Calcavecchia	*Missed the cut*	
1991	Nick Faldo	T17	-9
1992	Ian Baker-Finch	T19	-10
1993	Nick Faldo	2	-2
1994	Greg Norman	T11	-8
1995	Nick Price	T40	-9

Mark Calcavecchia, British Open winner in 1989 at Royal Troon, missed the cut 12 months later

UNITED STATES OPEN

Year	Player	Position	Margin
1896	Horace Rawlins	2	-3
1897	James Foulis	T3	-6
1898	Joe Lloyd	4	-11
1899	Fred Herd	T25	-35
1900	Willie Smith	5	-14
1901	Harry Vardon	*Did not defend*	
1902	Willie Anderson	T5	-11
1903	Laurie Auchterlonie	7	-14
1904	Willie Anderson	Won	+5
1905	Willie Anderson	Won	+2
1906	Willie Anderson	5	-12
1907	Alex Smith	*Did not defend*	
1908	Aleck Ross	T23	-25
1909	Fred McLeod	T13	-13
1910	George Sargent	T16	-11
1911	Alex Smith	T23	-14
1912	John J McDermott	Won	+2
1913	John J McDermott	8	-4
1914	Mr Francis Ouimet	T5	-8
1915	Walter Hagen	T10	-9
1916	Mr Jerome Travers	*Did not defend*	

Year	Player	Performance	Score
1917-18	*No tournament due to First World War*		
1919	Mr Charles Evans Jr	T9	-12
1920	Walter Hagen	11	-6
1921	Ted Ray	*Did not defend*	
1922	Jim Barnes	T24	-18
1923	Gene Sarazen	T16	-14
1924	Mr Bobby Jones	2	-3
1925	Cyril Walker	T47	-25
1926	Willie MacFarlane	T20	-14
1927	Mr Bobby Jones	T11	-8
1928	Tommy Armour	16	-7
1929	Johnny Farrell	*Missed the cut*	
1930	Mr Bobby Jones	Won	+2
1931	Mr Bobby Jones	*Did not defend*	
1932	Billy Burke	T7	-11
1933	Gene Sarazen	T26	-16
1934	Mr Johnny Goodman	T43	-18
1935	Olin Dutra	T12	-9
1936	Sam Parks Jr	*Missed the cut*	
1937	Tony Manero	T40	-19
1938	Ralph Guldahl	Won	+6
1939	Ralph Guldahl	T7	-4
1940	Byron Nelson	T5	-3
1941	Lawson Little	T17	-13
1942	*No tournament due to Second World War*		
1946	Craig Wood	Missed the cut	
1947	Lloyd Mangrum	T23	-11
1948	Lew Worsham	6	-9
1949	Ben Hogan	*Did not defend title due to injuries sustained in car accident*	
1950	Cary Middlecoff	T10	-5
1951	Ben Hogan	Won	+2
1952	Ben Hogan	3	-5
1953	Julius Boros	T17	-16
1954	Ben Hogan	T6	-5
1955	Ed Furgol	T45	-25
1956	Jack Fleck	*Missed the cut*	
1957	Cary Middlecoff	2	(Play-off)
1958	Dick Mayer	T23	-16
1959	Tommy Bolt	T38	-19
1960	Billy Casper	T12	-6
1961	Arnold Palmer	T14	-8
1962	Gene Littler	T8	-7
1963	Jack Nicklaus	*Missed the cut*	
1964	Julius Boros	*Missed the cut*	
1965	Ken Venturi	*Missed the cut*	
1966	Gary Player	T15	-15
1967	Billy Casper	4	-7
1968	Jack Nicklaus	2	-4
1969	Lee Trevino	*Missed the cut*	
1970	Orville Moody	*Missed the cut*	
1971	Tony Jacklin	*Missed the cut*	
1972	Lee Trevino	T4	-5
1973	Jack Nicklaus	T4	-3
1974	Johnny Miller	T35	-15
1975	Hale Irwin	T3	-1
1976	Lou Graham	T28	-17
1977	Jerry Pate	*Missed the cut*	
1978	Hubert Green	*Missed the cut*	
1979	Andy North	T11	-9
1980	Hale Irwin	T8	-10
1981	Jack Nicklaus	T6	-7
1982	David Graham	T6	-5
1983	Tom Watson	2	-1
1984	Larry Nelson	*Missed the cut*	
1985	Fuzzy Zoeller	T9	-4
1986	Andy North	67	-23
1987	Ray Floyd	T43	-13
1988	Scott Simpson	T6	-3
1989	Curtis Strange	Won	+1
1990	Curtis Strange	T21	-6
1991	Hale Irwin	T11	-8
1992	Payne Stewart	T51	-13
1993	Tom Kite	*Missed the cut*	
1994	Lee Janzen	*Missed the cut*	
1995	Ernie Els	*Missed the cut*	

USPGA CHAMPIONSHIP

Matchplay

Year	Player	Performance	(Losing Margin)
1917/18	*No tournament due to First World War*		
1919	Jim Barnes	Won	(5 matches)
1920	Jim Barnes	2nd Rd (16)	5&4 Clarence Hackney
1921	Jock Hutchison	2nd Rd (16)	8&7 Gene Sarazen
1922	Walter Hagen	*Did not defend*	
1923	Gene Sarazen	Won	(6 matches)
1924	Gene Sarazen	2nd Rd (16)	2&1 Larry Nabholtz
1925	Walter Hagen	Won	(5 matches)
1926	Walter Hagen	Won	(5 matches)

1927	Walter Hagen	Won	(5 matches)
1928	Walter Hagen	3rd Rd (8)	2&1 Leo Diegel
1929	Leo Diegel	Won	(5 matches)
1930	Leo Diegel	2nd Rd (16)	at 38th Harold Sampson
1931	Tommy Armour	3rd Rd (8)	3&1 Densmore Shute
1932	Tom Creavy	Semi-Fin (4)	at 38th Frank Walsh
1933	Olin Dutra	2nd Rd (16)	1 down Johnny Farrell
1934	Gene Sarazen	2nd Rd (16)	4&3 Al Watrous
1935	Paul Runyan	4th Rd (8)	3&2 Al Zimmermann
1936	Johnny Revolta	2nd Rd (32)	at 19th Harold McSpaden
1937	Densmore Shute	Won	(6 matches)
1938	Densmore Shute	3rd Rd (16)	2&1 Jimmy Hines
1939	Paul Runyan	4th Rd (8)	2&1 Dick Metz
1940	Henry Picard	3rd Rd (16)	1 down Gene Sarazen
1941	Byron Nelson	Runner-up	at 38th Vic Ghezzi
1942	Vic Ghezzi	1st Rd (32)	4&3 Jimmy Demaret
1943	No tournament due to Second World War		
1944	Sam Snead	Did not defend title due to injury	
1945	Bob Hamilton	1st Rd (32)	5&4 Jack Grout
1946	Byron Nelson	4th Rd (8)	1 down Ed Oliver
1947	Ben Hogan	1st Rd (64)	3&1 Toney Penna
1948	Jim Ferrier	2nd Rd (32)	1 down Claude Harmon
1949	Ben Hogan	Did not defend title because of injuries sustained in a car accident	
1950	Sam Snead	2nd Rd (32)	1 down Eddie Burke
1951	Chandler Harper	1st Rd (64)	at 23rd Jim Turnesa
1952	Sam Snead	1st Rd (64)	at 19th Lew Worsham
1953	Jim Turnesa	2nd Rd (32)	4&3 Felice Torza
1954	Walter Burkemo	Runner-up	4&3 Chick Harbert
1955	Chick Harbert	2nd Rd (32)	1 up Johnny Palmer
1956	Doug Ford	3rd Rd (32)	5&3 Walter Burkemo
1957	Jack Burke Jr	2nd Rd (64)	2&1 Milon Marusic

Gene Sarazen was only 19 years old when he beat title holder Jock Hutchison 8&7 in **1921**. Hutchinson had just been crowned British Open champion. However, the young Sarazen was beaten in his next match, 5&4, by Cyril Walker.

In **1922** Walter Hagen refused to defend the title because of exhibition engagements.

After winning 22 successive matches, Walter Hagen was finally beaten by Leo Diegel in the quarter-finals of the **1928** event at Five Farms Country Club in Baltimore, Maryland. During that unbeaten spell, Hagen had come close to defeat on a number of occasions. Six times he was either taken to the final hole, or pushed into extra-holes. In a quarter-final in 1925, Hagen was actually five down to Diegel after 18 holes of their 36-hole contest. But he fought back, squaring the match by winning the 36th hole and he finally sealed victory four holes into overtime.

Tom Creavy's reign went as far as the second extra-hole of his semi-final with Frank Walsh in **1932**. The match ended when the defending champion three-putted, including a miss from just three feet.

Denny Shute retained the title in **1937**, but only after a titanic struggle with Harold McSpaden who should have won the final. The challenger was two up with just three holes to play, but then lost the 34th and 35th holes when he was unable to make par. This brought the match back to all square. However, at the 36th, McSpaden was in pole position once again, as he stood over a four foot birdie putt for the title. But after being interupted by a number of photographers, McSpaden missed his chance. Shute won the first extra-hole after his shaken opponent bogeyed.

In one of the biggest upsets in the matchplay years of the US PGA Championship, defending champion Ben Hogan was dumped out in the first round of **1947** by Toney Penna. In their 18 hole encounter, Hogan was five under par through 17 holes when the match ended 3&1. Penna, for the same journey, was eight under.

Chandler Harper succumed at the fifth extra-hole of his first round match with Jim Turnesa in **1951**. Harper was three up with just three holes to play, before Turnesa made birdies at 16 and 17, as well as holing a five footer to stay in the match at the 18th. Turnesa clinched victory by sinking a 25-foot birdie putt on the 23rd green.

USPGA CHAMPIONSHIP

Strokeplay

Year	Player	Position	Margin
1958	Lionel Hebert	T16	-15
1959	Dow Finsterwald	4	-3
1960	Bob Rosburg	Missed 54-hole cut	
1961	Jay Hebert	13	-7
1962	Jerry Barber	Missed the cut	
1963	Gary Player	T8	-7
1964	Jack Nicklaus	T2	-3
1965	Bobby Nichols	T54	-20
1966	Dave Marr	T18	-11
1967	Al Geiberger	T5	-2
1968	Don January	T51	-15
1969	Julius Boros	T25	-11
1970	Ray Floyd	T8	-5
1971	Dave Stockton	T40	-13
1972	Jack Nicklaus	T13	-6
1973	Gary Player	T51	-17
1974	Jack Nicklaus	2	-1
1975	Lee Trevino	T60	-21
1976	Jack Nicklaus	T4	-2
1977	Dave Stockton	T31	-11
1978	Lanny Wadkins	T34	-15
1979	John Mahaffey	T51	-18
1980	David Graham	T26	-18
1981	Jack Nicklaus	T4	-6
1982	Larry Nelson	Missed the cut	
1983	Ray Floyd	T20	-10
1984	Hal Sutton	T6	-7
1985	Lee Trevino	2	-2
1986	Hubert Green	T41	-14
1987	Bob Tway	T47	-13
1988	Larry Nelson	T38	-15
1989	Jeff Sluman	T24	-8
1990	Payne Stewart	T8	-10
1991	Wayne Grady	T43	-14
1992	John Daly	82	-26
1993	Nick Price	T31	-11
1994	Paul Azinger	Missed the cut	
1995	Nick Price	T39	-13

UNITED STATES MASTERS

Year	Player	Position	Margin
1935	Horton Smith	T19	-14
1936	Gene Sarazen	3	-2
1937	Horton Smith	T19	-16
1938	Byron Nelson	5	-5
1939	Henry Picard	8	-10
1940	Ralph Guldahl	T14	-12
1941	Jimmy Demaret	T12	-12
1942	Craig Wood	T23	-22
1943-45	No tournament due to Second World War		
1946	Byron Nelson	T7	-8
1947	Herman Keiser	T24	-13
1948	Jimmy Demaret	T18	-16
1949	Claude Harmon	T11	-11
1950	Sam Snead	3	-4
1951	Jimmy Demaret	T30	-19
1952	Ben Hogan	T7	-7
1953	Sam Snead	T16	-18
1954	Ben Hogan	2(Play-Off)	
1955	Sam Snead	3	-8
1956	Cary Middlecoff	3	-2
1957	Jack Burke Jr	T7	-8
1958	Doug Ford	T2	-1
1959	Arnold Palmer	3	-2
1960	Art Wall		
	Did not defend due to a knee injury		
1961	Arnold Palmer	T2	-1
1962	Gary Player	T2(Play-Off)	
1963	Arnold Palmer	T9	-5
1964	Jack Nicklaus	T2	-6
1965	Arnold Palmer	T2	-9
1966	Jack Nicklaus	Won(Play-Off)	
1967	Jack Nicklaus	Missed the cut	
1968	Gay Brewer	T35	-14
1969	Bob Goalby	T40	-16
1970	George Archer	T31	-15
1971	Billy Casper	T13	-9
1972	Charles Coody	T12	-6
1973	Jack Nicklaus	T3	-2
1974	Tommy Aaron	Missed the cut	
1975	Gary Player	T30	-16

Bernhard Langer: finished 16th and 25th when defending his Masters title at Augusta in 1986 and 1994 respectively

1976	Jack Nicklaus	T3	-11	1986	Bernhard Langer	T16	-7
1977	Ray Floyd	T8	-9	1987	Jack Nicklaus	T7	-4
1978	Tom Watson	T2	-1	1988	Larry Mize	T45	-23
1979	Gary Player	T17	-8	1989	Sandy Lyle	*Missed the cut*	
1980	Fuzzy Zoeller	T19	-12	1990	Nick Faldo	Won(Play-off)	
1981	Seve Ballesteros	*Missed the cut*		1991	Nick Faldo	T12	-5
1982	Tom Watson	T5	-3	1992	Ian Woosnam	T19	-8
1983	Craig Stadler	T6	-6	1993	Fred Couples	T21	-11
1984	Seve Ballesteros	*Missed the cut*		1994	Bernhard Langer	T25	-14
1985	Ben Crenshaw	T57	-20	1995	Jose-Maria Olazabal	T14	-10

LOWEST ROUNDS IN MAJOR CHAMPIONSHIPS

ALL-TIME BEST IN MAJORS (18 HOLES)

Score	Player	Tournament	Course
63	JOHNNY MILLER	1973 US Open (Rd 4)	Oakmont CC
	BRUCE CRAMPTON	1975 USPGA (Rd 2)	Firestone CC (South)
	MARK HAYES	1977 Br Open (Rd 2)	Turnberry
	TOM WEISKOPF	1980 US Open (Rd 1)	Baltusrol GC
	JACK NICKLAUS	1980 US Open (Rd 1)	Baltusrol GC
	ISAO AOKI	1980 Br Open (Rd 3)	Muirfield
	RAY FLOYD	1982 USPGA (Rd 1)	Southern Hills CC
	GARY PLAYER	1984 USPGA (Rd 2)	Shoal Creek CC
	NICK PRICE	1986 Masters (Rd 3)	Augusta National
	GREG NORMAN	1986 Br Open (Rd 2)	Turnberry
	PAUL BROADHURST	1990 Br Open (Rd 3)	St Andrews
	JODIE MUDD	1991 Br Open (Rd 4)	Royal Birkdale
	NICK FALDO	1993 Br Open (Rd 2)	Royal St George's
	PAYNE STEWART	1993 Br Open (Rd 4)	Royal St George's
	VIJAY SINGH	1993 USPGA (Rd 2)	Inverness Club
	MICHAEL BRADLEY	1995 USPGA (Rd 1)	Riviera CC
	BRAD FAXON	1995 USPGA (Rd 4)	Riviera CC
64	LLOYD MANGRUM	1940 Masters (Rd 1)	Augusta National
	LEE MACKEY Jr	1950 US Open (Rd 1)	Merion GC
	TOMMY JACOBS	1964 US Open (Rd 2)	Congressional CC
	BOBBY NICHOLS	1964 USPGA (Rd 1)	Columbus CC
	JACK NICKLAUS	1964 USPGA (Rd 4)	Columbus CC
	JACK NICKLAUS	1965 Masters (Rd 3)	Augusta National
	RIVES McBEE	1966 US Open (Rd 2)	Olympic Club
	DON BIES	1969 USPGA (Rd 2)	NCR CC
	MILLER BARBER	1969 USPGA (Rd 3)	NCR CC
	MAURICE BEMBRIDGE	1974 Masters (Rd 4)	Augusta National
	GARY PLAYER	1974 USPGA (Rd 2)	Tanglewood GC
	HALE IRWIN	1975 Masters (Rd 4)	Augusta National
	GARY PLAYER	1978 Masters (Rd 4)	Augusta National
	MILLER BARBER	1979 Masters (Rd 2)	Augusta National
	HORACIO CARBONETTI	1980 Br Open (Rd 2)	Muirfield
	HUBERT GREEN	1980 Br Open (Rd 3)	Muirfield
	TOM WATSON	1980 Br Open (Rd 3)	Muirfield
	BEN CRENSHAW	1981 US Open (Rd 3)	Merion GC
	CRAIG STADLER	1983 Br Open (Rd 1)	Royal Birkdale
	GRAHAM MARSH	1983 Br Open (Rd 4)	Royal Birkdale
	HAL SUTTON	1984 USPGA (Rd 3)	Shoal Creek CC
	CHRISTY O'CONNOR Jr	1985 Br Open (Rd 1)	Royal St George's
	DOUG TEWELL	1985 USPGA (Rd1)	Cherry Hills CC
	SEVE BALLESTEROS	1986 Br Open (Rd 4)	Turnberry
	BOB TWAY	1986 USPGA (Rd 3)	Inverness Club
	KEITH CLEARWATER	1987 US Open (Rd 3)	The Olympic Club
	RODGER DAVIS	1987 Br Open (Rd 1)	Muirfield
	GREG NORMAN	1988 Masters (Rd 4)	Augusta National

Player	Tournament	Course
64 contd		
PETER JACOBSEN	1988 US Open (Rd 4)	The Country Club
DAVE RUMMELLS	1988 USPGA (Rd 2)	Oak Tree GC
CURTIS STRANGE	1989 US Open (Rd 2)	Oak Hill CC
GREG NORMAN	1989 Br Open (Rd 4)	Royal Troon
CRAIG STADLER	1989 USPGA (Rd 2)	Kemper Lakes GC
MIKE DONALD	1990 Masters (Rd 1)	Augusta National
IAN BAKER-FINCH	1990 Br Open (Rd 3)	St Andrews
IAN BAKER-FINCH	1991 Br Open (Rd 3)	Royal Birkdale
FRED COUPLES	1991 Br Open (Rd 4)	Royal Birkdale
STEVE PATE	1992 Br Open (Rd 1)	Muirfield
RAY FLOYD	1992 Br Open (Rd 1)	Muirfield
NICK FALDO	1992 Br Open (Rd 2)	Muirfield
WAYNE GRADY	1993 Br Open (Rd 3)	Royal St George's
GREG NORMAN	1993 Br Open (Rd 4)	Royal St George's
SCOTT SIMPSON	1993 USPGA (Rd 1)	Inverness Club
LOREN ROBERTS	1994 US Open (Rd 3)	Oakmont CC
MARK BROOKS	1994 Br Open (Rd 2)	Turnberry
LARRY MIZE	1994 Br Open (Rd 3)	Turnberry
FUZZY ZOELLER	1994 Br Open (Rd 3)	Turnberry
NICK FALDO	1994 Br Open (Rd 4)	Turnberry
ANDERS FORSBRAND	1994 Br Open (Rd 4)	Turnberry
BLAINE McCALLISTER	1994 USPGA (Rd 2)	Southern Hills CC
JAY HAAS	1995 Masters (Rd 2)	Augusta National
MARK O'MEARA	1995 USPGA (Rd 1)	Riviera CC
JIM GALLAGHER jr	1995 USPGA (Rd 1)	Riviera CC
STEVE STRICKER	1995 USPGA (Rd 2)	Riviera CC
JAY HAAS	1995 USPGA (Rd 3)	Riviera CC
STEVE ELKINGTON	1995 USPGA (Rd 4)	Riviera CC

Best of British

In 1974, England's Maurice Bembridge equalled, what was then, the course record at Augusta National, by shooting an eight-under-par 64. It remains the best single round score ever recorded by a British player in an American major championship. Bembridge covered the back nine in just 30 strokes and he completed his round by holing a birdie putt of over 25 feet on the 18th.

Jack's lost opportunity

During his glorious career, Jack Nicklaus rarely missed a chance to make history. Yet in the first round of the 1980 US Open at Baltusrol, he missed a three-foot birdie putt on the final green, which would have earned him a tournament record 62. However, Nicklaus tapped in for a 63 to tie Miller's record, going on to win the tournament.

From obscurity to Fame and back again

At the 1980 British Open at Muirfield, Horacio Carbonetti of Argentina made headline news when he fired a seven-under-par 64 in the second round, which, for a day at least, was the second lowest round in the tournament's history. The 64 was 14 strokes better than his first round 78, and after 36 holes he was tied for 18th. However, Carbonetti was still unable to make the 54-hole cut. His third round 78 gave him a three round total of 220, one stroke too many.

Could have been even better

When Greg Norman arrived at the 18th green in the second round of the 1986 British Open at Turnberry, he faced a 30 foot putt for a 61, and a chance to post the lowest ever single-round score in a major championship. But in typical Norman attacking style, he charged his first putt about six feet past the hole. However, he still had a great opportunity to card a 62 but also missed the return. Those three putts meant a round of 63 and only a share of the record. Yet disappointment was brief, two days later Norman lifted his first major title, winning by five strokes.

CHRONOLOGICAL IMPROVEMENT

BRITISH OPEN

Score	Player	Year	Course
91	3 players*	1873 (Rd 1)	St Andrews
88	Tom Kidd	1873 (Rd 2)	St Andrews
75	Mungo Park	1874 (Rd 1)	Musselburgh
74	Mr Horace Hutchinson	1892 (Rd 1)	Muirfield
72	Mr Harold Hilton**	1892 (Rd 3)	Muirfield
71	James Sherlock	1904 (Rd 2)	Royal St George's (Sandwich)
69	James Braid	1904 (Rd 3)	Royal St George's (Sandwich)
68	JH Taylor	1904 (Rd 4)	Royal St George's (Sandwich)
67	Walter Hagen	1929 (Rd 2)	Muirfield
65	Henry Cotton	1934 (Rd 2)	Royal St George's (Sandwich)
63	Mark Hayes ***	1977 (Rd 2)	Turnberry

* - Tom Kidd, Jamie Anderson and Bob Kirk
** - Hugh Kirkaldy shot 73 in the same round that Hilton lowered the tournament record by two strokes.
*** - Hayes needed a par four at the 431-yard, 18th hole, for a 62 - which would have been the lowest score ever recorded in a major championship, either side of the Atlantic. But after putting his tee shot (4 wood) into a fairway bunker, he still required a single-putt green for a five.

Note: The first 12 Opens were staged at Prestwick, which was a 12-hole course. It wasn't until 1873 at St Andrews that the tournament was first played over an 18-hole course.

UNITED STATES OPEN

Score	Player	Year	Course
76	Joe Lloyd	1896 (Rd 1)	Shinnecock Hills
74	James Foulis	1896 (Rd 2)	Shinnecock Hills
73	Gilbert Nicholls	1902 (Rd 3)	The Garden City GC
72	Willie Anderson/Alex Campbell	1904 (Rd 4)	Glen View Club
68	Dave Hunter *	1909 (Rd 1)	Englewood GC
67	Willie MacFarlane	1925 (Rd 2)	Worcester CC
66	Gene Sarazen	1932 (Rd 4)	Fresh Meadow CC
65	Mr James McHale	1947 (Rd 3)	St Louis CC
64	Lee Mackey Jr **	1950 (Rd 1)	Merion GC
63	Johnny Miller ***	1973 (Rd 4)	Oakmont CC

* - Andrew Campbell also beat the existing record for the championship in round one. He shot a 71. After his 68, Hunter needed 16 more shots in the second round and eventually wound up in a tie for 30th place with a four round total of 313.
** - Mackey followed his record-breaking 64 with an 81 in round two. He finished in a tie for 25th, 10 shots out of a play-off.
*** - Miller's final round 63, to win the 1973 US Open by one stroke, is still considered to be the finest major championship round in history. Oakmont, not a course usually associated with low scores, was taken apart by the 26-year-old Californian who started the final round with four straight birdies. He made nine birdies in all and his only bogey of the day came at the eighth hole which he three-putted. Miller began the final round six strokes off the pace. He hit all 18 greens in regulation thanks to a superb display of precision iron play. He took 29 putts in all and his putt for yet another birdie on 18 hit the hole and spun out.

Note: The first US Open in 1895 was played over a 9-hole course (Newport GC, Rhode Island)

UNITED STATES MASTERS

Score	Player	Year
70	3 players *	1934 (Rd 1)
69	Ed Dudley	1934 (Rd 2)
67	Henry Picard	1935 (Rd 1)
66	Byron Nelson	1937 (Rd 1)
64	Lloyd Mangrum	1940 (Rd 1)
63	Nick Price	1986 (Rd 3)

* - Horton Smith, Emmett French and Jimmy Hines had the honour of setting the pace in the first round of the first ever US Masters at Augusta in 1934. For that year only, what is now known as the front nine was played as the back nine and of course vice-versa.

USPGA CHAMPIONSHIP

Score	Player	Year	Course
67	Dow Finsterwald	1958 (Rd 1)	Llanerch CC
66	Walter Burkemo	1958 (Rd 3)	Llanerch CC
65	Jerry Barber	1959 (Rd 2)	Minneapolis GC
64	Bobby Nichols	1964 (Rd 1)	Columbus CC
63	Bruce Crampton	1975 (Rd 2)	Firestone CC (South)

Note: The USPGA Championship only became a strokeplay event in 1958.

LOWEST TOTALS IN MAJOR CHAMPIONSHIPS

ALL TIME BEST IN MAJORS (72 Holes)

Score	Player	Tournament	Course
267	GREG NORMAN	1993 Br Open	Royal St George's
	STEVE ELKINGTON	1995 USPGA	Riviera CC
	COLIN MONTGOMERIE	1995 USPGA	Riviera CC
268	TOM WATSON	1977 Br Open	Turnberry
	NICK PRICE	1994 Br Open	Turnberry
269	JACK NICKLAUS	1977 Br Open	Turnberry
	NICK FALDO	1993 Br Open	Royal St George's
	JESPER PARNEVIK	1994 Br Open	Turnberry
	NICK PRICE	1994 USPGA	Southern Hills CC
	JEFF MAGGERT	1995 USPGA	Riviera CC
	ERNIE ELS	1995 USPGA	Riviera CC
270	NICK FALDO	1990 Br Open	St Andrews
	BERNHARD LANGER	1993 Br Open	Royal St George's
271	BOBBY NICHOLS	1964 USPGA	Columbus CC
	JACK NICKLAUS	1965 Masters	Augusta National
	RAY FLOYD	1976 Masters	Augusta National
	TOM WATSON	1980 Br Open	Muirfield
	FUZZY ZOELLER	1994 Br Open	Turnberry
	BRAD FAXON	1995 USPGA	Riviera CC

272	DAVID GRAHAM	1979 USPGA	Oakland Hills CC
	BEN CRENSHAW	1979 USPGA	Oakland Hills CC
	JACK NICKLAUS	1980 US Open	Baltusrol GC
	RAY FLOYD	1982 USPGA	Southern Hills CC
	JEFF SLUMAN	1988 USPGA	Oak Tree GC
	IAN BAKER-FINCH	1991 Br Open	Royal Birkdale
	NICK FALDO	1992 Br Open	Muirfield
	LEE JANZEN	1993 US Open	Baltusrol GC
	PETER SENIOR	1993 Br Open	Royal St George's
	COREY PAVIN	1993 Br Open	Royal St George's
	PAUL AZINGER	1993 USPGA	Inverness Club
	GREG NORMAN	1993 USPGA	Inverness Club

EVOLUTION OF 72-HOLE SCORING RECORD

BRITISH OPEN

Score	Player	Year	Course
305	Mr Harold Hilton	1892	Muirfield
300	Harry Vardon	1903	Prestwick
296	Jack White*	1904	Royal St George's (Sandwich)
291	James Braid	1908	Prestwick
285	Mr Bobby Jones	1927	St Andrews
283	Gene Sarazen	1932	Prince's (Sandwich)
279	Bobby Locke **	1950	Troon
278	Peter Thomson/Dave Thomas	1958	Royal Lytham and St Anne's
276	Arnold Palmer	1962	Troon
268	Tom Watson ***	1977	Turnberry
267	Greg Norman	1993	Royal St George's

* - JH Taylor and James Braid (both 297) also broke the existing record in 1904. They tied for second.
** - The 1932 record was also bettered by Roberto de Vicenzo (281), Fred Daly (282) and Dai Rees (282
*** - Runner-up Jack Nicklaus (269) also smashed Palmer's 15-year record.
Note: It wasn't until 1892 that the British Open was first staged over 72 holes.

UNITED STATES OPEN

Score	Player	Year	Course
328	Fred Herd	1898	Myopia Hunt Club
315	Willie Smith	1899*	Baltimore CC
313	Harry Vardon	1900	Chicago GC
307	Laurie Auchterlonie	1902	The Garden City GC
303	Willie Anderson	1904	Glen View Club
295	Alex Smith	1906**	Onwentsia Club
290	George Sargent	1909***	Englewood GC
286	Mr Charles Evans Jr	1916****	Minikahda GC
282	Tony Manero	1936*****	Baltusrol GC
281	Ralph Guldahl	1937	Oakland Hills CC
276	Ben Hogan	1948******	Riviera CC
275	Jack Nicklaus	1967	Baltusrol GC
272	Jack Nicklaus	1980*******	Baltusrol GC

* - In 1899, four other players beat the previous lowest total set by Fred Herd one year earlier.
** - Alex Smith's brother Willie also broke the existing record in finishing second (302).
*** - Tom McNamara also bettered the previous best, shooting 294.
**** - The existing record was also broken by runner-up Jock Hutchison (288).
***** - As well as champion Tony Manero, Harry Cooper (284) was inside the existing record.
****** - In 1948 Jimmy Demaret (278) and Jim Turnesa (280) also bettered Ralph Guldahl's 281.
******* - Isao Aoki, who finished second to Nicklaus in 1980, carded a 72-hole total of 274.

Note: The first three tournaments (1895-97) were contested over 36 holes.

UNITED STATES MASTERS

Score	Player	Year
284	Horton Smith	1934
282	Craig Wood/Gene Sarazen	1935
279	Ralph Guldahl	1939 *
274	Ben Hogan	1953
271	Jack Nicklaus	1965

* - The previous lowest total was also beaten by runner-up Sam Snead (280).

USPGA CHAMPIONSHIP

Score	Player	Year	Course
276	Dow Finsterwald	1958	Llanerch CC
271	Bobby Nichols	1964 *	Columbus CC
269	Nick Price	1994	Southern Hills CC
267	Steve Elkington/Colin Montgomerie	1995	Riviera CC

* - Joint runners-up Jack Nicklaus and Arnold Palmer also beat the record with 72 hole totals of 274.

Note: The USPGA Championship only became a strokeplay event in 1958.

FOUR ROUNDS in the 60s

The following have all scored four sub-70 rounds in the same major championship:

Player	Rounds	Total	(Pos.)	Tournament	Venue
Arnold Palmer	68-68-69-69	274	T2	1964 USPGA	Columbus CC
Lee Trevino	69-68-69-69	275	Won	1968 US Open	Oak Hill CC
Ben Crenshaw	69-67-69-67	272	2	1979 USPGA	Oakland Hills CC
Lee Trevino	69-68-67-69	273	Won	1984 USPGA	Shoal Creek CC
Lee Janzen	67-67-69-69	272	Won	1993 US Open	Baltusrol GC
Ernie Els	68-69-69-68	274	T6	1993 Br Open	Royal St George's
Greg Norman	66-68-69-64	267	Won	1993 Br Open	Royal St George's
Nick Faldo	68-68-69-68	273	3	1993 USPGA	Inverness Club
Paul Azinger	69-66-69-68	272	Won	1993 USPGA	Inverness Club
Greg Norman	68-68-67-69	272	2	1993 USPGA	Inverness Club
Jesper Parnevik	68-66-68-67	269	2	1994 Br Open	Turnberry
Nick Price	69-66-67-66	268	Won	1994 Br Open	Turnberry

Player	Rounds	Total	(Pos.)	Tournament		Venue
Steve Lowery	69-68-68-69	274	T8	1995	USPGA	Riviera CC
Bob Estes	69-68-68-68	273	T6	1995	USPGA	Riviera CC
Steve Elkington	68-67-68-64	267	Won	1995	USPGA	Riviera CC
Colin Montgomerie	68-67-67-65	267	2	1995	USPGA	Riviera CC
Jeff Maggert	66-69-65-69	269	T3	1995	USPGA	Riviera CC

Note: No player has achieved this feat in the US Masters at Augusta National. But the table below lists those who have come closest to doing so.

Player	Rounds	Total	(Pos.)	Year
Ben Hogan	70-69-66-69	274	Won	1953
Arnold Palmer	69-68-69-70	276	Won	1964
Fred Couples	69-67-69-70	275	Won	1992
Ben Crenshaw	70-67-69-68	274	Won	1995

WIDEST MARGINS OF VICTORY

CHAMPIONSHIP WINS BY FIVE OR MORE STROKES

Margin	Player	Venue	Year
13 shots:	Tom Morris Snr	Prestwick	(1862 Br Open)
12 shots:	Tom Morris Jnr	Prestwick	(1870 Br Open)
11 shots:	Willie Smith	Baltimore CC	(1899 US Open)
9 shots:	Jim Barnes	Columbia CC	(1921 US Open)
	Jack Nicklaus	Augusta National	(1965 Masters)
8 shots:	JH Taylor	St Andrews	(1900 Br Open)
	James Braid	Prestwick	(1908 Br Open)
	JH Taylor	Royal Liverpool	(1913 Br Open)
	Ray Floyd	Augusta National	(1976 Masters)
7 shots:	Fred Herd	Myopia Hunt Club	(1898 US Open)
	Alex Smith	Onwentsia Club	(1906 US Open)
	Cary Middlecoff	Augusta National	(1955 Masters)
	Tony Jacklin	Hazeltine National GC	(1970 US Open)
	Jack Nicklaus	Oak Hill CC	(1980 USPGA)
6 shots:	Laurie Auchterlonie	The Garden City GC	(1902 US Open)
	Harry Vardon	Prestwick	(1903 Br Open)
	JH Taylor	Royal Cinque Ports	(1909 Br Open)
	Mr Bobby Jones	St Andrews	(1927 Br Open)
	Walter Hagen	Muirfield	(1929 Br Open)
	Ralph Guldahl	Cherry Hills CC	(1938 US Open)
	Ben Hogan	Oakmont CC	(1953 US Open)
	Arnold Palmer	Troon	(1962 Br Open)

6 shots contd	Player	Venue	Year
	Arnold Palmer	Augusta National	(1964 Masters)
	Johnny Miller	Royal Birkdale	(1976 Br Open)
	Nick Price	Southern HillS CC	(1994 USPGA)
5 shots:	Bob Ferguson	Musselburgh	(1880 Br Open)
	JH Taylor	Royal St George's	(1894 Br Open)
	Harry Vardon	Royal St George's	(1899 Br Open)
	Willie Anderson	Glen View Club	(1904 US Open)
	James Braid	St Andrews	(1905 Br Open)
	Gene Sarazen	Prince's	(1932 Br Open)
	Henry Cotton	Royal St George's	(1934 Br Open)
	Claude Harmon	Augusta National	(1948 Masters)
	Henry Cotton	Muirfield	(1948 Br Open)
	Ben Hogan	Augusta National	(1953 Masters)
	Tony Lema	St Andrews	(1964 Br Open)
	Greg Norman	Turnberry	(1986 Br Open)
	Nick Faldo	St Andrews	(1990 Br Open)

BEST MARGINS SINCE 1945

9 shots:	Jack Nicklaus	Augusta National	(1965 Masters)
8 shots:	Ray Floyd	Augusta National	(1976 Masters)
7 shots:	Cary Middlecoff	Augusta National	(1955 Masters)
	Tony Jacklin	Hazeltine National GC	(1970 US Open)
	Jack Nicklaus	Oak Hill CC	(1980 USPGA)
6 shots:	Ben Hogan	Oakmont CC	(1953 US Open)
	Arnold Palmer	Troon	(1962 Br Open)
	Arnold Palmer	Augusta National	(1964 Masters)
	Johnny Miller	Royal Birkdale	(1976 Br Open)
	Nick Price	Southern Hills CC	(1994 USPGA)
5 shots:	Claude Harmon	Augusta National	(1948 Masters)
	Henry Cotton	Muirfield	(1948 Br Open)
	Ben Hogan	Augusta National	(1953 Masters)
	Tony Lema	St Andrews	(1964 Br Open)
	Greg Norman	Turnberry	(1986 Br Open)
	Nick Faldo	St Andrews	(1990 Br Open)
4 shots:	Sam Snead	St Andrews	(1946 Br Open)
	Sam Snead	Augusta National	(1952 Masters)
	Julius Boros	Northwood Club	(1952 US Open)
	Ben Hogan	Carnoustie	(1953 Br Open)
	Tommy Bolt	Southern Hills CC	(1958 US Open)
	Ken Venturi	Congressional CC	(1964 US Open)
	Al Geiberger	Firestone CC	(1966 USPGA)
	Jack Nicklaus	Baltusrol GC	(1967 US Open)
	Lee Trevino	Oak Hill CC	(1968 US Open)

4 shots contd	Player	Venue	Year
	Jack Nicklaus	Canterbury GC	(1973 USPGA)
	Gary Player	Royal Lytham	(1974 Br Open)
	Seve Ballesteros	Augusta National	(1980 Masters)
	Tom Watson	Muirfield	(1980 Br Open)
	Bill Rogers	Royal St George's	(1981 Br Open)
	Larry Nelson	Atlanta Athletic Club	(1981 USPGA)
	Seve Ballesteros	Augusta National	(1983 Masters)
	Lee Trevino	Shoal Creek CC	(1984 USPGA)
	Bernhard Langer	Augusta National	(1993 Masters)

MOST RUNNER-UP FINISHES

The following table lists all players who have finished second or have tied for second on four or more occasions:

	Times	Period	(Major titles)
Jack Nicklaus	19	(1960-83)	(18)
Arnold Palmer	10	(1960-70)	(7)
Sam Snead	8	(1937-57)	(7)
Greg Norman	7	(1984-95)	(2)
JH Taylor	7	(1896-1914)	(5)
Tom Watson	7	(1978-87)	(8)
Ben Hogan	6	(1942-56)	(9)
Byron Nelson	6	(1939-47)	(5)
Gary Player	6	(1958-84)	(9)
Harry Vardon	6	(1900-20)	(7)
Ben Crenshaw	5	(1976-83)	(2)
Ray Floyd	5	(1976-92)	(4)
Tom Weiskopf	5	(1969-76)	(1)
Craig Wood	5	(1933-39)	(2)
James Braid	4	(1897-1909)	(5)
Billy Casper	4	(1958-71)	(3)
Harry Cooper	4	(1927-38)	(-)
Bruce Crampton	4	(1972-75)	(-)
Willie Fernie	4	(1882-91)	(1)
Alex Herd	4	(1892-1920)	(1)
Bobby Jones	4	(1922-28)	(7)
Cary Middlecoff	4	(1948-59)	(3)
Johnny Miller	4	(1971-81)	(2)
Willie Park	4	(1861-67)	(4)
Doug Sanders	4	(1959-70)	(-)
Gene Sarazen	4	(1928-40)	(7)
Macdonald Smith	4	(1910-32)	(-)
Lanny Wadkins	4	(1982-87)	(1)

The table below lists those players who have finished second or have tied for second most times but have never won a major title:

	Times	Period
Harry Cooper	4	(1927-38)
Bruce Crampton	4	(1972-75)
Doug Sanders	4	(1959-70)
Macdonald Smith	4	(1910-32)
Andy Bean	3	(1980-89)
Chip Beck	3	(1986-93)
Johnny Bulla	3	(1939-49)
Andrew Kirkaldy	3	(1879-91)
Tom McNamara	3	(1909-15)
Ed Oliver	3	(1946-53)
Dai Rees	3	(1953-61)
Mr Frank Stranahan	3	(1947-53)
David Strath	3	(1870-76)

MOST TOP-3 FINISHES

The following table lists all players who have had nine or more top-three finishes in major championships:

	Times	Period (Major titles)	
Jack Nicklaus	46	(1960-86)	(18)
Sam Snead	22	(1937-74)	(7)
Arnold Palmer	19	(1958-72)	(7)
Gary Player	18	(1958-84)	(9)
Ben Hogan	17	(1941-56)	(9)
Gene Sarazen	17	(1922-40)	(7)
Tom Watson	17	(1975-91)	(8)
Walter Hagen	16	(1914-35)	(11)
Harry Vardon	15	(1896-1920)	(7)
JH Taylor	13	(1894-1914)	(5)
Byron Nelson	12	(1937-47)	(5)
James Braid	11	(1897-1912)	(5)
Ben Crenshaw	11	(1975-95)	(2)
Nick Faldo	11	(1987-93)	(5)
Mr Bobby Jones	11	(1922-30)	(7)
Greg Norman	11	(1984-95)	(2)
Seve Ballesteros	10	(1976-88)	(5)
Ray Floyd	10	(1969-92)	(4)
Willie Park	10	(1860-76)	(4)
Leo Diegel	9	(1920-33)	(2)
Peter Thomson	9	(1952-69)	(5)
Lee Trevino	9	(1968-85)	(6)
Roberto De Vicenzo	9	(1948-69)	(1)
Lanny Wadkins	9	(1973-93)	(1)
Tom Weiskopf	9	(1969-77)	(1)

Note: 'Times' include '(Major Titles)'.

The table below lists those players who have had most top-three finishes without ever winning a major title:

	Times	Period
Harry Cooper	6	(1927-38)
Andrew Kirkaldy	6	(1879-99)
Doug Sanders	6	(1959-70)
Macdonald Smith	6	(1910-32)
Bruce Crampton	5	(1963-75)
Andy Bean	4	(1980-89)
Johnny Bulla	4	(1939-49)
Robert Cruickshank	4	(1923-37)
Tom McNamara	4	(1909-19)
Gil Morgan	4	(1980-90)
Ed Oliver	4	(1946-53)
Dai Rees	4	(1950-61)
Bert Yancey	4	(1967-74)

PLAY-OFFS

The table below, shows the win-loss record of all players who have contested two or more play-offs in major championships. This also includes USPGA Championship finals (matchplay years 1916-57) that went into sudden death.

	Play-offs		
	Won	Lost	(Period)
Jack Nicklaus	3	1	(1962-71)
Byron Nelson	2	3	(1939-46)
Bobby Jones	2	2	(1923-29)
Nick Faldo	2	1	(1988-90)
Gene Sarazen	2	1	(1923-40)
Densmore Shute	2	1	(1933-39)
Harry Vardon	2	1	(1896-1913)
Willie Anderson	2	0	(1901-03)
Billy Casper	2	0	(1966-70)
Fuzzy Zoeller	2	0	(1979-84)
Ben Hogan	1	3	(1942-55)
Arnold Palmer	1	3	(1962-66)
Tom Watson	1	2	(1975-79)
Victor Ghezzi	1	1	(1941-46)
Walter Hagen	1	1	(1919-23)
Don January	1	1	(1961-67)
John Mahaffey	1	1	(1975-78)
Lloyd Mangrum	1	1	(1946-50)
John J McDermott	1	1	(1910-11)
Gary Player	1	1	(1962-65)
Alex Smith	1	1	(1901-10)
Sam Snead	1	1	(1947-54)
Lanny Wadkins	1	1	(1977-87)
Mike J Brady	0	2	(1911-19)
Gene Littler	0	2	(1970-77)
Colin Montgomerie	0	2	(1994-95)
Greg Norman	0	4	(1984-93)
Craig Wood	0	4	(1933-39)

MAJOR CHAMPIONSHIP TOP TENS

FOUR TOP TENS IN THE SAME CALENDAR YEAR

Since the USPGA Championship became a 72-hole strokeplay tournament in 1958, the following golfers have had top-10 finishes in all four majors in the same calendar year:

YEAR	PLAYER	US MASTERS	US OPEN	BRITISH OPEN	USPGA
1960	Arnold Palmer	Won	Won	2	T7
1963	Gary Player	T5	T8	T7	T8
1966	Arnold Palmer	T4	2	T8	T6
1966	Doug Sanders	T4	T8	T2	T6
1969	Miller Barber	7	T6	10	T5
1971	Jack Nicklaus	T2	2	T5	Won
1973	Jack Nicklaus	T3	T4	4	Won
1974	Gary Player	Won	T8	Won	7
1974	Jack Nicklaus	T4	T10	3	2
1975	Jack Nicklaus	Won	T7	T3	Won
1975	Tom Watson	T8	T9	Won	9
1975	Hale Irwin	T4	T3	9	T5
1977	Tom Watson	Won	T7	Won	T6
1977	Jack Nicklaus	2	T10	2	3
1982	Tom Watson	T5	Won	Won	T9
1987	Ben Crenshaw	T4	T4	T4	T7

MOST TOP TENS IN MAJOR CHAMPIONSHIPS

The table below lists those golfers with most top 10 finishes in major championships:

PLAYER	MASTERS	US OPEN	BRITISH OPEN	USPGA	TOTAL	(Titles)
Jack Nicklaus	21	18	18	15	72	(18)
Sam Snead	15	12	2	17	46	(7)
Gary Player	15	9	12	8	44	(9)
Tom Watson	14	11	8	9	42	(8)
Ben Hogan	17	15	1	6	39	(9)
Arnold Palmer	12	13	7	6	38	(7)
Gene Sarazen	4	14	6	12	36	(7)
Walter Hagen	-	16	7	9	32	(11)
Ray Floyd	11	5	4	8	28	(4)
Byron Nelson	14	4	1	9	28	(5)

For the USPGA Championship, during its matchplay years between 1916 and 1957, top 10 finishes are credited to those golfers who reached the quarter-final stage.

EUROPE in the STATES

The following European players have all enjoyed top-10 finishes in American major championships since World War Two (1945-to date):

SEVE BALLESTEROS

Tournament	Scores	Total	Position	Margin
1980 Masters	66-69-68-72	275	Won	(+4)
1982 Masters	73-73-68-71	285	T3	(-1)
1983 Masters	68-70-73-69	280	Won	(+4)
1983 US Open	69-74-69-74	286	T4	(-6)
1984 USPGA	70-69-70-70	279	5	(-6)
1985 Masters	72-71-71-70	284	T2	(-2)
1985 US Open	71-70-69-71	281	T5	(-2)
1986 Masters	71-68-72-70	281	4	(-2)
1987 Masters *	73-71-70-71	285	T2	(-)
1987 US Open	68-75-68-71	282	3	(-5)
1987 USPGA	72-70-72-78	292	T10	(-5)
1989 Masters	71-72-73-69	285	5	(-2)
1990 Masters	74-73-68-71	286	T7	(-8)

MAURICE BEMBRIDGE

Tournament	Scores	Total	Position	Margin
1974 Masters	73-74-72-64	283	T9	(-5)

NICK FALDO

Tournament	Scores	Total	Position	Margin
1988 US Open *	72-67-68-71	278	2	(-)
1988 USPGA	67-71-70-71	279	T4	(-7)
1989 Masters *	68-73-77-65	283	Won	(-)
1989 USPGA	70-73-69-69	281	T9	(-5)
1990 Masters *	71-72-66-69	278	Won	(-)
1990 US Open	72-72-68-69	281	T3	(-1)
1992 US Open	70-76-68-77	291	T4	(-6)
1992 USPGA	68-70-76-67	281	T2	(-3)
1993 USPGA	68-68-69-68	273	3	(-1)
1994 USPGA	73-67-71-66	277	T4	(-8)

DAVID FEHERTY

Tournament	Scores	Total	Position	Margin
1991 USPGA	71-74-71-68	284	T7	(-8)

ANDERS FORSBRAND

Tournament	Scores	Total	Position	Margin
1992 USPGA	73-71-70-70	284	T9	(-6)

TONY JACKLIN

Tournament	Scores	Total	Position	Margin
1970 US Open	71-70-70-70	281	Won	(+7)

BERNHARD LANGER

Tournament	Scores	Total	Position	Margin
1985 Masters	72-74-68-68	282	Won	(+2)
1986 US Open	74-70-70-70	284	T8	(-5)

Ian Woosnam (left) succeeds Nick Faldo as Masters champion in 1991. Europeans have enjoyed considerable success at Augusta

1987 Masters	71-72-70-76	289	T7	(-4)
1987 US Open	69-69-73-72	283	T4	(-6)
1988 Masters	71-72-71-73	287	T9	(-6)
1990 Masters	70-73-69-74	286	T7	(-8)
1993 Masters	68-70-69-70	277	Won	(+4)

SANDY LYLE

Tournament	Scores	Total	Position	Margin
1988 Masters	71-67-72-71	281	Won	(+1)

COLIN MONTGOMERIE

Tournament	Scores	Total	Position	Margin
1992 US Open	70-71-77-70	288	3	(-3)
1994 US Open*	71-65-73-70	279	T2	(-)
1995 USPGA *	68-67-67-65	267	2	(-)

JOSE-MARIA OLAZABAL

Tournament	Scores	Total	Position	Margin
1989 Masters	77-73-70-68	288	T8	(-5)
1989 US Open	69-72-70-72	283	T9	(-5)
1990 US Open	73-69-69-73	284	T8	(-4)
1991 Masters	68-71-69-70	278	2	(-1)
1991 US Open	73-71-75-70	289	T8	(-7)
1993 Masters	70-72-74-68	284	T7	(-7)
1994 Masters	74-67-69-69	279	Won	(+2)
1994 USPGA	72-66-70-70	278	T7	(-9)

PETER OOSTERHUIS

Tournament	Scores	Total	Position	Margin
1973 Masters	73-70-68-74	285	T3	(-2)
1975 US Open	69-73-72-75	289	T7	(-2)
1977 US Open	71-70-74-70	285	T10	(-7)

STEVE RICHARDSON

Tournament	Scores	Total	Position	Margin
1991 USPGA	70-72-72-69	283	T5	(-7)

RAMON SOTA

Tournament	Scores	Total	Position	Margin
1965 Masters	71-73-70-72	286	T6	(-15)

IAN WOOSNAM

Tournament	Scores	Total	Position	Margin
1989 US Open	70-68-73-68	279	T2	(-1)
1989 USPGA	68-70-70-71	279	6	(-3)
1991 Masters	72-66-67-72	277	Won	(+1)
1992 US Open	72-72-69-79	292	T6	(-7)
1994 USPGA	68-72-73-66	279	T9	(-10)

* - Contested Play-Off

Sandy Lyle showed British golfers the way with his Masters win in 1988. Larry Mize (left) does the honours with the Green Jacket

MAJOR CHAMPIONSHIP PLAY-OFFS

A COMPLETE CHRONOLOGICAL LIST

Year	Event	Format	Winner	Loser(s)
1876	Br Open	Uncontested*	Bob Martin	David Strath
1883	Br Open	36 Holes	Willie Fernie (158)	Bob Ferguson (159)
1889	Br Open	36 Holes	Willie Park Jr (158)	Andrew Kirkaldy (163)
1896	Br Open	36 Holes	Harry Vardon (157)	JH Taylor (161)
1901	US Open	18 Holes	Willie Anderson (85)	Alex Smith (86)
1903	US Open	18 Holes	Willie Anderson (82)	David Brown (84)
1908	US Open	18 Holes	Fred McLeod (77)	Willie Smith (83)
1910	US Open	18 Holes	Alex Smith (71)	John J McDermott (75)/ Macdonald Smith (77)
1911	US Open	18 Holes	John J McDermott (80)	Mike J Brady (82)/ George O Simpson (85)
1911	Br Open	36 Holes**	Harry Vardon	Arnaud Massy
1913	US Open	18 Holes	Mr Francis Ouimet (72)	Harry Vardon (77)/ Ted Ray (78)
1919	US Open	18 Holes	Walter Hagen (77)	Mike J Brady (78)
1921	Br Open	36 Holes	Jock Hutchison (150)	Mr RH Wethered (159)
1923	US Open	18 Holes	Mr Bobby Jones (76)	Robert Cruickshank (78)
1925	US Open	18 Holes***	Willie MacFarlane (75, 72)	Mr Bobby Jones (75, 73)
1927	US Open	18 Holes	Tommy Armour (76)	Harry Cooper (79)
1928	US Open	36 Holes	Johnny Farrell (143)	Mr Bobby Jones (144)
1929	US Open	36 Holes	Mr Bobby Jones (141)	Al Espinosa (164)
1931	US Open	36 Holes****	Billy Burke (149-148)	George Von Elm (149-149)
1933	Br Open	36 Holes	Densmore Shute (149)	Craig Wood (154)
1935	Masters	36 Holes	Gene Sarazen (144)	Craig Wood (149)
1939	US Open	18 Holes***	Byron Nelson (68, 70)	Craig Wood (68, 73)/ Densmore Shute (76)
1940	US Open	18 Holes	Lawson Little (70)	Gene Sarazen (73)
1942	Masters	18 Holes	Byron Nelson (69)	Ben Hogan (70)
1946	US Open	18 Holes***	Lloyd Mangrum (72, 72)	Byron Nelson (72, 73)/ Victor Ghezzi (72, 73)
1947	US Open	18 Holes	Lew Worsham (69)	Sam Snead (70)
1949	Br Open	36 Holes	Bobby Locke (135)	Harry Bradshaw (147)
1950	US Open	18 Holes	Ben Hogan (69)	Lloyd Mangrum (73)/ George Fazio (75)
1954	Masters	18 Holes	Sam Snead (70)	Ben Hogan (71)
1955	US Open	18 Holes	Jack Fleck (69)	Ben Hogan (72)
1957	US Open	18 Holes	Dick Mayer (72)	Cary Middlecoff (79)
1958	Br Open	36 Holes	Peter Thomson (139)	Dave Thomas (143)
1961	USPGA	18 Holes	Jerry Barber (67)	Don January (68)
1962	Masters	18 Holes	Arnold Palmer (68)	Gary Player (71)/ Dow Finsterwald (77)
1962	US Open	18 Holes	Jack Nicklaus (71)	Arnold Palmer (74)
1963	US Open	18 Holes	Julius Boros (70)	Jacky Cupit (73)/ Arnold Palmer (76)
1963	Br Open	36 Holes	Bob Charles (140)	Phil Rodgers (148)
1965	US Open	18 Holes	Gary Player (71)	Kel Nagle (74)

1966	Masters	18 Holes	Jack Nicklaus (70)	Tommy Jacobs (72)/
				Gay Brewer (78)
1966	US Open	18 Holes	Billy Casper (69)	Arnold Palmer (73)
1967	USPGA	18 Holes	Don January (69)	Don Massengale (71)
1970	Masters	18 Holes	Billy Casper (69)	Gene Littler (74)
1970	Br Open	18 Holes	Jack Nicklaus (72)	Doug Sanders (73)
1971	US Open	18 Holes	Lee Trevino (68)	Jack Nicklaus (71)
1975	US Open	18 Holes	Lou Graham (71)	John Mahaffey (73)
1975	Br Open	18 Holes	Tom Watson (71)	Jack Newton (72)
1977	USPGA	Sudden-Death	Lanny Wadkins (4,4,3)	Gene Littler (4,4,4)
1978	USPGA	Sudden-Death	John Mahaffey (4,3)	Jerry Pate (4,4)/
				Tom Watson (4,4)
1979	Masters	Sudden-Death	Fuzzy Zoeller (4,3)	Ed Sneed (4,4)/
				Tom Watson (4,4)
1979	USPGA	Sudden-Death	David Graham (4,4,2)	Ben Crenshaw (4,4,4)
1982	Masters	Sudden-Death	Craig Stadler (4)	Dan Pohl (5)
1984	US Open	18 Holes	Fuzzy Zoeller (67)	Greg Norman (75)
1987	Masters	Sudden-Death	Larry Mize (4,3)	Greg Norman (4,4)
				Seve Ballesteros (5)
1987	USPGA	Sudden-Death	Larry Nelson (4)	Lanny Wadkins (5)
1988	US Open	18 Holes	Curtis Strange (71)	Nick Faldo (75)
1989	Masters	Sudden-Death	Nick Faldo (5,3)	Scott Hoch (5,4)
1989	Br Open	4 Holes	Mark Calcavecchia (4,3,3,3)	Wayne Grady/(4,4,4,4)
				Greg Norman (3,3,4,p-u)
1990	Masters	Sudden-Death	Nick Faldo (4,4)	Ray Floyd (4,5)
1990	US Open	18 Holes*****	Hale Irwin (74,3)	Mike Donald (74,4)
1991	US Open	18 Holes	Payne Stewart (75)	Scott Simpson (77)
1993	USPGA	Sudden-Death	Paul Azinger (4,4)	Greg Norman (4,5)
1994	US Open	18 Holes******	Ernie Els (74,4,4)	Loren Roberts (74,4,5)/
				Colin Montgomerie (78)
1995	Br Open	4 Holes	John Daly (4,3,4,4)	Costantino Rocca (5,4,7,3)
1995	USPGA	Sudden-Death	Steve Elkington (3)	Colin Montgomerie (4)

p-u = Picked-up

* Play-off wasn't staged. Bob Martin declared winner (see Play-off 'Short Putts')

** Harry Vardon claimed the title when Arnaud Massy conceded defeat on the 35th hole of the 36-hole play-off. At that stage Vardon enjoyed a comfortable lead.

*** An additional 18-hole play-off had to be staged when the first one was tied (See Play-off 'Short Putts').

**** An additional 36-hole play-off had to be staged when the first one was tied (See Play-off 'Short Putts').

***** When 18-hole play-off ended in a tie, it then became sudden-death. Irwin won on first sudden-death hole. (See Play-off 'Short Putts').

****** 18-hole play-off finished all square. Els and Roberts needed two sudden-death holes to decide a winner (See Play-off 'Short Putts').

US PGA CHAMPIONSHIP

(Matchplay years 1916-57)

The following finals went into extra-holes.

Year	Winner	Loser	Final Score
1923	Gene Sarazen	Walter Hagen	at the 38th
1934	Paul Runyan	Craig Wood	at the 38th
1937	Densmore Shute	Harold McSpaden	at the 37th
1939	Henry Picard	Byron Nelson	at the 37th
1941	Vic Ghezzi	Byron Nelson	at the 38th

PLAY-OFF 'SHORT PUTTS'

CONTROVERSIAL BEGINNING

The 'first' British Open play-off never took place because of a controversy involving David Strath, who had tied Bob Martin for first place at St Andrews in 1876. It was alleged that Strath had played his approach shot to the Road Hole (17th) before the green in front had cleared - his ball actually struck a golfer standing on the putting surface. 'The Scotsman' newspaper reported at the time: *The player ahead insisted on a disqualification, on the grounds of a breach of the rule providing that no one shall play to a green with players on it. It was also contended that Strath's card had not been accurately kept by the marker.*

The organisers decided that the two players should play-off for the title while they sat in judgement on Strath's alleged infringements. However, Strath refused to compete until a decision had been made. Thus the trophy was awarded to Martin.

FAMILY FORTUNES

At the Philadelphia Cricket Club, Pennsylvania, in 1910, the first three-way play-off in a major championship witnessed a family duel involving Alex Smith and his brother Macdonald. Alex claimed his second US Open crown with a round of 71, six lower than Macdonald. The pair were split by John J McDermott (75).

TURNING POINT

At the tender age of 20, and in his first appearance in a US Open, Francis Ouimet rocked the 'establishment' of British golf, by beating Harry Vardon and Ted Ray in a play-off at The Country Club, Brookline, Massachusetts in 1913. After finishing birdie-par over the regulation 72 holes, Ouimet won the 18-hole play-off by five strokes. He carded a one over par 72, against Vardon's 77 and Ray's 78. Many golf historians believe that this was the moment when the United States became a powerful force in world golf. Up until then, most of the leading exponents of the game had been British, many of whom had emigrated to the States and had dominated the US Open in the early years of the tournament. Ouimet was also the first amateur to win the title and had learned the game as a youngster when he caddied at the same Brookline course.

MAJOR BREAKTHROUGH

The great Bobby Jones landed his first major title, when he won an 18-hole play-off against Robert Cruickshank for the 1923 US Open at Inwood Country Club, New York. But the 21-year-old amateur should never have had to play-off for the title. On the last hole of regulation play, Jones made a double-bogey six, to Cruickshank's birdie three.

Yet 24 hours later, Jones exacted his revenge on the hole, hitting a magnificent two-iron shot from the rough to the putting surface over 200 yards away. The ball had to carry a lagoon in front of the green. Jones made his par four, while his opponent suffered a double-bogey six. Jones won the play-off 76-78.

SUPER SARAZEN

At the 38th hole (second extra-hole), in the final of the 1923 USPGA Championship, between Gene Sarazen and Walter Hagen, Sarazen produced one of the greatest shots of all time. After hitting his drive into thick rough, close to the out-of-bounds fence, Sarazen fired his next shot to within two feet of the hole. A stunned Hagen then hit his second into a greenside bunker and although he almost holed from the sand, Sarazen cooly sank his short birdie putt to successfully defend the title.

DOUBLE PLAY-OFF

At the 1925 US Open, a second 18-hole play-off had to be contested when the first one ended in a tie between Bobby Jones and the eventual champion Willie MacFarlane. In the second bout of overtime, MacFarlane trailed Jones by four shots with just nine holes to play before recovering superbly to win by one stroke, 72-73.

EASY OVERTIME

After holing a 12-footer on the final green of the 1929 US Open, to force a play-off with Al Espinosa, Bobby Jones enjoyed an easy ride in the 36 hole play-off the following day. In the most one-sided play-off in major championship history,

Jones coasted to a 23-stroke victory with rounds of 72 and 69, to Espinosa's 84 and 80.

LONGEST TOURNAMENT

The longest major championship of all time took place at the Inverness Club, Toledo, in 1931, when two 36-hole play-offs were required to produce a winner at the US Open. The tournament went into overtime when George Von Elm made a birdie three at the 72nd hole to tie Billy Burke. Twenty-four hours later, and after 36 more holes, the pair were still tied, thanks once again to a last hole birdie by Von Elm. So, incredibly, another 36 holes were needed the following day. Once again the players were difficult to separate, though on this occasion, Burke's final round 71 was enough to earn him a one-stroke victory and the title. Play-off scores read: Burke 73-76 (149), 77-71 (148); Von Elm 75-74 (149), 76-73 (149).

SHOT OF THE CENTURY

At the 1935 US Masters, Gene Sarazen played probably the most famous golf stroke of all time, when he holed out from 220 yards with a 4-wood for an albatross two at the par five, 15th, at Augusta. The three strokes saved to par at this one hole enabled Sarazen to force a play-off with Craig Wood. The 36-hole play-off was an anti-climax, Sarazen winning by five shots 144 (71-73) to 149 (75-74).

NELSON STEALS IT

Byron Nelson won the 1939 US Open following a play-off - but only after Sam Snead had thrown away a glorious opportunity to win. Needing a par five on the final hole for the title, Snead took eight. Densmore Shute, one of three players in the play-off, could also have won the title had he finished with two pars but he dropped a stroke at the 17th. In the 18-hole play-off, Shute slumped to a seven-over-par 76 and his chances were gone. The other two contestants were Nelson and Craig Wood. Wood looked all set to win, until Nelson drew level with a birdie at the final hole. Both players were round in 68, meaning another 18 holes were needed. This time Nelson eased home by three strokes (70 to 73). Nelson's 70 included an eagle two at the fourth, holing out with a one-iron.

DISQUALIFICATION COSTS PORKY PLAY-OFF PLACE

Ed (Porky) Oliver missed out on a play-off for teeing-up too early. Oliver was one of six players disqualified at the 1940 US Open for beginning the final round before their scheduled starting time. The six had decided to make an early start because of a threatening weather forecast. Despite being told he had broken the rules, Oliver carried on playing and completed his round. His unofficial 72-hole total of 287 equalled that of play-off contestants Lawson Little and Gene Sarazen.

LIVING ON HIS NERVES

Vic Ghezzi, winner of the 1941 US PGA Championship, after playing overtime in his final with Byron Nelson, couldn't have had a harder struggle in winning a major title. Four of his six matches in that tournament either went down the final fairway of regulation play or ended up in extra holes. In the title match with Nelson, Ghezzi missed a four footer for the Championship at the 36th, before finally ending the agony by holing a slightly shorter putt at the second extra hole to win.

BYRON'S FIGHTBACK

In what was described as one of the most exciting play-offs in major championship history, Byron Nelson pipped Ben Hogan by one shot to win the 1942 US Masters. But after just four holes of their 18-hole battle, a Nelson victory looked a million miles away. A double bogey at number one, followed by a bogey at the fourth, left Nelson three shots adrift even at this early stage. Yet within four holes Nelson had turned the tables and had grabbed the lead. There had been a two-shot swing at the par-three sixth, which Nelson birdied; and at the long eighth he sank a six-footer for an eagle three, a hole Hogan could only par. So with 10 holes left to play Nelson was now one stroke

ahead. This became a three-stroke cushion with a birdie at the treacherous par three 12th where Nelson played a glorious tee shot to within three feet of the flag. Hogan had earlier bogied 10. But back came Hogan reducing the gap to one, thanks to a birdie at 14 and three putts from Nelson at 15. But Hogan then made one mistake too many - his tee shot at the par-three 16th found sand. He was unable to get up and down from the bunker in two and Nelson's lead was once again stretched to two strokes. But there was still some drama left to come at 18, where both players put their second shots into greenside bunkers. Although Hogan managed to get down in two more for par, it left Nelson two putts from around 10 feet for the title. He needed both to win the play-off 69-70.

TRIPLE TIE

In the 1946 US Open at Canterbury GC, Ohio, all three players involved in the 18 hole play-off fired level par rounds of 72 - which meant yet another 18 holes of overtime. The second round was almost as tight - only one shot separated the threesome. Lloyd Mangrum (72-72), Byron Nelson (72-73), Victor Ghezzi (72-73).

PLAY IT AGAIN SAM

Sam Snead, who never did win the US Open, missed a putt of just under a yard on the final green of the play-off for the 1947 Championship. He lost by one shot to Lew Worsham, who holed out from a slightly shorter distance at the 18th to win with a 69.

WITHOUT DUE CARE AND ATTENTION

Lloyd Mangrum was penalised two strokes during the play-off for the 1950 US Open, when, after noticing an insect on his ball, he marked it, picked it up and blew away the insect. Under USGA rules cleaning a golf ball on the green was not permitted, despite being common practice on the USPGA Tour. At the time of this infringement Mangrum was only one stroke behind the eventual champion Ben Hogan. Mangrum finished with a 73, four more than Hogan.

FLECK OUTGUNS BEN

In possibly the biggest play-off shock of modern times, Jack Fleck denied Ben Hogan a record fifth US Open title at the Olympic Country Club in 1955. Fleck, who made two birdies in the final four holes of regulation play to tie Hogan, was never behind in the 18 hole play-off. However, his three-shot lead through 10 holes, had been reduced to just one when the pair stood on the 18th tee. But just when everyone expected Hogan to put pressure on the little-known Fleck, the former champion drove into thick rough. From there Hogan needed three attempts to get back on the fairway and he lost the play-off by three shots, 69 to 72.

BACK NINE BLITZ

Arnold Palmer produced one of his famous late-charges to wrestle the US Masters crown from defending champion Gary Player in a three-way play-off in 1962. Starting the back nine three strokes adrift of the South African, Palmer birdied the 10th, 12th, 13th and 14th. His sudden burst of form certainly shook Player, whose game quickly deteriorated. In the space of just five holes there had been a seven-shot swing. Palmer now led by four. He came home in 31, to Player's 37, to win by three strokes. Dow Finsterwald, the other play-off contestant, never figured in the title chase. Scores: Palmer 68, Player 71, Finsterwald 77.

JACK ARRIVES ON THE SCENE

At the age of 22 in 1962, Jack Nicklaus claimed the first of his 18 professional major titles, by beating Arnold Palmer in an 18-hole play-off at the US Open at Oakmont. Nicklaus raced into a four stroke lead as early as the sixth hole and eventually won by three (71-74). The clash also signalled the first of many enthralling battles between America's top two players, most of which were won by Nicklaus.

MAKING HISTORY

By winning the 1966 US Masters title after a play-off, Jack Nicklaus became the first golfer in the history of the tournament, to successfully defend his crown. Although the 18-hole play-off involved three players, it soon became apparent that it would be a straight fight between Nicklaus and Tommy Jacobs. Both reached the turn in 35 (one-under-par), three ahead of Gay Brewer, who the previous day had three-putted the 72nd green of regulation play. As it transpired, holes 10 and 11 (both par fours) settled the issue. Jacobs bogied the 10th, with Nicklaus holing a 25-foot birdie putt on the 11th, to open up a two stroke lead. Thereafter, Nicklaus and Jacobs matched each other hole-by-hole for the rest of the round, giving Nicklaus the title 70-72. A dispirited Brewer came home in 40 for a 78.

PALMER'S TRIPLE BOGEY

Arnold Palmer suffered the disappointment of losing three US Open play-offs in the space of five seasons. The first, in 1962, was to Jack Nicklaus (see JACK ARRIVES ON THE SCENE). Twelve months later he finished six strokes behind winner Julius Boros in a three-way play-off and in 1966 lost out by four strokes to Billy Casper, after throwing away a sizable lead over the final nine holes of regulation play.

PUTTING ON A DISPLAY

The play-off for the 1970 US Masters turned out to be a low key affair, due to an excellent display of putting by Billy Casper, who had six single-putt greens in the opening seven holes. Even at this early stage of the 18-hole play-off, Casper - who was three-under-par - led Gene Littler by five strokes, which turned out to be the final margin (Casper 69 - Littler 74)

FOR NORMAN, READ WOOD

Greg Norman of Australia and American Craig Wood have lost play-offs in all four major championships. Wood suffered his fate between 1933 and 1939, while Norman endured his misfortune between 1984 and 1993. And both players were at the wrong end of some outrageous strokes of luck. In 1935, Wood could only gasp in disbelief when told that Gene Sarazen had holed his now-famous albatross two at the par-five, 15th hole, in the final round of the US Masters. And 52 years later in the same tournament, Norman lost a play-off to Larry Mize who chipped-in from off the green at the second extra-hole. *Note that Wood's play-off defeats includes extra-holes in the final of the 1934 USPGA Championship which in those days was a matchplay event.*

TREVINO SHOCKS NICKLAUS

While waiting to tee-off in a play-off for the 1971 US Open, super joker Lee Trevino reached into his golf bag and pulled out a snake, which he lobbed at Jack Nicklaus. Momentarily, the Golden Bear looked worried, until he realised it was only a plastic one.

Nicklaus made a disappointing start to this head-to-head duel dropping three strokes in the first three holes. Four hours later Trevino had won his second US Open title by three shots 68-71.

A STAR IS BORN

Tom Watson's first major title came via a play-off at the 1975 British Open at Carnoustie. After sinking a 25 footer for a birdie three on the final hole (72nd) of regulation play, Watson edged home by a single stroke (71-72) against Australian Jack Newton in the following day's play-off. Despite Watson's chip-in for an eagle three at the 14th, the two 25 year olds were still tied by the time they reached the 18th tee. Both players hit good drives at the 448-yard par four, final hole, although Newton's ball had trailed off into some light rough. The Australian played first but left his 2-iron approach in a greenside bunker. Watson, also hitting a 2-iron, found the centre of the green. From sand, Newton could do no better than leave his ball 12 feet past the hole. Watson then two putted for his four, which meant Newton had to hole his tricky putt to keep the match alive. But alas, Newton's attempt slid wide, leaving Watson the champion.

FIRST EVER SUDDEN DEATH

The 1977 USPGA Championship at Pebble Beach was the first major tournament to be decided by sudden-death. Overtime between Lanny Wadkins and Gene Littler lasted three holes. At the first, Wadkins holed from 20 feet for par to extend the play-off; both players birdied the next (a par 5); before Wadkins secured the title by holing a six-foot par putt on the third. Earlier, 47-year-old Littler had blown a five-shot lead over the final nine holes of regulation play, coming home in 41 strokes.

AUSSIE RULES

David Graham of Australia looked an unlikely winner of the 1979 USPGA Championship when he faced Ben Crenshaw in a play-off at Oakland Hills. Standing on the first tee of overtime, Graham was in a despondent mood, having just taken a double-bogey six at the 72nd hole a few minutes earlier. But Graham is resilient if nothing else. At the first play-off hole he sank a 20-foot putt for par, while Crenshaw missed a shorter birdie opportunity for victory. At the next, a par five, Graham stayed alive by holing a 10-footer for birdie. After getting out of jail twice, the Australian finally claimed the title at the third play-off hole, a 204-yard par three. Graham holed out for a two after hitting a superb 4-iron shot to within six feet of the cup.

ONE HORSE RACE

In a one-sided encounter at Winged Foot, in 1984, American Fuzzy Zoeller strolled to an eight-stroke victory against Greg Norman in an 18-hole play-off for the US Open. Three strokes ahead after just two holes, Zoeller gradually pulled away from his Australian opponent. By the turn he led by five, was seven up after 14, and nine ahead through 16. Norman managed to pull one back at the penultimate hole but Zoeller was a comfortable winner. Final scores: Zoeller 67, Norman 75.

QUICK DEATH

Only three sudden-death play-offs have ended at the first extra-hole. At the 1982 US Masters, Dan Pohl missed a six-foot par putt (10th green) to hand Craig Stadler the title. Stadler had made a straight-forward par, while Pohl left his second shot on the fringe of the putting surface and needed three more to get down.

Five years later, in the USPGA Championship at Palm Beach National, a bogey by Lanny Wadkins gave Larry Nelson victory. Both players had missed the green with their approach shots from where Wadkins failed to get up and down in two. Nelson holed from six feet for a par, while Wadkins missed from four feet and had to settle for a one-over-par five.

And at the 1995 USPGA at Riviera, Steve Elkington beat Colin Montgomerie with a birdie three on their only play-off hole.

MIZE STUNNER

The 1987 US Masters provided one of the most dramatic play-offs in major championship history. Three players went into extra-holes: Greg Norman; former champion Seve Ballesteros and outsider Larry Mize. Three became two, when at the first hole (10th) Ballesteros three-putted from 20-feet for a bogey five - missing his second putt from five feet. At the second (11th), Mize pushed his approach shot off the green to the right, about 40 yards from the cup, while Norman's ball landed on the fringe, 40 feet from the hole. Then Mize stunned Norman by chipping-in for a birdie three from an almost impossible position. Norman, now needing to sink his birdie putt to force the play-off into a third extra-hole, never came close to making it, leaving Mize as the first Augusta-born player to win the Masters.

STRANGE VICTORY

After many years of near-misses in major championships, Curtis Strange finally came of age in the 1988 US Open at The Country Club, Brookline, Massachusetts, where he beat England's Nick Faldo in an 18-hole play-off. The turning point came at the 13th, where Strange rolled in an 18-foot birdie putt, while Faldo bogied. This two-shot swing gave the American a three-stroke cushion and although Faldo birdied the 14th, he then proceeded to drop three shots to par over the final four holes. Strange won 71-75.

NEW SYSTEM

By the time Mark Calcavecchia, Greg Norman and Wayne Grady contested a play-off for the 1989 British Open at Royal Troon, the Royal & Ancient had decided on a new format. Believing that an 18-hole play-off created an anti-climax to a tournament that should have ended 24 hours earlier, and feeling that sudden-death was a bit of a lottery, the R&A bravely decided to stage a four-hole play-off which would act as a perfect compromise between the two. The winner would be the player with the lowest total over those four holes. And using this historic new method, Mark Calcavecchia claimed the title three strokes ahead of Wayne Grady who never threatened to win the play-off. At one stage Greg Norman looked the most probable champion when he birdied the first two holes of overtime. But after dropping a shot at the next, he drove into a bunker at the last, from where he hit into another bunker and then played his third shot out of bounds. He then picked up conceding defeat to Calcavecchia.

FALDO'S DOUBLE

England's Nick Faldo won back-to-back play-offs at Augusta, lifting the US Masters title in 1989 and 1990. Both lasted two holes. In 1989, Faldo looked a beaten man when Scott Hoch stood over a 24-inch putt for victory at the first extra-hole (10th). But Hoch's tricky little putt slipped past the rim of the cup and both men had to settle for bogey fives (Faldo had bunkered his approach and took three more to hole out). At the next (11th, par 4), Faldo capitalised on Hoch's earlier mistake by rolling in a 25-foot birdie putt for the title.

And 12 months later, Faldo clinched his second green jacket at the same hole after opponent Ray Floyd had put his second shot into the pond which guards the front left of the green. Faldo safely reached the putting surface in two and when Floyd failed to hole his 20-yard pitch shot for a par four, the Englishman two-putted for victory.

RADICAL CHANGES AT THE US OPEN

Hale Irwin won his third major title at Medinah Country Club in 1990, when he beat Mike Donald in the first ever 19-hole play-off at the US Open. After remaining deadlocked through the scheduled 18 holes of overtime (both fired two over par 74s), the play-off had to be extended using sudden-death. Never before had the United States Golf Association, allowed their most important tournament to be decided by this format. But sudden-death lasted only one hole. Irwin sank a 10-foot birdie putt to end the hopes of Donald, who had gone into the tournament a lowly 126th in the world ranking. Donald had his chances to win - he held a two-stroke lead with just three holes to play. But an Irwin birdie at 16, followed by a Donald bogey at 18, where he hooked his drive into some trees, forced the contest into sudden-death.

NOT SO GREAT SCOTT

The normally consistent Scott Simpson played the last three holes of the 1991 US Open play-off at Hazeltine, bogey-bogey-bogey, to lose by two shots to Payne Stewart. Scores: Stewart 75, Simpson 77.

AZINGER'S DAY

American Paul Azinger claimed his first major title when he beat Greg Norman at the second extra-hole of the 1993 USPGA Championship at the Inverness Club in Toledo, Ohio. In the end, the destiny of the title revolved around three putts - all missed by Norman. First of all there was the 10-footer for victory on the final hole of regulation play. Then at the first play-off hole, also the 18th, Norman with an almost identical putt for birdie, once again rimmed the hole. At the second extra-hole Norman missed a four footer for par to hand Azinger the title.

LOW KEY AFFAIR

18-hole play-offs have a habit of being an anti-climax, and the three-man decider for the 1994 US Open at Oakmont was no exception. After just two holes, the leaderboard read: Loren Roberts (+1); Colin Montgomerie (+2); Ernie Els (+4). The latter had made a triple-bogey seven on the 342-yard second hole. Els did however recover to post a three-over par 74, to tie Roberts and send the play-off into sudden-death for the second time in five years. Two holes later, 24-year-old Els had secured the title with a couple of pars. But for Scotland's Colin Montgomerie the contest never got going. Out in 42 (six over), he recovered slightly coming home and finished with a 78 - four strokes too many.

THE CHAMPIONS

*Each champion selected for this chapter falls
into one of the following four categories:
a) winner of five or more Majors; b) winner of
three or more Majors since 1970; c) winner of
two majors since 1980; d) European player
with a Major victory since 1970.*
*Note: With the exception of those golfers still
competing on the main Tours, a player's major
championship record ceases 10 years after their
final victory, although other top 10 finishes are
listed in abbreviated form*

Seve BALLESTEROS

Born: April 1957
European Tour wins: 54
Ryder Cup appearances: 8 (1979, 83, 85, 87, 89, 91, 93, 95

There is little doubt that Seve Ballesteros is the most charismatic golfer the European Tour has ever produced. Since his spectacular arrival at Royal Birkdale, at the tender age of 19, the Spaniard has enjoyed the support of almost every golf fan this side of the Atlantic.

Whatever the occasion, whether it be major championship, Ryder Cup or just a run of the mill Tour event, Seve has never ceased to intrigue his vast following. Even on his bad days, the charm of the man has never failed to shine through.

Looking back on the great man's career, it's hard to believe that his number of major titles didn't reach double figures. His fourth major win, the British Open at St Andrews in 1984, came at

the age of 27. Few players are that successful so young. Compare this to Nick Faldo who won his first major, the 1987 British Open, the day after he turned 30, and Ben Hogan, winner of nine majors, who didn't claim his first big title until he was 34. Which all goes to show that what Seve achieved in his twenties was quite staggering. Sadly for him, his 30s have been more of an anti-climax but that shouldn't detract from what has been a remarkable career.

Ballesteros burst onto the scene in the hot summer of 1976. Only 19, and without any reasonable form behind him, he stunned the golfing world by taking a two-stroke lead into the final round of the British Open. While the pressure asserted by playing partner and eventual champion Johnny Miller proved too much for the Spanish youngster in the end, the style with which Seve bounced back from a potential final round disaster made everyone sit up and take notice. Seven over par through 12 holes, Ballesteros

A young Ballesteros hits out of deep rough during the final round of the 1976 British Open at Royal Birkdale

looked to be sliding into oblivion until he covered the final six holes in five under par to tie Jack Nicklaus for second place.

It sparked the start of a golden few weeks for Ballesteros. In his next four tournaments, there were three third place finishes and a debut victory at the Dutch Open. The amazing teenager ended the season as European number one and leader of the Order of Merit. And to prove that this was no flash in the pan, he topped the Order of Merit again in 1977 and 1978.

With Tony Jacklin long gone and Peter Oosterhuis playing most of his golf in the United States, Seve was clearly Europe's leading contender for major honours in the late 1970s and early 1980s.

And he didn't have to wait long to notch up his first success, the British Open at Royal Lytham in 1979, when he demoralised Hale Irwin with his great recovery play over the closing holes. Not once in the last six holes did Seve find the fairway with his tee shot, but he still played them in one under par. Irwin, his distraught playing partner, covered the same holes in three over.

Two more Open titles followed in 1984 and 1988. At St Andrews he finished par-birdie, to deny Tom Watson a third successive crown, and at Royal Lytham four years later he outduelled Nick Price down the final stretch. Price had began the final round two strokes ahead of Seve and despite carding a two-under-par 69 lost out by two shots to the Spaniard who played one of the great final rounds of all time in posting a 65.

In the spring of 1980, Seve became the youngest-ever Masters champion at 23 after leading from start to finish. But his victory was not as clear cut as the result looked on paper. Early on the back nine of his final round, a 10 stroke lead had been whittled down to just two. Yet in typical Seve fashion, he recovered bravely to claim the title by four strokes, which was the same winning margin for his second Augusta victory three years later.

Yet Seve probably feels aggrieved that he couldn't add to those two Masters wins. In 1986 a third green jacket looked a certainty until he found water at the par-5 15th. And in 1987, he three-putted the first play-off hole and was eliminated. But these were just two blemishes in an otherwise brilliant career that has sadly suffered from bouts of inconsistency in the 1990s.

In matchplay Seve was also a difficult opponent to beat. Five World Matchplay titles and a super Ryder Cup record pay testimony to

that. But like all great champions Ballesteros wanted to win every week not just the major championships. In over 20 years on Tour there have been more than 50 European victories, plus many more worldwide. Prize money has passed through £4m. Yet statistics alone can't really tell the story of Ballesteros. Personality and character is what made Seve the player he was and at times still is. Galleries are still enchanted and mesmerised by his Spanish flair regardless of their hero's form.

Year	T'ment	Scores	Total	Position
1975	Br Open	79-80	159	MC
1976	Br Open	69-69-73-74	285	**T2**
1977	Masters	74-75-70-72	291	T33
	Br Open	69-71-73-74	287	T15
1978	Masters	74-71-68-74	287	T18
	US Open	75-69-71-77	292	T16
	Br Open	69-70-76-73	288	T17
1979	Masters	72-68-73-74	287	T12
	US Open	79-81	160	MC
	Br Open	73-65-75-70	283	**Won**
1980	Masters	66-69-68-72	275	**Won**
	US Open	75-Dq	75	Disq.
	Br Open	72-68-72-74	286	T19
1981	Masters	78-76	154	MC
	US Open	73-69-72-75	289	T41
	Br Open	75-72-74-72	293	T39
	USPGA	71-73-72-70	286	T33
1982	Masters	73-73-68-71	285	**T3**
	US Open	81-79	160	MC
	Br Open	71-75-73-71	290	T13
	USPGA	71-68-69-73	281	13
1983	Masters	68-70-73-69	280	**Won**
	US Open	69-74-69-74	286	T4
	Br Open	71-71-69-68	279	T6
	USPGA	71-76-72-67	286	T27
1984	Masters	73-74	147	MC
	US Open	69-73-74-75	291	T30
	Br Open	69-68-70-69	276	**Won**
	USPGA	70-69-70-70	279	5
1985	Masters	72-71-71-70	284	**T2**
	US Open	71-70-69-71	281	T5
	Br Open	75-74-70-73	292	T39
	USPGA	73-72-68-76	289	T32
1986	Masters	71-68-72-70	281	4
	US Open	75-73-68-73	289	T24
	Br Open	76-75-73-64	288	T6
	USPGA	74-76	150	MC
1987	Masters**	73-71-70-71	285	**T2**
	US Open	68-75-68-71	282	3
	Br Open	73-70-77-75	295	T50
	USPGA	72-70-72-78	292	T10

1988	Masters	73-72-70-73	288	T11
	US Open	69-74-72-73	288	T32
	Br Open	67-71-70-65	273	**Won**
	USPGA	71-75	146	MC
1989	Masters	71-72-73-69	285	5
	US Open	75-70-76-69	290	T43
	Br Open	72-73-76-78	299	T77
	USPGA	72-70-66-74	282	T12
1990	Masters	74-73-68-71	286	T7
	US Open	73-69-71-76	289	T33
	Br Open	71-74	145	MC
	USPGA	77-83	160	MC
1991	Masters	75-70-69-70	284	T22
	US Open	72-77	149	MC
	Br Open	66-73-69-71	279	T9
	USPGA	71-72-71-73	287	T23

1992	Masters	75-68-70-81	294	T59
	US Open	71-76-69-79	295	T23
	Br Open	70-75	145	MC
1993	Masters	74-70-71-71	286	T11
	US Open	76-72	148	MC
	Br Open	68-73-69-71	281	T27
1994	Masters	70-76-75-71	292	T18
	US Open	72-72-70-73	287	T18
	Br Open	70-70-71-69	280	T38
	USPGA	78-76	154	MC
1995	Masters	75-68-78-75	296	T45
	US Open	74-73	147	MC
	Br Open	75-69-76-71	291	T40
	USPGA	76-75	151	MC

** - Lost Play-Off   MC = Missed Cut   T = Tied

James Braid, pictured at Walton Heath on his 80th birthday in February 1950

James BRAID

The name James Braid will always be linked with those of Harry Vardon and JH Taylor. The three were simply called the Great Triumvirate. All three were born within 14 months of each other, Braid being the oldest, Taylor the youngest. Between them they won a total of 16 British Opens, but unlike the other two, whose Open victories spanned 19 years (Taylor) and 18 years (Vardon), Braid packed his five successes into just nine. His first came in 1901, his last in 1910 and during this same period, there were three runner-up spots as well.

If Braid's character had to be summed up in just one word, then 'resilient' might well be it. He was never one to let a crisis get in his way. This was well illustrated at the 1908 Open at Prestwick, where he took an eight at the par-5 third after putting his second shot into the famous Cardinal Bunker in round three. This sandy nightmare can best be described as looking like a cliff face that runs across the middle of the fairway. And before holing out at that third hole, Braid had also gone out of bounds. Such an incident would have ended the chances of many less robust men but Braid put it all behind him to win the Championship by eight strokes. His 72-hole total of 291 was also a new record aggregate for the tournament.

Four years earlier another record had fallen to Braid as he became the first player ever to break 70 in the Open, posting a third round 69 at St George's.

But there was more to Braid than just his Open victories. He won the PGA Matchplay Championship four times and was a renowned golf course architect. Possibly his best known creations were the King's and Queen's courses at Gleneagles.

Born in Earlsferry, Fife, in 1870, Braid had a reputation for being a long hitter. Legend has it, that while playing one day at Walton Heath, where he was the club professional, he drove the ball 395 yards - albeit wind-assisted.

Braid stayed at Walton Heath for the rest of his life. He died in 1950, aged 80.

Year	T'ment	Scores	Total	Position
1894	Br Open	91-84-82-84	341	T10
1896	Br Open	83-81-79-80	323	6
1897	Br Open	80-74-82-79	315	2
1898	Br Open	80-82-84-75	321	T10
1899	Br Open	78-78-85-81	322	T5
1900	Br Open	82-81-80-79	322	3
1901	Br Open	79-76-74-80	309	Won
1902	Br Open	78-76-80-74	308	T2
1903	Br Open	77-79-79-75	310	5
1904	Br Open	77-80-69-71	297	T2
1905	Br Open	81-78-78-81	318	Won
1906	Br Open	77-76-74-73	300	Won
1907	Br Open	82-85-75-76	318	T5
1908	Br Open	70-72-77-72	291	Won
1909	Br Open	79-75-73-74	301	T2
1910	Br Open	76-73-74-76	299	Won
1911	Br Open	78-75-74-78	305	T5
1912	Br Open	77-71-77-78	303	3
1913	Br Open	80-79-82-80	321	T18
1914	Br Open	74-82-78-82	316	T10
1920	Br Open	79-80-79-82	320	T21

An action shot of Braid at Walton Heath in the early 1920s

Ben CRENSHAW

Born: January 1952, Austin, Texas
US Tour wins: 19
Ryder Cup appearances: 4, (1981, 83, 87, 95)
Up until winning his first important title in 1984, Crenshaw had acquired a reputation for being a major championship bridesmaid. Five times he'd been a runner-up and on two other occasions had finished third. Two particular moments must have hurt him badly. At the 1975 US Open he missed out on a play-off by one stroke, after hitting his tee shot into a lake at the 71st hole, which he double-bogied. Four years later at the USPGA Championship he did contest a play-off only to lose to David Graham.

■ After many years of disappointment, Crenshaw claimed his first major title at Augusta in 1984, beating Tom Watson into second place by two strokes. Crenshaw had started the final round two strokes behind leader Tom Kite, in third place. But Kite blew-up with a 75 to finish in a share for sixth, five strokes behind Crenshaw who'd closed with a four-under-par 68. The key

■ US Masters victory number two came 11 years later. Once again he carded a final round 68, but this time his winning margin was just one stroke. He birdied both the 16th (par 3) and 17th (par 4) in round four to take a two-shot lead up the last. Crenshaw could afford to bogey the final hole and after his winning putt had been sunk he broke down in tears. Seven days earlier, his mentor, teacher and close friend, Harvey Penick, had died at the age of 90. Crenshaw flew back to Austin, Texas, during Masters week to attend the funeral, where he was a pall-bearer.

■ Crenshaw has lost all eight play-offs he has contested on the US Tour (1978 Bing Crosby Pro-Am; 1979 Western Open; 1979 USPGA Championship; 1981 Bing Crosby Pro-Am; 1981 Texas Open; 1987 Los Angeles Open; 1989 World Series; 1992 Byron Nelson Classic)

Year	T'ment	Scores	Total	Position
1970	US Open	75-73-77-76	301	T36
1971	US Open	74-74-68-73	289	T27
1972	Masters	73-74-74-74	295	T19
	US Open	80-75	155	MC
1973	Masters	73-72-74-76	295	T24
	US Open	80-73	153	MC
1974	Masters	75-70-70-72	287	T22
	Br Open	74-80-76-70	300	T28
	USPGA	75-74-74-74	297	T63
1975	Masters	72-71-75-74	292	T30
	US Open	70-68-76-74	288	**T3**
	USPGA	73-72-71-70	286	T10
1976	Masters	70-70-72-67	279	**2**
	US Open	72-68-72-73	285	T8
	USPGA	71-69-74-70	284	T8
1977	Masters	71-69-69-76	285	T8
	US Open	74-71-72-79	296	T49
	Br Open	71-69-66-75	281	T5
1978	Masters	75-70-74-74	293	T37
	US Open	78-76	154	MC
	Br Open	70-69-73-71	283	**T2**
	USPGA	69-71-75-73	288	T16
1979	Masters	73-80	153	MC
	US Open	75-71-72-75	293	T11
	Br Open	72-71-72-71	286	**T2**
	USPGA*	69-67-69-67	272	**T2**
1980	Masters	76-70-68-69	283	T6
	US Open	72-73-71-72	288	T32
	Br Open	70-70-68-69	277	**3**
	USPGA	69-74-78-73	294	T41
1981	Masters	71-72-70-73	286	T8
	US Open	70-75-64-72	281	T11
	Br Open	72-67-76-71	286	T8
	USPGA	75-75	150	MC

Two time Masters champion Ben Crenshaw,
pictured at Augusta in 1990

moment of Crenshaw's final round came on the 10th green where he holed a monster 60-foot putt for a birdie three. It was his third birdie in a row.

Year	Event	Scores	Total	Pos
1982	Masters	74-80-70-71	295	T24
	US Open	76-74-68-73	291	T19
	Br Open	74-75-72-70	291	T15
	USPGA	73-76	149	MC
1983	Masters	76-70-70-68	284	T2
	US Open	74-78	152	MC
	Br Open	74-75	149	MC
	USPGA	68-66-71-77	282	T9
1984	Masters	67-72-70-68	277	Won
	US Open	80-71	151	MC
	Br Open	72-75-70-69	286	T22
	USPGA	80-73	153	MC
1985	Masters	70-76-77-79	302	T57
	US Open	78-72	150	MC
	Br Open	73-75-70-73	291	T35
	USPGA	73-72-75-75	295	T59
1986	Masters	71-71-74-70	286	T16
	US Open	76-69-69-69	283	T6
	Br Open	77-69-75-73	294	T21
	USPGA	72-73-72-67	284	T11
1987	Masters	75-70-67-74	286	T4
	US Open	67-72-72-72	283	T4
	Br Open	73-68-72-68	281	T4
	USPGA	72-70-74-74	290	T7
1988	Masters	72-73-67-72	284	4
	US Open	71-72-74-67	284	T12
	Br Open	73-73-68-72	286	T15
	USPGA	70-71-69-74	284	T17
1989	Masters	71-72-70-71	284	T3
	US Open	73-73	146	MC
	Br Open	73-73-74-71	291	T52
	USPGA	68-72-72-71	283	T17
1990	Masters	72-74-73-69	288	T14
	US Open	75-72	147	MC
	Br Open	74-69-68-73	284	T31
	USPGA	74-70-78-75	297	T31
1991	Masters	70-73-68-68	279	T3
	Br Open	71-75-72-71	289	T80
	USPGA	81	81	Wd
1992	Masters	72-71-71-74	288	46
	USPGA	75-71-78-74	298	T73
1993	Masters	74-74	148	MC
	Br Open	70-75	145	MC
	USPGA	70-70-73-74	287	T61
1994	Masters	74-73-73-72	292	T18
	US Open	71-74-70-78	293	T33
	Br Open	70-73-73-73	289	T77
	USPGA	70-67-70-72	279	T9
1995	Masters	70-67-69-68	274	Won
	US Open	72-71-79-75	297	T71
	Br Open	67-72-76-72	287	T15
	USPGA	68-73-73-67	281	T44

* Lost play-off

John DALY

Born: April 1966, Sacramento, California
US Tour wins: 3
Ryder Cup appearances: Nil

Whatever his haircut, John Daly is always a crowd pleaser

Despite being one of the game's biggest names, Daly is not noted for his consistency, which is reflected in his Sony Ranking. When he won his first major, the 1991 USPGA Championship, he was ranked 168th in the world. Four years later, when he added the British Open title to his list of achievements, his ranking was 109.

■ Daly's volatile temperament and well publicised drink problem has earned him a high profile.

■ At the beginning of 1993, Daly, a self-confessed alcoholic, underwent a rehabilitation programme to rid himself of this problem. And in May 1994, when he won the BellSouth Atlanta Classic he admitted: "This is the first time I've won sober and knowing I can do it sober means a lot."

■ In November 1993, at the Kapalua International in Hawaii, Daly got into trouble when he failed to complete the 11th hole of his second round. After missing a shortish putt for a birdie, he picked up his ball and walked off the green. This led to the US Tour revoking a probation order that had been issued against him earlier that year. As a result, he was suspended by the Tour and he didn't compete again until March 1994.

■ And at the World Series in August 1994, Daly got involved in a scuffle with the father of a fellow competitor. Bob Roth, 62, claimed that Daly had shown bad etiquette on the course during the final round. He said Daly had been dangerous and irresponsible, hitting a number of shots, when the group in front were still within range. He said that his son, Jeff, was nearly struck by one of Daly's drives. The incident with Roth senior took place in the car park.

■ When Daly won the 1991 USPGA Championship, he proved to be an excellent front-runner. He grabbed a one stroke lead at the end of round two, extended his advantage after 54 holes to three shots, which 24 hours later, was also his final winning margin.

Year	T'ment	Scores	Total	Position
1986	US Open	88-76	164	MC
1989	US Open	74-67-80-79	300	T69
1991	USPGA	69-67-69-71	276	**Won**
1992	Masters	71-71-73-68	283	T19
	US Open	74-75	149	MC
	Br Open	74-69-80-74	297	75
	USPGA	76-72-79-77	304	82
1993	Masters	70-71-73-69	283	**T3**
	US Open	72-68-72-72	284	T33
	Br Open	71-66-70-71	278	T14
	USPGA	71-68-73-73	285	T51
1994	Masters	76-73-77-78	304	T48
	US Open	81-73	154	MC
	Br Open	68-72-72-80	292	81
	USPGA	73-73	146	MC
1995	Masters	75-69-71-81	296	T45
	US Open	71-75-74-71	291	T45
	Br Open*	67-71-73-71	282	**Won**
	USPGA	76-73	149	MC

* Won after play-off

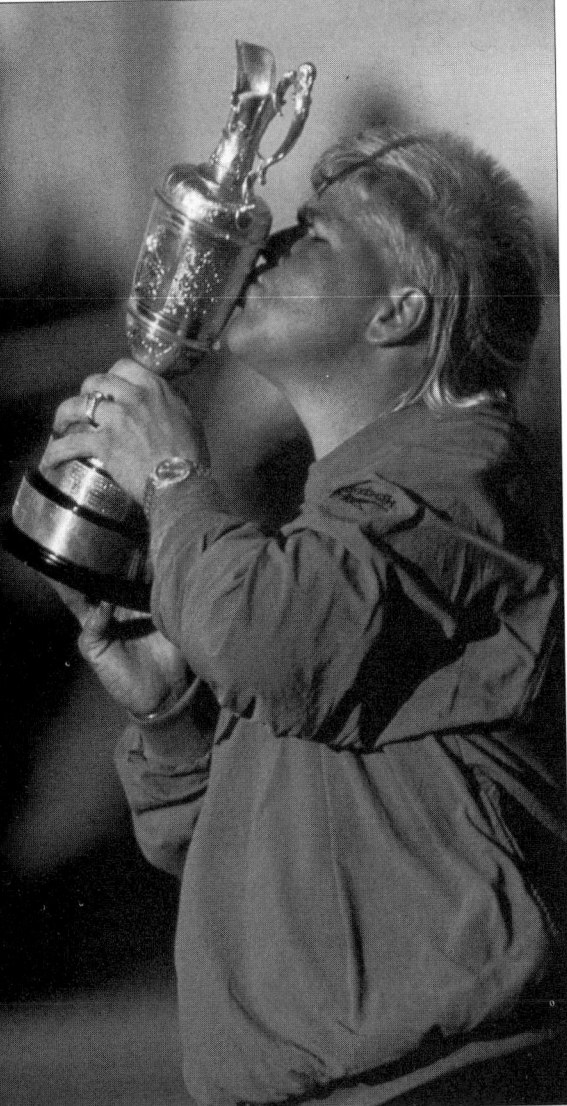

A play-off victory over Costantino Rocca in the 1995 British Open earned Daly his second Major title

Nick FALDO

Born: July 1957, Welwyn Garden City
European Tour wins: 29
Ryder Cup appearances: 10 (1977, 79, 81, 83, 85, 87, 89, 91, 93, 95)

There was never any doubt that Nick Faldo would become one of golf's great champions. Turning professional in 1976 at the age of 18, Faldo was marked down as a potential superstar of the future. To most golf followers it wasn't simply a question of whether Faldo would win a major championship in his career, but more a case of when. He had the temperament, guts and the talent needed to succeed. Yet, as it turned out, he finally reached that first major milestone a little later than had been forecast. Victory at Muirfield in July 1987, came one day after his 30th birthday, when his main European rivals, Seve Ballesteros, Sandy Lyle and Bernhard Langer, had already made their breakthrough in the major championship stakes. Langer and Lyle were both 27 when they won their first major title, while Ballesteros was only 22. However, once Faldo had claimed his first major scalp, there was certainly no stopping him. He now has five major titles to his credit.

But unlike many major champions, whose career paths have tended to follow a straight line, Faldo's didn't. Between 1976 and 1984 Faldo was most definitely upwardly mobile. Tournament victory followed tournament victory in Europe and by winning five events in 1983 he finished the year top of the European Order of Merit. Yet just when it seemed that Faldo was about to make his mark on world golf, his career took a downturn. Surprisingly this downturn was self-inflicted.

Self-doubt had crept into Faldo's mind. He didn't believe his swing was solid enough to cope with the pressures of winning a major championship. He pointed to two moments. At Birkdale in 1983 he was right there in the thick of the action going into the back nine. But a homeward journey of 40 (three over par) left him

five shots behind eventual champion Tom Watson who covered the same stretch in 34.

The following year at Augusta, Faldo was again well placed going into the final day only to shoot a 76, which was eight strokes worse than playing partner and winner Ben Crenshaw. These bitter experiences convinced Faldo that he had to change his swing if he was to win a major championship. So he called in David Leadbetter to make the alterations. Between May 1984 and May 1987 Faldo didn't win a single tournament. His lowest point must have been 1985, when he witnessed his contemporaries Langer and Lyle both join the major-winner's circle. That same year Faldo slumped to his lowest position in the European Order of Merit, 42nd. And in September played in the Ryder Cup as one of captain Tony Jacklin's wild cards. Although the Europeans won the Cup back for the first time in 28 years, Faldo lost both his matches at The Belfry. It couldn't have been easy for a player as proud as Faldo to join in whole-heartedly with the after match celebrations when his own game was not firing on all cylinders.

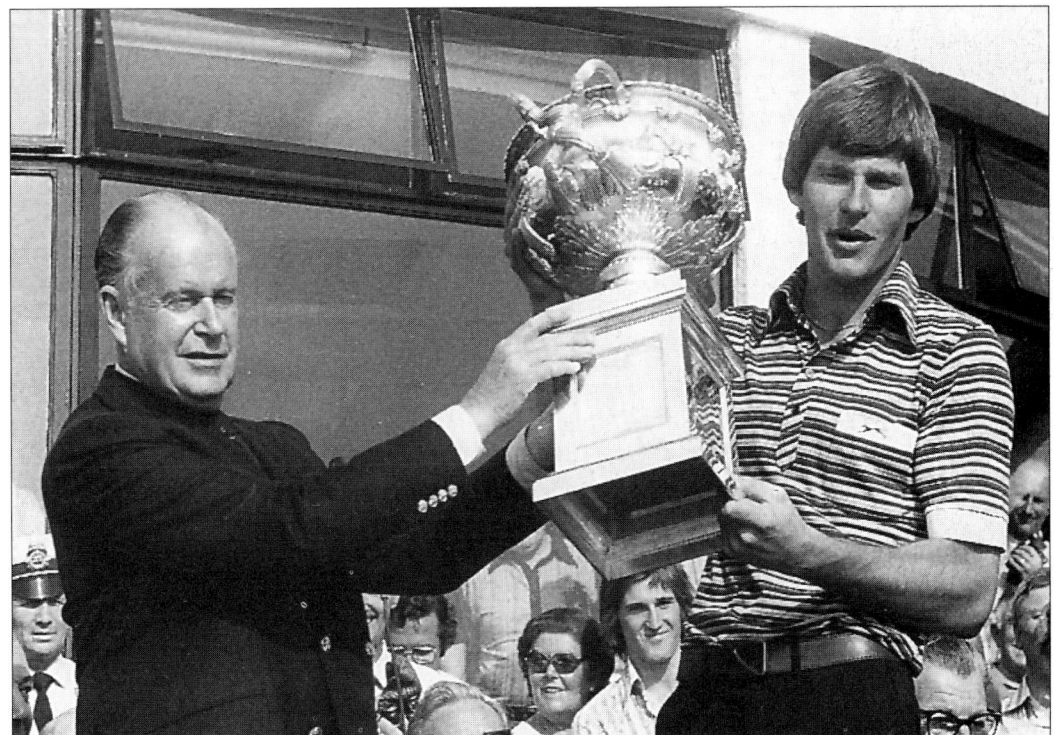

A young Nick Faldo shows off the PGA Championship trophy after winning at Royal Birkdale in 1978

But after three years in the wilderness, Faldo returned to winning ways at the 1987 Spanish Open. Two months later he'd won the biggest prize of them all, the British Open, where remarkably he made 18 straight pars in his final round of 71 to win by one stroke. It was this dogged consistency and his ability to wear down his opponents, that earned Faldo his reputation for being a tough competitor. At times, sadly, this tended to overshadow his massive flair and talent for the game.

The three-year slump Faldo had endured while mending his swing, was quickly put behind him. Between 1988 and 1992 Faldo dominated world golf. In 19 consecutive majors during that period, Faldo won four, had ten top-10 finishes and was not once outside the top-20. It was a high-level of consistency in the Nicklaus or Hogan mould

Four of Faldo's five majors were won by the narrowest of margins. Both Masters' titles were gained in sudden-death play-offs, with two British Open successes coming by a single stroke. All of which demonstrated his steely nerve when the going was tough. The odd-one out was the 1990 British Open at St Andrews where he won by five shots after playing almost flawless golf for four days. After 36 holes, he had been tied for the lead with Greg Norman, his arch-rival for the world number one spot at that time. Most expected a head-to-head shoot-out between these two top players over the final couple of days at the Old Course. But Faldo gunned down Norman in round three, shooting a 67 to the Australian's 76. The final round was almost a canter.

However, two years later, it was anything but easy at Muirfield when he won the Claret Jug for a third time. Starting the final round four strokes ahead of the field, Faldo looked to have let it slip by the time he had reached the 15th tee. Thanks in part to John Cook three-putting the par-5 17th and then bogeying 18, Faldo was back in the hunt. At the par-4 15th, he fired his second shot to within two feet of the cup for a birdie, then chipped brilliantly to save par at 16, made a two-putt birdie at 17 and parred 18 for a one-stroke victory.

Faldo went on to finish 1992 as European Order of Merit winner for a second time. Apart from his British Open success there were five other victories to savour that year. Four of them in Europe, plus a play-off win over Norman at the Johnnie Walker World Championship in Jamaica.

During his peak years in the late 80s and early 90s, Faldo came close to winning all four major championships. In the US Open at The Country Club, Brookline, he lost a play-off against Curtis Strange in 1988. Two years later at Medinah, his 12-foot putt on the final green, which had he sunk it would have put him in a play-off, grazed the outside of the hole. And in the other major championship which eludes him, the USPGA, Faldo has had four top-4 finishes.

In all, Faldo has savoured victory over 40 times around the world. As an amateur he won the English Championship in 1975. He also tasted life on a university golf scholarship in the United States but gave that up when he felt it wasn't helping his career. And so he joined the paid ranks in the spring of 1976 and played his first pro event at the French Open, where he carded four incredibly consistent rounds of 71-72-72-72, a sort of symbolic gesture for the future. With a start like that, how could he ever fail to impress.

Year	T'ment	Scores	Total	Position
1976	Br Open	78-71-76-69	294	T28
1977	Br Open	71-76-74-78	299	T62
1978	Br Open	71-72-70-72	285	T7
1979	Masters	73-71-79-73	296	40
	Br Open	74-74-78-69	295	T19
1980	Br Open	69-74-71-70	284	T12
1981	Br Open	77-68-69-73	287	T11
1982	Br Open	73-73-71-69	286	T4
	USPGA	67-70-73-72	282	T14
1983	Masters	70-70-76-76	292	T20
	Br Open	68-68-71-73	280	T8
	USPGA	74-77	151	MC
1984	Masters	70-69-70-76	285	T15
	US Open	71-76-77-72	296	T55
	Br Open	69-68-76-69	282	T6
	USPGA	69-73-74-70	286	T20
1985	Masters	73-73-75-71	292	T25
	Br Open	73-73-75-74	295	T53
	USPGA	70-77-73-74	294	T54
1986	Br Open	71-70-76-70	287	5
	USPGA	76-71	147	MC
1987	Br Open	68-69-71-71	279	Won
	USPGA	73-73-77-74	297	T28
1988	Masters	75-74-75-72	296	T30
	US Open**	72-67-68-71	278	2
	Br Open	71-69-68-71	279	3
	USPGA	67-71-70-71	279	T4
1989	Masters *	68-73-77-65	283	Won
	US Open	68-72-73-72	285	T18
	Br Open	71-71-70-69	281	T11
	USPGA	70-73-69-69	281	T9
1990	Masters *	71-72-66-69	278	Won
	US Open	72-72-68-69	281	T3

	Br Open	67-65-67-71	270	**Won**		Br Open	69-63-70-67	269	2
	USPGA	71-75-80-69	295	T19		USPGA	68-68-69-68	273	3
1991	Masters	72-73-67-70	282	T12	1994	Masters	76-73-73-74	296	32
	US Open	72-74-73-72	291	T16		US Open	73-75	148	MC
	Br Open	68-75-70-68	281	T17		Br Open	75-66-70-64	275	T8
	USPGA	70-69-71-76	286	T16		USPGA	73-67-71-66	277	T4
1992	Masters	71-72-68-71	282	T13	1995	Masters	70-70-71-75	286	T24
	US Open	70-76-68-77	291	T4		US Open	72-68-79-72	291	T45
	Br Open	66-64-69-73	272	**Won**		Br Open	74-67-75-75	291	T40
	USPGA	68-70-76-67	281	**T2**		USPGA	69-73-70-67	279	T31
1993	Masters	71-76-79-67	293	T39					
	US Open	70-74-73-72	289	T72					

** - Lost play-off
* - Won play-off

Ray Floyd pictured at the British Open, the only major championship to elude him, at Troon in 1982

Ray FLOYD

Born: September 1942, Fort Bragg, North Carolina
US Tour wins: 22
Ryder Cup appearances: 8 (1969, 75, 77, 81, 83, 85, 91, 93)
Victory in the St Petersburg Open in March 1963 made him the fourth youngest tournament winner ever on the US Tour at 20 years and six months. No one younger than that has won on Tour since.
■ Floyd has the reputation of being an excellent front runner. Three of his four major victories have been earned this way. In the 1976 US Masters he opened with a 65 to lead by one stroke. He followed that with a 66 to open-up a five-shot lead and thereafter was never caught. At the 1982 USPGA he started with a 63 and again led from start-to-finish. At the USPGA in 1969 he was tied for the lead after day one and then had sole possession of top spot after rounds two, three and four. The odd one out was the 1986 US Open in which he only moved into the lead during the final nine holes.
■ The only major he never won was the British Open. His best finish is tied second in 1978 at St Andrews where he trailed champion Jack Nicklaus by two strokes.
■ In 1992 he became the first player to win on both the 'Regular' Tour and Senior Tour in the same year. He won the Doral-Ryder Open in March on the main Tour, then the GTE North Classic on the Senior Tour in September.
■ Victory in the 1992 Doral-Ryder Open made him the fifth oldest Tour winner in history at 49 years and six months. It came only two weeks after his Miami home was burnt to the ground.

Year	T'ment	Scores	Total	Position
1963	USPGA	75-73-74-75	297	T57
1964	US Open	73-70-72-77	292	T14
1965	Masters	69-83	152	MC
	US Open	72-72-76-68	288	T6
	USPGA	68-73-72-77	290	T17
1966	Masters	72-73-74-74	293	T8
	US Open	80-80	160	Wd
	USPGA	74-75-74-68	291	T18
1967	Masters	74-77	151	MC
	US Open	74-74-73-73	294	T38
	USPGA	74-69-74-72	289	T20
1968	Masters	71-71-69-71	282	T7
	USPGA	79-70-73-71	293	T41
1969	Masters	73-71-78-74	296	T36
	US Open	79-68-68-72	287	T13
	Br Open	74-70-76-76	296	T34
	USPGA	69-66-67-74	276	**Won**
1970	Masters	76-76	152	MC
	US Open	78-73-70-76	297	T22
	Br Open	73-78	151	MC
	USPGA	71-73-65-75	284	T8
1971	USPGA	77-74	151	MC
	Masters	69-75-73-71	288	T13
	US Open	71-75-67-71	284	8
1972	Masters	76-82	158	MC
	US Open	75-81	156	MC
	USPGA	69-71-74-70	284	T4
1973	Masters	76-73-75-77	301	54
	US Open	70-73-75-71	289	16
	USPGA	70-73-73-74	290	T35
1974	Masters	69-72-76-70	287	T22
	US Open	72-71-78-75	296	T15
	USPGA	68-72-74-70	284	T11
1975	Masters	72-73-79-68	292	T30
	US Open	76-71-72-72	291	T12
	Br Open	71-72-76-71	290	T23
	USPGA	70-73-72-71	286	T10
1976	Masters	65-66-70-70	271	**Won**
	US Open	70-75-71-72	288	13
	Br Open	76-67-73-70	286	4
	USPGA	72-68-71-71	282	**T2**
1977	Masters	71-72-71-71	285	T8
	US Open	73-73-78-71	295	T47
	Br Open	70-73-68-72	283	8
	USPGA	74-72-73-76	295	T40
1978	Masters	76-71-71-68	286	T16
	US Open	75-70-76-70	291	T12
	Br Open	69-75-71-68	283	**T2**
	USPGA	76-72-73-73	294	T50
1979	Masters	70-68-73-77	288	T17
	US Open	76-76	152	MC
	Br Open	76-73-71-79	299	T36
	USPGA	74-70-77-72	293	T62
1980	Masters	75-70-74-67	286	T17
	US Open	67-79-71-75	292	T45
	USPGA	70-76-71-73	290	T17
1981	Masters	75-71-71-69	286	T8
	US Open	75-72-68-73	288	T37
	Br Open	74-70-69-70	283	**T3**
	USPGA	71-70-71-72	284	T19
1982	Masters	74-72-69-74	289	T7
	US Open	78-73-75-72	298	T49
	Br Open	74-73-77-67	291	T15
	USPGA	63-69-68-72	272	**Won**
1983	Masters	67-72-71-75	285	T4
	US Open	72-70-72-79	293	T13
	Br Open	72-66-69-75	282	T14
	USPGA	69-75-71-69	284	T20
1984	Masters	70-73-70-72	285	T15
	US Open	72-72-77-74	295	T52
	Br Open	74-74-73	221	MC
	USPGA	68-71-69-74	282	13
1985	Masters	70-73-69-72	284	**T2**
	US Open	72-67-73-75	287	T23
	USPGA	74-75	149	MC
1986	Masters	74-78	152	MC
	US Open	75-68-70-66	279	**Won**
	Br Open	78-67-73-74	292	T16
	USPGA	76-71	147	MC
1987	Masters	75-77	152	MC
	US Open	68-73-76-73	290	T43
	Br Open	72-68-70-76	286	T17
	USPGA	70-70-73-80	293	T14
1988	Masters	80-69-68-71	288	T11
	US Open	73-72-73-67	285	T17
	Br Open	76-77	153	MC
	USPGA	68-68-74-72	282	T9
1989	Masters	76-75-73-74	298	T38
	US Open	68-74-74-71	287	T26
	Br Open	73-68-73-74	288	T42
	USPGA	73-71-70-74	288	T46
1990	Masters**	70-68-68-72	278	**2**
	US Open	77-77	154	MC
	Br Open	72-71-71-71	285	T39
	USPGA	72-77-74-77	300	T49
1991	Masters	71-68-71-73	283	T17
	US Open	73-72-76-68	289	T8
	Br Open	80-78	158	MC
	USPGA	69-74-72-69	284	T7
1992	Masters	69-68-69-71	277	**2**
	US Open	71-69-76-81	297	T44
	Br Open	64-71-73-72	280	T12
	USPGA	69-75-69-79	292	T48
1993	Masters	68-71-74-73	286	T11
	US Open	68-73-70-68	279	T7
	Br Open	70-72-67-73	282	T34
	USPGA	71-73	144	MC

1994	Masters	70-74-71-72	287	T10
	USPGA	69-76-73-72	290	T61
1995	Masters	71-70-70-74	285	T17
	US Open	74-72-76-67	289	T36
	Br Open	72-74-72-76	294	T58

** - Lost Play-Off

Walter HAGEN

Born: Rochester, New York, December 1892
US Tour wins: 40
Ryder Cup appearances: 5 (1927, 29, 31, 33, 35)
Walter Hagen was golf's first extrovert character, flamboyant in everything he did. He had a chauffeur-driven limousine, enjoyed partying well into the early hours - even during tournaments - and he always wore the most fashionable clothes. He was a showman in every sense.

Yet behind that glitzy exterior lay a tough competitor. In a career that spanned over 20 years, Walter Hagen collected 11 professional major titles - only Jack Nicklaus has won more. And bear in mind that Hagen never had the opportunity to play in as many major tournaments as the likes of Nicklaus, Hogan, Palmer or Watson. When Hagen was at his peak, between 1913 and 1930, the US Masters didn't exist. He also lost a couple of years to the First World War. But his record was still outstanding.

Despite being one of golf's all-time greats, Hagen was never a particularly good ball striker. His driving was erratic and it was once said that he played more bad shots in one year than Harry Vardon did in his career. But his short game was a revelation. His powers of recovery were immense. If he missed a green in regulation he would usually get up and down in two. He was also an excellent putter and had great nerve on the green.

Hagen won two US Opens and four British Opens but where he really excelled was at

The smartly-attired Walter Hagen is congratulated by his wife after winning the British Open at Hoylake in June 1924

matchplay. He triumphed in five USPGA Championships including four in a row from 1924. And he holds the USPGA record for winning most successive matches - 22 in all.

He also had a good Ryder Cup record, winning seven of his nine contests and losing only once. That defeat came at the hands of George Duncan who thrashed Hagen 10&8 (over 36 holes) at Moortown, Leeds, in 1929.

Hagen was credited with raising the status of professional golf. In the early years of this century, professional golfers were simply servants of the clubs that employed them to teach wealthy members. When Hagen first came to England to play in the 1920 British Open at Deal, he shocked the game's establishment by ordering champagne to be delivered to his limousine which was parked in the club's driveway. At the time, professionals were not allowed to enter the clubhouse through the front door, they had to use either a side or back entrance. So Hagen made a point of not going into the clubhouse at all. Everything he needed was delivered to his car. He refused to accept second class treatment.

His clashes with the establishment, both sides of the Atlantic, was legendary yet it helped to give golf a higher profile, as did his colourful personality. This, in turn, brought greater sponsorship into the game. And as Hagen's great friend and rival, Gene Sarazen, once commented: "All the players who have a chance to go after big money should say a silent prayer to Walter Hagen. It was Walter who made professional golf what it is."

Hagen, who lived life to the full, died in October 1969, aged 76.

Year	T'ment	Scores	Total	Position
1913	US Open	73-78-76-80	307	T4
1914	US Open	68-74-75-73	290	**Won**
1915	US Open	78-73-76-79	306	T10
1916	US Open	73-76-75-71	295	7
1919	US Open*	78-73-75-75	301	**Won**
1920	Br Open	84-82-78-85	329	T53
	US Open	74-73-77-77	301	11
1921	Br Open	74-79-72-77	302	T6
	US Open	79-73-72-74	298	**T2**
1922	Br Open	76-73-79-72	300	**Won**
	US Open	68-77-74-72	291	5
1923	Br Open	76-71-74-75	296	2
	US Open	77-75-73-86	311	T18
1924	US Open	75-75-76-77	303	T4
	Br Open	77-73-74-77	301	**Won**

Year	T'ment	Scores	Total	Position
1925	US Open	72-76-71-74	293	T5
1926	Br Open	68-77-74-76	295	**T3**
	US Open	73-77-74-74	298	7
1927	US Open	77-73-76-81	307	6
1928	Br Open	75-73-72-72	292	**Won**
	US Open	75-72-73-76	296	T4
1929	Br Open	75-67-75-75	292	**Won**
	US Open	76-81-74-78	309	T19
1930	US Open	72-75-76-80	303	T17
1931	US Open	74-74-73-76	297	T7
1932	US Open	75-73-79-71	298	10
1933	US Open	73-76-77-66	292	T4
	Br Open	68-72-79-82	301	T22
1934	Masters	71-76-70-77	294	T13
	US Open	76-79-83-80	318	T58
1935	Masters	73-69-72-79	293	T15
	US Open	77-76-73-76	302	3
1936	Masters	77-74-73-72	296	T11
	US Open	74-72-73-78	297	T33
1937	Br Open	76-72-80-81	309	T26
1939	Masters	76-76-76-76	304	T33

* - Won Play-Off

HAGEN AT THE USPGA CHAMPIONSHIP

(Matchplay years 1916-57)

Year	Position	Final Match		(W-L)
1916	Semi-Final	Lost 2 up	Jock Hutchison	(3-1)
1921	**Champion**	Won 3&2	Jim Barnes	(5-0)
1923	**Runner-Up**	Lost at 38th	Gene Sarazen	(5-1)
1924	**Champion**	Won 2 up	Jim Barnes	(5-0)
1925	**Champion**	Won 6&5	Bill Mehlhorn	(5-0)
1926	**Champion**	Won 5&3	Leo Diegel	(5-0)
1927	**Champion**	Won 1 up	Joe Turnesa	(5-0)
1928	Qtr-Final	Lost 2&1	Leo Diegel	(2-1)
1929	Semi-Final	Lost 3&2	Leo Diegel	(3-1)
1931	1st Rd (32)	Lost 4&3	Peter O'Hara	(0-1)
1932	1st Rd (32)	Lost at 43rd	Johnny Golden	(0-1)
1934	1st Rd (32)	Lost 4&3	Densmore Shute	(0-1)
1935	1st Rd (64)	Lost 1 up	Johnny Revolta	(0-1)
1939	1st Rd (64)	Lost 1 up	Tony Manero	(0-1)
1940	3rd Rd (16)	Lost 1 up	Harold McSpaden	(2-1)

Ben Hogan practising before the 1956 Canada Cup at Wentworth

Ben HOGAN

Born: August 1912, Dublin, Texas
US Tour wins: 63
Ryder Cup appearances: 2 (1947, 51)

Ben Hogan was one of golf's late developers. Despite winning his first Tour event in 1938, at the age of 26, it was another eight years before Hogan finally became a major star. Even taking into account the years lost to the Second World War, Hogan didn't reach his peak until well into his 30s.

Yet once he'd landed that first, almost elusive, major title - the 1946 USPGA Championship - there was no stopping him.

Many claim that Hogan at his best was the greatest golfer the game has ever seen. And if you examine his major championship record between 1948 and 1953 it's hard to disagree. Of the 11 majors that Hogan contested from the 1948 USPGA through to the 1953 British Open, he won eight of them. That's an incredible strike rate of 72.73%. Of the three he didn't win during this period, his worst finish was tied 7th. Even the great Jack Nicklaus in his prime couldn't match that.

Had a world ranking system been in existence at the time, Hogan would most certainly have been miles ahead of the rest.

As a man, Hogan was an extremely private individual. Born in Dublin, Texas, in August 1912, few people ever really got to know him well. And even after he retired from the game, he still continued to limit his appearances in public, confining himself to a few close friends. He almost became a recluse.

As a golfer he was a perfectionist, practising for hours almost every day and his contemporaries considered him to be the finest ball striker in the game.

Yet what Hogan achieved in the early 1950s might never have happened at all. On February 2nd, 1949, he was involved in a near-fatal road accident, when his Cadillac was struck head-on by a 10-ton greyhound bus. For over an hour, Hogan lay unconscious by the side of a dark Texas highway, while his wife, Valerie, waited for an ambulance. His injuries were considerable and it was touch-and-go whether he would survive.

Somehow, Hogan pulled through. However, his legs had taken terrible punishment and it wasn't clear he would ever walk again, let alone play golf. All of which made it even more astounding that when Hogan did return to the competitive arena in 1950, he won the US Open.

In 1953, at the age of 40, Hogan produced the single greatest season in golf history, winning the US Masters, US Open and British Open. He still remains the only golfer to win three professional majors in the same year. Unfortunately, due to a clash of dates, Hogan was unable to complete the Grand Slam. The USPGA Championship was only scheduled to finish the day before the British Open was due to start. As it happened he chose to play in Carnoustie, Scotland.

After his car accident, Hogan never again played in the USPGA. As a matchplay event, he could have been required to play 36 holes a day for four successive days, which would have put too much strain on his badly mangled legs.

In 1951, a film was made about Hogan. It was called 'Follow the Sun' and starred Glenn Ford. It was too early to include his great year of 1953 but there is little doubt that Hogan's life story of pain and achievement was a remarkable one indeed.

Year	T'ment	Scores	Total	Position
1934	US Open	79-79	158	MC
1936	US Open	75-79	154	MC
1938	Masters	75-76-78-72	301	T25
	US Open	77-79	156	MC
1939	Masters	75-71-72-72	290	9
	US Open	76-74-78-80	308	T62
1940	Masters	73-74-69-74	290	T10
	US Open	70-73-74-73	290	T5
1941	Masters	71-72-75-68	286	4
	US Open	74-77-68-70	289	T3
1942	Masters**	73-70-67-70	280	2
1946	Masters	74-70-69-70	283	2
	US Open	72-68-73-72	285	T4
1947	Masters	75-68-71-70	284	T4
	US Open	70-75-70-74	289	T6
1948	Masters	70-71-77-71	289	T6
	US Open	67-72-68-69	276	Won
1950	Masters	73-68-71-76	288	T4
	US Open*	72-69-72-74	287	Won
1951	Masters	70-72-70-68	280	Won
	US Open	76-73-71-67	287	Won
1952	Masters	70-70-74-79	293	T7
	US Open	69-69-74-74	286	3
1953	Masters	70-69-66-69	274	Won
	US Open	67-72-73-71	283	Won
	Br Open	73-71-70-68	282	Won
1954	Masters**	72-73-69-75	289	2
	US Open	71-70-76-72	289	T6
1955	Masters	73-68-72-73	286	2
	US Open**	72-73-72-70	287	2
1956	Masters	69-78-74-75	296	T8
	US Open	72-68-72-70	282	T2
1957	Masters	76-75	151	MC
1958	Masters	72-77-69-73	291	T14
	US Open	75-73-75-71	294	T10
1959	Masters	73-74-76-72	295	T30
	US Open	69-71-71-76	287	T8
1960	Masters	73-68-72-76	289	T6
	US Open	75-67-69-73	284	T9
	USPGA	74-73-78	225	MC
1961	Masters	74-73-72-79	298	T32
	US Open	71-72-73-73	289	T14
1962	Masters	78-71-75-73	297	38

Other Top 10 finishes

1964	Masters	T9	(287)
	USPGA	T9	(282)
1967	Masters	T10	(290)

* - Won play-off ** - Lost play-off

HOGAN AT THE USPGA

(Matchplay years 1916-57)

Year	Position	Final Match		(W-L)
1939	3rd Rd (16)	Lost 3&2	Paul Runyan	(2-1)
1940	Qtr-Final	Lost 3&2	Ralph Guldahl	(3-1)
1941	Qtr-Final	Lost 2up	Byron Nelson	(3-1)
1942	Qtr-Final	Lost 2&1	Jim Turnesa	(2-1)
1946	**Champion**	Won 6&4	Ed Oliver	(6-0)
1947	1st Rd (64)	Lost 3&1	Toney Penna	(0-1)
1948	**Champion**	Won 7&6	Mike Turnesa	(6-0)

Hale IRWIN

Born: June 1945, Joplin, Missouri
US Tour wins: 20
Ryder Cup appearances: 5, (1975, 77, 79, 81, 91)

All three of his major victories have come in the US Open (1974-79-90). But despite having an excellent US Open record, Irwin has only once finished under par in the tournament. That was in 1990, when he was 8-under and went on to take the title in a play-off. In 1979 he was level par, and in 1974, 7-over-par. By the end of 1995 he had played in 26 US Opens.

■ The key moment of Irwin's march to glory in 1974 at Winged Foot came on the 71st hole. After driving into the rough at the 444-yard, par-4, 17th, Irwin could only move his ball another 100 yards down the fairway. But from there, he pitched to within 10 feet of the flag and holed a vital par-saving putt. A par at the last earned him a two-shot victory over Forrest Fezler who had bogied 18.

■ In 1990, Irwin received a special exemption from the USGA to play in the US Open and went on to win the championship. At the 72nd hole he sank a monster 45-foot putt for a birdie three. He'd covered the last eight holes in just 26 strokes. But he then had to wait almost two hours before finding out he had forced a play-off with joint third-round leader Mike Donald.

■ Irwin has built-up a reputation for being a fine matchplayer. He is one of only two golfers to reach the World Matchplay final at Wentworth three years in a row (the other is Sandy Lyle). Irwin won the title in 1974 and 1975, before losing the 1976 Championship after sudden-death.

■ In the Ryder Cup, Irwin has won 13 of his 20 matches, losing only five times. In 1991, it was his singles with Bernhard Langer that decided the fate of the trophy. Langer's missed putt from six-feet on the final green allowed Irwin to grab the vital half-point that regained the Cup for the United States.

Hale Irwin pictured at St Andrews in 1990,
the year of his third win in the US Open

Year	T'ment	Scores	Total	Position
1966	US Open	75-75-78-77	305	T61
1970	USPGA	72-69-76-75	292	T30
1971	USPGA	73-72-72-74	291	T22
	Masters	69-72-71-76	288	T13
	US Open	72-73-72-70	287	T19
1972	Masters	81-71	152	MC
	US Open	78-72-73-83	306	T36
	USPGA	71-69-75-71	286	T11
1973	US Open	73-74-75-71	293	T20
	USPGA	76-72-68-68	284	T9
1974	Masters	68-70-72-71	281	T4
	US Open	73-70-71-73	287	**Won**
	Br Open	76-73-79-71	299	T24
1975	Masters	73-74-71-64	282	T4
	US Open	74-71-73-70	288	T3
	Br Open	69-70-69-75	283	9
	USPGA	72-65-73-73	283	T5

Year	Event	Scores	Total	Place
1976	Masters	71-77-67-70	285	T5
	US Open	75-72-75-71	293	T26
	Br Open	74-72-77-73	296	T32
	USPGA	69-73-77-72	291	T34
1977	Masters	70-74-70-68	282	5
	US Open	73-71-77-72	293	T41
	Br Open	70-71-73-80	294	T46
	USPGA	74-75-73-75	297	T44
1978	Masters	73-67-71-71	282	8
	US Open	69-74-75-70	288	T4
	Br Open	75-71-76-68	290	T24
	USPGA	73-71-73-70	287	T12
1979	Masters	72-70-74-74	290	T23
	US Open	74-68-67-75	284	Won
	Br Open	68-68-75-78	289	6
	USPGA	73-75	148	MC
1980	Masters	74-73	147	MC
	US Open	70-70-73-69	282	T8
	USPGA	69-76-74-74	293	T30
1981	Masters	73-74-70-74	291	T25
	US Open	72-75-73-72	292	T58
	USPGA	71-74-68-69	282	T16
1982	Masters	80-78	158	MC
	US Open	76-75-68-77	296	T39
	USPGA	73-69-73-73	288	T42
1983	Masters	72-73-72-69	286	T6
	US Open	72-76-75-76	299	T39
	Br Open	69-68-72-67	276	T2
	USPGA	72-70-73-68	283	T14
1984	Masters	70-71-74-72	287	T21
	US Open	68-68-69-79	284	6
	Br Open	75-68-70-72	285	T14
	USPGA	71-70-74-72	287	T25
1985	Masters	78-71-73-72	294	T36
	US Open	73-72-70-70	285	14
	USPGA	71-73-72-73	289	T32
1986	Masters	76-76	152	MC
	US Open	77-74	151	MC
	USPGA	76-70-73-68	287	T26
1987	US Open	79-71	150	MC
1988	US Open	71-71-72-71	285	T17
	USPGA	74-70-72-71	287	T38
1989	US Open	74-70-79-70	293	T54
1990	US Open	69-70-74-67	280	Won
	Br Open	72-68-75-72	287	T53
	USPGA	77-72-70-74	293	T12
1991	Masters	70-70-75-66	281	T10
	US Open	71-75-70-74	290	T11
	Br Open	74-70-73-69	286	T57
	USPGA	70-76-74-78	298	T73
1992	Masters	72-70-72-75	289	47
	US Open	73-70-78-77	298	T51
	Br Open	70-73-67-72	282	T19
	USPGA	71-77-72-75	295	T66
1993	Masters	74-69-74-72	289	T27
	US Open	73-71-71-72	287	T62
	USPGA	68-69-67-73	277	T6
1994	Masters	73-68-79-72	292	T18
	US Open	69-69-71-78	287	T18
	USPGA	75-69-68-74	286	T39
1995	Masters	69-72-71-72	284	T14
	US Open	75-72	147	MC
	USPGA	71-68-71-73	283	T54

Tony JACKLIN

Born: July 1944, Scunthorpe, England
European Tour wins: 14
US Tour wins: 3
Ryder Cup appearances: 7, (1967, 69, 71, 73, 75, 77, 79)

The only Ryder Cup captain to taste victory over the United States more than once, Jacklin guided Europe to victory in 1985 and 1987, and then retained the trophy in 1989 when the match was tied 14-all. His only loss as captain came in 1983 in Florida. In those four matches in charge, Jacklin's European team amassed a total of 59 points, to the 53 scored by the Americans.

■ Despite being Europe's leading player between 1968 and 1972, Jacklin never topped the European Order of Merit. During this period, he spent most of his time on the US Tour. His highest ever finish in the European OM was 5th in 1966.

■ When Jacklin won the US Open in 1970, he led the tournament after each round. He led by two strokes after day one; by three strokes after 36 holes; and by four after round three. He eventually won by seven, which is the widest winning margin in the US Open since 1921. Yet in the final round, Jacklin did have one scary moment. After posting successive bogies at the 7th and 8th holes his seemingly unassailable lead was down to three. Then, at the 400-yard, par 4, 9th, he faced a birdie putt of around 25 feet. Jacklin struck it hard. The ball was on line but travelling at quite a pace. Fortunately for Jacklin, the ball rammed against the back of the cup, jumped about nine inches into the air and fell into the hole. What could have turned out to be a bogey-five, was instead a birdie-three. He was back to four strokes ahead and the title was his.

■ Jacklin won both his major titles at the age of 25. But while many expected him to win more majors, his career took a downturn in 1973, when he started to devote more time to the European Tour. After finishing third in the 1972 British Open at Muirfield, Jacklin never registered another top-10 finish in a major championship.

■ His last European victory came at Hillside, Southport, in May 1982, when he won the Sun Alliance PGA Championship, beating Bernhard Langer in a play-off. At the first extra-hole, Jacklin fired a 6-iron shot that actually touched the edge of the cup, before coming to rest two feet from the flag. The resulting birdie-three secured the title. Jacklin joined the US Senior Tour in 1994.

Year	T'ment	Scores	Total	Position
1963	Br Open	73-72-76-74	295	T30
1965	Br Open	75-73-73-77	298	T25
1966	Br Open	74-76-72-76	298	T30
1967	Masters	71-70-74-77	292	T16
	Br Open	73-69-73-70	285	5
1968	Masters	69-73-74-72	288	T22
	Br Open	72-72-75-80	299	T18
1969	Masters	73-76	149	MC
	US Open	71-70-73-75	289	T25
	Br Open	68-70-70-72	280	**Won**
	USPGA	73-70-73-71	287	T25
1970	Masters	73-74-70-71	288	T12
	US Open	71-70-70-70	281	**Won**
	Br Open	67-70-73-76	286	5
	USPGA	74-79	153	MC
1971	USPGA	71-74-74-73	292	T29
	Masters	73-76-76-72	297	T36
	US Open	75-77	152	MC
	Br Open	69-70-70-71	280	3
1972	Masters	72-76-75-74	297	T27
	US Open	75-78-71-83	307	T40
	Br Open	69-72-67-72	280	3
1973	Masters	77-75	152	MC
	US Open	75-75-73-77	300	T52
	Br Open	75-73-72-70	290	T14
	USPGA	70-71-76-75	292	T46
1974	Masters	81-71	152	MC
	US Open	78-76	154	MC
	Br Open	74-77-71-75	297	T18
	USPGA	73-72-76-74	295	T55
1975	Masters	77-74	151	MC
	US Open	76-74	150	MC
1976	Br Open	73-77-76-72	298	T42
1977	Br Open	72-70-74-77	293	T43
1978	Br Open	75-74	149	MC
1979	Br Open	73-74-76-73	296	T24
1980	Br Open	72-74-71-73	290	T32

In 1969, Tony Jacklin became the first home winner of the British Open for 18 years. He followed this success by winning the US Open the following year

Bobby Jones on his way to winning the 1927 British Open at St Andrews

Mr Bobby JONES

Between 1926 and 1930, no one had a finer major championship record than Bobby Jones. Despite being an amateur, Jones was the supreme champion.

He played in four British Opens winning three of them, he also won four US Opens. And in a total of 12 US and British Opens in which he played from 1922 to 1930, he only once finished lower than second.

Jones, however, is best remembered for achieving, what used to be referred to, as the old Grand Slam. In 1930, he won, the British Amateur Championship, British Open, US Open and US Amateur Championship, in that order.

Nowadays, being an amateur champion is considered as merely the final step before turning professional. Yet back in the 1920s and 30s, many of the world's best players held amateur status throughout their golfing life.

After completing the Grand Slam, Jones retired from tournament golf. He was only 28. A successful career in law followed, not that Jones turned his back on golf completely. Together with Clifford Roberts, he founded Augusta National and in the early years of the US Masters he made rare appearances in the tournament. He also made a number of instructional films on golf.

Jones, born in Atlanta, Georgia in March 1902, was a clean cut, modest, American hero, unlike the more flamboyant figures of his contemporaries Walter Hagen and Gene Sarazen.

Looking back on Jones' career, both on and off the golf course, it seemed as if everything came easy to him. In addition to his golfing prowess, Jones held degrees in engineering, science and law. Extremely gifted, he was, but there were still one or two traumatic moments. In his first appearance at the British Open, in 1921, at St Andrews, Jones tore up his card in anger in round three. He'd taken 46 strokes to reach the turn, then made sixes at both the 10th and short par-3, 11th holes, before petulantly walking off the course. Jones apologised for his behaviour. He was still only 19.

Jones also found the tension of tournament golf quite a strain and he would often be physically sick before an important round.

Sadly, Jones' health deteriorated in his 50s and he spent his last years confined to a wheel chair, as a cripple. He died in December 1971.

Year	T'ment	Scores	Total	Position
1920	US Open	78-74-70-77	299	T8
1921	Br Open	Withdrew during 3rd Round		
	US Open	78-71-77-77	303	T5
1922	US Open	74-72-70-73	289	T2
1923	US Open*	71-73-76-76	296	Won
1924	US Open	74-73-75-78	300	2
1925	US Open**	77-70-70-74	291	2
1926	Br Open	72-72-73-74	291	Won

	US Open	70-79-71-73	293	**Won**
1927	US Open	76-77-79-77	309	T11
	Br Open	68-72-73-72	285	**Won**
1928	US Open**	73-71-73-77	294	2
1929	US Open*	69-75-71-79	294	**Won**
1930	Br Open	70-72-74-75	291	**Won**
	US Open	71-73-68-75	287	**Won**
1934	Masters	76-74-72-72	294	T13
1935	Masters	74-72-73-78	297	T25
1936	Masters	78-78-73-77	306	33
1937	Masters	79-74-73-77	303	T28
1938	Masters	76-74-72-75	297	T16
1939	Masters	76-77-78-73	304	T33
1940	Masters	79-76-Wd	155	Wd

* - Won Play-Off
** - Lost Play-Off

British Amateur Championship
Won: 1930

US Amateur Championship
Won: 1924-25-27-28-30
Runner-Up: 1919-26

Bernhard LANGER

Born: August 1957, Anhausen, Germany
European Tour wins: 34
Ryder Cup appearances: 8, (1981, 83, 85, 87, 89, 91, 93, 95)

When the inaugural Sony Ranking was published in April 1986, Langer had the honour of being the first-ever world number one. He remained there for the first three weeks.

■ Has yet to win the British Open despite finishing in the top-3 on five occasions. Three of his top-3 finishes were at Royal St. George's (1981, 85 & 93).

■ Through to the end of 1995, Langer had won at least one official European Tour event every year, for the past 16 years.

■ Both his major victories have come at Augusta. In 1985, the key moment came at the par-4, 17th in the final round, when Langer holed a birdie putt from 14-feet. It allowed him the luxury of taking a bogey five at the final hole and still winning the title. Eight years later, Langer won by four shots. The decisive moment was an eagle three at the 13th, when Langer sank

Bernhard Langer: twice the Masters champion at Augusta

a tricky downhill putt. Once again he bogied the 72nd hole.

■ By the end of 1995, he had won nine European Tour events in his own country - German Open (1981, 82, 85, 86, 93); German Masters (1989, 91); Honda Open (1992); Deutsche Bank Open (1995).

■ Led Germany to a famous victory in the 1990 World Cup in Orlando, Florida, when his teammate was Torsten Giedeon.

Year	T'ment	Scores	Total	Position
1976	Br Open	82-79	161	MC
1978	Br Open	78-73	151	MC
1980	Br Open	73-72-72-76	293	T51
1981	Br Open	73-67-70-70	280	2
1982	Masters	77-78	155	MC
	US Open	80-79	159	MC
	Br Open	70-69-78-73	290	T13
1983	Br Open	67-72-76-74	289	T56
1984	Masters	73-70-74-72	289	T31
	Br Open	71-68-68-71	278	**T2**
1985	Masters	72-74-68-68	282	**Won**
	US Open	76-76	152	MC
	Br Open	72-69-68-75	284	**T3**
	USPGA	69-72-76-72	289	T32
1986	Masters	74-68-69-75	286	T16
	US Open	74-70-70-70	284	T8
	Br Open	72-70-76-68	286	**T3**
	USPGA	73-74	147	MC
1987	Masters	71-72-70-76	289	T7
	US Open	69-69-73-72	283	T4
	Br Open	69-69-76-72	286	T17
	USPGA	70-78-77-70	295	T21
1988	Masters	71-72-71-73	287	T9
	US Open	75-72	147	MC
	Br Open	73-75-75-80	303	70
	USPGA	74-77	151	MC
1989	Masters	74-75-71-73	293	T26
	US Open	66-78-77-73	294	T59
	Br Open	71-73-83-82	309	80
	USPGA	74-71-75-72	292	T61
1990	Masters	70-73-69-74	286	T7
	US Open	78-70	148	MC
	Br Open	74-69-75-68	286	T48
	USPGA	75-78	153	MC
1991	Masters	71-68-74-74	287	T32
	US Open	75-74	149	MC
	Br Open	71-71-70-67	279	T9
	USPGA	75-74	149	MC
1992	Masters	69-73-69-74	285	T31
	US Open	73-72-75-75	295	T23
	Br Open	70-72-76-73	291	T59
	USPGA	72-74-72-73	291	T40
1993	Masters	68-70-69-70	277	**Won**
	US Open	74-71	145	MC
	Br Open	67-66-70-67	270	3
	USPGA	75-69	144	MC
1994	Masters	74-74-72-73	293	T25
	US Open	72-72-73-72	289	T23
	Br Open	72-70-70-72	284	T60
	USPGA	73-71-67-72	283	T25
1995	Masters	71-69-73-75	288	T31
	US Open	74-67-74-74	289	T36
	Br Open	72-71-73-73	289	T24

Sandy LYLE

Born: February 1958, Shrewsbury, England
European Tour wins: 19
Ryder Cup appearances: 5, (1979, 81, 83, 85, 87)

In 1985 Sandy Lyle followed Tony Jacklin as the first home winner of the British Open for 16 years

Sandy Lyle has topped the European Order of Merit three times (1979, 80, 85).

His golden year was 1988 when he won three times on the US Tour, including the US Masters at Augusta. Back in Europe he won the British Masters at Woburn and the World Matchplay Championship at Wentworth.

During 1988, Lyle reached number two in the Sony World Ranking - his highest position to date.

In winning the World Matchplay title in 1988, Lyle enjoyed a rich vein of form in his matches with Seve Ballesteros and Nick Faldo. In his semi-final with Ballesteros, Lyle was 13-under-par for the 30 holes played. He won the contest 7&6. And in his 2&1 victory over Faldo in the final, he was 9-under-par for 35 holes. Lyle closed out his clash with Faldo by making four consecutive birdies, from the 32nd.

■ Lyle's first major title came at Royal St George's in 1985. After sinking birdies putts at the 14th (35 feet) and 15th (12 feet), he arrived at the final hole needing a par for victory. But his second shot at the par-4, 18th, trickled off the left side of the green. He took three more shots to hole out, and his bogey-five allowed David Graham and Bernhard Langer the opportunity to force a play-off. Both came to the final hole needing a birdie to tie Lyle. But Graham found a greenside bunker with his approach and Langer overshot the green. Both made bogies. Lyle had become the first British winner of the British Open for 16 years.

■ Three years later Lyle won the US Masters in more spectacular fashion, when he birdied the final hole for a one-stroke victory. After driving into a fairway trap, Lyle lofted a 7-iron bunker shot to within 10 feet of the flag and then sank the putt for a three.

■ In 1987, he became the first, and so far only, European golfer to win the prestigious Players' Championship at TPC at Sawgrass in Florida. Lyle parred the third play-off hole to beat Jeff Sluman.

Year	T'ment	Scores	Total	Position
1974	Br Open	75-77-84	236	MC
1977	Br Open	75-80	155	MC
1978	Br Open	72-78	150	MC
1979	Br Open	74-76-75-70	295	T19
1980	Masters	76-70-70-78	294	48
	US Open	73-76	149	MC
	Br Open	70-71-70-73	284	T12
1981	Masters	73-70-76-73	292	T28
	US Open	74-74	148	MC
	Br Open	73-73-71-71	288	T14
	USPGA	76-73	149	MC
1982	Br Open	74-66-73-74	287	T8
1983	Masters	74-74	148	MC
	Br Open	73-71-74	218	MC
1984	Br Open	75-71-72-67	285	T14
1985	Masters	78-65-76-73	292	T25
	Br Open	68-71-73-70	282	Won
1986	Masters	76-70-68-71	285	T11
	US Open	78-71-72-72	293	T45

	Br Open	78-73-70-74	295	T30
1987	Masters	77-74-68-72	291	T17
	US Open	70-74-72-73	289	T36
	Br Open	76-69-71-70	286	T17
1988	Masters	71-67-72-71	281	Won
	US Open	68-71-75-73	287	T25
	Br Open	73-69-67-74	283	T7
1989	Masters	77-76	153	MC
	US Open	78-74	152	MC
	Br Open	73-73-71-72	289	T46
1990	Masters	77-74	151	MC
	US Open	78-72	150	MC
	Br Open	72-70-67-72	281	T16
1991	Masters	77-76	153	MC
	US Open	72-70-74-75	291	T16
	Br Open	79-Dq	79	MC
	USPGA	68-75-71-72	286	T16
1992	Masters	72-69-70-75	286	T37
	US Open	73-74-75-76	298	T51
	Br Open	68-70-70-72	280	T12
	USPGA	74-78	152	MC
1993	Masters	73-71-71-73	288	T21
	US Open	70-74-70-72	286	T52
	Br Open	70-76	146	MC
	USPGA	69-73-70-74	286	T56
1994	Masters	75-73-78-73	299	T38
	Br Open	71-72-72-72	287	74
	USPGA	75-70-76-76	297	T73
1995	Masters	75-71	146	MC
	Br Open	71-71-79-75	296	T79
	USPGA	67-73-69-71	280	T39

Byron NELSON

Born: February 1912, Fort Worth, Texas
US Tour wins: 52
Ryder Cup appearances: 2 (1937, 47)

In 1946, having just completed the three most successful years of his life, Byron Nelson announced his retirement from golf aged 34.

In three glorious seasons he had won 32 tournaments on the US Tour, including 18 in 1945 alone. But the strain of competition was getting too much for Nelson. He wasn't scared to admit that the tension of playing week-in, week-out, on Tour was affecting his health. Financially secure from his exploits on the fairways, he bought a ranch and settled back into family life.

Nelson captured five major titles in his career. And in that superb summer of 1945, won 11

Byron Nelson was one of the game's great exponents of matchplay, winning two USPGA titles

consecutive tournaments between March 11th and August 4th, easily a Tour record (the next best is four successive wins). This run included his second USPGA title.

It's amazing to think that when Nelson won his fifth and final major, at the age of 33, fellow Texan Ben Hogan, who was only six months his junior, had yet to land his first. Hogan's great future lay just around the corner.

Nelson made his name in 1937, when he won the Masters by two strokes after opening with, what was then, a course record 66. Five years later there was a second Augusta title, after pipping Hogan by one shot in an exciting 18-hole play-off. His US Open triumph in 1939 also came via a play-off.

But Nelson's greatest success came in matchplay. He won two USPGA titles and was runner-up on three occasions. Between 1939 and 1946, Nelson won 31 of his 36 matches in the USPGA Championship. And in those five defeats, he never once failed to go the distance. Three times he lost in extra-holes and was twice beaten on the 36th green. Only the great Walter Hagen

had a matchplay record to compare with Nelson, who also won three of his four Ryder Cup matches, the only reverse being a 3&1 loss to Dai Rees in 1937.

After 1946, Nelson continued to play in selected tournaments, such as the US Masters. He was also a great student of the swing, writing many instructional books on golf and in the mid-1970s became Tom Watson's mentor. Nelson was always popular with fans and fellow-competitors and has a US Tour event named after him, the Byron Nelson Classic staged in Texas since 1968.

In reviewing Nelson's career, many golf historians point out that his most productive years came at the end of the Second World War, when many of the game's leading players were away on active service. Nelson, himself, had been turned down by the military forces because of a blood disorder. Yet to underestimate Nelson's achievements would be foolish. In his hot streak of 1945 he posted 19 successive rounds under 70 and had an exceptional stroke average of 68.33, a great performance whatever the quality of the field.

Year	T'ment	Scores	Total	Position
1934	US Open	79-83	162	MC
1935	Masters	71-74-72-74	291	T9
	US Open	75-81-82-77	315	T32
1936	Masters	76-71-77-74	298	T13
	US Open	79-74	153	MC
1937	Masters	66-72-75-70	283	Won
	US Open	73-78-71-73	295	T20
	Br Open	75-76-71-74	296	5
1938	Masters	73-74-70-73	290	5
	US Open	77-71-74-72	294	T5
1939	Masters	71-69-72-75	287	7
	US Open*	72-73-71-68	284	Won
1940	Masters	69-72-74-70	285	3
	US Open	72-74-70-74	290	T5
1941	Masters	71-69-73-70	283	2
	US Open	73-73-74-77	297	T17
1942	Masters*	68-67-72-73	280	Won
1946	Masters	72-73-71-74	290	T7
	US Open**	71-71-69-73	284	T2
1947	Masters	69-72-72-70	283	T2
1948	Masters	71-73-72-74	290	T8
1949	Masters	75-70-74-73	292	T8
	US Open	74-77	151	MC
1950	Masters	75-70-69-74	288	T4
1951	Masters	71-73-73-74	291	T8
1952	Masters	72-75-78-77	302	T24
1953	Masters	73-73-78-73	297	T29
1954	Masters	73-76-74-73	296	T12
1955	Masters	72-75-74-72	293	T10
	US Open	77-74-80-75	306	T28
	Br Open	72-75-78-71	296	T32

* - Won Play-Off ** - Lost Play-Off

BYRON NELSON AT THE USPGA

(Matchplay years 1916-57)

Year	Position	Final Match		(W-L)
1934	1st Rd (32)	Lost 4&3	Tommy Armour	(0-1)
1937	Qtr-Final	Lost 2 up	Ky Laffoon	(3-1)
1938	Qtr-Final	Lost 2&1	Jimmy Hines	(3-1)
1939	**Runner-Up**	Lost at 37th	Henry Picard	(5-1)
1940	**Champion**	Won 1up	Sam Snead	(6-0)
1941	**Runner-Up**	Lost at 38th	Vic Ghezzi	(5-1)
1942	Semi-Final	Lost at 37th	Jim Turnesa	(3-1)
1944	**Runner-up**	Lost 1up	Bob Hamilton	(4-1)
1945	**Champion**	Won 4&3	Sam Byrd	(5-0)
1946	Qtr-Final	Lost 1 up	Ed Oliver	(3-1)

Does not include years when player failed to qualify for matchplay stages

Larry NELSON

Born: September 1947, Ft. Payne, Alabama
US Tour wins: 10
Ryder Cup appearances: 3, (1979, 81, 87)
Between August 1981 and August 1987, Nelson won 'only' four US Tour events - yet three of them were major championships.

■ His favourite day is August 9. Both his USPGA titles (1981 & 1987) were won on Sunday 9th August.

■ Didn't start playing golf until he was 21 years old, after serving two years in the military service.

■ Has an excellent Ryder Cup record, winning his first nine matches in the series.

■ In winning the 1983 US Open at Oakmont, he played the last two rounds in 132 strokes (65-67), which is still a tournament record for the final 36 holes. Nelson had started the third round seven strokes off the pace.

■ The quiet, unassuming, Nelson has a reputation for being a steely competitor. When he won his first major title in 1981 (USPGA Championship), he started the final day four strokes ahead of Fuzzy Zoeller in second place. Eighteen holes later, the cool, calm, Nelson had maintained that margin over the rest of the field after firing a final day 71.

Year	T'ment	Scores	Total	Position
1976	US Open	75-74-70-72	291	T21
	USPGA	75-71-74-71	291	T34
1977	US Open	69-75-78-77	299	T54
	USPGA	77-69-79-76	301	T54
1978	US Open	77-78	155	MC
	USPGA	76-71-70-70	287	T12
1979	Masters	70-75-70-77	292	T31
	US Open	71-68-76-73	288	T4
	USPGA	70-75-70-70	285	T28
1980	Masters	69-72-73-69	283	T6
	US Open	70-74-76-79	299	T60
	Br Open	72-70-71-71	284	T12
	USPGA	79-74	153	MC
1981	Masters	78-73	151	MC
	US Open	70-73-69-72	284	T20
	USPGA	70-66-66-71	273	Won
1982	Masters	79-71-70-69	289	T7
	US Open	74-72-74-71	291	T19
	Br Open	77-69-77-74	297	T32
	USPGA	74-75	149	MC
1983	Masters	73-75	148	MC
	US Open	75-73-65-67	280	Won
	Br Open	70-73-73-72	288	T53

Larry Nelson, pictured here at Troon in 1989, has won three major titles

	USPGA	72-68-68-80	288	T36		1991	Masters	74-69-76-75	294	55
1984	Masters	76-69-66-70	281	5			US Open	73-72-72-68	285	T3
	US Open	82-76	158	MC			USPGA	75-77	152	MC
	Br Open	75-69-76	220	MC		1992	Masters	Disq	-----	Disq
	USPGA	72-77	149	MC			US Open	77-76	153	MC
1985	Masters	73-75-74-72	294	T36			USPGA	72-68-75-74	289	T28
	US Open	71-71-77-71	290	T39		1993	US Open	70-71-71-73	285	T46
	Br Open	70-75-75-77	297	T56			USPGA	73-67-74-72	286	T56
	USPGA	70-74-71-72	287	T23		1994	US Open	75-73	148	MC
1986	Masters	73-73-71-76	293	T36			USPGA	75-71	146	MC
	US Open	75-73-70-73	291	T35		1995	USPGA	70-75	145	MC
	Br Open	81-75	156	MC						
	USPGA	74-74	148	MC						
1987	Masters	75-79	154	MC						
	US Open	76-75	151	MC						
	Br Open	70-75-76-73	294	T48						
	USPGA	70-72-73-72	287	**Won**						
1988	Masters	69-78-75-75	297	T33						
	US Open	78-67-80-72	297	T62						
	Br Open	73-71-68-73	285	T13						
	USPGA	70-71-76-70	287	T38						
1989	Masters	77-76	153	MC						
	US Open	68-73-68-75	284	T13						
	Br Open	73-74	147	MC						
	USPGA	71-74-68-75	288	T46						
1990	Masters	74-73-79-74	300	48						
	US Open	74-67-69-75	285	T14						
	USPGA	77-75	152	MC						

Jack NICKLAUS

Born: January 1940, Columbus, Ohio
US Tour wins: 70
Ryder Cup appearances: 6 (1969, 71, 73, 75, 77, 81)

Arguably the greatest player in the history of the game. From the moment he joined the US Tour in January 1962, right through to the early 1980s, almost everything Jack touched turned to gold.

While players such as Walter Hagen, Bobby Jones, Ben Hogan, Arnold Palmer and Tom

Watson were clearly the leading golfers of their generation, none of them dominated the game for as long a period as the Golden Bear. Eighteen professional major titles, 70 US Tour wins, plus many more victories worldwide, are testimony to Nicklaus' claim to being the greatest of all time.

And what a dramatic entrance he made, by making the 1962 US Open, his first professional success. Thereafter, every time he teed up, Nicklaus was clearly the man to beat. But it was his high level of consistency week-in, week-out, that made him such a formidable player. He might have won as many as 18 majors but he also finished in the top three on another 28 occasions.

The following set of data speaks for itself:

o - For 17 successive seasons between 1962 and 1978 inclusive, he never once finished outside the top four in the US Money List and he led that eight times.

o - During the same period he won at least two US tournaments a year and a total of 65 in all.

o - In 33 major championships from the 1970 British Open through to the 1978 British Open, there were a staggering 31 top-10 finishes, including eight victories. His worst finish in that time was tied 13th.

During his career Nicklaus has had many challengers to his crown as world number one. Yet what captivated American golf for so many years in the early 1960s was his rivalry with Arnold Palmer, the man Nicklaus deposed as the world's best player.

Palmer had been unofficial world number one for just four years, between 1958 and 1962, when a man 10 years his junior snatched the 'title' away. For many of Palmer's followers, known as Arnie's Army, this was unthinkable that their man had been displaced as the world's leading golfer. For a short period of time this made Nicklaus extremely unpopular with many golf fans. Not that this affected the Golden Bear's form, it just made him more determined to succeed.

When Nicklaus won the US Open at Oakmont in 1962, it was Palmer he defeated in a play-off. For the next four years the competition between the two was incredibly fierce. During that period Nicklaus won 19 US Tour events to Palmer's 14. But where it really mattered, in the major championships, the balance was clearly in Nicklaus' favour, six wins to two.

After winning the US Open for a second time in 1967, Nicklaus had, what was for him, a minor decline in major form, not winning another until

Jack Nicklaus pictured at St Andrews in 1970

1970 at St Andrews. But that play-off victory over luckless Doug Sanders was the start of another golden period, which lasted the best part of the decade, until Tom Watson emerged as the game's leading player.

But even in his 40s, there were still some great moments ahead. Two majors titles came in 1980 and six years later there was his emotional victory at Augusta when a final round of 65, and a back nine of 30, saw him claim a record sixth Green Jacket in the most dramatic of circumstances.

Nicklaus has also left his mark as a golf

course architect. While still a leading player back in the mid-1970s, he co-designed the beautiful but exacting Muirfield Village course in his home state. The complex was named after the famous Scottish course, where Nicklaus represented the United States at the 1959 Walker Cup match and where seven years later he won the first of his three British Opens.

Probably the biggest disappointment of Jack's career came not as a player but as non-playing captain of the 1987 US Ryder Cup team which lost to Europe 15-13. Not only was this the first time that an American side had been beaten on home soil, it happened at Jack's own Muirfield Village. But even the greatest can't win every time.

Year	T'ment	Scores	Total	Position
1957	US Open	80-80	160	MC
1958	US Open	79-75-73-77	304	T41
1959	Masters	76-74	150	MC
	US Open	77-77	154	MC
1960	Masters	75-71-72-75	293	T13
	US Open	71-71-69-71	282	2
1961	Masters	70-75-70-72	287	T7
	US Open	75-69-70-70	284	T4
1962	Masters	74-75-70-72	291	T15
	US Open*	72-70-72-69	283	Won
	Br Open	80-72-74-79	305	T34
	USPGA	71-74-69-67	281	T3
1963	Masters	74-66-74-72	286	Won
	US Open	76-77	153	MC
	Br Open	71-67-70-70	278	3
	USPGA	69-73-69-68	279	Won
1964	Masters	71-73-71-67	282	T2
	US Open	72-73-77-73	295	T23
	Br Open	76-74-66-68	284	2
	USPGA	67-73-70-64	274	T2
1965	Masters	67-71-64-69	271	Won
	US Open	78-72-73-76	299	T32
	Br Open	73-71-77-73	294	T12
	USPGA	69-70-72-71	282	T2
1966	Masters*	68-76-72-72	288	Won
	US Open	71-71-69-74	285	3
	Br Open	70-67-75-70	282	Won
	USPGA	75-71-75-71	292	T22
1967	Masters	72-79	151	MC
	US Open	71-67-72-65	275	Won
	Br Open	71-69-71-69	280	2
	USPGA	67-75-69-71	282	T3
1968	Masters	69-71-74-67	281	T5
	US Open	72-70-70-67	279	2
	Br Open	76-69-73-73	291	T2
	USPGA	71-79	150	MC
1969	Masters	68-75-72-76	291	T24
	US Open	74-67-75-73	289	T25
	Br Open	75-70-68-72	285	T6
	USPGA	70-68-74-71	283	T11
1970	Masters	71-75-69-69	284	8
	US Open	81-72-75-76	304	T51
	Br Open*	68-69-73-73	283	Won
	USPGA	68-76-73-66	283	T6
1971	USPGA	69-69-70-73	281	Won
	Masters	70-71-68-72	281	T2
	US Open**	69-72-68-71	280	2
	Br Open	71-71-72-69	283	T5
1972	Masters	68-71-73-74	286	Won
	US Open	71-73-72-74	290	Won
	Br Open	70-72-71-66	279	2
	USPGA	72-75-68-72	287	T13
1973	Masters	69-77-73-66	285	T3
	US Open	71-69-74-68	282	T4
	Br Open	69-70-76-65	280	4
	USPGA	72-68-68-69	277	Won
1974	Masters	69-71-72-69	281	T4
	US Open	75-74-76-69	294	T10
	Br Open	74-72-70-71	287	3
	USPGA	69-69-70-69	277	2
1975	Masters	68-67-73-68	276	Won
	US Open	72-70-75-72	289	T7
	Br Open	69-71-68-72	280	T3
	USPGA	70-68-67-71	276	Won
1976	Masters	67-69-73-73	282	T3
	US Open	74-70-75-68	287	T11
	Br Open	74-70-72-69	285	T2
	USPGA	71-69-69-74	283	T4
1977	Masters	72-70-70-66	278	2
	US Open	74-68-71-72	285	T10
	Br Open	68-70-65-66	269	2
	USPGA	69-71-70-73	283	3
1978	Masters	72-73-69-67	281	7
	US Open	73-69-74-73	289	T6
	Br Open	71-72-69-69	281	Won
	USPGA	79-74	153	MC
1979	Masters	69-71-72-69	281	4
	US Open	74-77-72-68	291	T9
	Br Open	72-69-73-72	286	T2
	USPGA	73-72-78-71	294	T65
1980	Masters	74-71-73-73	291	T33
	US Open	63-71-70-68	272	Won
	Br Open	73-67-71-69	280	T4
	USPGA	70-69-66-69	274	Won
1981	Masters	70-65-75-72	282	T2
	US Open	69-68-71-72	280	T6
	Br Open	83-66-71-70	290	T23
	USPGA	71-68-71-69	279	T4
1982	Masters	69-77-71-75	292	T15
	US Open	74-70-71-69	284	2
	Br Open	77-70-72-69	288	T10

	USPGA	74-70-72-67	283	T16
1983	Masters	73-Wd	73	Wd
	US Open	73-74-77-76	300	T43
	Br Open	71-72-72-70	285	T29
	USPGA	73-65-71-66	275	2
1984	Masters	73-73-70-70	286	T18
	US Open	71-71-70-77	289	T21
	Br Open	76-72-68-72	288	T31
	USPGA	77-70-71-69	287	T25
1985	Masters	71-74-72-69	286	T6
	US Open	76-73	149	MC
	Br Open	77-75	152	MC
	USPGA	66-75-74-74	289	T32
1986	Masters	74-71-69-65	279	Won
	US Open	77-72-67-68	284	T8
	Br Open	78-73-76-71	298	T46
	USPGA	70-68-72-75	285	T16
1987	Masters	74-72-73-70	289	T7
	US Open	70-68-76-77	291	T46
	Br Open	74-71-81-76	302	T72
	USPGA	76-73-74-73	296	T24
1988	Masters	75-73-72-72	292	T21
	US Open	74-73	147	MC
	Br Open	75-70-75-68	288	T25
	USPGA	72-79	151	MC
1989	Masters	73-74-73-71	291	T18
	US Open	67-74-74-75	290	T43
	Br Open	74-71-71-70	286	T30
	USPGA	68-72-73-72	285	T27
1990	Masters	72-70-69-74	285	6
	US Open	71-74-68-76	289	T33
	Br Open	71-70-77-71	289	T63
	USPGA	78-74	152	MC
1991	Masters	68-72-72-76	288	T35
	US Open	70-76-77-74	297	T46
	Br Open	70-75-69-71	285	T44
	USPGA	71-72-73-71	287	T23
1992	Masters	69-75-69-74	287	T42
	US Open	77-74	151	MC
	Br Open	75-73	148	MC
	USPGA	72-78	150	MC
1993	Masters	67-75-76-71	289	T27
	US Open	70-72-76-71	289	T72
	Br Open	69-75	144	MC
	USPGA	71-73	144	MC
1994	Masters	78-74	152	MC
	US Open	69-70-77-76	292	T28
	Br Open	72-73	145	MC
	USPGA	79-71	150	MC
1995	Masters	67-78-70-75	290	T35
	US Open	71-81	152	MC
	Br Open	78-70-77-71	296	T79
	USPGA	69-71-71-76	287	T67

* - Won Play-Off   ** - Lost Play-Off

Greg NORMAN

Born: February 1955, Queensland, Australia
European Tour wins: 18
US Tour wins: 15

Has yet to win a major title in the United States, where he has finished second on six occasions (Masters 1986, 1987; US Open 1984, 1995; USPGA 1986, 1993).

■ In 1986 he led all four major championships after 54 holes, but only won one of them - the British Open. Because of this rare occurrence the press said Norman had achieved the 'Saturday Slam.'

Greg Norman blasts out of trouble en route to victory at the 1993 British Open at Royal St George's

Victory in the 1993 British Open brought the popular Norman his second major title

■ Since the start of the Sony World Ranking in April 1986, Norman has never been out of the top 10. He is the only golfer to retain a top-10 place throughout the history of the Ranking. Was ranked world number one at the end of 1986, 1987, 1989, 1990 and 1995.

■ Has lost play-offs in all four major championships.

■ Has won over $9m on the US Tour alone.

■ His first victory as a professional was the West Lakes Classic in Australia in October 1976.

■ Produced one of the great finishing rounds in major championship history when winning the

1993 British Open at Royal St George's. Norman started the final day one stroke behind co-leaders Corey Pavin and Nick Faldo. Defending champion, Faldo, fired a three-under-par 67 but this failed to contain the brilliance of Norman who carded a 64 to win by two strokes.

■ Topped the US Money List in 1986, 1990 and 1995. He also won the European Order of Merit in 1982.

Year	T'ment	Scores	Total	Position
1977	Br Open	78-72-74	224	MC
1978	Br Open	72-73-74-72	291	T29
1979	US Open	76-74-74-78	302	T48
	Br Open	73-71-72-76	292	T10
1980	Br Open	74-74-76	224	MC
1981	Masters	69-70-72-72	283	4
	US Open	71-67-73-76	287	T33
	Br Open	72-75-72-72	291	T31
	USPGA	73-67-68-71	279	T4
1982	Masters	73-75-73-79	300	T36
	Br Open	73-75-76-72	296	T27
	USPGA	66-69-70-72	277	T5
1983	Masters	71-74-70-79	294	T30
	US Open	74-75-81-72	302	T50
	Br Open	75-71-70-67	283	T19
	USPGA	72-72-70-75	289	T42
1984	Masters	75-71-73-69	288	T25
	US Open**	70-68-69-69	276	2
	Br Open	67-74-74-67	282	T6
	USPGA	75-72-73-71	291	T39
1985	Masters	73-72-75-78	298	T47
	US Open	72-71-71-72	286	T15
	Br Open	71-72-71-73	287	T16
	USPGA	75-73	148	MC
1986	Masters	70-72-68-70	280	T2
	US Open	71-68-71-75	285	T12
	Br Open	74-63-74-69	280	Won
	USPGA	65-68-69-76	278	2
1987	Masters**	73-74-66-72	285	T2
	US Open	72-69-74-77	292	T51
	Br Open	71-71-74-75	291	T35
	USPGA	73-78-79-79	309	70
1988	Masters	77-73-71-64	285	T5
	US Open	74-Wd	74	Wd
	USPGA	68-71-72-71	282	T9
1989	Masters	74-75-68-67	284	T3
	US Open	72-68-73-76	289	T33
	Br Open**	69-70-72-64	275	T2
	USPGA	74-71-67-70	282	T12
1990	Masters	78-72	150	MC
	US Open	72-73-69-69	283	T5
	Br Open	66-66-76-69	277	T6
	USPGA	77-69-76-73	295	T19

1991	Masters	78-69	147	MC
	US Open	78-Wd	78	Wd
	Br Open	74-68-71-66	279	T9
	USPGA	70-74-72-73	289	T32
1992	Masters	70-70-73-68	281	T6
	Br Open	71-72-70-68	281	18
	USPGA	71-74-71-70	286	T15
1993	Masters	74-68-71-77	290	T31
	US Open	73-74	147	MC
	Br Open	66-68-69-64	267	**Won**
	USPGA**	68-68-67-69	272	2
1994	Masters	70-70-75-77	292	T18
	US Open	71-71-69-72	283	T6
	Br Open	71-67-69-69	276	T11
	USPGA	71-69-67-70	277	T4
1995	Masters	73-68-68-68	277	**T3**
	US Open	68-67-74-73	282	2
	Br Open	71-74-72-70	287	T15
	USPGA	66-69-70-72	277	T20

** - Lost Play-off   Wd - Withdrew

Jose Maria OLAZABAL

Born: February 1966, Fuenterrabia, Spain
European Tour wins: 15
Ryder Cup appearances: 4, (1987, 89, 91, 93)

Had the most remarkable rookie year in 1986, winning two tournaments (European Masters and Sanyo Open) and finishing second in the European Order of Merit - the highest ever finish by a rookie.

■   As an 18-year-old he beat Colin Montgomerie 5&4 in the final of the 1984 British Amateur Championship at Formby.

■   Produced one of the great performances of all time to win the 1990 World Series in Akron, Ohio, by 12 shots, the widest winning margin on the US Tour since 1975. He opened with a 61, to lead by four, before adding three successive 67s for a 72-hole total of 262.

Jose-Maria Olazabal takes a break during his Ryder Cup debut in 1987 at Muirfield Village

■ Finally rid himself of that unwanted tag 'best player never to win a major', with victory at Augusta in 1994. The key moment in his two-stroke victory came at the par-5 15th where he holed a 30-foot eagle putt from the front of the green. Moments later playing partner and main challenger Tom Lehman missed his eagle attempt from 15 feet giving Ollie a two-stroke cushion.

■ In his Ryder Cup debut at Muirfield Village, Ohio, in 1987, Olazabal won his first three matches when he was paired with close-friend and fellow-countryman Seve Ballesteros in two foursomes and one four-ball.

Year	T'ment	Scores	Total	Position
1984	Br Open	74-75	149	MC
1985	Masters	81-76	157	MC
	Br Open	72-76-71-70	289	T25
1986	Br Open	78-69-72-73	292	T16
1987	Masters	79-75	154	MC
	US Open	76-69-76-74	295	T68
	Br Open	70-73-70-72	285	T11
	USPGA	79-77	156	MC
1988	Br Open	73-71-73-75	292	T36
1989	Masters	77-73-70-68	288	T8
	US Open	69-72-70-72	283	T9
	Br Open	68-72-69-75	284	T23
	USPGA	73-74	147	MC
1990	Masters	72-73-68-74	287	13
	US Open	73-69-69-73	284	T8
	Br Open	71-67-71-72	281	T16
	USPGA	73-77-72-72	294	T14
1991	Masters	68-71-69-70	278	2
	US Open	73-71-75-70	289	T8
	Br Open	74-67-74-74	289	T80
	USPGA	77-73	150	MC
1992	Masters	76-69-72-70	287	T42
	US Open	73-77	150	MC
	Br Open	70-67-69-68	274	3
	USPGA	73-77	150	MC
1993	Masters	70-72-74-68	284	T7
	US Open	74-74	148	MC
	Br Open	73-74	147	MC
	USPGA	73-69-73-71	286	T56
1994	Masters	74-67-69-69	279	Won
	US Open	76-74	150	MC
	Br Open	72-71-69-68	280	T38
	USPGA	72-66-70-70	278	T7
1995	Masters	66-74-72-72	284	T14
	US Open	73-70-72-73	288	T28
	Br Open	72-72-74-72	290	T31
	USPGA	72-66-70-71	279	T31

Arnold PALMER

Born: September 1929, Latrobe, Pennsylvania
US Tour wins: 60
Ryder Cup appearances: 6 (1961, 63, 65, 67, 71, 73)

If major titles were decided on popularity alone, then Arnold Palmer would have more Championships to his credit than any other golfer in the history of the game.

For more than four decades, Palmer's massive following has been legendary. 'Arnie's Army', as his supporters are called, have been incredibly loyal and at times fanatical. Even now, some 30 years after the last of his seven major victories, the support for Palmer has hardly dipped. His fans just get younger.

Joining the US Tour in 1955, Palmer quickly attracted large galleries through his go-for-broke style of play as well as his charismatic and highly emotional personality. His fans lived every shot and every moment with him and there were plenty of highs and lows in Palmer's golfing life.

While his attacking, gambling instincts were certainly instrumental in helping him win four US Masters, one US Open and two British Opens, they also lost him a few majors as well. His roller-coaster performances certainly make interesting reading.

o 1959 US Masters - Takes a three-over par 6 at Augusta's 12th hole in round four and eventually loses out by two strokes.

o 1960 US Masters - Sinks birdie putts of 35 feet at 17 and six feet at 18 to win by one.

o 1960 US Open - Starts final round seven shots off the pace but birdies six of the opening seven holes, en route to a 65 and the title.

o 1961 US Masters - Needing a par four at 18 to win, he shoots a double-bogey six.

o 1966 US Open - Despite taking a seven-shot lead into the final nine holes, Palmer is caught after coming home in 39 strokes. He loses the play-off the following day - it was his third play-off defeat in the US Open since 1962.

The Rodman Wanamaker trophy (USPGA Championship) is the only major prize missing from Palmer's collection of valuables. In this he was second three times. In 1964, Bobby Nichols beat him by three shots, although Palmer did have the consolation of becoming the first player in history to shoot four sub-70 rounds in the same major championship. In 1968 he trailed home one stroke

An expectant gallery watches Arnold Palmer drive off during the 1961 Ryder Cup match at Royal Lytham

behind Julius Boros and two years later at Southern Hills, Dave Stockton edged him out by two.

By the law of averages Palmer should have won more majors than he actually did. He was a runner-up on no fewer than 10 occasions - only Nicklaus has had more. Yet at times it was his vulnerability in his moment of truth, that made him such a fascinating personality. You could never tell how he would react to a given situation. He could win from seemingly impossible positions but could also snatch defeat from the jaws of victory.

Born in Latrobe, Pennsylvania, in September 1929, Palmer turned professional soon after winning the 1954 US Amateur Championship. Powerful arms and big hands made him one of the longest hitters on Tour. His first victory came at the 1955 Canadian Open, his last and 60th at the 1973 Bob Hope Desert Classic. He also topped the US Money List four times (1958, 60, 62 & 63).

One of the most puzzling aspects of Palmer's career was his failure to win any more major titles after the 1964 US Masters. It wasn't as if his game was in decline. Between 1964 and 1973 there were 19 Tour wins, plus six runner-up finishes in major championships. But probably the greatest contribution he ever made was attracting thousands of fans to the game of golf through his dynamic personality and his exciting brand of play. Even now, well into his 60s, he can still create quit a stir among his large army of supporters.

Year	T'ment	Scores	Total	Position
1953	US Open	84-78	162	MC
1954	US Open	81-73	154	MC
1955	Masters	76-76-72-69	293	T10
	US Open	77-76-74-76	303	T21
1956	Masters	73-75-74-79	301	21
	US Open	72-70-72-73	287	7
1957	Masters	73-73-69-76	291	T7

	US Open	76-76	152	MC
1958	Masters	70-73-68-73	284	Won
	US Open	75-75-77-72	299	T23
	USPGA	76-71-77-74	298	T40
1959	Masters	71-70-71-74	286	3
	US Open	71-69-72-74	286	T5
	USPGA	72-72-71-71	286	T14
1960	Masters	67-73-72-70	282	Won
	US Open	72-71-72-65	280	Won
	Br Open	70-71-70-68	279	2
	USPGA	67-74-75-70	286	T7
1961	Masters	68-69-73-71	281	T2
	US Open	74-75-70-70	289	T14
	Br Open	70-73-69-72	284	Won
	USPGA	73-72-69-68	282	T5
1962	Masters*	70-66-69-75	280	Won
	US Open**	71-68-73-71	283	2
	Br Open	71-69-67-69	276	Won
	USPGA	71-72-73-72	288	T17
1963	Masters	74-73-73-71	291	T9
	US Open**	73-69-77-74	293	2
	Br Open	76-71-71-76	294	T26
	USPGA	74-73-73-73	293	T40
1964	Masters	69-68-69-70	276	Won
	US Open	68-69-75-74	286	T5
	USPGA	68-68-69-69	274	T2
1965	Masters	70-68-72-70	280	T2
	US Open	76-76	152	MC
	Br Open	70-71-75-79	295	16
	USPGA	72-75-74-73	294	T33
1966	Masters	74-70-74-72	290	T4
	US Open**	71-66-70-71	278	2
	Br Open	73-72-69-74	288	T8
	USPGA	75-73-71-68	287	T6
1967	Masters	73-73-70-69	285	4
	US Open	69-68-73-69	279	2
	USPGA	70-71-72-74	287	T14
1968	Masters	72-79	151	MC
	US Open	73-74-79-75	301	59
	Br Open	77-71-72-77	297	T10
	USPGA	71-69-72-70	282	T2
1969	Masters	73-75-70-74	292	27
	US Open	70-73-69-72	284	T6
	USPGA	82-Wd	82	Wd
1970	Masters	75-73-74-73	295	T36
	US Open	79-74-75-77	305	T54
	Br Open	68-72-76-74	290	12
	USPGA	70-72-69-70	281	T2
1971	USPGA	75-71-70-73	289	T18
	Masters	73-72-71-73	289	T18
	US Open	73-68-73-74	288	T24
1972	Masters	70-75-74-81	300	T33
	US Open	77-68-73-76	294	3
	Br Open	73-73-69-71	286	T6

	USPGA	69-75-72-73	289	T16
1973	Masters	77-72-76-70	295	T24
	US Open	71-71-68-72	282	T4
	Br Open	72-76-70-72	290	T14
	USPGA	76-74	150	MC
1974	Masters	76-71-70-67	284	T11
	US Open	73-70-73-76	292	T5
	USPGA	72-75-70-72	289	T28

Other Top 10 finishes:

1975	US Open	T9	(290)
1977	Br Open	7	(282)

* - Won Play-Off
** - Lost Play-Off

Gary PLAYER

Born: November 1935, Johannesburg
US Tour wins: 21

Few golfers have had to travel as far in their career as Gary Player. In his search for top class competitive golf, the diminutive South African was forced to leave his homeland in his early 20s. Having turned professional as a teenager, Player quickly discovered that the level of opposition needed to test his extraordinary abilities to the full didn't exist in his native South Africa.

He first came to Britain in 1955, before taking his talents to the toughest breeding ground of all, the United States, when still only 21.

Player never rattled up major victories with the same frequency of say a Hogan, Nicklaus or Palmer. But that shouldn't detract from his greatness because history shows it is far more difficult for a foreigner to dominate in the United States than a home grown American.

His nine major victories covered a 19-year spell (1959-78) during which time he won at regular intervals. The longest gap between major wins being just over four years from the 1968 British Open to the 1972 USPGA Championship.

Throughout his career, Player always had the ability to dig deep into his powers of concentration to produce tournament-winning shots at crucial times.

One such moment came on the 70th hole (par 4) at the 1972 USPGA Championship at Oakland Hills. Having blocked his tee shot down the right, Player had his path to the green shut out by a

Gary Player seems to be the master of all he surveys at the 1974 British Open, which he won for the third time

large tree. He also had a greenside pond to negotiate. But taking a lofted club, Player fired his ball over the tree to within four feet of the hole. The ensuing birdie helped him secure a two-stroke victory.

Two years later, Player made another vital birdie at the 71st hole (par 4) of the US Masters, hitting a nine iron to less than a foot from the cup. He won by two shots.

And who'll forget his final major title at Augusta in 1978, at the age of 42, when he came home in 30 (six-under-par) for a 64 and a one-stroke victory. He'd started the day seven strokes off the pace, yet his successful 15 foot birdie putt on 18 meant a third Green Jacket.

Player also had a few problems when winning majors. At Muirfield in 1959 he finished with a double-bogey six. He then had to wait for two nerve-racking hours before being told he'd won his first major title - the British Open.

And in 1961 at Augusta he played the final nine holes in 40 shots (four-over-par) but still won the Masters by one when Arnold Palmer double-bogeyed the final hole.

Player was particularly good at matchplay. He won the World Matchplay Championship five times - a record he jointly holds with Seve Ballesteros -between 1965 and 1973. The highlights of these Wentworth years must have been the trouncing of Jack Nicklaus twice in the final (6&4 in 1966; 5&4 in 1971).

His thirst for competition has taken him far and wide. He's won the Australian Open seven times, as well as his home National Championship on an incredible 13 occasions. And during a career that has touched five different decades, Player's boyish enthusiasm for the game has never waned.

Despite passing his 60th birthday in November 1995, Player's competitive desire is almost as strong now on the US Senior Tour as it was back in the 1960s. And the day Player decides to call a halt to his globe-trotting activities will be a sad one indeed for all his many followers who have admired the South African's energy, bravery and courage throughout his glorious career.

Year	T'ment	Scores	Total	Position		Year	T'ment	Scores	Total	Position
							Br Open	71-70-71-72	284	7
1956	Br Open	71-76-73-71	291	4		1972	Masters	73-75-72-71	291	T10
1957	Masters	77-72-75-73	297	T24			US Open	72-74-75-80	301	T15
	Br Open	71-74-75-73	293	T24			Br Open	71-71-76-67	285	6
1958	Masters	74-76	150	MC			USPGA	71-71-67-72	281	**Won**
	US Open	75-68-73-71	287	2		1973	US Open	67-70-77-73	287	12
	Br Open	68-74-70-71	283	7			Br Open	76-69-76-69	290	T14
1959	Masters	73-75-71-71	290	T8			USPGA	73-72-71-78	294	T51
	US Open	71-69-76-76	292	T15		1974	Masters	71-71-66-70	278	**Won**
	Br Open	75-71-70-68	284	**Won**			US Open	70-73-77-73	293	T8
1960	Masters	72-71-72-74	289	T6			Br Open	69-68-75-70	282	**Won**
	US Open	70-72-71-76	289	T19			USPGA	73-64-73-70	280	7
	Br Open	72-71-72-69	284	7		1975	Masters	72-74-73-73	292	T30
1961	Masters	69-68-69-74	280	**Won**			US Open	75-73-72-77	297	T43
	US Open	75-72-69-71	287	T9			Br Open	75-71-73-73	292	T32
	Br Open	73-77-Wd	150	Wd			USPGA	72-70-73-76	291	T33
	USPGA	72-74-71-73	290	T29		1976	Masters	73-73-70-79	295	T28
1962	Masters**	67-71-71-71	280	**T2**			US Open	72-77-73-70	292	T23
	US Open	71-71-72-74	288	T6			Br Open	72-72-79-71	294	T28
	Br Open	74-79	153	MC			USPGA	70-69-72-75	286	T13
	USPGA	72-67-69-70	278	**Won**		1977	Masters	71-70-72-74	287	T19
1963	Masters	71-74-74-70	289	T5			US Open	72-67-71-75	285	T10
	US Open	74-75-75-72	296	T8			Br Open	71-74-74-69	288	T22
	Br Open	75-70-72-70	287	T7			USPGA	74-77-68-74	293	T31
	USPGA	74-75-67-70	286	T8		1978	Masters	72-72-69-64	277	**Won**
1964	Masters	69-72-72-73	286	T5			US Open	71-71-70-77	289	T6
	US Open	75-74-72-74	295	T23			Br Open	74-71-76-71	292	T34
	Br Open	78-71-73-70	292	T8			USPGA	76-72-71-71	290	T26
	USPGA	70-71-71-71	283	T13		1979	Masters	71-72-74-71	288	T17
1965	Masters	65-73-69-73	280	**T2**			US Open	73-73-72-68	286	**T2**
	US Open*	70-70-71-71	282	**Won**			Br Open	77-74-69-75	295	T19
	Br Open	76-71-79-Wd	226	Wd			USPGA	73-70-70-71	284	T23
	USPGA	74-72-74-74	294	T33		1980	Masters	71-71-71-70	283	T6
1966	Masters	74-77-76-72	299	T28			US Open	77-72	149	MC
	US Open	78-72-74-69	293	T15			Br Open	77-71-72	220	MC
	Br Open	72-74-71-69	286	T4			USPGA	72-74-71-75	292	T26
	USPGA	73-70-70-73	286	**T3**		1981	Masters	73-73-71-71	288	T15
1967	Masters	75-69-72-71	287	T6			US Open	72-72-71-71	286	T26
	US Open	69-73-73-71	286	T12			Br Open	81-68-75	224	MC
	Br Open	72-71-67-74	284	**T3**			USPGA	75-72-71-71	289	T49
1968	Masters	72-67-71-72	282	T7		1982	Masters	74-73-71-74	292	T15
	US Open	76-69-70-73	288	T16			US Open	78-78	156	MC
	Br Open	74-71-71-73	289	**Won**			Br Open	75-74-76-75	300	T42
1969	Masters	74-70-75-76	295	T33			USPGA	76-70	146	MC
	US Open	71-75-72-77	295	T48		1983	Masters	73-78	151	MC
	Br Open	74-68-76-74	292	T23			US Open	73-74-76-71	294	T20
	USPGA	71-65-71-70	277	2			Br Open	76-71	147	MC
1970	Masters	74-68-68-70	280	3			USPGA	74-68-73-74	289	T42
	US Open	80-73-75-74	302	T44		1984	Masters	71-72-73-71	287	T21
	Br Open	74-75-75	224	MC			US Open	74-72-72-76	294	T43
	USPGA	74-68-74-70	286	T12			Br Open	74-75	149	MC
1971	USPGA	71-73-68-73	285	T4			USPGA	74-63-69-71	277	**T2**
	Masters	72-72-71-69	284	T6		1985	Masters	71-75-73-75	294	T36
	US Open	76-71-72-70	289	T27			Br Open	72-77-73	222	MC

	USPGA	72-76	148	MC
1986	Masters	77-73	150	MC
	Br Open	75-72-73-76	296	T35
1987	Masters	75-75-71-76	297	T35
	Br Open	72-74-79-75	300	T66
1988	Masters	78-75	153	MC
	US Open	77-72	149	MC
	Br Open	72-76-73-76	297	T61

* - Won after Play-Off
** - Lost after Play-Off

Nick PRICE

Born: January 1957, Durban, South Africa
US Tour wins: 14
Between August 1992 and September 1994, he won 11 US Tour events. This golden run of form included three major championships. By the end of 1994 he was the undisputed world number one.
■ Didn't win his first major title, the 1992 USPGA Championship, until he was 35 years old.
■ Has represented South Africa and Zimbabwe in the World Cup. In 1978 he played for South Africa, while 15 years later turned out for Zimbabwe.
■ Should have won the 1982 British Open at Royal Troon, where he led by two strokes with five holes to play. But he covered the final four holes in three over par to finish in a tie for second, one stroke behind champion Tom Watson. Price had dropped two shots at the par-4 15th, then three-putted the par-3 17th for a bogey-four. Price was also second in 1988, when Seve Ballesteros won at Royal Lytham.
■ At Turnberry in 1994, Price finally won the British Open, covering the last seven holes in four-under-par, to pip Jesper Parnevik by one stroke. Parnevik had bogied the final hole.

A young Nick Price pictured during the British Open at Royal Troon in 1982, when he narrowly missed out on the title

Year	T'ment	Scores	Total	Position
1978	Br Open	74-73-74-72	293	T39
1980	Br Open	72-71-71-74	288	T28
1981	Br Open	77-68-76-69	290	T23
1982	Br Open	69-69-74-73	285	**T2**
1983	US Open	72-77-72-80	301	T48
	Br Open	76-74	150	MC
	USPGA	72-74-74-74	294	T67
1984	Masters	77-76	153	MC
	Br Open	74-73-72-71	290	T44
	USPGA	73-74-71-75	293	T54
1985	US Open	82-74	156	MC
	Br Open	74-77	151	MC
	USPGA	73-73-65-71	282	5
1986	Masters	79-69-63-71	282	5
	USPGA	75-78	153	MC
1987	Masters	73-73-71-76	293	T22
	US Open	69-74-69-74	286	T17

	Br Open	68-71-72-73	284	T8
	USPGA	76-71-70-75	292	T10
1988	Masters	75-76-72-66	289	T14
	US Open	72-74-71-73	290	T40
	Br Open	70-67-69-69	275	2
	USPGA	74-70-67-73	284	T17
1989	Masters	76-82	158	MC
	US Open	74-72	146	MC
	Br Open	74-73	147	MC
	USPGA	70-72-72-74	288	T46
1990	Br Open	70-67-71-75	283	T25
	USPGA	75-71-81-76	303	T63
1991	Masters	72-73-72-74	291	T49
	US Open	74-69-71-78	292	T19
	Br Open	69-72-73-71	285	T44
1992	Masters	70-71-67-73	281	T6
	US Open	71-72-77-71	291	T4
	Br Open	69-73-73-74	289	T51
	USPGA	70-70-68-70	278	Won
1993	Masters	72-81	153	MC
	US Open	71-66-70-73	280	T11
	Br Open	68-70-67-69	274	T6
	USPGA	74-66-72-71	283	T31
1994	Masters	74-73-74-77	298	T35
	US Open	76-72	148	MC
	Br Open	69-66-67-66	268	Won
	USPGA	67-65-70-67	269	Won
1995	Masters	76-73	149	MC
	US Open	66-73-73-74	286	T13
	Br Open	70-74-70-77	291	T40
	USPGA	71-71-70-68	280	T39

Gene SARAZEN

Born: February 1902, Harrison, New York
US Tour wins: 38
Ryder Cup appearances: 6 (1927, 29, 31, 33, 35, 37)

Gene Sarazen was an overnight sensation. By the time he'd reached his 22nd birthday, he already had three major titles to his credit. He won two of them when he was still only 20 (1922 US Open & USPGA Championship). And in winning his third, by successfully defending his USPGA crown in 1923, he claimed the biggest scalp of them all. Sarazen beat matchplay specialist Walter Hagen, the world's best player of that era, in an exciting final which ended on the 38th green (second extra-hole).

But just when it seemed that Sarazen might soon replace Hagen as the world's leading golfer, his run of major success slowed down. While Sarazen still continued to win many run-of-the-mill tournaments, almost nine years passed before he landed another major title. One possible reason for this 'dry period' was the emergence of the great Bobby Jones. And it was only after Jones' retirement in 1930, that Sarazen's major championship career picked up again. Between 1932 and 1935, he added another four major titles to his list of successes.

Sarazen, whose father was an Italian carpenter, was christened Eugene Saraceni, but changed his surname to avoid being confused with a violin player. Despite being small in stature, Sarazen was an extremely confident, often brash, young man. He had discovered golf while caddying at New York's Apawamis Club.

He was always a most popular visitor to Britain, although his first stab at 'our' Open ended in failure. When he arrived at Troon in June 1923, he was the holder of both the US Open and USPGA titles and was rightly considered one of the favourites for the Championship. But in one of the greatest shocks of all time, he failed to qualify for the tournament by one stroke. In those days every player, even the defending champion, had to pre-qualify for the British Open. After a run of near-misses, Sarazen finally won the British Open in his golden summer of 1932. Fifteen days later he won his second US Open crown, after covering the last 28 holes in eight-under-par.

Although Sarazen was never the greatest player of his generation, these are just a few of the achievements for which he will be remembered:

o - First player to win two majors in the same year (1922 US Open/USPGA Championship).

o - By winning the 1935 US Masters, became the first golfer to collect all four professional major titles.

o - Played, what is possibly, the most famous single golf stroke of all time at the 1935 Masters, when he holed out with a 4-wood for an albatross two at Augusta's par-5 15th. The following day he won the title after a play-off with Craig Wood.

o - Is the youngest USPGA Champion of all time - 20 yrs, 5 mths in 1922.

o - Invented the sand iron.

Year	T'ment	Scores	Total	Position
1920	US Open	79-79-76-77	311	T30
1921	US Open	83-74-77-77	311	17
1922	US Open	72-73-75-68	288	Won
1923	US Open	79-78-73-80	310	T16

1924	US Open	74-80-80-79	313	T17
	Br Open	83-75-84-81	323	41
1925	US Open	72-72-75-74	293	T5
1926	US Open	78-77-72-70	297	T3
1927	US Open	74-74-80-74	302	3
1928	Br Open	72-76-73-73	294	2
	US Open	78-76-73-72	299	T6
1929	Br Open	73-74-81-76	304	T8
	US Open	71-71-76-78	296	T3
1930	US Open	76-78-77-75	306	T28
1931	Br Open	74-76-75-73	298	T3
	US Open	74-78-74-70	296	T4
1932	Br Open	70-69-70-74	283	Won
	US Open	74-76-70-66	286	Won
1933	US Open	74-77-77-75	303	T26
	Br Open	72-73-73-75	293	T3
1934	US Open	73-72-73-76	294	2
	Br Open	75-73-74-80	302	T21
1935	Masters*	68-71-73-70	282	Won
	US Open	75-74-78-79	306	T6
1936	Masters	78-67-72-70	287	3
	US Open	75-72-75-74	296	T28
	Br Open	73-75-70-73	291	T5
1937	Masters	74-80-73-73	300	T24
	US Open	78-69-71-74	292	T10
1938	Masters	78-70-68-79	295	T13
	US Open	74-74-75-73	296	10
1939	Masters	73-66-72-72	283	5
	US Open	74-72-79-76	301	T47
1940	Masters	74-71-77-73	295	T21
	US Open**	71-74-70-72	287	2
1941	Masters	76-72-74-75	297	T19
	US Open	74-73-72-75	294	T7
1942	Masters	75-74-76-79	304	T29

Other Top 10 finishes:
1950 Masters   T10   (294)

* - Won Play-Off
** - Lost Play-Off

Gene Sarazen drives at the 1924 British Open at Royal Hoylake

SARAZEN AT THE USPGA CHAMPIONSHIP

(Matchplay years 1916-57)

Year	Position	Final Match		(W-L)
1921	Qtr-Final	Lost 5&4	Cyril Walker	(2-1)
1922	**Champion**	Won 4&3	Emmett French	(6-0)
1923	**Champion**	Won at 38th	Walter Hagen	(6-0)
1924	2nd Rd (16)	Lost 2&1	Larry Nabholtz	(1-1)
1925	1st Rd (32)	Lost 8&7	Jack Burke	(0-1)
1926	2nd Rd (16)	Lost 4&3	Johnny Golden	(1-1)
1927	Qtr-Final	Lost 3&2	Joe Turnesa	(2-1)
1928	Semi-Final	Lost 9&8	Leo Diegel	(3-1)
1929	Qtr-Final	Lost 3&2	Leo Diegel	(2-1)
1930	**Runner-Up**	Lost 1 up	Tommy Armour	(4-1)
1931	Semi-Final	Lost 5&3	Tom Creavy	(3-1)
1933	**Champion**	Won 5&4	Willie Goggin	(5-0)
1934	2nd Rd (16)	Lost 4&3	Al Watrous	(1-1)
1935	2nd Rd (32)	Lost 2&1	Alvin Krueger	(1-1)
1936	1st Rd (64)	Lost 1 up	Jack Patroni	(0-1)
1937	2nd Rd (32)	Lost 1 up	Jim Foulis	(1-1)
1938	Qtr-Final	Lost 3&2	Henry Picard	(3-1)
1939	1st Rd (64)	Lost 1 up	Jack Ryan	(0-1)
1940	Qtr-Final	Lost 1 up	Sam Snead	(3-1)
1941	Semi-Final	Lost 2&1	Byron Nelson	(4-1)
1945	1st Rd (32)	Lost 4&3	Byron Nelson	(0-1)

Sam SNEAD

Born: May 1912, Hot Springs, Virginia
US Tour wins: 81
Ryder Cup appearances: 7 (1937, 47, 49, 51, 53, 55, 59)

Has won more US Tour events than any other golfer. Between 1936 and 1965, Samuel Jackson Snead compiled 81 official victories, a record that is unlikely to be beaten.

Snead played the Tour for 40 years, longer than any other leading player. The secret to his longevity was a natural athleticism, coupled with an effortless and rhythmical swing, arguably the best in the business. Snead never got bogged down with mechanics - he didn't need to. And his swing looked as graceful in his 70s as it had at the start of his career.

He still holds the record for being the oldest winner on Tour, capturing the 1965 Greater Greensboro Open at 52 years and 10 months.

Even at the age of 62, Snead put together rounds of 69-71-71-68 to finish in a tie for third at the 1974 USPGA Championship. Only Lee Trevino and Jack Nicklaus finished above him.

And when the tournament was over Snead said: "I could have won if I could only putt."

In his peak years, between 1942 and 1954, he won seven major titles. But his one big disappointment, was that he never managed to land the US Open crown. Four times he came second in his National Championship. His run of US Open near-misses reads as follows:

1937: On his first appearance in the Championship, Snead shared the lead after round one. He wound up in second place two strokes behind champion Ralph Guldahl.

1939: Took a triple bogey eight at the final hole and finished two strokes out of a play-off in fifth spot. A par would have won him the title, although when Snead came to the 72nd hole he thought he had to make a birdie to win.

1947: Lost an 18-hole play-off to Lew Worsham. On the final green Snead missed from 30 inches, while Worsham holed from a marginally shorter distance for a one stroke victory (69-70).

1949: Bogied the 71st hole to finish one shot behind champion Cary Middlecoff who had teed off 48 minutes before Snead.

Sam Snead: famous for his near-misses at the US Open

1953: Second for the fourth and final time. Snead trailed Ben Hogan by one stroke with 18 holes to play but a final round 76 left him six strokes behind his great rival.

1955: One stroke off the pace after 54 holes, Snead could only shoot a 74 in the final round to finish in a tie for third.

Snead was a country boy from Virginia and was often looked upon as a bit of a hillbilly in his early years on Tour. Not that this bothered him. He won three US Masters and three USPGA Championships. A reluctant traveller, Snead only played in four British Opens between 1937 and 1976, winning it once at St Andrews in 1946. He also played in seven Ryder Cup contests between 1937 and 1959.

Year	T'ment	Scores	Total	Position
1937	Masters	76-72-71-79	298	18
	US Open	69-73-70-71	283	2
	Br Open	75-74-75-76	300	T11
1938	Masters	78-78-75-73	304	T31
	US Open	77-76-76-80	309	T38
1939	Masters	70-70-72-68	280	2
	US Open	68-71-73-74	286	5
1940	Masters	71-72-69-76	288	T7
	US Open	67-74-73-81	295	T16
1941	Masters	73-75-72-69	289	T6
	US Open	76-70-77-73	296	T13
1942	Masters	78-69-72-73	292	T7
1946	Masters	74-75-70-71	290	T7
	US Open	69-75-74-74	292	T19
	Br Open	71-70-74-75	290	Won
1947	Masters	72-71-75-75	293	T22
	US Open**	72-70-70-70	282	2
1948	Masters	74-75-72-73	294	T16
	US Open	69-69-73-72	283	5
1949	Masters	73-75-67-67	282	Won
	US Open	73-73-71-70	287	T2
1950	Masters	71-74-70-72	287	3
	US Open	73-75-72-74	294	T12
1951	Masters	69-74-68-80	291	T8
	US Open	71-78-72-74	295	T10
1952	Masters	70-67-77-72	286	Won
	US Open	70-75-76-72	293	T10
1953	Masters	71-75-71-75	292	T16
	US Open	72-69-72-76	289	2
1954	Masters*	74-73-70-72	289	Won
	US Open	72-73-72-73	290	T11
1955	Masters	72-71-74-70	287	3
	US Open	79-69-70-74	292	T3
1956	Masters	73-76-72-71	292	T4
	US Open	75-71-77-73	296	T24
1957	Masters	72-68-74-72	286	2
	US Open	74-74-69-73	290	T8
1958	Masters	72-71-68-79	290	13
	US Open	75-80	155	MC
	USPGA	73-67-67-73	280	3
1959	Masters	74-73-72-74	293	T22
	US Open	73-72-67-75	287	T8
	USPGA	71-73-68-70	282	T8
1960	Masters	73-74-72-73	292	T11
	US Open	72-69-73-75	289	T19
	USPGA	68-73-70-72	283	T3
1961	Masters	74-73-69-73	289	T15
	US Open	73-70-74-73	290	T17
	USPGA	72-71-71-75	289	T27
1962	Masters	72-75-70-74	291	T15
	US Open	76-74-78-74	302	T38
	Br Open	76-73-72-71	292	T6
	USPGA	75-70-71-72	288	T17
1963	Masters	70-73-74-71	288	T3
	US Open	74-75-79-83	311	T42
	USPGA	71-73-70-76	290	T27
1964	Masters	79-73	152	MC
	US Open	77-72-75-75	299	T34

Other Top 10 finishes:

1965	USPGA	T6	(285)
1966	USPGA	T6	(287)
1967	Masters	T10	(290)
1968	US Open	T9	(286)
1972	USPGA	T4	(284)
1973	USPGA	T9	(284)
1974	USPGA	T3	(279)

USPGA CHAMPIONSHIP

(Snead's matchplay years 1916-57)

Year	Position	Final Match		(W-L)
1937	3rd Rd (16)	Lost 3&2	Harold McSpaden	(2-1)
1938	**Runner-Up**	Lost 8&7	Paul Runyan	(5-1)
1940	**Runner-up**	Lost 1up	Byron Nelson	(5-1)
1941	Qtr-Final	Lost 6&4	Lloyd Mangrum	(3-1)
1942	**Champion**	Won 2&1	Jim Turnesa	(5-0)
1946	2nd Rd (32)	Lost 6&5	George Schneiter	(1-1)
1947	2nd Rd (32)	Lost 2&1	Gene Sarazen	(1-1)
1948	Qtr-Final	Lost at 42nd	Claude Harmon	(3-1)
1949	**Champion**	Won 3&2	Johnny Palmer	(6-0)
1950	2nd Rd (32)	Lost 1up	Eddie Burke	(1-1)
1951	**Champion**	Won 7&6	Walter Burkemo	(6-0)
1952	1st Rd (64)	Lost at 19th	Lew Worsham	(0-1)
1953	2nd Rd (32)	Lost at 19th	Dave Douglas	(1-1)
1954	Qtr-Final	Lost at 39th	Tommy Bolt	(3-1)
1955	2nd Rd (32)	Lost 3&2	Tommy Bolt	(1-1)
1956	Qtr-Final	Lost 2&1	Ted Kroll	(4-1)
1957	4th-Rd (16)	Lost 3&1	Dow Finsterwald	(3-1)

Does not include years when player failed to qualify for matchplay stage

* - Won Play-Off
** - Lost Play-Off

Payne STEWART

Payne Stewart, two times a major championship winner

Born: January 1957, Springfield, Missouri
US Tour wins: 9
Ryder Cup appearances: 4, (1987, 89, 91, 93)
Almost sneaked in unnoticed to finish second in the 1985 British Open at Royal St George's. Starting the final round six strokes off the pace, Stewart carded a joint best-of-day 68 (2-under-par) to finish one shot behind champion Sandy Lyle. It was his first top-3 performance in a major championship. At that point in his career, Stewart had only won two US Tour events, but it was this performance in Kent that marked him down as a potential major star of the future.

■ After turning professional in 1979, Stewart failed to win his US Tour player's card at the qualifying school in the autumn of that year. So he headed off to Asia to learn his trade there. His time in the far east yielded victories in the Indian and Indonesian Opens, both in 1981. While competing on the Asian circuit he met and married his Australian wife Tracey. A more experienced Stewart returned to the States in 1981 when he was successful in earning his US Tour card.

■ Stewart fought back twice to beat Scott Simpson in their head-to-head duel at the 1991 US Open at Hazeltine, Minnesota. Firstly, in regulation play, Stewart trailed Simpson by two shots with just three holes remaining. A Simpson bogey at 16 reduced the gap to one as they headed down the last. Here, Simpson drove into deep rough and was unable to reach the green in two, at the 452-yard, par 4, 18th, while Stewart's second shot had run off the back of the putting surface. But Stewart got up and down in two for par to force a play-off with Simpson who two-putted from 30 feet for a bogey.

Again, in the play-off, Simpson led Stewart by two strokes with three holes to play. The whole tournament turned on the 16th (384-yard, par 4). Simpson had left his second shot just short of the green but then played an excellent third to within three feet of the flag. However, Stewart rattled home a 20-footer for a birdie three. This unnerved Simpson who then missed his short putt, leaving him to contemplate a bogey five. The two-shot swing meant the players were now level. Simpson then hit his tee shot at the par-3, 17th, into a greenside pond and made bogey. Stewart carded pars at both the final two holes to win by two shots over Simpson who made yet another bogey at 18. In the play-off, Stewart had played the last three holes in one-under-par to Simpson's three-over.

■ After winning the 1987 Hertz Bay Hill Classic, he donated his $108,000 winner's cheque to the Florida Hospital 'Golden Circle of Friends Home'. This gift was in memory of his father William Louis Stewart who died of cancer two years earlier. His father was a former Missouri State Amateur Champion.

Year	T'ment	Scores	Total	Position
1981	Br Open	73-75-74-77	299	T58
1982	USPGA	76-72	148	MC
1983	Masters	70-76-78-71	295	T32
	USPGA	78-71	149	MC
1984	Masters	76-69-68-74	287	T21
	US Open	75-78	153	MC
	Br Open	74-72-74	220	MC
	USPGA	80-73	153	MC
1985	Masters	69-71-76-76	292	T25
	US Open	70-70-71-70	281	T5
	Br Open	70-75-70-68	283	2
	USPGA	72-72-73-68	285	T12
1986	Masters	75-71-69-69	284	T8
	US Open	76-68-69-70	283	T6
	Br Open	76-69-75-76	296	T35
	USPGA	70-67-72-72	281	T5
1987	Masters	71-75-74-78	298	T42
	US Open	74-74	148	MC
	Br Open	71-66-72-72	281	T4
	USPGA	72-75-75-74	296	T24
1988	Masters	75-76-71-72	294	T25
	US Open	73-73-70-67	283	T10
	Br Open	73-75-68-67	283	T7
	USPGA	70-69-70-73	282	T9
1989	Masters	73-75-74-70	292	T24
	US Open	66-75-72-71	284	T13
	Br Open	72-65-69-74	280	T8
	USPGA	74-66-69-67	276	**Won**
1990	Masters	71-73-77-74	295	T36
	US Open	73-75	148	MC
	Br Open	68-68-68-71	275	**T2**
	USPGA	71-72-70-79	292	T8
1991	US Open*	67-70-73-72	282	**Won**
	Br Open	72-72-71-68	283	T32
	USPGA	74-70-71-70	285	T13
1992	Masters	74-75	149	MC
	US Open	73-70-72-83	298	T51
	Br Open	70-73-71-72	286	T34
	USPGA	76-69-79-72	296	T69
1993	Masters	74-70-72-69	285	T9
	US Open	70-66-68-70	274	2
	Br Open	71-72-70-63	276	12
	USPGA	71-70-70-73	284	T44
1994	Masters	78-78	156	MC
	US Open	74-75	149	MC
	Br Open	74-74	148	MC
	USPGA	72-73-72-74	291	T66
1995	Masters	71-72-72-78	293	T41
	US Open	74-71-73-69	287	T21
	Br Open	72-68-75-71	286	T11
	USPGA	69-70-69-67	275	T13

* Won after a play-off

Curtis STRANGE

Born: January 1955, Norfolk, Virginia
US Tour wins: 17
Ryder Cup appearances: 5, (1983, 85, 87, 89, 95)
Between 1985 and 1989, Strange was America's leading player. He topped the US Money list three times (1985, 87 and 88) and in 1988 became the first golfer to win over $1million in one season on the US Tour.

■ By winning the US Open in 1988 and 1989, he was the first back-to-back champion since Ben Hogan in 1950 and 1951.

■ Has an identical twin brother called Allen, who often caddies for him at tournaments.

■ Started playing golf at the age of seven. His late father Tom was the golf professional and

Curtis Strange pictured in action during the 1989 Memorial Tournament at Muirfield Village

one of the greatest bunker shots of all time, his ball finished about 12 inches from the cup. Faldo two-putted for his par from 25 feet and in the following day's play-off Strange won by four shots (71-75).

■ In winning the 1989 championship, at Oak Hill, Strange parred the first 15 holes of his final round. He then made a crucial birdie on 16 (par 4), parred the 17th and could afford the luxury of a bogey-five at 18, to win by one stroke. Strange had started the final round three strokes behind leader Tom Kite. But Kite took a triple-bogey 7 at the fifth hole, went on to shoot an 8-over-par 78 and finished in a tie for 9th - five strokes behind Strange. When asked what it takes to win the US Open twice, Strange replied: "Guts and pars."

Year	T'ment	Scores	Total	Position
1975	Masters	75-77	152	MC
1976	Masters	71-76-73-71	291	T15
	Br Open	79-74	153	MC
1977	Masters	79-74	153	MC
	US Open	77-74	151	MC
1978	USPGA	72-74-71-79	296	T58
1979	USPGA	74-76	150	MC
1980	Masters	77-70	147	MC
	US Open	69-74-71-70	284	T16
	USPGA	68-72-72-72	284	T5
1981	Masters	69-79-70-71	289	T19
	US Open	71-69-72-71	283	T17
	USPGA	73-72-74-66	285	T27
1982	Masters	74-70-73-72	289	T7
	US Open	74-73-74-75	296	T39
	Br Open	72-73-76-70	291	T15
	USPGA	72-70-71-69	282	T14
1983	Masters	77-72	149	MC
	US Open	74-72-78-72	296	T26
	Br Open	74-68-70-73	285	T29
	USPGA	71-74-85-74	304	86
1984	Masters	71-74-75-77	297	T46
	US Open	69-70-74-68	281	3
	USPGA	79-79	158	MC
1985	Masters	80-65-68-71	284	T2
	US Open	71-68-76-73	288	T31
	USPGA	77-76	153	MC
1986	Masters	73-74-68-72	287	T21
	US Open	76-79	155	MC
	Br Open	79-69-74-69	291	T14
	USPGA	74-75	149	MC
1987	Masters	71-70-73-76	290	T12
	US Open	71-72-69-71	283	T4
	USPGA	70-76-71-74	291	9
1988	Masters	76-70-72-74	292	T21
	US Open*	70-67-69-72	278	**Won**

owner of White Sands Country Club in Virginia Beach. His father played in five US Opens.

■ Until he won the 1988 US Open, Strange had adopted that unfavourable tag of being called 'the best player yet to win a major.' On reaching the 72nd hole of that year's championship, he and Nick Faldo were tied for the lead at six-under-par. While playing-partner Faldo safely hit the green in two, at the 438-yard, par-4 18th, Strange bunkered his approach. Yet from sand, he played

	Br Open	79-69-69-68	285	T13		US Open	67-78-76-74	295	T23
	USPGA	72-72-73-69	286	T31		Br Open	74-73	147	MC
1989	Masters	74-71-74-72	291	T18		USPGA	74-78	152	MC
	US Open	71-64-73-70	278	**Won**	1993	Masters	77-Wd	77	Wd
	Br Open	70-74-74-74	292	T61		US Open	73-68-75-67	283	T25
	USPGA	70-68-70-69	277	**T2**		USPGA	72-73	145	MC
1990	Masters	70-73-71-72	286	T7	1994	Masters	74-70-75-75	294	T27
	US Open	73-70-68-75	286	T21		US Open	70-70-70-70	280	4
	Br Open	74-71	145	MC		USPGA	73-71-68-70	282	T19
	USPGA	79-76	155	MC	1995	Masters	72-71-65-73	281	9
1991	Masters	72-74-72-71	289	T42		US Open	70-72-76-71	289	T36
	US Open	77-74	151	MC		Br Open	73-76	149	MC
	Br Open	70-73-69-72	284	T38		USPGA	72-68-68-68	276	T17
	USPGA	81-Wd	81	Wd					
1992	Masters	73-72-71-69	285	T31					

* - Won Play-Off

JH TAYLOR

JH Taylor: a great British champion and a founder member of the PGA

Five-time British Open winner JH Taylor was always a worthy and convincing champion. His smallest winning margin was four strokes and twice he won by as many as eight. Taylor was also runner-up on six occasions, including four years in a row from 1904.

Compared to the elegant Harry Vardon, his friend and rival, Taylor was not a great stylist. But his short, punchy swing was extremely accurate and efficient. He had the perfect game to cope with the windy conditions associated with British links courses.

John Henry Taylor, who was born in Northam, Devon, in March 1871, won the first British Open to be staged outside Scotland. His 1894 triumph came at St George's in Kent. After leaving school at 11, he became a caddie at Westward Ho! where, later, he worked as a greenkeeper. Later he was appointed professional/greenkeeper at Burnham in Somerset.

Taylor was a founder-member of the British PGA in 1901 and was non-playing captain of Britain & Ireland's Ryder Cup winning team at Southport & Ainsdale in 1933. He died in 1963 at the grand old age of 91.

He also had a great opportunity to become the first, and so far only, golfer to win six British Open titles. After three rounds of the 1914 Championship at Prestwick, he held a two-stroke lead over Vardon. But in the final round Taylor slumped to an 83, allowing Vardon to wear the crown with a 78. So instead of Taylor holding a record sixth title, the name of Vardon was written into the history books.

Year	T'ment	Scores	Total	Position
1893	Br Open	75-89-86-83	333	T10
1894	Br Open	84-80-81-81	326	Won
1895	Br Open	86-78-80-78	322	Won
1896	Br Open**	77-78-81-80	316	2
1897	Br Open	82-80-82-86	330	T10
1898	Br Open	78-78-77-79	312	4
1899	Br Open	77-76-83-84	320	4
1900	Br Open	79-77-78-75	309	Won
	US Open	76-82-79-78	315	2
1901	Br Open	79-83-74-77	313	3
1902	Br Open	81-76-77-80	314	T6
1903	Br Open	80-82-78-76	316	T9
1904	Br Open	77-78-74-68	297	T2
1905	Br Open	80-85-78-80	323	T2
1906	Br Open	77-72-75-80	304	2
1907	Br Open	79-79-76-80	314	2
1908	Br Open	79-77-76-75	307	T7
1909	Br Open	74-73-74-74	295	Won
1910	Br Open	76-80-78-78	312	T14
1911	Br Open	72-76-78-79	305	T5
1912	Br Open	75-76-77-84	312	T11
1913	Br Open	73-75-77-79	304	Won
	US Open	81-80-78-84	323	T30
1914	Br Open	74-78-74-83	309	2
1920	Br Open	78-79-80-79	316	12
1921	Br Open	80-80-75-74	309	T26
1922	Br Open	73-78-76-77	304	6
1923	Br Open	80-78-79-79	316	T44

** - Lost after play-off

Peter Thomson en route to a third successive British Open title at Hoylake in 1956

Peter THOMSON

During the 1950s, no one had a better British Open record than Peter Thomson. In seven successive Championships, between 1952 and 1958, he was never lower than second, and this included four victories.

No one ever doubted Thomson's ability to improvise on fast running links courses, where he won five British Open titles in all, the fifth coming after a seven-year gap in 1965. But he did have his critics in the United States, where Thomson was unable to reproduce his British Open form. Many Americans believed that Thomson's game wasn't suited to the lush well-watered fairways of the US Tour, where the chip and run is rarely needed.

Between 1952 and 1958, Thomson was a frequent visitor to the States, during which period he managed seven top-3 finishes, including a victory at the 1956 Texas Open. That same year he also finished ninth in the US Money List.

Yet where it really mattered, in major championships, Thomson rarely covered himself in glory outside Britain. During his career, Thomson played in 13 American majors, yielding just two top-10 finishes. The nearest he came to winning was the 1956 US Open which he led after 36 holes. He eventually finished in a tie for fourth, four strokes behind champion Cary Middlecoff. A year later he was fifth in the US Masters.

It was also said that four of his five British Open successes occurred during a period when American participation in the event was poor. Not that he had any control over the quality of his opposition. Yet when he triumphed for a fifth time at Royal Birkdale in 1965, Jack Nicklaus, Arnold Palmer, Gary Player and defending champion Tony Lema were all in the field.

Ironically, Thomson produced some of his best American performances when he was a senior. In 1985 he won an astonishing nine times, ending the year as the US Senior Tour's leading money winner. A year earlier he'd captured the USPGA Seniors Championship, one of four senior majors. Yet whatever his American detractors may think, Thomson was always the coolest of customers, with an easy, unhurried swing.

Born in Melbourne, Australia, in August 1929, his first important victory was the 1950 New Zealand Open, a tournament he won a record nine times. He's also won in Italy, Spain, Germany, China, Hong Kong, Philippines, India and Japan, as well as his own national open on three occasions.

He was certainly an international champion revered everywhere he went, with the exception of the United States. Not that this should take anything away from the only man this century to win three successive British Open titles (1954-56).

Year	T'ment	Scores	Total	Position
1951	Br Open	70-75-73-75	293	T6
1952	Br Open	68-73-77-70	288	2
1953	Masters	77-76-74-73	300	T36
	US Open	80-73-73-75	301	T26
	Br Open	72-72-71-71	286	T2
1954	Masters	76-72-76-73	297	T16
	US Open	77-76	153	MC
	Br Open	72-71-69-71	283	Won
1955	Masters	74-73-74-76	297	T18
	Br Open	71-68-70-72	281	Won
1956	US Open	70-69-75-71	285	T4
	Br Open	70-70-72-74	286	Won
1957	Masters	72-73-73-71	289	5
	US Open	71-72-74-77	294	T22
	Br Open	73-69-70-70	282	2
1958	Masters	72-74-73-76	295	T23
	Br Open*	66-72-67-73	278	Won
1959	Masters	72-74-72	218	Dq
	Br Open	74-74-72-74	294	T23
1960	Br Open	72-69-75-70	286	T9
1961	Masters	73-76-68-74	291	T19
	US Open	78-75	153	MC
	Br Open	75-72-70-73	290	7
1962	Br Open	70-77-75-70	292	T6
1963	Br Open	67-69-71-78	285	5
1964	Br Open	79-73-72-75	299	T24
1965	Br Open	74-68-72-71	285	Won
1966	Br Open	73-75-69-71	288	T8
1967	Br Open	71-74-70-72	287	T8
1968	Br Open	77-71-78-75	301	T24
1969	Masters	78-75	153	MC
	Br Open	71-70-70-72	283	T3
1970	Br Open	68-74-73-74	289	T9
1971	Br Open	70-73-73-69	285	T9
1972	Br Open	71-72-74-77	294	T31
1973	Br Open	76-75-70-73	294	T31
1974	Br Open	79-81	160	MC
1975	Br Open	73-75-81	229	MC

* - Won after a play-off

Lee Trevino at the 1971 US Open at Merion where he beat Jack Nicklaus in a play-off

Lee TREVINO

Born: December 1939, Dallas, Texas
US Tour wins: 27
Ryder Cup appearances: 6 (1969, 71, 73, 75, 79, 81)

Lee Buck Trevino was a winner of the highest quality. He might not have been the most dominant player of his generation but whenever Trevino got a whiff of victory few would bet against him. Unlike many players, who would let the pressure of contention over run them down the final stretch, Trevino simply revelled in it. He was made for the big occasion. Always ready with a humorous quip, Trevino once said: "There's no pressure playing for a couple of hundred thousand dollars. Pressure is playing for 100 bucks when you've only ten in your pocket."

This was clearly a reference to his modest beginnings. Trevino was brought-up in an old shack by his mother and grand-mother. He got his first taste of golf before his 10th birthday, caddying at a local public course where he also got the opportunity to hit a few balls.

He left school early to work as a handyman, before spending four years in the Marines. But golf was Trevino's real love and at the age of 20 he turned professional to take up a club job in El Paso. Having endured much early hardship, Trevino realised there was nothing to fear on a golf course. Standing over a short putt to win a major championship was nothing compared to the problems he had faced in his early years.

He finally made it onto the US Tour in 1967, by which time he was married with two young children. Uncertain about whether he should play in the 1967 US Open, Trevino's wife went behind his back and made an entry for him. After surviving the normal strenuous qualifying procedures, he made it to Baltusrol where he finished a stunning fifth. He was the surprise package of the tournament and it was this performance that changed his career.

Twelve months later he was on the winner's rostrum at Oak Hill, after four rounds in the 60s and a four-stroke victory over Jack Nicklaus. His US Open win was his first on Tour.

By the early 1970s he was clearly America's number two behind Nicklaus. He was the leading

Money Winner in 1970, and in 1971 had one of those golden spells most golfers can only dream of. Within three weeks he had won the Opens of America, Canada and Britain. And when Trevino won his second successive British Open at Muirfield in 1972 he had triumphed in three of the last five major championships to be held. He was at the peak of his powers.

His victory at Muirfield had produced one of the most stunning climaxes in Championship golf. Arriving at the par-5 17th level with Tony Jacklin, Trevino had looked to have blown his chances by driving into a bunker. He then played a poor second shot, hooked his third into the rough and then topped a sand wedge across the green. From there he holed his chip shot for a par five, when a seven looked to be on the cards. Moments later a visibly shaken Jacklin three-putted from close range for a bogey six. Trevino was now one ahead and a par at 18 secured the title.

After winning the 1974 USPGA Championship, Trevino's career was hit by a number of injuries. Many believed these problems were the result of an incident at the 1975 Western Open where Trevino was one of three players hit by lightning.

But Trevino still had one big win left in him. Ten years after his fifth major victory, he recaptured the USPGA title thanks to a stunning display with the putter, at the age of 44.

In all, Trevino won 27 times on Tour. The only major he didn't win was the Masters. He often said that he never really fancied his chances at Augusta and at best could only manage a couple of tenth place finishes there. His game, he believed, just wasn't suited to the course.

His other blank spot came in the 1985 Ryder Cup at The Belfry where he was non-playing captain to the United States team which lost the trophy for the first time in 28 years.

But these blemishes aside, Trevino's career was one of the most remarkable in what is traditionally a mid-class sport, a game that rarely witnesses a rags-to-riches story such as his.

Year	T'ment	Scores	Total	Position
1966	US Open	74-73-78-78	303	T54
1967	US Open	72-70-71-70	283	5
1968	Masters	71-72-69-80	292	T40
	US Open	69-68-69-69	275	Won
	USPGA	69-71-72-76	288	T23
1969	Masters	72-74-75-69	290	T19
	US Open	74-75	149	MC
	Br Open	75-72-71-78	296	T34
	USPGA	73-71-72-76	292	T48
1970	US Open	77-73-74-70	294	T8
	Br Open	68-68-72-77	285	T3
	USPGA	72-77-77-65	291	T26
1971	USPGA	71-73-75-69	288	T13
	US Open*	70-72-69-69	280	Won
	Br Open	69-70-69-70	278	Won
1972	Masters	75-76-77-72	300	T33
	US Open	74-72-71-78	295	T4
	Br Open	71-70-66-71	278	Won
	USPGA	73-71-71-71	286	T11
1973	Masters	74-75-75-75	299	T43
	US Open	70-72-70-70	282	T4
	Br Open	75-73-73-68	289	T10
	USPGA	76-70-73-67	286	T18
1974	US Open	78-78	156	MC
	Br Open	79-70-78-74	301	T31
	USPGA	73-66-68-69	276	Won
1975	Masters	71-70-74-71	286	T10
	US Open	72-69-75-79	295	T29
	Br Open	76-69-73-75	293	T40
	USPGA	73-72-78-74	297	T60
1976	Masters	75-75-69-76	295	T28
	USPGA	70-80	150	MC
1977	US Open	74-70-73-73	290	T27
	Br Open	68-70-72-70	280	4
	USPGA	71-73-71-73	288	T13
1978	Masters	70-69-72-74	285	T14
	US Open	72-71-75-73	291	T12
	Br Open	75-72-73-71	291	T29
	USPGA	69-73-70-72	284	T7
1979	Masters	73-71-70-73	287	T12
	US Open	77-73-73-72	295	T19
	Br Open	71-73-74-76	294	T17
	USPGA	70-73-72-72	287	T35
1980	Masters	74-71-70-74	289	T26
	US Open	68-72-69-74	283	T12
	Br Open	68-67-71-69	275	2
	USPGA	74-71-71-69	285	7
1981	Masters	77-77	154	MC
	US Open	72-76	148	MC
	Br Open	77-67-70-73	287	T11
	USPGA	Dq	-----	Dq
1982	Masters	75-78-75-73	301	T38
	US Open	78-76	154	MC
	Br Open	78-72-71-75	296	T27
1983	Masters	71-72-72-77	292	T20
	Br Open	69-66-73-70	278	5
	USPGA	70-68-74-71	283	T14
1984	Masters	68-73-74-79	294	43
	US Open	71-72-69-74	286	T9
	Br Open	70-67-75-73	285	T14
	USPGA	69-68-67-69	273	Won
1985	Masters	70-73-72-72	287	T10

	US Open	76-72	148	MC
	Br Open	73-76-68-71	288	T20
	USPGA	66-68-75-71	280	2
1986	Masters	76-73-73-77	299	47
	US Open	74-68-69-71	282	T4
	Br Open	80-71-75-75	301	T59
	USPGA	71-74-69-70	284	T11
1987	Masters	80-76	156	MC
	US Open	73-78	151	MC
	Br Open	67-74-73-72	286	T17
1988	Masters	81-83	164	MC
	US Open	73-73-73-71	290	T40
	Br Open	75-74	149	MC
	USPGA	77-71	148	MC
1989	Masters	67-74-81-69	291	T18
	US Open	74-79	153	MC
	Br Open	68-73-73-74	288	T42
	USPGA	74-75	149	MC
1990	Masters	78-69-72-72	291	T24
	Br Open	69-70-73-71	283	T25
	USPGA	77-75	152	MC
1991	Masters	71-72-77-71	291	T49
	US Open	77-72	149	MC
	Br Open	71-72-71-67	281	T17
1992	Br Open	69-71-73-74	287	T39
1994	Br Open	75-72	147	MC

* - Won after Play-Off

Harry VARDON

To this day, no one has won the British Open as often as Harry Vardon. His six triumphs between 1896 and 1914 is still a record and his rivalry with JH Taylor was one of the great talking points around the turn of the century.

Indeed, this rivalry began at Muirfield in 1896, when Vardon denied Taylor a third successive Open title following a play-off between the two men. Vardon won the 36-hole play-off by four strokes to secure the Claret Jug for the first time. And in doing so created a bit of history as well. After just one round, Vardon was 11 strokes off the pace, set by Alex Herd who had fired a 72. No eventual Open champion has ever come from so far behind after 18 holes to win.

In golfing terms, the next few years belonged to Vardon. He won the British Open twice more before the turn of the century and in 1900 made a rare visit to America to win the US Open, where he once again beat Taylor into second place, this

time by two shots.

Born in Jersey in May 1870, Vardon moved to England in November 1890. His first golfing position was as greenkeeper/professional at Studley Royal GC, in Ripon, Yorkshire. Yet by the time he had teed off in his first British Open in 1893, he was at Bury which was where he fine-tuned his game for the successes ahead.

Vardon was one of the straightest hitters of his generation. But he did have two weaknesses - his

Harry Vardon, winner of six British Open titles

putting and his health. Not long after winning his fourth title in 1903, he contracted tuberculosis. It took Vardon another eight years before he won the British Open again.

He will also be remembered for his graceful swing and the man who invented the overlapping grip, which was revolutionary at the time but is still the most common way of holding a club today. Vardon was a fine all-round sportsman too. Cricket was a favourite pastime when he first moved to England and he also broke an arm playing football for Ganton.

When Vardon won his last Open (1914) shortly before the outbreak of World War One, he was 44 years old. Once again it was a battle between him and Taylor, who began the final round two strokes ahead of his great rival. But a final round 83 by Taylor let in Vardon to win his sixth Championship, a record that still stands today.

Year	T'ment	Scores	Total	Position
1893	Br Open	84-90-81-89	344	T23
1894	Br Open	86-86-82-80	334	T5
1895	Br Open	80-85-85-88	338	T9
1896	Br Open*	83-78-78-77	316	Won
1897	Br Open	84-80-80-76	320	6
1898	Br Open	79-75-77-76	307	Won
1899	Br Open	76-76-81-77	310	Won
1900	Br Open	79-81-80-77	317	2
	US Open	79-78-76-80	313	Won
1901	Br Open	77-78-79-78	312	2
1902	Br Open	72-77-80-79	308	T2
1903	Br Open	73-77-72-78	300	Won
1904	Br Open	76-73-79-74	302	5
1905	Br Open	80-82-84-83	329	T9
1906	Br Open	77-73-77-78	305	3
1907	Br Open	84-81-74-80	319	T7
1908	Br Open	79-78-74-75	306	T5
1909	Br Open	82-77-79-78	316	T26
1910	Br Open	77-81-75-80	313	T16
1911	Br Open*	74-74-75-80	303	Won
1912	Br Open	75-72-81-71	299	2
1913	Br Open	79-75-79-80	313	T3
	US Open**	75-72-78-79	304	T2
1914	Br Open	73-77-78-78	306	Won
1920	Br Open	78-81-81-78	318	T14
	US Open	74-73-71-78	296	T2
1921	Br Open	77-77-80-74	308	T23
1922	Br Open	79-79-74-75	307	T8

* - Won after play-off
** - Lost after play-off

Tom WATSON

Born: September 1949, Kansas City, Missouri
US Tour victories: 32
Ryder Cup appearances: 4 (1977, 81, 83, 89)

Tom Watson holds up the claret jug after out-duelling Jack Nicklaus at Turnberry in the 1977 British Open

Thomas Sturges Watson had to experience bitter defeat before he could fully appreciate the art of winning. Twice, early in his career, the Kansas Swinger was in the driving seat at the US Open but on both occasions he let the pressure of the moment wear him down.

In 1974 at Winged Foot he led going into the final day, only to shoot a nine-over-par 79. He finished in joint fifth spot, five strokes behind champion Hale Irwin. Twelve months later at Medinah, Watson opened with rounds of 67 and 68, which gave him a three stroke lead. But closing scores of 78 and 77 pushed him down into ninth place and three strokes out of a play-off with Lou Graham and John Mahaffey. Unfairly, the media of the day dubbed him a choker.

But Watson has a tough competitive streak behind the calm, smiling and friendly exterior. Within a month of his second US Open disappointment, still only 25, he bounced back to win the 1975 British Open at Carnoustie in a play-off. Then between 1975 and 1983, Watson captured eight major titles, including five British Opens, and during which period he took over from Jack Nicklaus as the world's leading player. In fact, in four of his major wins, Nicklaus was relegated to second place.

The Saga of Tom v Jack:

o 1977 US Masters - The pair were tied for the lead with just two holes remaining. Playing one group behind Nicklaus, Watson's birdie at 17 forces a mistake out of Nicklaus up on 18. Watson wins by two.

o 1977 British Open - The famous duel in the sun at Turnberry. Watson plays the last six holes in four under par, while Nicklaus covers the same stretch in one under. Watson wins by one stroke after carding 65-65 for the last two rounds. Nicklaus closed 65-66. Third placed Hubert Green is a distant 10 shots behind Nicklaus.

o 1981 US Masters - Watson's last round 71 is enough to beat Nicklaus by two, after the latter had fired a 72.

o 1982 US Open - With Nicklaus already finished at four-under-par, the only player who can beat him is Watson, who is also at minus four but in deep trouble at 17 where his ball is in rough just off the green. But Watson produces the shot of his life by chipping in for a birdie two. He then birdies 18 for good measure for a two stroke victory.

In major terms, Watson's big disappointment was in never winning the USPGA Championship. How he lost in 1978 at Oakmont is a mystery. With nine holes to play, he held a four-stroke lead. But bogey followed bogey coming home and Watson eventually lost in a play-off. He never came as close again to winning the USPGA.

With eight majors under his belt at the age of 33, Watson looked well placed to challenge Nicklaus' record total of 18 professional major

victories. But after winning the 1983 British Open at Royal Birkdale, Watson's run of successes came to an abrupt end.

Yet to fully appreciate Watson's impact on world golf one has to look beyond his major titles. He's been leading money winner on the US Tour five times, including a record four years in a row between 1977 and 1980 - not even Nicklaus achieved that. He also won 32 times on Tour between 1974 and 1987.

In his hey-day, Watson was absolutely brilliant close to the green, he was also a wonderful putter. But since 1985, Watson has only won one tournament in the States. While his tee-to-green game is still as good as ever, if not better, his putting has let him down, particularly from short range.

In terms of being a major challenger Watson's day may be over yet what he achieved in those golden years from 1975 to 1984, leaves no one in any doubt that he is one of the greatest golfers the game has ever seen.

Year	T'ment	Scores	Total	Position
1970	Masters	77-76	153	MC
1972	US Open	74-79-76-76	305	T29
1973	US Open	81-73	154	MC
	USPGA	75-70-71-69	285	T12
1974	US Open	73-71-69-79	292	T5
	USPGA	69-72-73-70	284	T11
1975	Masters	70-70-72-73	285	T8
	US Open	67-68-78-77	290	T9
	Br Open*	71-67-69-72	279	**Won**
	USPGA	70-71-71-73	285	9
1976	Masters	77-73-76-70	296	T33
	US Open	74-72-68-70	284	7
	Br Open	75-72-80	227	MC
	USPGA	70-74-70-73	287	T15
1977	Masters	70-69-70-67	276	**Won**
	US Open	74-72-71-67	284	T7
	Br Open	68-70-65-65	268	**Won**
	USPGA	68-73-71-74	286	T6
1978	Masters	73-68-68-69	278	**T2**
	US Open	74-75-70-70	289	T6
	Br Open	73-68-70-76	287	T14
	USPGA**	67-69-67-73	276	**T2**
1979	Masters**	68-71-70-71	280	**T2**
	US Open	75-77	152	MC
	Br Open	72-68-76-81	297	T26
	USPGA	66-72-69-74	281	T12
1980	Masters	73-69-71-71	284	T12
	US Open	71-68-67-70	276	**T3**
	Br Open	68-70-64-69	271	**Won**
	USPGA	75-74-72-67	288	T10

1981	Masters	71-68-70-71	280	**Won**
	US Open	70-69-73-73	285	T23
	Br Open	73-69-75-73	290	T23
	USPGA	75-73	148	MC
1982	Masters	77-69-70-71	287	T5
	US Open	72-72-68-70	282	**Won**
	Br Open	69-71-74-70	284	**Won**
	USPGA	72-69-71-68	280	T9
1983	Masters	70-71-71-73	285	T4
	US Open	72-70-70-69	281	2
	Br Open	67-68-70-70	275	**Won**
	USPGA	75-67-78-70	290	T47
1984	Masters	74-67-69-69	279	**2**
	US Open	72-72-74-69	287	T11
	Br Open	71-68-66-73	278	**T2**
	USPGA	74-72-74-71	291	T39
1985	Masters	69-71-75-72	287	T10
	US Open	75-72	147	MC
	Br Open	72-73-72-77	294	T47
	USPGA	67-70-74-72	283	T6
1986	Masters	70-74-68-71	283	T6
	US Open	72-71-71-75	289	T24
	Br Open	77-71-77-71	296	T35
	USPGA	72-69-72-72	285	T16
1987	Masters	71-72-74-72	289	T7
	US Open	72-65-71-70	278	2
	Br Open	69-69-71-74	283	7
	USPGA	70-79-73-71	293	T14
1988	Masters	72-71-73-71	287	T9
	US Open	74-71-69-75	289	T36
	Br Open	74-72-72-72	290	T28
	USPGA	72-68-74-72	286	T31
1989	Masters	72-73-74-71	290	T14
	US Open	76-69-73-73	291	T46
	Br Open	69-68-68-72	277	4
	USPGA	67-69-74-71	281	T9
1990	Masters	77-71-67-71	286	T7
	US Open	74-75	149	MC
	Br Open	72-73	145	MC
	USPGA	74-71-77-73	295	T19
1991	Masters	68-68-70-73	279	**T3**
	US Open	73-71-77-70	291	T16
	Br Open	69-72-72-69	282	T26
	USPGA	74-75	149	MC
1992	Masters	73-70-76-71	290	T48
	US Open	75-73	148	MC
	Br Open	73-75	148	MC
	USPGA	72-71-73-78	294	T62
1993	Masters	71-75-73-75	294	T45
	US Open	70-66-73-69	278	T5
	Br Open	71-73	144	MC
	USPGA	69-65-70-72	276	5
1994	Masters	70-71-73-74	288	13
	US Open	68-73-68-74	283	T6

	Br Open	68-65-69-74	276	T11
	USPGA	69-72-67-71	279	T9
1995	Masters	73-70-69-72	284	T14
	US Open	70-73-77-73	293	T56
	Br Open	67-76-70-77	290	T31
	USPGA	71-71-72-70	284	T58

** - Lost Play-Off
* - Won Play-Off

Ian WOOSNAM

Born: March 1958, Oswestry, England (near to the Welsh border)
European Tour wins: 27
Ryder Cup appearances: 7, (1983, 85, 87, 89, 91, 93, 95)

In 1987 became the first British player to win the World Matchplay Championship at Wentworth. He beat Nick Faldo (quarter-finals), Seve Ballesteros (semi-finals) and Sandy Lyle (final). All three 36-hole matches were won by the margin of 1 up. He also won the title in 1990.

■ Topped the European Order of Merit in both 1987 and 1990.

■ Has yet to win a Ryder Cup singles in seven attempts. 1983 Craig Stadler (lost 3&2); 1985 Craig Stadler (lost 2&1); 1987 Andy Bean (lost one up); 1989 Curtis Strange (lost two up); 1991 Chip Beck (lost 3&1); 1993 Fred Couples (halved); 1995 Fred Couples (halved)

■ Held his nerve superbly to hold off the challenge of Tom Watson and Jose-Maria Olazabal to win the 1991 US Masters. With one hole left to play, all three were tied for the lead at 11 under par. Olazabal, playing one group ahead of Watson and Woosnam, bogied the par-4 72nd hole after finding sand with both his drive and second shot. Watson drove into the trees down the right and took six (double-bogey), while Woosnam bravely got down in two for par from just off the putting surface to pip Olazabal by one stroke.

■ Was ranked number one in the world at the end of 1991 - his big year.

Year	T'ment	Scores	Total	Position
1982	Br Open	78-73-80	231	MC
1983	Br Open	77-73	150	MC
1984	Br Open	72-69-79	220	MC

1985	Br Open	70-71-71-75	287	T16		Br Open	70-72-69-70	281	T17
1986	Br Open	70-74-70-72	286	**T3**		USPGA	67-72-76-76	291	T48
	USPGA	72-70-75-71	288	T30	1992	Masters	69-66-73-75	283	T19
1987	Br Open	71-69-72-72	284	T8		US Open	72-72-69-79	292	T6
	USPGA	86-75	161	MC		Br Open	65-73-70-71	279	T5
1988	Masters	81-74	155	MC		USPGA	73-80	153	MC
	Br Open	76-71-72-69	288	T25	1993	Masters	71-74-73-69	287	T17
	USPGA	78-79	157	MC		US Open	70-74-72-70	286	T52
1989	Masters	74-76-71-69	290	T14		Br Open	72-71-72-70	285	T51
	US Open	70-68-73-68	279	**T2**		USPGA	70-71-68-72	281	T22
	Br Open	74-72-73-71	290	T49	1994	Masters	76-73-77-75	301	T46
	USPGA	68-70-70-71	279	6		US Open	77-75	152	MC
1990	Masters	72-75-70-76	293	T30		Br Open	79-73	152	MC
	US Open	70-70-74-72	286	T21		USPGA	68-72-73-66	279	T9
	Br Open	68-69-70-69	276	T4	1995	Masters	69-72-71-73	285	T17
	USPGA	74-75-70-78	297	T31		US Open	72-71-69-75	287	T21
1991	Masters	72-66-67-72	277	**Won**		Br Open	71-74-76-71	292	T49
	US Open	73-68-79-80	300	T55		USPGA	71-72	143	MC

Woosnam sinks the putt that signals victory in the 1991 US Masters

PROFESSIONAL TEAM EVENTS

RYDER CUP

The most famous team competition in golf. In 1926, Samuel Ryder (born 1858), the son of a Manchester corn merchant, agreed to donate a trophy, for an international match between the leading professionals from Great Britain & Ireland, and those of the United States. The solid gold cup was worth £250. A year later the first Ryder Cup was staged in America. For 50 years, the match remained a contest between these two teams. However, between 1935 and 1977, GB&I

George Duncan, who skippered Great Britain in 1929

could only muster one victory in 18 meetings. So when the match was held in 1979, GB&I had become Europe. By including golfers from the continent of Europe, it was hoped that the series would become competitive again. And the change certainly worked. From 1985, through to 1991, Europe held the trophy. The golfers don't get paid for playing in the Ryder Cup and yet, it is one of the most fiercely contested of all sporting occasions. To most golf fans it's the fifth major.

1927
Worcester, Mass.

	USA 9½	**GB&I** 2½
Captains:	Walter Hagen	Ted Ray

Britain's original choice as captain, Abe Mitchell, was forced to withdraw with an appendicitis before the team set sail from Southampton. Ted Ray took over his duties. The two-day contest consisted of four foursomes and eight singles, each game played over 36 holes. This format remained until 1961. The hosts led 3-1 after the first day foursomes and then romped through the singles 6½-1½. GB&I's only victory in the singles came from George Duncan who beat Joe Turnesa one up.

1929
Moortown, Leeds

	GB&I 7	**USA** 5
Captains:	George Duncan	Walter Hagen

Despite trailing 2½-1½ after the foursomes, the hosts bounced back to win by two points. Their hero was captain George Duncan who beat his opposite number, Walter Hagen, 10&8 in the singles. Two weeks earlier Hagen had won the British Open at Muirfield. Other vital wins included Archie Compston over Gene Sarazen (6&4) and Charles Whitcombe's victory against Johnny Farrell (8&6). Farrell, who'd finished second behind Hagen at Muirfield, was the reigning US Open champion.

1931
Scioto, Ohio

	USA 9	**GB&I** 3
Captains:	Walter Hagen	Charles Whitcombe

Walter Hagen gained partial revenge over George Duncan when they met in the foursomes. Hagen

United States captain Walter Hagen drives during the 1933 match at Southport & Ainsdale

and partner Densmore Shute crushed Duncan and Arthur Havers 10&9. Five of America's nine victories were achieved by a margin of 7&6 or greater. In the battle of the captains, Hagen beat Charles Whitcombe 4&3.

1933
Southport & Ainsdale

GB&I 6½	USA 5½

Captains: JH Taylor   Walter Hagen

With the series standing at 5½ points each, and only one singles left on the course, Britain's Syd Easterbrook gave the home supporters a rousing finale, by beating Densmore Shute one up. Easterbrook and Shute had reached the final green all square, and both had putts of around 30 feet. Easterbrook left his approach putt within tap-in range, before Shute raced four feet past and then missed the return, giving Easterbrook the match and Britain the Cup.

As it transpired, this was Britain's last victory until 1957, 24 years on. Less than two weeks later, Shute won the British Open at St Andrews.

1935
Ridgewood, N. Jersey

USA 9	GB&I 3

Captains: Walter Hagen   Charles Whitcombe

Three brothers represented Britain - Charles, Reg and Ernest Whitcombe. But there was no family celebration as America swept through the foursomes 3-1 and the singles 6-2. Two matches were halved, while Britain's only two successes were both slender one hole victories.

1937
Southport & Ainsdale

GB&I 4	USA 8

Captains: Charles Whitcombe Walter Hagen

After five successive victories for the home team, the visitors finally won a Ryder Cup series. At one point during the final afternoon the match score was tied at 4-4, before the Americans mopped-up the last four singles. Britain's most successful player was Dai Rees, who was making his debut. Rees, partnered by Charles Whitcombe, halved his foursomes with Gene Sarazen and Densmore Shute.

September 1949: US captain Ben Hogan is presented with the Ryder Cup by Lord Wardington, president of Britain's PGA

He then beat reigning US Masters champion Byron Nelson 3&1 in the singles.

1947
Portland, Oregon

	USA	11	GB&I	1

Captains: Ben Hogan   Henry Cotton

Britain's worst performance in Ryder Cup history. Four defeats in the foursomes followed by a 7-1 drubbing in the singles. The visitors' only victory came from Sam King, a 4&3 winner over 1946 US Masters champion Herman Keiser. The American team contained Ben Hogan (who didn't even pick himself for the singles), Sam Snead, Byron Nelson, Lloyd Mangrum and Jimmy Demaret.

1949
Ganton, Scarborough

	GB&I	5	USA	7

Captains: Charles Whitcombe Ben Hogan

Britain were well placed after winning the opening foursomes 3-1. But the States fought back to take the singles 6-2. Dai Rees again performed well in the singles, beating former USPGA Champion Bob Hamilton 6&4.

1951
Pinehurst, N.Carolina

	USA	9½	GB&I	2½

Captains: Sam Snead   Arthur Lacey

Another clear-cut home victory for the States. Two of Britain's points were won by Arthur Lees

- both by 2&1 margins. Ed Oliver was his victim in both singles and foursomes, when Lees partnered Charles Ward and Oliver teamed-up with Henry Ransom.

1953

Wentworth, Surrey

GB&I	5½	**USA**	6½

Captains: Henry Cotton   Lloyd Mangrum

Britain snatched defeat from the jaws of victory. Youngsters Peter Alliss and Bernard Hunt would have clinched the Cup for the hosts but for last hole mistakes. Alliss drove out of bounds at the 17th to go one down against Jim Turnesa, but he looked all set to redeem himself at the last (par 5) where his American opponent had driven into the trees. Turnesa was still well short of the green in three, while Alliss was close to the putting surface in two. But Alliss fluffed his chip and later missed his par putt from just over a yard. Turnesa claimed a half with a bogey six to win the game one up.

Coming up next, in the penultimate match, was Bernard Hunt, who was one up on the last tee. But he three-putted from the back of the green to allow Dave Douglass to win the hole and halve the match with a par five. Had Hunt and Alliss both parred the final hole, Britain would have won the Cup back.

1955

Thunderbird, California

USA	8	**GB&I**	4

Captains: Chick Harbert   Dai Rees

John Jacobs, playing in his only Ryder Cup match for GB&I, won both his games on the final hole. He was the only visitor to earn two points. In the foursomes, he and John Fallon beat Chandler Harper and Jerry Barber one up, a scoreline Jacobs repeated in his singles against reigning US Masters champion Cary Middlecoff.

1957

Lindrick, Sheffield

GB&I	7½	**USA**	4½

Captains: Dai Rees   Jack Burke

A great fightback by the hosts who had trailed 3-1 after the foursomes. But on the final afternoon, Britain won six of the eight singles, with another halved. The Cup-clinching point arrived when Ken Bousfield beat Lionel Hebert 4&3.

1959

Eldorado, California

USA	8½	**GB&I**	3½

Captains: Sam Snead   Dai Rees

Revenge for the Americans in a contest that almost never happened. While flying between Los Angeles and Palm Springs, the British and Irish team experienced a journey of sheer terror. Their charter flight was tossed around in a violent storm. Ronald Heager, of the Daily Express, was on board. He wrote: "From our flying height of 13,000 feet, we dropped like a stone to 9,000 feet. It was like falling in a giant lift when the cable had snapped." After this brush with death, the result hardly seemed to matter.

1961

Royal Lytham, Lancs

GB&I	9½	**USA**	14½

Captains: Dai Rees   Jerry Barber

For the 14th staging of the Ryder Cup there was a new format. All matches were played over 18 holes, rather than 36. Instead of four foursomes on the first day there were now eight (four in the morning/four in the afternoon). The number of second day singles was also doubled from eight to 16. But this made little difference to the outcome. The States led 6-2 after day one, and by the end of the first series of eight singles had moved 11-5 in front. This meant only one point was needed from the second round of eight singles to retain the trophy. British captain Dai Rees claimed 3 points out of 4, while Arnold Palmer won 3½ out of 4 for the States.

1963

East Lake, Georgia

USA	23	**GB&I**	9

Captains: Arnold Palmer   John Fallon

Four-ball matches were included for the first time, as the contest was extended from two days to three. Eight foursomes on day one; eight four-balls on day two and 16 singles on day three. Yet another easy win for the hosts who were 12-4 ahead after day two. They needed just 4 points from the 16 singles to keep the Cup. Billy Casper led the American charge with 4½ points out of 5, while teammate Dow Finsterwald won 4½ out of 6.

1965

Royal Birkdale, Lancs.

GB&I	12½	**USA**	19½

Captains: Harry Weetman   Byron Nelson

A battling performance by the hosts who went

into the final day only 9-7 down. Peter Alliss was Britain's leading player, winning five of his six matches, including singles victories over Billy Casper (1 up) and Ken Venturi (3&1). But once again, the Americans showed they had greater strength in depth winning 10½ points out of 16 on the final day.

1967
Champions, Texas

USA	23½	GB&I 8½
Captains:	Ben Hogan	Dai Rees

Just another stroll in the park for the States. At the end of the second day, the hosts enjoyed a 13-3 lead. And going into the final series of eight singles they were already uncatchable. Arnold Palmer and Gardner Dickinson both had 100% records from five matches.

1969
Royal Birkdale, Lancs.

GB&I 16	USA	16
Captains:	Eric Brown	Sam Snead

One of the most exciting clashes in Cup history, with 18 of the 32 matches going down to the final hole. The match erupted on day two in a four-ball game involving America's Dave Hill and Ken Still, against Britain's Brian Huggett and Bernard Gallacher. For most of the front nine, there was constant squabbling between the four players. At the first, Hill was told to stand still as Huggett putted. On the second green Gallacher was just about to putt when Still shouted to his own caddie not to hold the flag for the Scottish player. Still remarked that Gallacher's own caddie should be attending the flag. At the seventh, the British pair protested that Still had putted out of turn and at the eighth the Americans were furious that they had been conceded a putt. Still had wanted to hole-out in order to show his partner the line. The match quietened down on the back nine. Hill and Still finally won 2&1.

Going into the final day, the match was level at 8 all. In the first series of singles, reigning British Open champion Tony Jacklin beat Jack Nicklaus 4&3. And when the two captains nominated their players for the second round of eight singles, Jacklin and Nicklaus were once again drawn to face each other - in the last match of the series.

By holing an enormous eagle putt to win the 17th, Jacklin had drawn level with Nicklaus. And, as they teed-up on the par-5 18th, their game was the only one left on the course. The

match score at this point was 15½-15½. Everything depended on this final hole. Both reached the 18th green in two. Jacklin was at the back of the green, Nicklaus was slightly closer and to the right of the flag. Jacklin, putting first, ran his ball to within 20 inches of the cup. Nicklaus, with a putt to win the Ryder Cup for America, overshot by three feet before holing the return for a birdie four. Nicklaus immediately picked-up Jacklin's ball marker and conceded him his putt. The match ended in a tie, 16 all. As Nicklaus handed Jacklin back his marker, he said: "I don't think you would have missed but under the circumstances I'm not giving you the opportunity." This was a fine sporting gesture by Nicklaus, one that will always be treasured. Jacklin ended the match unbeaten - four wins and two halves.

1971
Old Warson, Missouri

USA	18½	GB&I 13½
Captains:	Jay Hebert	Eric Brown

After the emotional, gripping finale of 1969, normal service was resumed two years later. The visitors had managed to grab a one point advantage at the end of the first day foursomes (4½-3½). But on day two, the Americans took complete control. They won all four morning four-balls, before adding another 2½ points in the afternoon. Britain's quota of four-ball points was a meagre 1½ out of 8. The contest ended there.

However, there was one unsavoury incident on the second morning, involving Arnold Palmer and Gardner Dickinson for the States, against Britain's Bernard Gallacher and Peter Oosterhuis. Palmer, with the honour, had just played his tee shot at the par-3, seventh, when Gallacher's caddie, an American called Jack McLeod, innocently shouted: "Great shot, what did you hit?" Palmer replied "A five iron". But McLeod's instinctive inquiry had infringed the rules. Technically he had asked his opponents for advice, which is not permitted even as a caddie.

The outcome was that the British pair lost the hole. Gallacher claimed that instead of turning a blind eye to the incident, Palmer had complained to the referee while leaving the green after both sides had made par 3s. Palmer denied Gallacher's accusation. Whatever the truth, the referee had no option but to award the Americans the hole. As a result of this penalty, the Americans went 2 up, and finally won the contest 5&4.

1973
Muirfield, Scotland
    GB&I 13   USA 19
Captains: Bernard Hunt Jack Burke
Hopes were high for a home victory midway through the second day, when Britain led 7½-4½ after the second round of foursomes. But that was the end of the dream. Once again, the Americans proved invincible in the singles, which they swept through 11-5. However, Britain's Peter Oosterhuis and Maurice Bembridge emerged with great credit. Oosterhuis claimed 4 points out of 6, including a halved singles with Lee Trevino, and a 4&2 victory over Arnold Palmer on the final afternoon. Bembridge, meanwhile, had two memorable singles matches against Jack Nicklaus, both of which went the distance. The morning clash was halved, while Nicklaus won the afternoon encounter 2 up. To date, this is the only occasion in which the Ryder Cup has been held in Scotland. One final note, Peter Butler became the first player to hole in one at the Ryder Cup when he aced the 16th on day two.

1975
Laurel Valley, Penn.
    USA 21   GB&I 11
Captains: Arnold Palmer Bernard Hunt
The visitors were never in the hunt after losing all four foursomes on the first morning. By the end of the second day, the Americans led 12½-3½, and by lunch on singles day they couldn't be caught. Hale Irwin captured 4½ points out of 5 for the States, while teammate Tom Weiskopf won all four of his games. Britain's big moment came on singles day when Brian Barnes beat Jack Nicklaus twice. In the morning he won 4&2, in the afternoon it was 2&1.

1977
Royal Lytham, Lancs.
    GB&I 7½   USA 12½
Captains: Brian Huggett Dow Finsterwald
Another change to the format. Five foursomes on day one, five four-balls on day two, with 10 singles on the third day. For a couple of hours on the first afternoon, it looked as if Britain might grab an early lead. But from two-up with three to play, Peter Dawson and Neil Coles were beaten by Dave Stockton and Jerry McGee; while Eamonn Darcy and Tony Jacklin lost a two hole lead with three to play, to halve their game with Ed Sneed

and Don January. So instead of leading 3-2, which looked a distinct possibility, Britain suddenly trailed 3½-1½.

Britain's only stars over the three days were Peter Oosterhuis and 20-year-old Nick Faldo, making his debut. In foursomes, Oosterhuis and Faldo beat Ray Floyd and Lou Graham 2&1; they then defeated Jack Nicklaus and Floyd 3&1 in the four-balls, and both went on to win their respective singles matches on the final day. Faldo was particularly impressive in beating the reigning US Masters and British Open champion Tom Watson 1 up.

The match also witnessed an unfortunate incident on day two between Britain's non-playing captain Brian Huggett and Jacklin. Huggett confronted Jacklin in public for not going back on to the course to support his teammates, after his own match had ended. He then dropped Jacklin from the following day's singles. Jacklin complained that Huggett had failed to consult any of his players about pairings.

1979
The Greenbrier, W.Va.
    USA 17   Europe 11
Captains: Billy Casper John Jacobs
The first contest to include players from the continent of Europe. Spaniards Seve Ballesteros and Antonio Garrido had the honour of being the first non-British, Irish or American golfers to play in the Ryder Cup. And, after two days, the match was finely balanced in favour of the Americans, 8½-7½. But the singles was a different story, America taking 8½ points out of 12. Yet Europe would have run the hosts closer, had they not lost four of the five singles that went down to the 18th green. The meeting's leading player was Larry Nelson who won all five of his matches on his debut, including four victories over Ballesteros.

1981
Walton Heath, Surrey
    Europe 9½   USA 18½
Captains: John Jacobs Dave Marr
Prospects looked hopeful for the hosts when they took a 4½-3½ lead after day one. However, on day two, the States won 7 of the 8 points at stake, and increased their advantage even more in the singles for a most comprehensive victory. Once again, Larry Nelson led the way winning all four of his matches for the visitors.

1983
PGA National, Florida
USA 14½   Europe 13½
Captains: Jack Nicklaus   Tony Jacklin
This meeting signalled the start of the modern era of Ryder Cup matches. From now on, there would be no easy games for either side. With just two singles left on the course, on the last day, the match score was tied at 13 all. With one hole to play, Spain's Jose-Maria Canizares led Lanny Wadkins 1 up; while Bernard Gallacher, bringing up the rear, trailed American Tom Watson by one hole after 16. But, sadly for Europe, Wadkins knocked a 60-yard chip to within 12 inches of the pin to halve his match; and shortly afterwards Watson won the 17th with a bogey-four to defeat Gallacher 2&1. Watson won four of his five matches over the three days.

1985
The Belfry, Midlands
Europe 16½   USA 11½
Captains: Tony Jacklin   Lee Trevino
Victory for Europe at last and America's first defeat for 28 years. But it was the visitors who made the best start, by taking a 3-1 lead after the opening series of foursomes. The turning point came on the second morning when Craig Stadler (playing with Curtis Strange) missed a putt of around 18 inches on the final green of a four-ball clash against Europe's Bernhard Langer and Sandy Lyle. The game was halved, allowing Europe to draw level in the match for the first time at 6-6. From here, Europe took control. They won three of the afternoon's four foursomes and the following day collected 7½ points out of 12 in the singles. The Cup was regained when Sam Torrance holed from around 20-feet to beat Andy North 1-up. Manuel Pinero was the unsung hero of the European team, winning four of his five games.

1987
Muirfield Village, Ohio
USA 13   Europe 15
Captains: Jack Nicklaus   Tony Jacklin
America's first-ever defeat on home soil. After two days, Europe held a commanding 10½-5½ advantage. But on singles day, the hosts struck back winning 7½ points. But it was too late to deny Europe a famous win. Fittingly, Seve Ballesteros secured the vital point, by beating Curtis Strange 2&1. Ballesteros won four of his five games, three of them in partnership with his 21-year-old compatriot Jose-Maria Olazabal.

1989
The Belfry, Midlands
Europe 14   USA 14
Captains: Tony Jacklin   Ray Floyd
Only the second tie in 28 meetings. Trailing 9-7, going into the singles, the visitors fought back to square the series 14 all, although a draw was good enough for Europe to retain the trophy. The most dramatic moment of an emotional final afternoon was Christy O'Connor jr's 2-iron shot to within four feet of the flag at 18. It enabled him to beat

European captain Tony Jacklin with the trophy in 1989

American Fred Couples by one hole. The putt that retained the Cup for Europe belonged to 42-year-old Jose Maria Canizares. He holed from close range to beat Ken Green 1-up. Green had three-putted the final hole. Europe's big guns - Bernhard Langer, Seve Ballesteros, Nick Faldo and Ian Woosnam - all lost their singles. Jose-Maria Olazabal was Europe's key player, picking-up 4½ points out of 5. Chip Beck contributed 3½ points out of 4 to the American cause.

1991

Kiawah Island, S Car.

	USA 14½	Europe 13½

Captains: Dave Stockton   Bernard Gallacher

The destiny of the Cup depended on the very last putt. With the match score 14-13 to the hosts, Bernhard Langer needed to hole a six-foot par putt to beat Hale Irwin and tie the series at 14 all. A draw would have retained the trophy for Europe but his ball rolled agonisingly wide. Irwin had escaped with a half and the States had won back the Ryder Cup by a single point. Earlier, on the last afternoon, Colin Montgomerie had fought back from four down with four to play, to halve his game with America's Mark Calcavecchia. Over those last four holes, Calcavecchia made two bogeys and two triple-bogeys. Montgomerie had played the same holes in a total of three-over-par. For Europe, Seve Ballesteros won 4½ points out of 5.

1993

The Belfry, Midlands

	Europe 13	USA 15

Captains: Bernard Gallacher Tom Watson

Europe was left to rue the singles defeats of Barry Lane and Costantino Rocca. Lane was 3-up on Chip Beck on the 14th tee, but lost four of the final five holes and was beaten 1-up. Rocca, 1-up on Davis Love III after 16, lost the last two holes. At 17 he three-putted, missing his second putt from three feet. Rocca then bogied 18 to hand Love an unlikely victory.

Nick Faldo gave European fans something to cheer about by making a hole-in-one at the par-3 14th. He halved his singles match with Paul Azinger. For the record, Ray Floyd, 51, became the oldest competitor in Cup history. He won three of his four matches, including a singles success over Jose-Maria Olazabal (2-up). The best individual record belonged to Ian Woosnam, who won 4½ points out of 5.

1995

Oak Hill, New York

	USA 13½	Europe 14½

Captains: Lanny Wadkins Bernard Gallacher

When Corey Pavin (playing with Loren Roberts) chipped-in from just off the back of the green at 18 to beat Europe's Nick Faldo and Bernhard Langer, 1-up, in the final fourball game of the second day, the United States held a 9-7 lead. With just 12 singles remaining, few people gave the visitors much of a chance of winning the trophy back. Only once

Philip Walton is hugged by his captain Bernard Gallacher after securing a dramatic victory for Europe in 1995

America's Jay Haas (right) congratulates Walton after their decisive singles match at Oak Hill in 1995

since 1957, had Europe (or GB&I) claimed most points on singles day, and never on American soil. Yet Europe performed one of the greatest Ryder Cup fightbacks of all time to sneak a one point victory. Every game was vital, but two in particular turned out to be crucial - Brad Faxon v David Gilford; and Curtis Strange v Nick Faldo. One up with one to play, Gilford was in trouble at the final hole (par 4) where he pulled his second shot left of the green and then fluffed a chip. In the end he salvaged a bogey-five by holing a tough eight footer. However, Faxon still had a chance to halve the match, if only he could sink his par putt from five feet. But Faxon, considered one of the best putters on the US Tour, failed in his attempt. Gilford had escaped with a narrow victory. In the other key match, Faldo was one down with two to play. The Englishman, however, got back to all square when he won the 17th (par 4), where he got down in two from a greenside bunker to save par. Strange had also missed the green at 17 with his second, chipped

to 10 feet but missed the putt. At the final hole Faldo drove into rough, from where he had to lay-up short of the green with his second. Strange, meanwhile, had hit an excellent drive only for his second shot to finish in the grassy bank short of the green. Faldo then produced one of the best shots he's ever played under pressure, a high wedge to within four feet of the flag. Strange found this an impossible act to follow. He chipped to six feet, missed the putt and had to settle for another bogey. Faldo held his nerve brilliantly to make par and snatch an unlikely win.

Now, with just one point needed for victory, Philip Walton clinched the Cup for Europe when he beat Jay Haas 1-up in a nervous finish. Corey Pavin was the leading points scorer over the three days, collecting 4 out of 5 for the States. There were also holes in one for Costantino Rocca (167-yard, 6th) in a second day foursomes and Howard Clark (192-yard, 11th) in his singles with Peter Jacobsen which Clark won 1-up.

Changes in format

1927-59 Day One: 4 foursomes;   Day Two 8 singles. All games 36 holes.

1961 Day One: Morning, 4 foursomes;   Afternoon, 4 foursomes.
Day Two: Morning, 8 singles; Afternoon, 8 singles. All games 18 holes.

1963-71 Day One: Morning, 4 foursomes;   Afternoon, 4 foursomes.
Day Two: Morning, 4 four-balls; Afternoon, 4 four-balls.
Day Three: Morning, 8 singles; Afternoon, 8 singles. All games 18 holes.

1973 Day One: Morning, 4 foursomes;   Afternoon, 4 four-balls.
Day Two: Morning, 4 foursomes;   Afternoon, 4 four-balls.
Day Three: Morning, 8 singles; Afternoon, 8 singles. All games 18 holes.

1975 Day One: Morning, 4 foursomes;   Afternoon, 4 four-balls.
Day Two: Morning, 4 four-balls;   Afternoon, 4 foursomes.
Day Three: Morning, 8 singles; Afternoon, 8 singles. All games 18 holes.

1977 Day One: 5 foursomes;   Day Two 5 four-balls.
Day Three: 10 singles. All games 18 holes.

1979 Day One: Morning 4 four-balls; Afternoon 4 foursomes.
Day Two: Morning 4 foursomes; Afternoon 4 four-balls.
Day Three: 12 singles. All games 18 holes.

1981-85 Day One: Morning, 4 foursomes;   Afternoon, 4 four-balls.
Day Two: Morning, 4 four-balls;   Afternoon, 4 foursomes.
Day Three: 12 singles. All games 18 holes.

1987-95 Day One: Morning, 4 foursomes;   Afternoon, 4 four-balls.
Day Two: Morning, 4 foursomes;   Afternoon, 4 four-balls.
Day Three: 12 singles. All games 18 holes.

RYDER CUP STATISTICS

	Pld	Won	Hlvd	Lost
United States	31	23	2	6
Europe/GB&I	31	6	2	23

Most appearances:

United States	8 times	Lanny Wadkins (1977-79-83-85-87-89-91-93)
		Ray Floyd (1969-75-77-81-83-85-91-93)
		Billy Casper (1961-63-65-67-69-71-73-75)
Europe/GB&I	10 times	Christy O'Connor sr. (1955-57-59-61-63-65-67-69-71-73)
		Nick Faldo (1977-79-81-83-85-87-89-91-93-95)

Youngest competitors:

United States	Horton Smith (21 yrs, 4 dys in 1929)
Europe/GB&I	Nick Faldo (20 yrs, 1 mth, 28 dys in 1977)

Oldest competitors:

United States	Ray Floyd (51 yrs, 20 dys in 1993)
	Don January (47 yrs, 9 mths, 26 dys in 1977)
Europe/GB&I	Ted Ray (50 yrs, 2 mths, 6 dys in 1927)
	Christy O'Connor sr (48 yrs, 8 mths, 30 dys in 1973)

Most matches played:

United States	37	Billy Casper (1961-75)
	34*	Lanny Wadkins (1977-93)
	32	Arnold Palmer (1961-73)

* - Includes singles that was credited as a half, although not played in 1993, when Sam Torrance withdrew injured.

Europe/GB&I	41	Nick Faldo (1977-95)
	40	Neil Coles (1961-77)
	37	Seve Ballesteros (1979-95)

Most points won:

United States	23½	Billy Casper (Max. 37, 63.51%)
	23	Arnold Palmer (Max 32, 71.88%)
	21½*	Lanny Wadkins (Max 34, 63.24%)

* - Includes singles that was credited as a half, although not played in 1993, when Sam Torrance withdrew injured.

Europe/GB&I:	23	Nick Faldo (Max. 41, 56.10%)
	22½	Seve Ballesteros (Max. 37, 60.81%)
	17½	Bernhard Langer (Max. 34, 51.47%)

Most singles points won:

United States	7	Billy Casper (Max. 10)
	7	Lee Trevino (Max. 10)
	7	Arnold Palmer (Max. 11)

Note: Tom Kite and Sam Snead have each won 6 points from 7 singles matches.

Europe/GB&I	7	Neil Coles (Max. 15)
	6½	Peter Oosterhuis (Max. 9)
	6½	Peter Alliss (Max. 12)
	6½	Nick Faldo (Max. 10)

Most matches lost:

United States	16	Ray Floyd (out of 31)
	12	Curtis Strange (20)
	11	Lanny Wadkins (34)

Europe/GB&I	21	Christy O'Connor sr (out of 36)
	21	Neil Coles (40)

Most singles matches lost:

United States	4	Ray Floyd (out of 8)
	4	Jack Nicklaus (10)

Europe/GB&I	10	Christy O'Connor sr (out of 14)
	8	Tony Jacklin (11)

Biggest winning margins (team, 36 holes)

United States	10&9	Walter Hagen & Densmore Shute (beat Duncan/Havers, 1931)
	10&9	Lew Worsham & Ed Oliver (Cotton/Lees, 1947)

Europe/GB&I	7&5	Aubrey Boomer & Charles Whitcombe (Diegel/Mehlhorn, 1927)

Biggest winning margins (team, 18 holes)

United States	7&6	Hale Irwin & Tom Kite (Brown/Smyth, 1979)
	7&6	Paul Azinger & Mark O'Meara (Faldo/Gilford, 1991)

Europe/GB&I	7&5	J-M Canizares & Jose Rivero (Kite/Peete, 1985)
	7&5	Bernhard Langer & Ian Woosnam (Azinger/Stewart, 1993)

Biggest winning margins (singles, 36 holes)

United States	9&8	Leo Diegel (beat Abe Mitchell, 1929)

Europe/GB&I	10&8	George Duncan (beat Walter Hagen, 1929)
	9&8	Abe Mitchell (beat Olin Dutra, 1933)

Biggest winning margins (singles, 18 holes)

United States	8&7	Tom Kite (beat Howard Clark, 1989)
	7&6	Miller Barber (beat Maurice Bembridge, 1969)
	7&6	Lee Trevino (beat Brian Huggett, 1971)
Europe/GB&I	5&4	Bernard Hunt (beat Jerry Barber, 1961)
	5&4	Christy O'Connor sr (beat Frank Beard, 1969)
	5&4	Peter Dawson (beat Don January, 1977)
	5&4	Bernhard Langer (beat Hal Sutton, 1985)

Most times captain:

United States	6	Walter Hagen (1927-29-31-33-35-37)
Europe/GB&I	5	Dai Rees (1955-57-59-61-67)

America's Curtis Strange en route to a record 10-under-par 62 during the 1987 Dunhill Cup at St Andrews

ALFRED DUNHILL CUP

First staged in 1985, this international event is contested by 16 three-man teams. Upto and including 1991, the tournament was played on a knock-out basis. Since then teams have been divided into four groups of four to contest a round robin stage, with each group winner qualifying for the semi-finals.

Each match is made up of three head-to-head singles, using the medal matchplay format. The player with the lowest 18-hole score in each individual game is deemed the winner. The team that collects most individual game victories is the overall winner of that match.

St Andrews in Scotland has hosted every tournament since its inception.

FINAL RESULTS (winning team members listed first)

1985	AUSTRALIA	bt USA	3-0	G Norman	65-71	M O'Meara	
				G Marsh	71-74	R Floyd	
				D Graham	69-72	C Strange	
1986	AUSTRALIA	bt JAPAN	3-0	R Davis	76-81	T Ozaki	
				D Graham	81-82	N Ozaki	
				G Norman	73-76	T Nakajima	
1987	ENGLAND	bt SCOTLAND	2-1	N Faldo	66-69	A Lyle	
				GJ Brand	64-69	S Torrance	
				H Clark	73-68	G Brand jr	
1988	IRELAND	bt AUSTRALIA	2-1	D Smyth	71-73	R Davis	
				R Rafferty	69-74	D Graham	
				E Darcy	71-63	G Norman	
1989	USA	bt JAPAN	3½-2½	M Calcavecchia	67-68	H Meshiai	
				T Kite	68-68	N Ozaki	
				C Strange	72-75	K Suzuki	
				M Calcavecchia	66-68	H Meshiai	
				T Kite	74-71	K Suzuki	
				C Strange	71-69	N Ozaki	
1990	IRELAND	bt ENGLAND	3½-2½	P Walton	72-72	M James	
				R Rafferty	71-73	R Boxall	
				D Feherty	74-73	H Clark	
				P Walton	77-76	M James	
				R Rafferty	71-77	R Boxall	
				D Feherty*	75-75	H Clark	
				* - Won at 3rd play-off hole			
1991	SWEDEN	bt SOUTH AFRICA	2-1	A Forsbrand	68-69	J Bland	
				P-U Johansson	74-68	D Frost	
				M Lanner*	74-74	G Player	
				* - Won at 1st play-off hole			
1992	ENGLAND	bt SCOTLAND	2½-1½	S Richardson	71-73	G Brand jr	
				J Spence	69-69	C Montgomerie	
				D Gilford	71-74	A Lyle	

1993	USA	bt	ENGLAND	2-1	P Stewart	74-70	M James
					F Couples	68-69	N Faldo
					J Daly	70-73	P Baker
1994	CANADA	bt	USA	2-1	D Barr	70-71	T Kite
					R Gibson	74-67	C Strange
					R Stewart	71-72	F Couples
1995	SCOTLAND	bt	ZIMBABWE	2-1	A Coltart	67-71	T Johnstone
					S Torrance	68-70	M McNulty
					C Montgomerie	74-68	N Price

Lowest scores: 62 **C Strange (USA)** v G Norman (Aus) (70) - 3rd place play-off, 1987

        63 **R Davis (Aus)** v D Halldorson (Can) (73) - 2nd round, 1987
           G Norman (Aus) v E Darcy (Ire) (71) - Final, 1988

Highest Score: 87 **C Espinoza (Mex)** v CH Chung (Tai) (79) - Group match, 1993

WORLD CUP

The tournament is run by the International Golf Association (IGA). Each competing nation is represented by two players whose four round totals are added together to give the team score. First played in 1953, the event was called the Canada Cup until 1967 when it became known as the World Cup.

    The first tournament in 1953 was staged over 72 holes (36 by each player) and contested by seven countries. In addition to the team event, the player with the lowest gross score is awarded the International Trophy for winning the individual competition.

Note: Home countries are in bold.

Year	Host	Champions	Second	Third
1953	Canada	ARGENTINA 287	CANADA 297	AUSTRALIA 298
1954	Canada	AUSTRALIA 556	ARGENTINA 560	USA 565
1955	USA	USA 560	AUSTRALIA 569	**SCOTLAND** 571
1956	England	USA 567	SOUTH AFRICA 581	CANADA 583
1957	Japan	JAPAN 557	USA 566	SOUTH AFRICA 569
1958	Mexico	**IRELAND** 579	SPAIN 582	SOUTH AFRICA 584
1959	Australia	AUSTRALIA 563	USA 573	CANADA 574
1960	Ireland	USA 565	**ENGLAND** 573	AUSTRALIA 574
1961	Puerto Rico	USA 560	AUSTRALIA 572	CANADA 579
1962	Argentina	USA 557	ARGENTINA 559	AUSTRALIA 569
1963	France	USA 482**	SPAIN 485	SOUTH AFRICA 492
1964	USA	USA 554	ARGENTINA 565	SOUTH AFRICA 568
1965	Spain	SOUTH AFRICA 571	SPAIN 579	USA 582
1966	Japan	USA 548	SOUTH AFRICA 553	CHINA 554
1967	Mexico	USA 557	NEW ZEALAND 570	MEXICO 574
1968	Italy	CANADA 569	USA 571	ITALY 573
1969	Singapore	USA 552	JAPAN 560	ARGENTINA 561
1970	Argentina	AUSTRALIA 544	ARGENTINA 554	SOUTH AFRICA 563
1971	USA	USA 555	SOUTH AFRICA 567	NEW ZEALAND 569

1972	Australia	TAIWAN 438***	JAPAN 440	SOUTH AFRICA 444
1973	Spain	USA 558	SOUTH AFRICA 564	TAIWAN 568
1974	Venezuela	SOUTH AFRICA 554	JAPAN 559	UNITED STATES 563
1975	Thailand	USA 554	TAIWAN 564	JAPAN 565
1976	USA	SPAIN 574	USA 576	TAIWAN 581
1977	Philippines	SPAIN 591	PHILIPPINES 594	CANADA 595
1978	USA	USA 564	AUSTRALIA 574	CANADA/**ENGLAND** 577
1979	Greece	USA 575	**SCOTLAND** 580	SPAIN 590
1980	Colombia	CANADA 572	**SCOTLAND** 575	TAIWAN 578
1981	Not Held			
1982	Mexico	SPAIN 563	USA 566	ITALY 574
1983	Indonesia	USA 565	AUSTRALIA/CANADA 572	
1984	Italy	SPAIN 414***	**SCOTLAND**/TAIPEI 422	
1985	USA	CANADA 559	**ENGLAND** 563	USA 564
1986	Not held			
1987	USA	**WALES** 574*	**SCOTLAND** 574	USA 576
1988	Australia	USA 560	JAPAN 561	AUSTRALIA 562
1989	Spain	AUSTRALIA 278****	SPAIN 281	USA/SWEDEN 287
1990	USA	GERMANY 556	**ENGLAND/IRELAND** 559	
1991	Italy	SWEDEN 563	**WALES** 564	**SCOTLAND** 567
1992	Spain	USA 548	SWEDEN 549	AUSTRALIA/**WALES** 555
1993	USA	USA 556	ZIMBABWE 561	**SCOTLAND** 565
1994	Puerto Rico	USA 536	ZIMBABWE 550	SWEDEN 551
1995	China	USA 543	AUSTRALIA 557	JAPAN/**SCOTLAND** 558

Fred Couples (left) and Davis Love III, winners of four successive World Cups for the United States in the 1990s

International Trophy

Year	Winner	Runners-up
1953	A Cerda (Arg) 140	S Leonard (Can) 144
1954	S Leonard (Can) 275	P Thomson(Aus)/A Cerda (Arg) 277
1955	E Furgol (US) 279*	P Thomson (Aus)/F Van Donck (Bel) 279
1956	B Hogan (US) 277	R de Vicenzo (Mex^) 282
1957	T Nakamura (Jap) 274	G Player (SA)/S Snead (USA)/**D Thomas (Wal)** 281
1958	A Miguel (Sp) 286*	**H Bradshaw (Ire)** 286
1959	S Leonard (Can) 275*	P Thomson (Aus) 275
1960	F Van Donck (Bel) 279	S Snead (USA) 281
1961	S Snead (USA) 272	P Thomson (Aus) 280
1962	R de Vicenzo (Arg) 276	**P Alliss (Eng)**/A Palmer (USA) 278
1963	J Nicklaus (USA) 237**	S Miguel (Sp)/G Player (SA) 242
1964	J Nicklaus (USA) 276	A Palmer (USA) 278
1965	G Player (SA) 281	J Nicklaus (USA) 284
1966	G Knudsen (Can) 272*	H Sugimoto (Jap) 272
1967	A Palmer (USA) 276	J Nicklaus (USA)/B Charles (NZ) 281
1968	A Balding (Can) 274	R Bernardini (It) 279
1969	L Trevino (USA) 275	R de Vicenzo (Arg) 276
1970	R de Vicenzo (Arg) 269	D Graham (Aus) 270
1971	J Nicklaus (USA) 271	G Player (SA) 278
1972	H Min-Nan (Tai) 217***	T Kono (Jap) 219
1973	J Miller (USA) 277	G Player (SA) 280
1974	B Cole (SA) 271	M Ozaki (Jap) 276
1975	J Miller (USA) 275	B Shearer (Aus)/H Min-Nan (Tai)/B Arda (Phil) 277
1976	E Acosta (Mex) 282	M Pinero (Sp)/J Pate (USA)/C-H Kuo (Tai)/ S Owen (NZ)/**B Barnes (Sco)**/D Hayes (SA) all 285
1977	G Player (SA) 289	R Lavares (Phil)/H Green (USA) 292
1978	J Mahaffey (USA) 281	A North (USA) 283
1979	H Irwin (USA) 285	**A Lyle (Sco)**/B Langer (WG) 287
1980	**A Lyle (Sco)** 282	B Langer (WG) 283
1981	Not held	
1982	M Pinero (Sp) 281	J-M Canizares (Sp)/B Gilder (USA) 282
1983	D Barr (Can) 276	R Caldwell (USA) 279
1984	J-M Canizares (Sp) 205***	**G Brand jr (Sco)** 207
1985	**H Clark (Eng)** 272	**C O'Connor jr (Ire)** 277
1986	Not held	
1987	**I Woosnam (Wal)** 274	**A Lyle (Sco)** 279
1988	B Crenshaw (USA) 275	T Ozaki (Jap) 276
1989	P Fowler (Aus) 137****	A Sorensen (Den)/J-M Canizares (Sp) 138
1990	P Stewart (USA) 271	A Sorensen (Den) 273
1991	**I Woosnam (Wal)** 273	B Langer (Ger) 276
1992	B Ogle (Aus) 270*	**I Woosnam (Wal)** 270
1993	B Langer (Ger) 272	F Couples (USA) 275
1994	F Couples (USA) 265	C Rocca 270
1995	D Love III (USA) 267*	H Sasaki (Jap) 267

* - Won play-off
** - Tournament reduced to 63 holes
*** - Tournament reduced to 54 holes
**** - Tournament reduced to 36 holes
^ - Argentina's Roberto de Vicenzo was representing Mexico at the time

WORLD CUP RECORDS

Most victories:
21 - USA
4 - Spain & Australia

Most times member of winning team:
6 - Jack Nicklaus (USA) 1963, 64, 66, 67, 71, 73
  - Arnold Plamer (USA) 1960, 62, 63, 64, 66, 67
4 - Sam Snead (USA) 1956, 60, 61, 62
  Fred Couples (USA) 1992, 93, 94, 95
  Davis Love III (USA) 1992, 93, 94, 95

Most Individual titles:
3 - Jack Nicklaus (USA) 1963, 64, 71

2 - Stan Leonard (Can) 1954, 59
  Roberto de Vicenzo (Arg) 1962, 70
  Gary Player (SA) 1965, 77
  Johnny Miller (USA) 1973, 75
  Ian Woosnam (Wal) 1987, 91

Note: On the only occasion England hosted the World Cup in 1956 the event was staged at Wentworth in Surrey. Portmarnock in Dublin was the venue in 1960 when Ireland held the competition.

THE PROFESSIONAL TOURS

EUROPEAN TOUR

THE GROWTH OF THE EUROPEAN TOUR

Although professional golf was in existence well before the turn of the 20th century, tournaments were few and far between, especially on this side of the Atlantic. For most of Britain's golf professionals, the chance to play in a 36 or 54 hole strokeplay event, in pursuit of modest cash prizes, was a welcome relief from the day-to-day grind of teaching amateurs at their local clubs.

In 1901 the pros got together to form the Professional Golfers' Association of Great Britain with its first offices being in Bishopgate, London.

The purpose of this body was to look after the interest of its members whose main duties were club based. Organising tournaments was of lesser importance.

Even when the first official Order of Merit was conducted in 1937 most of Britain's leading golfers were still very much club professionals. And this was the way it stayed until well after World War II, despite the advent of a flourishing Tour in the United States.

But as the number of events slowly increased, the best club professionals started to devote more and more time to tournament play. Thus the opportunity of earning a living from tournament golf alone became a distinct possibility, if only for a privileged few.

Yet in time, it became clear that two distinct types of golf professional existed. Ones that played

Wentworth in Surrey, headquarters of the PGA European Tour since April 1981

tournaments and those who taught in the clubs. And the dividing line was clearly getting wider. It wasn't long before the tournament pros felt that the PGA of Great Britain was failing to look after their interests properly, so a special Tournament Players' Division of the PGA was set-up in 1971 under the guidance of John Jacobs. In 1972 tournaments from the continent of Europe were included in the Order of Merit for the first time. Since 1981, the Tour has been based at Wentworth in Surrey and in 1984 the Tour became a limited company. The club pros (PGA of Great Britain) now have their own headquarters at The Belfry in the Midlands.

As for the increasingly continental flavour of the Tour, that also developed slowly over the years. Up until the early 1970s, most tournaments in Europe were staged in Britain because most of

the leading professionals were either British or Irish. Such was the dominance of British and Irish events that the word 'European' wasn't actually used in the title until 1977 when it became known as the PGA European Tournament Players' Division. In 1979 it became the PGA European Golf Tour.

By the mid-1980s there were more tournaments staged on the continent of Europe than in Great Britain and Ireland and that is still the case today. The fields have become more international as well.

Today's leading tournament players can earn millions of pounds by playing golf. But that wasn't always the case. In 1963, the leading money winner was Bernard Hunt with £7,209. Compare that to the $128,230 earned by Arnold Palmer on the US Tour that same year. Even by

Peter Oosterhuis pictured during a tournament at Stoke Poges in 1971, the year he led the Order of Merit for the first time

the monetary values of the day, Europe's best golfers were poorly paid back in the 1950s and 60s. Yet if it wasn't for these pioneers who improved the standard of golf with each decade, it is doubtful whether today's superstars would be making such an excellent living.

EUROPEAN ORDER OF MERIT

The leader of the Order of Merit (OM) receives the Harry Vardon Trophy. It was first awarded in 1937, although the method for selecting the OM winner has changed over the years.

At one time the Trophy was contested on a points basis. The higher-up a player finished in an official OM tournament, the greater the number of points he received. Nowadays, the OM position is decided on money won in official events. The full list of OM leaders are listed as follows:

Year	Leader	Country
1937	Charles Whitcombe	England
1938	Henry Cotton	England
1939	Reg Whitcombe	England
1940-45	*Not contested due to World War II*	
1946	Bobby Locke	South Africa
1947	Norman von Nida	Australia
1948	Charlie Ward	England
1949	Charlie Ward	England
1950	Bobby Locke	South Africa
1951	John Panton	Scotland
1952	Harry Weetman	England
1953	Flory van Donck	Belgium
1954	Bobby Locke	South Africa
1955	Dai Rees	Wales
1956	Harry Weetman	England
1957	Eric Brown	Scotland
1958	Bernard Hunt	England
1959	Dai Rees	Wales
1960	Bernard Hunt	England
1961	Christy O'Connor	Ireland
1962	Christy O'Connor	Ireland
1963	Neil Coles	England
1964	Peter Alliss	England
1965	Bernard Hunt	England
1966	Peter Alliss	England
1967	Malcolm Gregson	England
1968	Brian Huggett	Wales
1969	Bernard Gallacher	Scotland
1970	Neil Coles	England
1971	Peter Oosterhuis	England
1972	Peter Oosterhuis	England
1973	Peter Oosterhuis	England
1974	Peter Oosterhuis	England
1975	Dale Hayes	South Africa
1976	Seve Ballesteros	Spain
1977	Seve Ballesteros	Spain
1978	Seve Ballesteros	Spain
1979	Sandy Lyle	Scotland
1980	Sandy Lyle	Scotland
1981	Bernhard Langer	West Germany
1982	Greg Norman	Australia
1983	Nick Faldo	England
1984	Bernhard Langer	West Germany
1985	Sandy Lyle	Scotland
1986	Seve Ballesteros	Spain
1987	Ian Woosnam	Wales
1988	Seve Ballesteros	Spain
1989	Ronan Rafferty	Ireland
1990	Ian Woosnam	Wales
1991	Seve Ballesteros	Spain
1992	Nick Faldo	England
1993	Colin Montgomerie	Scotland
1994	Colin Montgomerie	Scotland
1995	Colin Montgomerie	Scotland

Most times OM leader:

6 - Seve Ballesteros (1976, 77, 78, 86, 88, 91)

4 - Peter Oosterhuis (1971, 72, 73, 74)

European Tour facts and figures

Most Tournament wins:
54   Seve Ballesteros (1976-95)

Most wins in one season:
7   Norman Von Nida (1947)
      Flory Van Donck (1953)

Youngest tournament winner:
Dale Hayes (18 yrs 290 dys) 1971 Spanish Open

Oldest tournament winner:
Neil Coles (48 yrs 14 dys) 1982 Sanyo Open

Lowest 18-hole score:
60   7 times (first by Baldovino Dassu,
      1971 Swiss Open

Lowest 72-hole total:
258   David Llewellyn 1988 Biarritz Open
      Ian Woosnam, 1990 Monte Carlo Open

Peter Alliss, three-time winner of the PGA Championship, pictured during the 1961 event at Royal Mid-Surrey

PGA CHAMPIONSHIP

The PGA Championship is the second most important tournament in Europe, earning the winner a 10-year exemption on Tour. The British Open is the only other European event to offer such a grand reward to its champion.

First staged in 1955, the tournament was restricted to British and Irish professionals until 1967, when for the next two years only, both a 'closed' and an 'open' championship were held. Since 1969 the event has been Open.

The tournament has been staged at Wentworth, the European Tour's headquarters, since 1984.

Year	Venue	Champion	Score
1955	Pannal	K Bousfield	277
1956	Maesdu	C Ward	282
1957	Maesdu	P Alliss	286
1958	Llandudno	H Bradshaw	287
1959	Ashburnham	D Rees	283
1960	Coventry	A Stickley	247*
1961	Royal Mid-Surrey	B Bamford	266
1962	Little Aston	P Alliss	287
1963	Royal Birkdale	P Butler	306
1964	Western Gailes	A Grubb	287
1965	Prince's	P Alliss	286
1966	Saunton	G Wolstenholme	278
1967	Hunstanton	M Gregson	275 (O)
1967	Thorndon Park	B Huggett	271 (C)
1968	Dunbar	D Talbot	276 (O)
1968	Royal Mid-Surrey	P Townsend	275 (C)
1969	Ashburnham	B Gallacher	293
1970-71		No Tournament	
1972	Wentworth	A Jacklin	279
1973	Wentworth	P Oosterhuis	280
1974	Wentworth	M Bembridge	278

Year	Venue	Champion	(Score)	Runners-up	(Score)
1975	Royal St George's	Arnold Palmer	285	Eamonn Darcy	287
1976	Royal St George's	Neil Coles**	280	Eamonn Darcy/Gary Player	280
1977	Royal St George's	Manuel Pinero	283	Peter Oosterhuis	286
1978	Royal Birkdale	Nick Faldo	278	Ken Brown	285
1979	St Andrews	Vicente Fernandez	288	Gary Player/Baldovino Dassu	289
1980	Royal St George's	Nick Faldo	283	Ken Brown	284
1981	Ganton	Nick Faldo	274	Ken Brown/Neil Coles	278
1982	Hillside	Tony Jacklin**	284	Bernhard Langer	284
1983	Royal St George's	Seve Ballesteros	278	Ken Brown/Sandy Lyle	280
1984	Wentworth	Howard Clark***	204	Bernhard Langer/Gordon J Brand	206
1985	Wentworth	Paul Way**	282	Sandy Lyle	282
1986	Wentworth	Rodger Davis**	281	Des Smyth	281
1987	Wentworth	Bernhard Langer	270	Seve Ballesteros	274
1988	Wentworth	Ian Woosnam	274	Seve Ballesteros/Mark James	276
1989	Wentworth	Nick Faldo	272	Ian Woosnam	274
1990	Wentworth	Mike Harwood	271	Nick Faldo/John Bland	272
1991	Wentworth	Seve Ballesteros**	271	Colin Montgomerie	271
1992	Wentworth	Tony Johnstone	272	J-M Olazabal/Gordon Brand jr	274
1993	Wentworth	Bernhard Langer	274	Gordon Brand jr/Frank Nobilo	280
				Colin Montgomerie	280
1994	Wentworth	Jose-Maria Olazabal	271	Ernie Els	272
1995	Wentworth	Bernhard Langer	279	Michael Campbell/P-U Johansson	280

* - Tournament reduced to 63 holes
** - Won after a play-off
*** - Tournament reduced to 54 holes
(O) - Open; (C) - Closed

Sponsors:

1967-69	Schweppes
1972-74	Viyella
1975-77	Penfold
1978-79	Colgate
1980-83	Sun Alliance
1984-87	Whyte & Mackay
1988-95	Volvo

Most wins:
4 Nick Faldo (1978, 80, 81, 89)
3 Peter Alliss (1957, 62, 65)
   Bernhard Langer (1987, 93, 95)

WORLD MATCHPLAY CHAMPIONSHIP

Annually contested at Wentworth, Surrey, since 1964

Year	Champion	Runner-Up	Final Score
1964	Arnold Palmer (USA)	Neil Coles (GB&I)	2&1
1965	Gary Player (SA)	Peter Thomson (Aus)	3&2
1966	Gary Player (SA)	Jack Nicklaus (USA)	6&4
1967	Arnold Palmer (USA)	Peter Thomson (Aus)	1 up
1968	Gary Player (SA)	Bob Charles (NZ)	1 up
1969	Bob Charles (NZ)	Gene Littler (USA)	at 37th

Hale Irwin, World Matchplay champion in 1974 and 1975, was runner-up to David Graham in 1976

1970	Jack Nicklaus (USA)	Lee Trevino (USA)	2&1
1971	Gary Player (SA)	Jack Nicklaus (USA)	5&4
1972	Tom Weiskopf (USA)	Lee Trevino (USA)	4&3
1973	Gary Player (SA)	Graham Marsh (Aus)	at 40th
1974	Hale Irwin (USA)	Gary Player (SA)	3&1
1975	Hale Irwin (USA)	Al Geiberger (USA)	4&2
1976	David Graham (Aus)	Hale Irwin (USA)	at 38th
1977	Graham Marsh (Aus)	Ray Floyd (USA)	5&3
1978	Isao Aoki (Jap)	Simon Owen (NZ)	3&2
1979	Bill Rogers (USA)	Isao Aoki (Jap)	1 up
1980	Greg Norman (Aus)	Sandy Lyle (GB&I)	1 up
1981	Seve Ballesteros (Sp)	Ben Crenshaw (USA)	1 up
1982	Seve Ballesteros (Sp)	Sandy Lyle (GB&I)	at 37th
1983	Greg Norman (Aus)	Nick Faldo (GB&I)	3&2
1984	Seve Ballesteros (Sp)	Bernhard Langer (Ger)	2&1
1985	Seve Ballesteros (Sp)	Bernhard Langer (Ger)	6&5

David Graham during his epic World Matchplay final against defending champion Hale Irwin in 1976

1986	Greg Norman (Aus)	Sandy Lyle (GB&I)	2&1
1987	Ian Woosnam (GB&I)	Sandy Lyle (GB&I)	1 up
1988	Sandy Lyle (GB&I)	Nick Faldo (GB&I)	2&1
1989	Nick Faldo (GB&I)	Ian Woosnam (GB&I)	1 up
1990	Ian Woosnam (GB&I)	Mark McNulty (Zim)	4&2
1991	Seve Ballesteros (Sp)	Nick Price (Zim)	3&2
1992	Nick Faldo (GB&I)	Jeff Sluman (USA)	8&7
1993	Corey Pavin (USA)	Nick Faldo (GB&I)	1 up
1994	Ernie Els (SA)	Colin Montgomerie (GB&I)	4&2
1995	Ernie Els (SA)	Steve Elkington (Aus)	3&1

Note: All finals played over 36 holes

Sponsors: 1964-76 Piccadilly; 1977-78 Colgate; 1979-90 Suntory; 1991-95 Toyota.

Most titles:
5 - Gary Player (1965, 66, 68, 71, 73)
    Seve Ballesteros (1981, 82, 84, 85, 91)

Most appearances in final:
6 - Gary Player (1965, 66, 68, 71, 73, 74)
5 - Sandy Lyle (1980, 82, 86, 87, 88)
    Seve Ballesteros (1981, 82, 84, 85, 91)
    Nick Faldo (1983, 88, 89, 92, 93)

Biggest winning margin (36 holes):

11&9	Tom Watson beat Dale Hayes (1st rd, 1978)

(In Final):

8&7	Nick Faldo beat Jeff Sluman (1992)

Longest match:

At 40th	Gary Player beat Graham Marsh (Final, 1973) Isao Aoki beat Seve Ballesteros (Semi-Final, 1979)

Most appearances in tournament:

20 -	Gary Player (1964-84)
19 -	Seve Ballesteros (1976-94)
15 -	Nick Faldo (1977-94)

Seve's miracle shot

To celebrate the 20th staging of the World Matchplay Championship in 1983, the organisers decided to invite all former winners. One player who accepted was inaugural champion Arnold Palmer who was drawn to face title-holder Seve Ballesteros in the first round. For that year only, first round matches were contested over 18 holes, not the usual 36. And what a game Palmer v Ballesteros turned out to be. Fifty-four year-old Palmer rolled back the years with some inspired golf. He reached the turn 1 up, and standing on the 17th (par 5) tee he led by two. A fighting birdie by Seve, where he holed from seven feet, took this intriguing contest down the 18th (par 5). Yet the Spaniard's chances of tieing the match didn't look good when he was 80 yards short of the 18th green in two. But Ballesteros then played the shot of his life - a perfect chip and run which rolled purposely into the hole for an eagle three to square the match. Poor Arnie was stunned. Despite shooting a three-under-par 69, without a single bogey on his card, he was forced into extra-holes. After both players made par at the 19th and 20th, Seve's birdie four at the next proved too much for Palmer, who finally succumbed on the 21st green.

Fighting Player

Possibly the most famous match of all time was Gary Player's semi-final with American Tony Lema in 1965. Six down at lunch, Player's prospects quickly got worse when he bogied the first hole in the afternoon to trail Lema by seven, with 17 holes to play. Although Player won both the 20th and 21st, he was still five down with nine to play. This, however, became two down, when

Player won three of the next four holes. Lema conceded the 34th, so with two holes to play, his lead had been cut to just one. At the 35th, where both men made birdie 4s, Player had to hole from six feet to stay alive. At the 36th (par 5), Player's 4-wood second shot finished 12 feet from the flag. Lema's second missed the green and he took three more to get down. Player two-putted for a birdie-four, to square the contest. At the first and only extra-hole (37th), the par-4, 1st, Player made a routine par to close out the match and complete a remarkable comeback. Lema had cracked. His second shot at the 37th found a greenside bunker and his 15-footer to take the match into a second extra-hole stayed above ground. The next day Player returned to the West Course to beat Australian Peter Thomson 3&2 in the final and claim the first of his five World Matchplay titles.

Jacklin's 29

It is doubtful that back in 1972, you'd find the name of Lee Trevino on Tony Jacklin's Christmas card list. Firstly at Muirfield, in the British Open, Trevino broke Jacklin's heart by chipping-in on a number of occasions to deny the British player a second Open title. Three months later at Wentworth the two were at each other's throats again in the semi-final stage. The morning session went the American's way, as Trevino opened-up a four-hole lead. But back came Jacklin with an outward half of 29 after lunch, winning five holes out of six starting at the 4th (22nd) where he holed from 30-feet for an eagle three. At the 23rd he fired a 6-iron to four feet and grabbed a birdie-two; he made another birdie at the par-4, 24th, after stroking a wedge to within four feet of the flag; then his 6-iron second shot at the 26th (par 4) finished no more than 12 inches away and he completed the outward half with yet another birdie by firing a 5-iron to within 6-feet of the cup at the par-4, 27th. Amazingly, Jacklin was now one-up. But Trevino has always been famed for his fighting qualities. Supermex levelled matters early on the back nine before the pair halved five successive holes through to the end of the 35th. Once again, Trevino came up with the killer blow. His 3-wood second shot to the par-5, 36th, came to rest 10 feet from the flag. Jacklin, who had played his second shot first, missing the green on the left, had to settle for a par 5. Trevino two-putted for a famous victory. Despite shooting a nine-under-par 63 after lunch, Jacklin had lost by one hole. Trevino's two rounds of 67 had put him into the final.

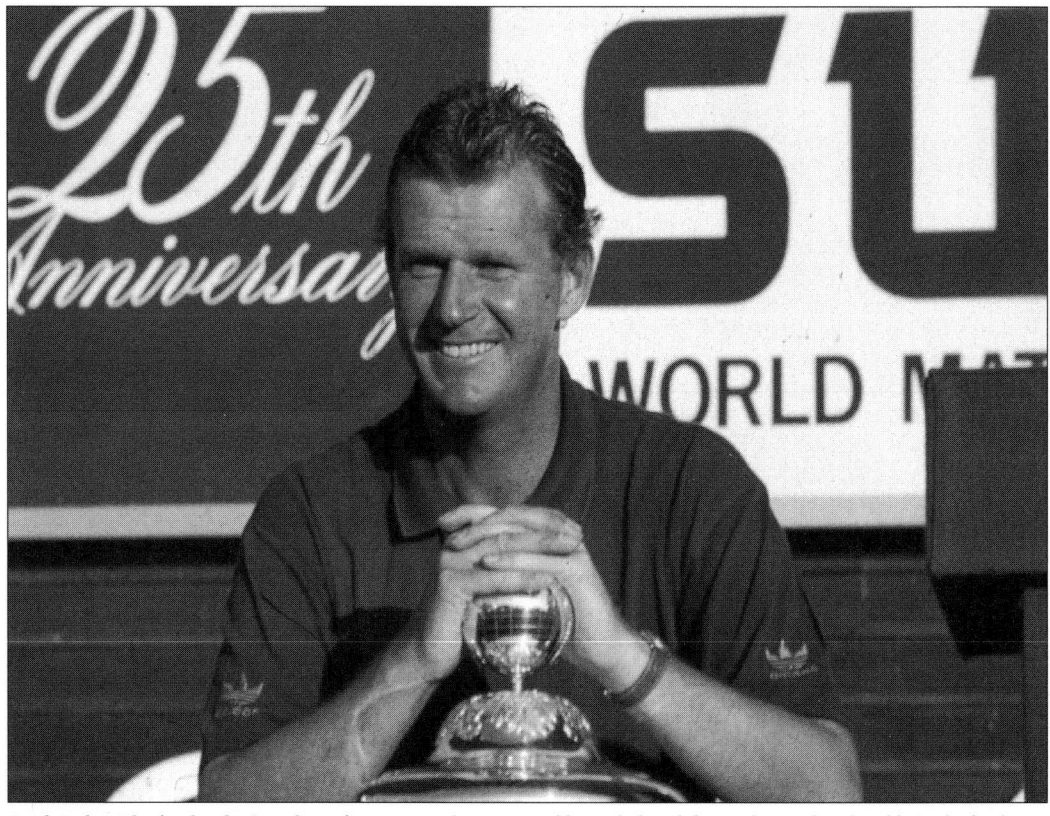

Sandy Lyle smiles for the photographers after winning the 1988 World Matchplay, defeating his rival Nick Faldo in the final

Prize-Money

Arnold Palmer's winning cheque at the 1964 Championship was £5,000. Yet 30 years later invitees were guaranteed £25,000 for losing in the first round - that's £9,000 more than the entire purse in the first year.

Year	Total Purse	First Prize
1964:	£16,000	£5,000
1974:	£30,000	£10,000
1984:	£150,000	£45,000
1994:	£600,000	£160,000

Raining birdies

The 1986 quarter-final encounter between Japan's Tommy Nakajima and Sandy Lyle of Scotland was by anyone's standards, a most remarkable match. In 36 holes of regulation play, the pair fired a total of four eagles and 27 birdies. Both carded 65s in the morning and 64s after lunch. Lyle had trailed by two with just two holes to play. A birdie four at the 17th (35th) reduced the gap to one, before Lyle sank a 45-foot eagle putt at the 36th to take the match into extra-holes. However, overtime lasted only one hole (the par-5, 17th) where a dispirited Nakajima three-putted for a bogey six, leaving Lyle the victor with a straightforward par.

Faldo's 'friendly' assistance

One of the less savoury moments in World Matchplay history came in a first round clash between Nick Faldo and Australian Graham Marsh in 1983. All square through 15 holes of this 18-hole encounter, Faldo's second shot at the 16th ran through the green and into a section of crowd, only for his ball to surprisingly reappear moments later trundling back on to the putting surface. It eventually finished around 40 feet from the hole. The situation was now in the hands of referee Bill McCrea. Was Faldo's ball deflected while it was still in motion? Or had it been kicked or thrown by a spectator who wanted to assist Faldo's chances of winning this match? Unable to confirm exactly what had happened, McCrea had no option but to allow the British golfer to play his third shot from where it had finally come to rest. An aggrieved Marsh, slightly further away than Faldo, left his birdie attempt three-feet short. Faldo then two-putted for par but failed to concede Marsh his putt. The Australian missed, leaving Faldo one-up with two holes to play. Faldo then birdied the 17th to clinch the match 2&1 but he had reached the quarter-finals in extremely controversial circumstances.

Graham comes late

No one has ever won three consecutive titles, although in 1976, Hale Irwin came mighty close. Standing on the 33rd tee in the final against David Graham, the American was 2-up. He was also six-under-par for the 32 holes he'd played that day. But Graham is Australian, therefore a fighter by trade. On the 33rd green he holed from 40 feet for a winning birdie three, to reduce the gap to one. At the 35th (par 5), Graham looked in danger of losing 2&1. But he rolled in a 20-foot birdie putt which proved good enough for a half when Irwin made his four from 8 feet. At the 36th (par 5), Graham was again in trouble after his second shot finished in a greenside bunker. Yet from here, he blasted out to within four feet of the cup and cooly made his birdie four to level the match after Irwin's conservative par. Both made pars at the first play-off hole, before Graham secured the title at the par-3, 38th. His tee shot finished 12 feet from the cup and Graham duly holed out for a winning birdie. Irwin was left to rue a missed opportunity. Despite being seven-under-par for 38 holes and without a single bogey all day, the champion of 1974 and 1975 was denied a third successive title.

EUROPEAN OPEN

The winner earns a five-year exemption on Tour.

Year	Venue	Champion	(Score)	Runners-up	(Score)
1978	Walton Heath	Bobby Wadkins*	283	Bernard Gallacher	283
				Gil Morgan	283
1979	Turnberry	Sandy Lyle	275	Dale Hayes	282
				Peter Townsend	282
1980	Walton Heath	Tom Kite	284	Leonard Thompson	285
				Lon Hinkle	285
1981	Hoylake	Graham Marsh	275	Seve Ballesteros	277
1982	Sunningdale	Manuel Pinero	266	Sam Torrance	268
1983	Sunningdale	Isao Aoki	274	Seve Ballesteros	276
				Carl Mason/Nick Faldo	276
1984	Sunningdale	Gordon Brand jr	270	Seve Ballesteros	273
				Noel Ratcliffe	273
1985	Sunningdale	Bernhard Langer	269	John O'Leary	272
1986	Sunningdale	Greg Norman *	269	Ken Brown	269
1987	Walton Heath	Paul Way	279	Gordon Brand jr/	
				John Bland	281
1988	Sunningdale	Ian Woosnam	260	Nick Faldo	263
1989	Walton Heath	Andrew Murray	277	Frank Nobilo	278
1990	Sunningdale	Peter Senior	267	Ian Woosnam	268
1991	Walton Heath	Mike Harwood	277	Sandy Lyle	279
1992	Sunningdale	Nick Faldo	262	Robert Karlsson	265
1993	East Sussex	Gordon Brand jr	275	Phillip Price/	
				Ronan Rafferty	282
1994	East Sussex	David Gilford	275	Costantino Rocca	280
				Jose Maria Olazabal	280
1995	The K Club	Bernhard Langer*	280	Barry Lane	280

* - Won after a play-off

Most titles: 2 Gordon Brand jr (1984-93), Bernhard Langer (1985-95)

UNITED STATES TOUR

Detailed tournament records have been kept in the United States since 1916, the year that Cornish-born American Jim Barnes and New York's Walter Hagen led the way with three victories apiece. For more than 60 years now, men's golf in the United States has been big business. Even in the mid 1920s, America's leading professionals could play tournament golf most weeks of the year, which unfortunately wasn't the case for their British counterparts. Yet it wasn't until 1934 that the first official Money List was compiled. The inaugural winner was Paul Runyan who won six times and had 16 top 10-finishes. While topping the Money List does not enjoy the same prestige as winning one of the four major championships, it is generally accepted as being the perfect yardstick for judging a player's form over an entire season. Since 1981, the Money Leader has been presented with the Arnold Palmer Trophy.

MONEY LIST LEADERS

Year	Leader
1934	Paul Runyan
1935	Johnny Revolta
1936	Horton Smith
1937	Harry Cooper
1938	Sam Snead
1939	Henry Picard
1940	Ben Hogan
1941	Ben Hogan
1942	Ben Hogan
1943	No statistics recorded
1944	Byron Nelson
1945	Byron Nelson
1946	Ben Hogan
1947	Jimmy Demaret
1948	Ben Hogan
1949	Sam Snead
1950	Sam Snead
1951	Lloyd Mangrum
1952	Julius Boros
1953	Lew Worsham
1954	Bob Toski
1955	Julius Boros
1956	Ted Kroll
1957	Dick Mayer
1958	Arnold Palmer
1959	Art Wall
1960	Arnold Palmer
1961	Gary Player
1962	Arnold Palmer
1963	Arnold Palmer
1964	Jack Nicklaus
1965	Jack Nicklaus
1966	Billy Casper
1967	Jack Nicklaus
1968	Billy Casper
1969	Frank Beard
1970	Lee Trevino
1971	Jack Nicklaus
1972	Jack Nicklaus
1973	Jack Nicklaus
1974	Johnny Miller
1975	Jack Nicklaus
1976	Jack Nicklaus
1977	Tom Watson
1978	Tom Watson
1979	Tom Watson
1980	Tom Watson
1981	Tom Kite
1982	Craig Stadler
1983	Hal Sutton
1984	Tom Watson
1985	Curtis Strange
1986	Greg Norman
1987	Curtis Strange
1988	Curtis Strange
1989	Tom Kite
1990	Greg Norman
1991	Corey Pavin
1992	Fred Couples
1993	Nick Price
1994	Nick Price
1995	Greg Norman

Money List Milestones:

- Paul Runyan topped the first Money List with $6,767 in 1934.

- The first player to break the $100,000 barrier for a season was Arnold Palmer in 1963, winning $128,230.

- Tom Watson was the first to pass half-a-million dollars with earnings of $530,808 in 1980.

- And the first million dollar man was Curtis Strange in 1988 ($1,147,644).

PGA TOUR FACTS AND FIGURES

Most times Money List leader:
8 -   Jack Nicklaus
      (1964, 65, 67, 71, 72, 73, 75, 76)
Most Tournament wins:
81 - Sam Snead (1936-65)
70 - Jack Nicklaus (1962-86)
63 - Ben Hogan (1938-59)
Most wins in one season:
18 - Byron Nelson (1945)
13 - Ben Hogan (1946)
11 - Sam Snead (1950)
Youngest tournament winners:
Johnny McDermott (19 yrs 10 mths),
1911 US Open
Gene Sarazen (20 yrs 4 mths),
1922 US Open

Oldest tournament winners:
Sam Snead (52 yrs 10 mths, 1965
Gt Greensboro' Open)
Art Wall (51 yrs 7 mths, 1975
Gt Milwaukee Open)
Lowest 18-hole scores:
59 - Al Geiberger (1977 Memphis Classic)
59 - Chip Beck (1991 Las Vegas Invitational)
Lowest 72-hole totals:
257 - Mike Souchak
(1955 Texas Open - 60-68-64-65)
258 - Donnie Hammond
(1989 Texas Open - 65-64-65-64)
Widest winning margin (strokes):
16 - Bobby Locke
(1948 Chicago Victory Championship)
14 - Ben Hogan (1945 Portland Invitational)
14 - Johnny Miller (1975 Phoenix Open)

WORLD SERIES of GOLF

The World Series of Golf is one of the most sought after titles on the PGA Tour. It is also one of only five American tournaments to offer its winner a 10-year exemption on Tour (the others are the Masters, US Open, USPGA Championship & Players' Championship).

To play in the World Series, a golfer has to win one of the designated qualifying tournaments from around the world and this select field is normally no more than 50 in total.

Year	Champion	Score	Runners-Up	Score
1976	Jack Nicklaus	275	Hale Irwin	279
1977	Lanny Wadkins	267	Hale Irwin/Tom Weiskopf	272
1978	Gil Morgan *	278	Hubert Green	278
1979	Lon Hinkle	272	Bill Rogers/Larry Nelson/Lee Trevino	273
1980	Tom Watson	270	Ray Floyd	272
1981	Bill Rogers	275	Tom Kite	276
1982	Craig Stadler *	278	Ray Floyd	278
1983	Nick Price	270	Jack Nicklaus	274
1984	Denis Watson	271	Bruce Lietzke	273
1985	Roger Maltbie	268	Denis Watson	272
1986	Dan Pohl	277	Lanny Wadkins	278
1987	Curtis Strange	275	Fulton Allem	278
1988	Mike Reid *	275	Tom Watson	275
1989	David Frost *	276	Ben Crenshaw	276
1990	Jose-Maria Olazabal	262	Lanny Wadkins	274
1991	Tom Purtzer *	279	Davis Love III/Jim Gallagher jr	279
1992	Craig Stadler	273	Corey Pavin	274
1993	Fulton Allem	270	Craig Stadler/Jim Gallagher jr/Nick Price	275
1994 **	Jose-Maria Olazabal	269	Scott Hoch	270
1995	Greg Norman*	278	Billy Mayfair/Nick Price	278

Note: The tournament is staged on the South Course at Firestone CC, Akron, Ohio.

* - Won after a play-off
** - For one year only the tournament was held on the North Course at Firestone.

Most titles:
2 - Craig Stadler (1982-92)
     Jose-Maria Olazabal (1990-94)
Note: Between 1962 and 1975 an unofficial tournament called the World Series was played at Firestone. It featured a select four-man field (the four major champions of that year) and was held over 36 holes.

THE PLAYERS' CHAMPIONSHIP

The Players' Championship is the brainchild of the PGA Tour. While yet to attain the status of a major championship, there is little doubt that it is the fifth most prestigious title in golf, with the champion earning a 10-year exemption on Tour. Since 1982, it has been staged at the Tournament Players' Club at Sawgrass, the administrative home of the PGA Tour.

Year	Champion	Score	Runners-Up	Score
1974	Jack Nicklaus	272	JCSnead	274
1975	Al Geiberger	270	Dave Stockton	273
1976	Jack Nicklaus	269	JC Snead	272
1977	Mark Hayes	289	Mike McCullough	291
1978	Jack Nicklaus	289	Lou Graham	290
1979	Lanny Wadkins	283	Tom Watson	288
1980	Lee Trevino	278	Ben Crenshaw	279
1981	Ray Floyd *	285	Curtis Strange/Barry Jaeckel	285
1982	Jerry Pate	280	Scott Simpson/Brad Bryant	282
1983	Hal Sutton	283	Bob Eastwood	284
1984	Fred Couples	277	Lee Trevino	278
1985	Calvin Peete	274	DA Weibring	277
1986	John Mahaffey	275	Larry Mize	276
1987	Sandy Lyle *	274	Jeff Sluman	274
1988	Mark McCumber	273	Mike Reid	277
1989	Tom Kite	279	Chip Beck	280
1990	Jodie Mudd	278	Mark Calcavecchia	279
1991	Steve Elkington	276	Fuzzy Zoeller	277
1992	Davis Love III	273	Tom Watson/Ian Baker-Finch	277
			Nick Faldo/Phil Blackmar	277
1993	Nick Price	270	Bernhard Langer	275
1994	Greg Norman	264	Fuzzy Zoeller	268
1995	Lee Janzen	283	Bernhard Langer	284

* - Won after a play-off

Most titles:
3 -   Jack Nicklaus (1974-76-78)

European Top 10s:

Seve Ballesteros	T3 (1980); T6 (1982); T3 (1984)
Nick Faldo	T2 (1992); 5 (1994)
Bernhard Langer	T7 (1985); T6 (1991); 2 (1993); 2 (1995)
Sandy Lyle	Won (1987)
Colin Montgomerie	9 (1994)
Jose-Maria Olazabal	T9 (1992)
Peter Oosterhuis	T9 (1978)

Courses used:

1974	Atlanta CC, Georgia

1976	Inverrary G&CC, Lauderhill, Florida
1977-81	Sawgrass CC, Jacksonville, Florida
1982-95	TPC at Sawgrass, Ponte Vedra, Florida
1975	Colonial CC, Fort Worth, Texas

OTHER TOURNAMENTS

AUSTRALIAN OPEN

First played: 1904

Is the most important tournament in the Southern Hemisphere and usually attracts a good quality field. Some of the big name overseas players to win the title include Bobby Locke, Jack Nicklaus, Arnold Palmer, Gary Player, Gene Sarazen and Tom Watson. The event is part of the Australasian Tour. *Winners since 1970:*

Year	Venue	Champion	Score
1970	Kingston Heath	Gary Player	280
1971	Royal Hobart	Jack Nicklaus	269
1972	Kooyonga	Peter Thomson	281
1973	Royal Queensland	JC Snead	280
1974	Lake Karrinyup	Gary Player	277
1975	The Australian	Jack Nicklaus	279
1976	The Australian	Jack Nicklaus	286
1977	The Australian	David Graham	284
1978	The Australian	Jack Nicklaus	284
1979	Metropolitan	Jack Newton	288
1980	The Lakes	Greg Norman	284
1981	Victoria	Bill Rogers	282
1982	The Australian	Bob Shearer	287
1983	Kingston Heath	Peter Fowler	285
1984	Royal Melbourne	Tom Watson	281
1985*	Royal Melbourne	Greg Norman	212
1986	Metropolitan	Rodger Davis	278
1987	Royal Melbourne	Greg Norman	273
1988	Royal Sydney	Mark Calcavecchia	269
1989	Kingston Heath	Peter Senior	271
1990	The Australian	John Morse	283
1991	Royal Melbourne	Wayne Riley	285
1992	The Lakes	Steve Elkington	280
1993	Metropolitan	Brad Faxon	275
1994	Royal Sydney	Robert Allenby	280
1995	Kingston Heath	Greg Norman	278

* - Reduced to 54 holes

Most wins:
7-Gary Player (1958, 62, 63, 65, 69, 70, 74)
6-Jack Nicklaus (1964, 68, 71, 75, 76, 78)
5-Ivo Whitton (Am) (1912, 13, 26, 29, 31)

Lowest 72-hole total:
264 (Gary Player, 1965 at Kooyonga)

CANADIAN OPEN

First played: 1904 (Currently part of the PGA Tour in the United States). Winners since 1970:

Year	Venue	Champion	Score
1970	London Hunt	Kermit Zarley	279
1971	Richelieu Valley	Lee Trevino	275
1972	Cherry Hill	Gay Brewer	275
1973	Richelieu Valley	Tom Weiskopf	278
1974	Mississauga	Bobby Nichols	270
1975	Royal Montreal	Tom Weiskopf	274
1976	Essex	Jerry Pate	267
1977	Glen Abbey	Lee Trevino	280
1978	Glen Abbey	Bruce Lietzke	283
1979	Glen Abbey	Lee Trevino	281
1980	Royal Montreal	Bob Gilder	274
1981	Glen Abbey	Peter Oosterhuis	280
1982	Glen Abbey	Bruce Lietzke	277
1983	Glen Abbey	John Cook	277
1984	Glen Abbey	Greg Norman	278
1985	Glen Abbey	Curtis Strange	279
1986	Glen Abbey	Bob Murphy	280
1987	Glen Abbey	Curtis Strange	276
1988	Glen Abbey	Ken Green	275
1989	Glen Abbey	Steve Jones	271
1990	Glen Abbey	Wayne Levi	278
1991	Glen Abbey	Nick Price	273
1992	Glen Abbey	Greg Norman	280
1993	Glen Abbey	David Frost	279
1994	Glen Abbey	Nick Price	275
1995	Glen Abbey	Mark O'Meara	274

Most Wins:
4 - Leo Diegel (1924, 25, 28, 29)
3 - Tommy Armour (1927, 30, 34)
 - Sam Snead (1938, 40, 41)
 - Lee Trevino (1971, 77, 79)

Lowest 72-hole total:
263 (Johnny Palmer, 1952 at St Charles CC in Winnipeg)

SOUTH AFRICAN OPEN

First played: 1903 (currently part of the South African PGA tour). Winners since 1970:

Year	Venue	Champion	Score
1970	Royal Durban	Tommy Horton	285
1971	Mowbray	Simon Hobday	276
1972	Royal Johannesburg	Gary Player	274
1973	Royal Durban	Bob Charles	282
1974	Royal Johannesburg	Bobby Cole	272
1975	Mowbray	Gary Player	278
1976	Houghton	Dale Hayes	287
1976*	Royal Durban	Gary Player	280
1977	Royal Johannesburg	Gary Player	273
1978	Mowbray	Hugh Baiocchi	285
1979	Houghton	Gary Player	279
1980	Durban	Bobby Cole	279
1981	Royal Johannesburg	Gary Player	272
1982	Not played owing to switch of dates for Championship		
1983	Mowbray	Charles Bolling	278
1984	Houghton	Tony Johnstone	274
1985	Royal Durban	Gavin Levenson	280
1986	Royal Johannesburg	David Frost	275
1987	Mowbray	Mark McNulty	278
1988	Durban	Wayne Westner	275
1989	Glendower	Fred Wadsworth	278
1990	Royal Cape	Trevor Dodds	285
1991	Durban	Wayne Westner	272
1992	Houghton	Ernie Els	273
1993	Glendower	Clinton Whitelaw	279
1993*	Durban	Tony Johnstone	267
1994	Not played owing to switch of dates for Championship		
1995	Randpark	Retief Goosen	275

* - Played twice in same year owing to switch of dates for Championship

Most wins:
13-Gary Player (1956, 60, 65, 66, 67, 68, 69, 72, 75, 76, 77, 79, 81)
9-Bobby Locke (1935 (Am), 37 (Am), 38, 39, 40, 46, 50, 51, 55)

Lowest 72-hole total:
267 (Tony Johnstone, 1993 at Durban CC)

NEW ZEALAND OPEN

First played: 1907 (Currently part of the Australasian Tour). Winners since 1970:

Year	Venue	Champion	Score
1970	Auckland	Bob Charles	271
1971	Dunedin	Peter Thomson	276
1972	Paraparaumu	Bill Dunk	279
1973	Palmerston North	Bob Charles	288
1974	Christchurch	Bob Gilder	283
1975	Hamilton	Bill Dunk	272
1976	Wellington	Simon Owen	284
1977	Auckland	Bob Byman	290
1978	Wanganui	Bob Shearer	277
1979	Dunedin	Stewart Ginn	278
1980	New Plymouth	Bud Allin	274
1981	Wellington	Bob Shearer	285
1982	Christchurch	Terry Gale	284
1983	Auckland	Ian Baker-Finch	280
1984	Paraparaumu	Corey Pavin	269
1985	Russley	Corey Pavin	277
1986	Auckland	Rodger Davis	262
1987	Dunedin	Ronan Rafferty	279
1988	Wanganui	Ian Stanley	273
1989	Wellington	Greg Turner	277
1990	Not played		
1991	Paraparaumu	Rodger Davis	273
1992	Paraparaumu	Grant Waite	268
1993	Paraparaumu	Peter Fowler	274
1994	Auckland	Craig Jones	277
1995	Wellington	Lucas Parsons	282

Most Wins:
9-Peter Thomson (1950, 51, 53, 55, 59, 60, 61, 65, 71)
7-Kel Nagle (1957, 58, 62, 64, 67, 68, 69)
7-Andy Shaw (1926, 29, 30, 31, 32, 34, 36)

Lowest 72-hole total:
262 (Rodger Davis, 1986 in Auckland)

JAPAN OPEN

First played: 1927 (part of the Japanese Tour) Winners since 1970:

Year	Venue	Champion	Score
1970	Musashi	M Kitta	282
1971	Aichi	Y Fujii	282
1972	Iwai City	H Chang-Sang	278
1973	Osaka	B Arda	278
1974	Central	M Ozaki	279
1975	Kasugai	T Murakami	278
1976	Central	K Shimada	288
1977	Narashino	S Ballesteros	284
1978	Yokohama	S Ballesteros	281
1979	Hino	K Chie-Hsiung	285
1980	Sagamihara	K Kikuchi	296
1981	Nihon Rhine	Y Hagawa	280
1982	Musashi	A Yabe	277
1983	Rokkokokusai	I Aoki	281
1984	Ranzan	K Uehara	283

Fred Couples savours victory at the first Johnnie Walker World Championship in 1991

1985	Higashinagoya	T Nakajima	285
1986	Tozuka	T Nakajima	284
1987	Arima	I Aoki	279
1988	Tokyo	M Ozaki	288
1989	Nagoya	M Ozaki	274
1990	Otaru	T Nakajima	281
1991	Shimonoseki	T Nakajima	290
1992	Ryugaski	M Ozaki	277
1993	Biwako	S Okuda	281

| 1994 | Biwako | M Ozaki | 270 |
| 1995 | Saitama Pref | T Izawa | 277 |

Most Wins:
6-Tomekichi Miyamoto (1929, 30, 32, 35, 36, 40)
5-Masashi 'Jumbo' Ozaki (1974, 88, 89, 92, 94)

Lowest 72-hole total:
270 (Masashi 'Jumbo' Ozaki, 1994 at Biwako)

JOHNNIE WALKER WORLD CHAMPIONSHIP

Has been played at Tryall GC in Jamaica since its inception in 1991. Even though the tournament is just five years old, it has already become one of golf's most prestigious titles. This select field is usually made up of around 28 players. Golfers qualify by either winning one of the nominated important tournaments from around the world or have been specially chosen by an international advisory panel. The tournament is played in December.

Year	Champion	Score	Runners-up	Score
1991	Fred Couples	281	Bernhard Langer	285
1992	Nick Faldo *	274	Greg Norman	274
1993	Larry Mize	266	Fred Couples	276
1994	Ernie Els	268	Mark McCumber/Nick Faldo	274
1995	Fred Couples *	279	Vijay Singh/Loren Roberts	279

* - Won after a play-off

WOMEN'S PROFESSIONAL GOLF

THE MAJORS

Similar to the men, the women currently have four designated major championships, although the nominated tournaments have changed over the years. The Ladies Professional Golf Association (LPGA), which run the women's tour in the United States list six events as being of major status, although two of these no longer exist.

UNITED STATES OPEN

First staged in 1946 and run by the USGA, the US Open is undoubtedly the most prestigious title in women's golf today. Mickey Wright and Betsy Rawls share the record for winning it most times. The first US Open winner was Patty Berg and for that year only the final stages of the tournament was matchplay. Since then, the event has been 72 holes of strokeplay.

Winners since 1980:

1980	Amy Alcott
1981	Pat Bradley
1982	Janet Alex
1983	Jan Stephenson
1984	Hollis Stacy
1985	Kathy Baker
1986	Jane Geddes *
1987	Laura Davies *
1988	Liselotte Neumann
1989	Betsy King
1990	Betsy King
1991	Meg Mallon
1992	Patty Sheehan *
1993	Lauri Merten
1994	Patty Sheehan
1995	Annika Sorenstam

* - Won after 18-hole play-off

Most wins: 4 - Betsy Rawls (1951, 53, 57, 60)
Mickey Wright (1958, 59, 61, 64)

Sweden's Annika Sorenstam during the final round of the 1995 US Open

Sorenstam pictured with the US Open trophy after her success

LPGA CHAMPIONSHIP

Was first held in 1955 when Beverly Hanson won the title. It is the second most important event in women's golf and is played over 72 holes of strokeplay.

Winners since 1980:
1980   Sally Little
1981   Donna Caponi
1982   Jan Stephenson
1983   Patty Sheehan
1984   Patty Sheehan
1985   Nancy Lopez
1986   Pat Bradley
1987   Jane Geddes
1988   Sherri Turner
1989   Nancy Lopez

1990   Beth Daniel
1991   Meg Mallon
1992   Betsy King
1993   Patty Sheehan
1994   Laura Davies
1995   Kelly Robbins
Most wins: 4 - Mickey Wright (1958, 60, 61, 63)

DU MAURIER CLASSIC

Although first staged in 1973, the Du Maurier did not earn major status until 1979 when the winner was Amy Alcott. It is the only women's major to be held outside the United States. This 72-hole strokeplay tournament is played in Canada.

Winners since 1980:
1980   Pat Bradley
1981   Jan Stephenson
1982   Sandra Haynie
1983   Hollis Stacy
1984   Juli Inkster
1985   Pat Bradley
1986   Pat Bradley *
1987   Jody Rosenthal
1988   Sally Little
1989   Tammie Green
1990   Cathy Johnston
1991   Nancy Scranton
1992   Sherri Steinhauer
1993   Brandie Burton *
1994   Martha Nause
1995   Jenny Lidback
* - Won after a play-off
Most wins: 3 - Pat Bradley (1980, 85, 86)

DINAH SHORE TOURNAMENT

First played in 1972, the Dinah Shore was awarded major status in 1983. It is a 72-hole strokeplay event.

Winners since 1983:
1983   Amy Alcott
1984   Juli Inkster *
1985   Alice Miller
1986   Pat Bradley
1987   Betsy King *
1988   Amy Alcott
1989   Juli Inkster
1990   Betsy King
1991   Amy Alcott

1992   Dottie Mochrie *
1993   Helen Alfredsson
1994   Donna Andrews
1995   Nanci Bowen
* - Won after a play-off
Most wins: 3 -   Amy Alcott (1983, 88, 91)

WESTERN OPEN

Was first contested in 1937 but ceased to be a
major championship after 1967.

Most wins:
7 -Patty Berg (1941, 43, 48, 51, 55, 57, 58)

TITLEHOLDERS

Another former major which was held annually
between 1937 and 1966 (minus the war years
1943 to 1945). After 1966 it stopped for five
years before making a one-off farewell
appearance in 1972.

Most wins:
7 -   Patty Berg (1937, 38, 39, 48, 53, 55, 57)

THE GREATEST MAJOR CHAMPIONS

	US Open	LPGA	Maurier	Dinah	T'holders	Western	Total
Patty Berg	1				7	7	15
Mickey Wright	4	4			2	3	13
Louise Suggs	2	1			4	4	11
Babe Zaharias	3				3	4	10
Betsy Rawls	4	2				2	8
Kathy Whitworth		3			2	1	6
Pat Bradley	1	1	3	1			6
Amy Alcott	1		1	3			5
Betsy King	2	1		2			5
Patty Sheehan	2	3					5
Donna Caponi	2	2					4
Sandra Haynie	1	2	1				4
Hollis Stacy	3		1				4
Susie Berning	3					1	4

LPGA TOUR

Back in 1944, Betty Hicks, Hope Seignious and
Ellen Griffin founded the Women's Professional
Golf Association with the aim of promoting the
pro side of the game in the United States.

However, its early years met with little success
and in 1948 the WPGA was rescued by Wilson
Sporting Goods, whose marketing director, Fred
Corcoran, was given the task of turning the
women's game into a prosperous business.

The WPGA changed its name to the Ladies
Professional Golf Association (LPGA) and in
1950 organised its first official Tour. The wheels
had started to turn.

In that first year, the total purse for nine
events was $50,000 and Babe Zaharias ended the
season as top money winner with $14,800.

The number of tournaments on offer has risen steadily and since 1972 there have been over 30 events every year. The first million dollar Tour arrived in 1973 and since 1992 the women have been chasing annual prize money of over $20m. When Laura Davies, Britain's leading player, became the first European to top the Money List in 1994, she earned a cool $687,201. The record for a single year, however, belongs to Beth Daniel who made $863,578 in 1990.

Nowadays, the LPGA Tour is a year long success story. And while it still can't compare with its male counterpart - the PGA Tour - in terms of exposure and prestige, many of today's top players have achieved millionairess status out of the game.

Money Leaders (since 1980):

1980	Beth Daniel
1981	Beth Daniel
1982	JoAnne Carner
1983	JoAnne Carner
1984	Betsy King
1985	Nancy Lopez
1986	Pat Bradley
1987	Ayako Okamoto
1988	Sherri Turner
1989	Betsy King
1990	Beth Daniel
1991	Pat Bradley
1992	Dottie Mochrie
1993	Betsy King
1994	Laura Davies
1995	Annika Sorenstam

Most times top Money Leader:
8 - Kathy Whitworth (1965, 1966, 1967, 1968, 1970, 1971, 1972, 1973)

Most Tour wins:
88 - Kathy Whitworth
82 - Mickey Wright
57 - Patty Berg
Most wins in one season:
13 - Mickey Wright (1963)

THE SOLHEIM CUP

The Solheim Cup is the women's equivalent of the Ryder Cup and is played every two years. First held in 1990, the contest pits together the best professionals of the United States against the leading pros from Europe. So far, all three matches have been won by the hosts.

Year	Venue	Hosts	Visitors	Score
1990	Lake Nona, Florida	UNITED STATES	EUROPE	11½ - 4½
1992	Dalmahoy, Edinburgh	EUROPE	UNITED STATES	11½ - 6½
1994	The Greenbrier, West Virginia	UNITED STATES	EUROPE	13 - 7

Note: Mickey Walker has been Europe's non-playing captain for all three meetings. For the United States, Kathy Whitworth was non-playing captain in both 1990 and 1992, while JoAnne Carner took over duties in 1994.

WOMEN PROFESSIONAL GOLFERS' EUROPEAN TOUR

The WPGET has been in existence since 1979. Despite, at times, finding it difficult to attract major sponsors, the standard of the women's game in Europe has improved dramatically and far quicker than most believed possible. Due to the likes of Laura Davies, Liselotte Neumann, Annika Sorenstam and Helen Alfredsson, the WPGET has grown in stature and thanks to an unlikely but thoroughly deserved victory over the Americans in the Solheim Cup at Dalmahoy in October 1992, the Tour currently enjoys a reasonably high profile amongst golf fans. The Tour is currently sponsored by American Express.

ORDER of MERIT WINNERS

1979	Catherine Panton
1980	Muriel Thomson
1981	Jenny Lee-Smith
1982	Jenny Lee-Smtih
1983	Muriel Thomson
1984	Dale Reid
1985	Laura Davies
1986	Laura Davies
1987	Dale Reid
1988	Marie-Laure Taya
1989	Marie-Laure Taya de Lorenzi

Swedish success: (left to right) Catrin Nilsmark, Helen Alfredsson and Liselotte Neumann celebrate Europe's Solheim Cup win over the United States in 1992

1990	Trish Johnson
1991	Corinne Dibnah
1992	Laura Davies
1993	Karen Lunn
1994	Liselotte Neumann
1995	Annika Sorenstam

Most Times OM leader:
3 - Laura Davies (1985, 86, 92)

Most Tour wins:
22 - Laura Davies (1985-95

Most wins in one season:
7 - Marie-Laure Taya (1988)

LADIES BRITISH OPEN

The Ladies British Open is Europe's blue riband event. It was first held in 1976, three years before the birth of the WPGET. (winners British & Irish unless stated)

Year	Venue	Winner	(Score)
1976	Fulford	Jenny Lee-Smith (a)	299
1977	Lindrick	Vivien Saunders	306
1978	Foxhills	Janet Melville (a)	310
1979	Southport & A.	Alison Sheard (SA)	301
1980	Wentworth	Debbie Massey (USA)	294
1981	Ganton	Debbie Massey (USA)	295
1982	Royal Birkdale	Marta Figueras-Dotti (a) (Spa)	296
1983	*Not held*		
1984	Woburn	Ayako Okamoto (Jap)	289
1985	Moor Park	Betsy King (USA)	300
1986	Royal Birkdale	Laura Davies	283
1987	St Mellion	Alison Nicholas	296
1988	Lindrick	Corinne Dibnah (Aus)*	295
1989	Ferndown	Jane Geddes (USA)	274
1990	Woburn	Helen Alfredsson (Swe)*	288
1991	Woburn	Penny Grice-Whittaker	284
1992	Woburn **	Patty Sheehan (USA)	207
1993	Woburn	Karen Lunn (Aus)	275
1994	Woburn	Liselotte Neumann (Swe)	280
1995	Woburn	Karrie Webb (Aus)	278

(a) - amateur   * - Won after a play-off   ** - reduced to 54 holes

AMATEUR GOLF

THE AMATEUR GAME

There was a time when the leading amateurs were capable of winning major championships. Players such as John Ball, Harold Hilton, Francis Ouimet, and of course, the incomparable Bobby Jones, are legendary champions.

They took on the top professionals of their day and beat them. Hilton won the British Open twice, while Jones won four US Opens and three British Opens.

Those were the days when players made 'careers' out of being an amateur. But all that happened before the Second World War.

Although Billy Joe Patton and Ken Venturi came close to wearing Augusta's Green Jacket in the 1950s, the day when the talented amateur was capable of winning a major professional title is over.

For most of today's top amateurs, winning a British or an American Amateur Championship is just the final icing on the cake before joining the paid ranks.

However, both these amateur events are still regarded as highly coveted titles, earning its champions invitations to major tournaments.

It is also an honour to be selected for the Walker Cup and Curtis Cup. In this brief chapter we celebrate the most important events in the amateur game.

BRITISH AMATEUR CHAMPIONSHIP

First staged in 1885 at Royal Liverpool, Hoylake, the inaugural champion was Allan MacFie. Various systems have been used, although the final stages of all Championships have been matchplay. At present, the tournament starts with 36 holes of strokeplay qualifying, with the lowest 64 scores contesting a knock-out matchplay phase. Final results since 1970 are as follows. All players are British and Irish unless stated:

Year	Venue	Winner	Runner-Up	Score
1970	Newcastle, Co. Down	M Bonallack	W Hyndman (USA)	8&7
1971	Carnoustie	S Melnyk (USA)	J Simons (USA)	3&2
1972	Royal St George's	T Homer	A Thirlwell	4&3
1973	Royal Porthcawl	R Siderowf	P Moody	5&3
1974	Muirfield	T Homer	J Gabrielsen (USA)	2 up
1975	Royal Liverpool	M Giles (USA)	M James	8&7
1976	St Andrews	R Siderowf	J Davies	at 37th
1977	Ganton	P McEvoy	H Campbell	5&4
1978	Royal Troon	P McEvoy	P McKellar	4&3
1979	Hillside	J Sigel (USA)	S Hoch (USA)	3&2
1980	Royal Porthcawl	D Evans	D Suddards (SA)	4&3
1981	St Andrews	P Ploujoux (Fr)	J Hirsch (USA)	4&2
1982	Royal Cinque Ports	M Thompson	A Stubbs	4&3
1983	Turnberry	P Parkin	J Holtgrieve (USA)	5&4
1984	Formby	J-M Olazabal (Sp)	C Montgomerie	5&4
1985	Royal Dornoch	G McGimpsey	G Homewood	8&7
1986	Royal Lytham	D Curry	G Birtwell	11&9
1987	Prestwick	P Mayo	P McEvoy	3&1
1988	Royal Porthcawl	C Hardin (Swe)	B Fouchee (SA)	1 up
1989	Royal Birkdale	S Dodd	C Cassells	5&3
1990	Muirfield	R Muntz (Holl)	A Macara	7&6
1991	Ganton	G Wolstenholme	B May (USA)	8&6
1992	Carnoustie	S Dundas	B Dredge	7&6
1993	Royal Portrush	I Pyman	P Page	at 37th
1994	Nairn	L James	G Sherry	2&1
1995	Royal Liverpool	G Sherry	M Reynard	7&6

Most titles:

8-John Ball jr (1888-90-92-94-99-1907-10-12)   4-Harold Hilton (1900-01-11-13)
5-Michael Bonallack (1961-65-68-69-70)

Tiger Woods, US Amateur champion in 1994 and 1995

UNITED STATES AMATEUR CHAMPIONSHIP

Charles Macdonald won the first tournament in 1895 at Newport, Rhode Island. Except for eight events, between 1965 and 1972 when the Championship was staged over 72 holes of strokeplay, the final stages of all tournaments have been contested using matchplay. Final results since 1970 are as follows:

Year	Venue	Winner	Runner-Up	Score
1970	Waverley, Oregon	L Wadkins (279)	T Kite (280)	Strokeplay
1971	Wilmington, Delaware	G Cowan (280)	E Pearce (283)	Strokeplay
1972	Charlotte, N Carolina	M Giles (285)	M Hayes (288)	Strokeplay
1973	Inverness, Ohio	C Stadler	D Strawn	6&5
1974	Ridgewood, N Jersey	J Pate	J Grace	2&1
1975	CC of Virginia	F Ridley	K Fergus	2 up
1976	Bel-Air, California	B Sander	C Moore jr	8&6
1977	Aronimink, Penn.	J Fought	D Fischesser	9&8
1978	Plainfield, N Jersey	J Cook	S Hoch	5&4
1979	Canterbury, Ohio	M O'Meara	J Cook	8&7
1980	CC of North Carolina	H Sutton	B Lewis	9&8
1981	Olympic Club, Cal.	N Crosby	B Lindley	at 37th
1982	The Country Club, Mass.	J Sigel	D Tolley	8&7
1983	North Shore, Illinois	J Sigel	C Perry	8&7
1984	Oak Tree, Oklahoma	S Verplank	S Randolph	4&3
1985	Montclair, New Jersey	S Randolph	P Persons	1 up
1986	Shoal Creek, Alabama	B Alexander	C Kite	5&3
1987	Jupiter Hills, Florida	B Mayfair	E Rebmann	4&3
1988	Hot Springs, Virginia	E Meeks	D Yates	7&6
1989	Merion, Pennsylvania	C Patton	D Green	3&1
1990	Cherry Hills, Colorado	P Mickelson	M Zerman	5&4
1991	Honors Course, Tenn.	M Voges	M Zerman	7&6
1992	Muirfield Village, Ohio	J Leonard	T Scherrer	8&7
1993	Champions, Texas	J Harris	D Ellis	5&3
1994	TPC at Sawgrass, Fl.	T Woods	T Kuehne	2 up
1995	Newport, Rhode Island	T Woods	B Marucci	2 up

Most titles:
5 - Bobby Jones jr (1924-25-27-28-30)
4 - Jerome Travers (1907-08-12-13)
3 - Walter Travis (1900-01-03)

WALKER CUP

The trophy was donated by former president of the USGA, George Walker, to be contested between the leading amateurs of the United States and those of Great Britain and Ireland. Since 1924 this international match has been played every two years (except for Second World War years). The inaugural contest was in 1922. Winners in bold:

Year	Venue	Hosts		Visitors	
1922	National GL, New York	**USA**	8	GB&I	4
1923	St Andrews, Scotland	GB&I	5½	**USA**	6½
1924	Garden City, New York	**USA**	9	GB&I	3
1926	St Andrews, Scotland	GB&I	5½	**USA**	6½
1928	Chicago, Illinois	**USA**	11	GB&I	1
1930	Royal St George's, Kent	GB&I	2	**USA**	10
1932	The Country Club, Mass.	**USA**	9½	GB&I	2½
1934	St Andrews, Scotland	GB&I	2½	**USA**	9½
1936	Pine Valley, New Jersey	**USA**	10½	GB&I	1½
1938	St Andrews, Scotland	**GB&I**	7½	USA	4½
1947	St Andrews, Scotland	GB&I	4	**USA**	8
1949	Winged Foot, New York	**USA**	10	GB&I	2
1951	Royal Birkdale, Lancashire	GB&I	4½	**USA**	7½
1953	Kittansett, Mass.	**USA**	9	GB&I	3
1955	St Andrews, Scotland	GB&I	2	**USA**	10
1957	Minikahda, Minnesota	**USA**	8½	GB&I	3½
1959	Muirfield, Scotland	GB&I	3	**USA**	9
1961	Seattle, Washington	**USA**	11	GB&I	1
1963	Turnberry, Scotland	GB&I	10	**USA**	14
1965	Baltimore, Maryland	USA	12	**GB&I**	12
1967	Royal St George's, Kent	GB&I	9	**USA**	15
1969	Milwaukee, Wisconsin	**USA**	13	GB&I	11
1971	St Andrews, Scotland	**GB&I**	13	USA	11
1973	The Country Club, Mass.	**USA**	14	GB&I	10
1975	St Andrews, Scotland	GB&I	8½	**USA**	15½
1977	Shinnecock Hills, NY	**USA**	16	GB&I	8
1979	Muirfield, Scotland	GB&I	8½	**USA**	15½
1981	Cypress Point, California	**USA**	15	GB&I	9
1983	Royal Liverpool	GB&I	10½	**USA**	13½
1985	Pine Valley, New Jersey	**USA**	13	GB&I	11
1987	Sunningdale, Berkshire	GB&I	7½	**USA**	16½
1989	Peachtree, Georgia	USA	11½	**GB&I**	12½
1991	Portmarnock, Ireland	GB&I	10	**USA**	14
1993	Interlachen, Minnesota	**USA**	19	GB&I	5
1995	Royal Porthcawl, Wales	**GB&I**	14	USA	10

Summary: United States won 30; Great Britain & Ireland won 4; with one match halved.

CURTIS CUP

The women's equivalent of the Walker Cup. The trophy was presented by American sisters Harriet and Margaret Curtis, and has been staged every two years since 1932, apart from those years affected by the Second World War. Winners are indicated in bold:

Year	Venue	Hosts		Visitors	
1932	Wentworth, Surrey	GB&I	3½	**USA**	5½
1934	Chevy Chase, Maryland	**USA**	6½	GB&I	2½
1936	Gleneagles, Scotland	**GB&I**	4½	USA	4½
1938	Essex, Massachusetts	**USA**	5½	GB&I	3½
1948	Royal Birkdale, Lancashire	GB&I	2½	**USA**	6½
1950	CC of Buffalo, New York	**USA**	7½	GB&I	1½
1952	Muirfield, Scotland	**GB&I**	5	USA	4
1954	Merion, Pennsylvania	**USA**	6	GB&I	3
1956	Prince's, Kent	**GB&I**	5	USA	4
1958	Brae Burn, Massachusetts	USA	4½	**GB&I**	4½
1960	Lindrick, Yorkshire	GB&I	2½	**USA**	6½
1962	Broadmoor, Colorado	**USA**	8	GB&I	1
1964	Royal Porthcawl, Wales	GB&I	7½	**USA**	10½
1966	Hot Springs, Virginia	**USA**	13	GB&I	5
1968	Royal Co. Down, N.Ireland	GB&I	7½	**USA**	10½
1970	Brae Burn, Massachusetts	**USA**	11½	GB&I	6½
1972	Western Gailes, Scotland	GB&I	8	**USA**	10
1974	San Francisco, California	**USA**	13	GB&I	5
1976	Royal Lytham, Lancashire	GB&I	6½	**USA**	11½
1978	Apawamis, New York	**USA**	12	GB&I	6
1980	St Pierre, Wales	GB&I	5	**USA**	13
1982	Denver, Colorado	**USA**	14½	GB&I	3½
1984	Muirfield, Scotland	GB&I	8½	**USA**	9½
1986	Prairie Dunes, Kansas	USA	5	**GB&I**	13
1988	Royal St George's, Kent	**GB&I**	11	USA	7
1990	Somerset Hills, New Jersey	**USA**	14	GB&I	4
1992	Royal Liverpool	**GB&I**	10	USA	8
1994	Honors Course, Tenn.	USA	9	**GB&I**	9

Summary: United States won 20; Great Britain & Ireland won 5; with three matches halved.

CURIOSITIES

CURIOSITIES

Ex-President's message
Gerald Ford, President of the United States between 1974 and 1976, is a keen golfer, although not a particularly good one, despite being a frequent competitor in pro-ams. But Ford is not too proud to admit his lack of ability with the clubs. He once said: "I know I'm getting better at golf because I'm hitting fewer spectators."

Lightning Lee
In 1975, Lee Trevino was one of three golfers struck by lightning at the Western Open in Illinois. His description of this life-threatening moment included his usual tongue in cheek quip. He said: "There was a thunderous crack like cannonfire and suddenly I was lifted a foot and a half off the ground. Damn it, I thought to myself, this is one helluva penalty for slow play."

Hagen's humour
Walter Hagen has always been renowned for his quick-wit. One of his most famous one-liners was: "Miss a putt for two thousand dollars? Not likely."

Bachelor boy
When Ernie Els won the 1994 US Open at Oakmont, he was the first bachelor to win the title since 1935 when Sam Parks triumphed at the same Pennsylvania course.

Dizzy heights
Little-known professional Andy Dillard, competing in his first US Open in 1992 at Pebble Beach, birdied the first six holes in round one. This represented the best start in the tournament's history. He went on to post a four-under-par 68 in the first round, good enough for a share of third place. On day two he carded a 70, which moved him up into second position. However, Dillard fell away over the closing 36 holes, with rounds of 79-77 to leave him in a tie for 17th.

Take your woolies
The world's most northerly golf course is Akureyri GC in Iceland, which stands over 65 degrees north of the equator. The most southerly is Scott Base Country Club in Antarctica where golfers use orange balls.

Sorry guv'nor
The evening before the start of the 1962 US Open, club pro Charles Smith was informed that he was needed as a late replacement, after another competitor had withdrawn. So Smith jumped into his car and at great speed headed down the Ohio Turnpike to travel to Pittsburgh, Pennsylvania. At about 3 am he was stopped by a highway patrolman who did not believe his story and detained him for almost an hour before issuing the golfer with a $20 fine. Smith managed to get to the first tee on time but failed to make the cut after shooting 83-84 for the worst 36-hole total of the tournament.

Should have done better
In a career that lasted almost 20 years, Fred Hawkins was always a consistent performer. In all, he had 107 top-10 finishes on the US Tour. Twelve times he was third, 19 times a runner-up, but only once did he win. That was the Oklahoma City Open in September 1956. He also played in one Ryder Cup match, at Lindrick in 1957 when, yes you've guessed it, the Americans finished 'second' for the only time between 1935 and 1983. However, there was one bright moment for Hawkins in that 1957 contest. He was the only American to win a singles, beating Peter Alliss 2&1.

Consecutive aces
London-based pro John Hudson was the first golfer to score successive holes-in-one at a British professional tournament. The 25-year-old, competing in the 1971 Martini International at Royal Norwich, aced the 11th and 12th holes during the second round. At the 195-yard, 11th, he used a 4-iron; while taking a driver on the 311-yard, par-4, 12th.

What's in a name
There are some weird and wonderful names given to golf holes, and at times some strange and barmy explanations for why holes got their name in the first place. One of the best concerns Carnoustie's 10th hole, called 'South America.' While the name itself is nothing remarkable, the story behind it is quite amusing. Around the turn of the century, one Carnoustie member decided he would emigrate to South America, and the evening before he was due to leave he hosted a farewell party at a local hostelry. It is not known how much alcohol this man consumed that night, but the following morning he was discovered fast asleep on the 10th

fairway. He never did get to South America but the hole was still named in his honour.

Another one from Hagen
"Give me a man with big hands, big feet and no brains and I will make a golfer out of him."

Watch out there's a thief about
While playing the final (72nd) hole of the 1936 US Open at Baltusrol, Leslie Madison had his wallet stolen, which contained $55. A 15 minute search for the thief took place close to the 18th green but he or she was never found. The delay in play didn't help Madison's playing partner Harry Cooper who finished second.

Changing values
In winning the 1995 Senior British Open at Royal Portrush, Northern Ireland, Brian Barnes earned £58,330. That was more money than he'd ever won in a single season on the European Tour during his illustrious career. His best haul for one year on the regular Tour was £51,722. And when Barnsey finished fourth in the Order of Merit back in 1971, his total earnings for the season was a mere £2,652.

Getting older
Explaining the difference between playing golf in his 20s and in his 40s, Lee Trevino once remarked: "I still swing the way I used to but when I look up the ball is going in a different direction."

Making history
In 1978, Bob Impaglia became the first competitor in US Open history to be penalised for slow play, after taking four and a half minutes to play one shot on the 9th hole, during his second round, at Cherry Hills. After being told of his infringement, Impaglia remarked to reporters: "That's OK, I love the exposure." He missed the cut by 17 shots after rounds of 83-84.

Endurance test
In 1940, American professional Harry Gonder hit over 1,800 balls in just under 17 hours in an attempt to make a hole in one at a par 3. He didn't achieve it, although one shot touched the edge of the hole and finished an inch away.

Steady on mate
At the 1968 French Open at St Cloud, Brian Barnes took 15 shots to complete the 8th hole in his second round. In anger he stabbed at the ball 12 times from no more than three feet, hitting the ball while it was still moving on a number of occasions.

Senior attraction
When asked if he was looking forward to joining the US Senior Tour at the age of 50, Lee Trevino replied, "Why play with the flat bellies when you can play with the round bellies."

Mr 59
On June 10th, 1977, Al Geiberger became the first player to break 60 on the US Tour, shooting a 13-under-par 59 at Colonial Country Club, Cordova, Tennessee. It came in the second round of the Danny Thomas Memphis Classic, a tournament 39-year-old Geiberger went on to win by three shots. Yet strangely, Geiberger's four rounds did not include another score under 70. His scores read: 72-59-72-70 (273). Since then he has been known on Tour as 'Mr 59'.

Television award
Only two golfers have ever won the coveted BBC Sports Personality of the Year award. In 1957, Dai Rees enjoyed the honour after leading Great Britain & Ireland to victory in the Ryder Cup; while Nick Faldo took the spoils in 1989, the year of his first US Masters triumph.

Ed's major duck
American Ed Dudley has the unenviable honour of having most top-10 finishes in major championships without ever winning one. Between 1928 and 1944, Dudley compiled 19 such finishes (US Masters 7; US Open 4; British Open 2; USPGA 6).

Good old boy
Sam Snead holds the US Tour record for winning most titles after the age of 40. Starting with the Inverness Round Robin Invitational in June 1952, Snead won 19 tournaments through to the 1965 Greater Greensboro Open. Born May 27, 1912, Snead won 81 official Tour events in his career.

Wealthy 'loser'
Despite having never won on the US Tour, American Bobby Wadkins has earned over $2m in prize money. By the end of the 1995 season, his 21st on Tour, he had accumulated $2,448,213. Wadkins has finished second three times (1979 Philadelphia Classic (lost play-off); 1985 Heritage

Classic (lost play-off); 1994 Kemper Open). Wadkins did, however, travel to England in 1978 to win the inaugural European Open at Walton Heath. Bobby is the younger brother of 1995 US Ryder Cup captain Lanny.

Four in the 70s
Tom Kite is the most recent major champion not to break 70 in any of his four rounds. In winning the 1992 US Open at Pebble Beach, Kite fired rounds of 71-72-70-72 (285, 3-under-par).

Top dog
The Sony World Ranking was established in April 1986. The table below lists those players who occupied the number one position at the end of each calendar year.

1986	Greg Norman (Australia)
1987	Greg Norman (Australia)
1988	Seve Ballesteros (Spain)
1989	Greg Norman (Australia)
1990	Greg Norman (Australia)
1991	Ian Woosnam (Wales)
1992	Nick Faldo (England)
1993	Nick Faldo (England)
1994	Nick Price (Zimbabwe)
1995	Greg Norman (Australia)

Note: The only other two golfers to hold the number one spot since the Ranking was formed are Bernhard Langer (three weeks in 1986) and Fred Couples (16 weeks in 1992).

Fabulous finish
Australian Peter O'Malley produced a remarkable burst of scoring to win the 1992 Scottish Open at Gleneagles. With just five holes remaining, O'Malley was four strokes off the pace. However, he then proceeded to play the last five in seven-under-par (eagle-birdie-birdie-birdie-eagle) to win the tournament by two strokes from Colin Montgomerie. On the last five greens he sank putts of 20, 20, 10, 8 and 25 feet. This gave him a final round of 62 (8-under-par) and his first victory on the European Tour.

Day to remember
Mancunian Denis Durnian never did win on the European Tour. Yet in 1983, he enjoyed his finest moment by setting a new British Open record for the lowest 9-hole score (28 strokes, - 6). At Royal Birkdale, Durnian grabbed birdies at the 2nd, 3rd, 4th, 5th, 7th and 8th holes. He also lipped out for birdie at the 6th. He came home in 38 shots to post a second round score of 66. He went

on to finish in a tie for eighth, after rounds of 73-66-74-67 (280), five strokes behind winner Tom Watson. The previous lowest score for nine holes in the British Open was 29, carded by Peter Thomson (1958), Tom Haliburton (1958), Tony Jacklin (1970) and Bill Longmuir (1979).

Day to forget
Standing on the 13th tee in the final round of the 1950 US Masters, Australian Jim Ferrier looked a certain winner. With his nearest challenger Jimmy Demaret already in the clubhouse, having posted a 72-hole total of 283, Ferrier could play the final six holes in two-over-par and still wear the Green Jacket. But disaster struck. Ferrier parred only one of these last six holes. He finished second, two strokes behind Demaret. Ferrier's six of the worst reads as follows:

Hole	13th	14th	15th	16th	17th	18th	
Par	5	4	5	3	4	4	(25)
Score	6	5	5	4	5	5	(30)

What a caddie
Between 1991 and 1994, caddie Jeff 'Squeaky' Medlen brought home three of the four winners of the USPGA Championship. In 1992 and 1994, he carried the bag of his regular player Nick Price, while in 1991 he helped out John Daly, when Price withdrew from the tournament.

Give us a break Jack!
Australian Bruce Crampton is one of the best players never to have won a major championship. Four times he had to settle for the runners-up spot and amazingly on all four occasions, the only golfer to beat him was Jack Nicklaus. Crampton was the bridesmaid at the 1972 US Masters; 1972 US Open; 1973 USPGA and 1975 USPGA - all won by the Golden Bear. Crampton was also third in the 1963 USPGA Championship, when, yet again, Nicklaus grabbed the spoils.

Play-off king
Arnold Palmer holds the US Tour record for contesting most play-offs. Between 1956 and 1971, Palmer reached 24 play-offs winning 14 of them. Just one behind Palmer, on 23, is Jack Nicklaus (1962-84) who has won 13.

Sad end for Young Tom
The youngest British Open champion of all time, Tom Morris jr, had a tragic end to his life. Young Tom died from a lung haemorrhage on Christmas

Day 1875, at the age of 24. Three months earlier his wife had died giving birth to their still-born child. Young Tom, who won the first of his four British Open titles at 17, never recovered from the death of his wife.

Lengthy overtime

The longest sudden-death play-off in US Tour history lasted 11 holes - and it still failed to produce a champion. After sharing 11 consecutive extra holes at the 1949 Motor City Open, Cary Middlecoff and Lloyd Mangrum were declared co-winners by mutual agreement.

Bad light stops play

And at the 1986 Lancome Trophy, Seve Ballesteros and Bernhard Langer also agreed to share the title when bad light curtailed play after four holes of their play-off.

Consolation prize

In 1994, Fuzzy Zoeller became the first player to win over $1million in a US Tour season, without recording a victory. Zoeller earned $1,016,804 after finishing second five times - Players' Championship, Tour Championship, Bob Hope Classic, Nestle Invitational and Walt Disney Classic.

Double whammy

While golf can't be classified as a physical contact sport, it can at times be dangerous. Brett Ogle will vouch for that. Twice, the Australian has been injured in freak golfing accidents. At the 1990 Australian Open in Sydney, Ogle was just one stroke off the lead playing the penultimate hole. But after driving into some trees at the 17th, he attempted to fade a shot back on to the fairway, only for his ball to rebound off a trunk and strike him on his left kneecap. He collapsed to the ground in agony and play was held up while he received medical attention. As Ogle was so near the end of his round, he decided to limp on. To add insult to injury, he was penalised two shots, because he'd been struck by his own golf ball. He completed the hole in nine strokes and went on to finish joint eighth, seven shots behind the winner. A subsequent X-ray revealed a hairline fracture.

Five years later, on Friday the 13th of January at the 13th hole in the second round of the 1995 Hawaiian Open, Ogle attempted to punch a shot from behind another tree, but the shaft of his 5-iron caught the trunk and broke

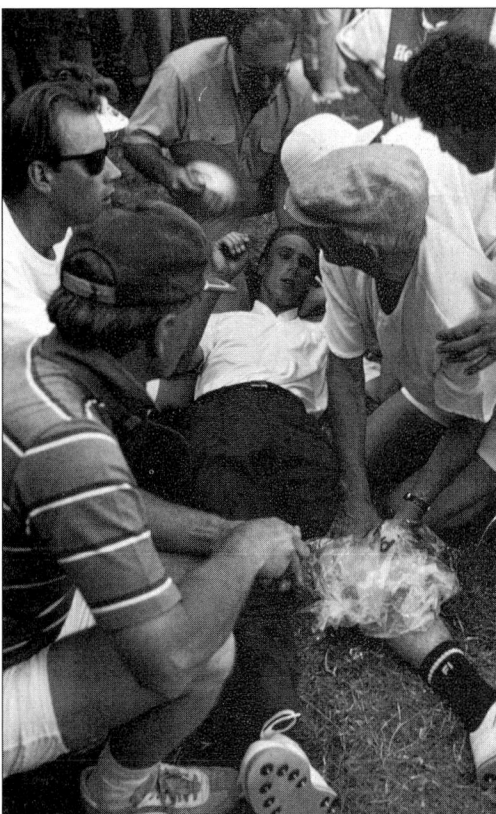

Brett Ogle receives attention after his freak accident in 1990

into three pieces. One of these flew into Ogle's face, smashing his sun glasses and hitting him just below his left eye. Ogle admitted afterwards: "I thought I had lost my eye. I'm glad I was wearing the glasses. Thank god it didn't catch me square on." He withdrew from the event suffering from blurred vision. And what made these incidents particularly spooky, was that both tournaments were won by the same golfer - little known American John Morse.

Lancaster prevails

The most number of golfers to contest a play-off on the US Tour is six. This occurred at the 1994 Byron Nelson Classic in Irving, Texas, when Neal Lancaster triumphed at the only extra-hole where he sank a four foot birdie putt to clinch the title. The five losers were David Edwards, Tom Byrum, Yoshinori Mizumaki, David Ogrin and Mark Carnevale. The tournament, scheduled for four rounds, had to be reduced to just 36 holes because of heavy rain.

Major dates

The 1971 USPGA Championship at PGA National, Palm Beach Gardens, Florida, was held from February 25-28. This is the earliest date on the calendar in which a major championship has been staged. The latest date for a major was the 1929 USPGA Championship (December 2-7) at Hillcrest Country Club, Los Angeles, California.

If at first you don't succeed...

In 1976, Maurice Flitcroft from Barrow-in-Furness, made headline news, when he took 121 strokes to play 18 holes at Formby in the first qualifying round of the British Open. At the time, 46-year-old Flitcroft was not a member of any club, he didn't have a handicap and he'd only started playing golf two years before. Yet on his entry form, he'd stated that he was an unattached professional. Understandably, Royal & Ancient officials, who had accepted his bogus application, were not amused. Flitcroft, a former crane driver, had made them look extremely silly. Following this embarrassment, the R&A made stringent efforts to prevent a similar incident happening again. Yet seven years later, Flitcroft made another attempt at qualifying. Under the assumed name Gerald Hoppy, and stating he was from Switzerland, he teed-up at Pleasington. This time he got as far as the ninth hole, before R&A officials caught up with him, by which stage he'd played 63 strokes. Afterwards Flitcroft said: "Everything was going well and according to plan until I five-putted the 2nd."

Fall from grace

Back in 1991, Scott Verplank, had one of those seasons all professional golfers dread. In 26 events on the US Tour, he missed 23 cuts and withdrew from two others. His only cheque came at the Las Vegas Invitational where he finished a lowly 63rd. That same year he was last in four Tour categories (Driving Distance, Driving Accuracy, Greens in Regulation & Scoring Average). Yet only six years earlier, Verplank had been tipped for greatness. He had won the 1984 US Amateur Championship, represented the United States in their victorious Walker Cup team of 1985, and, while still an amateur, had won on the US Tour at the age of 21 (1985 Western Open). Verplank still competes on Tour but is now relegated to the also-rans.

For my next trick

In the summer of 1985, at Little Chalfont, Adrian Donkersley, played six successive holes in 6-5-4-3-2-1. Holes 9th-14th have a par of 4-4-3-4-3-3.

Low 9s

The lowest 9-hole score for an official European Tour event is 27. This figure has been achieved three times and, remarkably, twice by the same golfer. That player is England's Robert Lee. At the Monte Carlo Open in 1985, his seven-under-par 27 at Mont Agel enabled him to fire a first round 61, en route to finishing fourth. Two years later, Lee was at it again, this time in the Portuguese Open at Estoril, where he compiled yet another 61 on day one. On this occasion his record-equalling 27 was six-under-par and Lee went on to win the tournament. The first player, however, to card 27 for 9 holes in Europe, was Spain's Jose Maria Canizares. It came in the third round of the 1978 Swiss Open at Crans-sur-Sierre, where Canizares covered the front nine in 9-under-par (one eagle, seven birdies). He finished the tournament in a tie for third.

US Tour career earnings

Top 10 at Jan. 1st 1996

1	Greg Norman	$9,592,829
2	Tom Kite	$9,337,998
3	Payne Stewart	$7,389,479
4	Nick Price	$7,338,119
5	Fred Couples	$7,188,408
6	Corey Pavin	$7,175,523
7	Tom Watson	$7,072,113
8	Paul Azinger	$6,957,324
9	Ben Crenshaw	$6,845,235
10	Curtis Strange	$6,791,618

European Tour career earnings

Top 10 at Jan. 1st 1996

1	Bernhard Langer	£5,092,579
2	Nick Faldo	£4,887,191
3	Seve Ballesteros	£4,340,370
4	Ian Woosnam	£4,176,787
5	Colin Montgomerie	£4,159,956
6	Sam Torrance	£3,439,762
7	Jose-Maria Olazabal	£3,140,347
8	Barry Lane	£2,596,813
9	Mark McNulty	£2,522,873
10	Ronan Rafferty	£2,491,672

THE 60 SHOOTERS

As yet, no one has broken 60 in a single round on the European Tour, although seven golfers couldn't have come closer. In chronological order, the 60 shooters are:

Player	Tournament	Venue	Final Pos.
Baldovino Dassu (Italy)	1971 Swiss Open	Crans-sur-Sierre	3
David Llewellyn (Wales)	1988 Biarritz Open	Biarritz	Won
Ian Woosnam (Wales)	1990 Monte Carlo Open	Mont Agel	Won
Darren Clarke (N.Ireland)	1992 Monte Carlo Open	Mont Agel	4
Johan Rystrom (Sweden)	1992 Monte Carlo Open	Mont Agel	T2
Paul Curry (England)	1992 Scottish Open	Gleneagles	T17
Jamie Spence (England)	1992 European Masters	Crans-sur-Sierre	Won

Notes:
Of all the above scores, Jamie Spence, at 12-under, was the lowest to par. Spence began the final round 10 shots off the pace, before firing his record-equalling round and then winning the tournament after a play-off.

David Llewellyn had a great opportunity to break 60. He arrived at the final green in round three needing two putts from 45 feet for a 59 but then three-putted for a bogey five. He missed his second putt from five feet.

Johan Rystrom needed to birdie the final hole for a 59 but his 12-footer to make history narrowly missed.

Acknowledgements for illustrations

Allsport 172

Allsport Historical Collection 10, 11, 15, 16 left, 16 bottom, 17,
    31, 60, 117, 123, 124, 131, 139, 149, 161, 183, 185, 186

Allsport/Hobbs Collection 137

Allsport/Simon Bruty 39 right, 167

Allsport/Jeremy Campion 24 top

Allsport/David Cannon 23, 39 left, 44, 51, 54, 64, 80, 93, 95,
    111, 125, 126, 134, 146, 158, 175, 180, 202, 215

Allsport/JD Cuban 56 bottom, 198, 199

Allsport/Matthew Harris 195

Allsport/Stephen Munday 133

Allsport/Joe Patronite 76

Allsport/Steve Powell 141

Hulton-Deutsch 128, 143

Popperfoto 18 left, 18 right, 20 left, 20 right, 21, 24 bottom, 35, 36,
    40, 42, 46, 56 top, 63, 67, 106, 108, 109, 110, 112, 113, 115, 119,
    121, 130, 135, 145, 148, 150, 152, 154, 155, 160, 162, 166, 168,
    181, 188, 207

INDEX

Note: Major subject entries are listed in bold type.